THE PROFITS OF NATURE

The Profits of Nature

COLONIAL DEVELOPMENT AND THE
QUEST FOR RESOURCES IN
NINETEENTH-CENTURY CHINA

Peter B. Lavelle

Columbia University Press
New York

Columbia University Press
Publishers Since 1893
New York   Chichester, West Sussex
cup.columbia.edu

Library of Congress Cataloging-in-Publication Data
Names: Lavelle, Peter B., author.
Title: The profits of nature : colonial development and the quest for resources
in nineteenth-century China / Peter B. Lavelle.
Description: New York : Columbia University Press, [2020] | Includes
bibliographical references and index.
Identifiers: LCCN 2019026955 (print) | LCCN 2019026956 (ebook) |
ISBN 9780231194709 (cloth) | ISBN 9780231550956 (ebook)
Subjects: LCSH: Zuo, Zongtang, 1812–1885. | Economic development—China—
History—19th century. | Natural resources—Government policy—China. | China—Economic
policy—19th century. | China—Politics and government—19th century.
Classification: LCC HC427.7 .L38 2020 (print) | LCC HC427.7 (ebook) |
DDC 333.70951/09034—dc23
LC record available at https://lccn.loc.gov/2019026955
LC ebook record available at https://lccn.loc.gov/2019026956

Columbia University Press books are printed on permanent and durable acid-free paper.
Printed in the United States of America

Cover image: Transplanting mulberry trees. From Wei Jie, *Cansang tushuo* (Illustrated guide
to sericulture), 1895. Courtesy of Columbia University Library.

Cover design: Chang Jae Lee

For my parents

Contents

Conventions and Measures

I n this book, Chinese words and names have been transliterated according to the *pinyin* system of romanization. For names of Manchus, Mongols, or Turkestanis derived from their Chinese transcriptions, hyphens
have been added between the syllables (e.g., Bu-yan-tai). Place names have
been written with spellings that reflect common usage (e.g., Khotan). All
dates have been rendered according to the Gregorian calendar.

Readers who are unfamiliar with units of measurement in Qing China
may benefit from knowing the following equivalences, which are derived
from information in Wilkinson, *Chinese History.*

One *mu*, a measure of land area, was roughly one-sixth of an acre.
One *li*, a measure of distance, was roughly one-third of a mile.
One catty (*jin*), a measure of weight, was roughly 1.3 pounds.
One picul, a measure of weight, was 120 catties, or about 156 pounds.
One ounce (*liang*), a measure of weight, was 1/16 of a catty, or about 1.3 U.S.
ounces.
One tael (*liang*), a unit of accounting for money, was about 1.3 U.S. ounces.
One inch (*cun*), a measure of length, was roughly 1.3 U.S. inches.
One *sheng*, a measure of volume, was roughly 35 U.S. fluid ounces.
One *dan*, a measure of volume, was 100 *sheng*, or about 27 U.S. fluid gallons.

THE PROFITS OF NATURE

Introduction

In the final month of 1853, Wang Shiduo fled the city of Nanjing and headed for the hills. Less than a year earlier, he had witnessed an unimaginable tragedy. Tens of thousands of armed insurgents had stormed eastward down the Yangzi River, capturing his hometown and throwing the entire region into turmoil. After enduring nine months of rebel rule, the former schoolteacher abandoned the city and took refuge in the mountains of nearby Anhui province. While living there, Wang pondered the roots of a crisis that had engulfed his home and destroyed his family. As he searched for answers, he began reading the landscape for clues. "In old times, there were old-growth forests deep in the mountains where one could escape the chaos," he observed. "But now, even remote mountains and desolate valleys all have highways running through them."[1] Such changes alarmed Wang, leading him to identify the country's enormous population and its insatiable appetite for resources as one of its most troubling problems. In his eyes, the environmental repercussions of overpopulation were widespread, extending well beyond the scenery right in front of him. "The harm of having so many people," he wrote, "is that mountaintops have been planted with grain and islets in rivers are being used as farmland. In Sichuan, old-growth forests have been exploited, and in places where Miao people live, deep groves of bamboo have been opened up." Wang worried that not everyone could find sustenance despite the exploitation of even marginal lands and remote stands of timber. There were just too many people consuming the country's resources, leaving the "strength of heaven and earth exhausted."[2]

Further down the river in Shanghai, other people saw things quite differently. Feng Guifen retreated to the urban environs of the bustling entrepôt in the spring of 1860 as insurgents advanced on his hometown.[3] From the relative safety of the city, the former government official and school headmaster drafted a series of essays ruminating on the tumultuous changes swirling around him. In one essay, Feng celebrated the size and immense resource wealth of his country. "China is the largest country on earth with ample, fertile plains and marshes, numerous people and abundant resources. Naturally the mouths of all nations are watering with desire," he wrote, revealing a hint of trepidation.[4] He called attention to his country's prodigious output of agricultural commodities, and he contemplated its enormous potential for mineral exploitation, noting how foreign books extolled its underground riches.[5] Feng may have had a unique perspective, but he was hardly alone in having such thoughts. Some years later, a letter printed in one of the country's most widely read newspapers proclaimed that China was indeed a wealthy country, owing to its massive size, its immense population, and its plentiful resources. Not only was China several times more populous than Europe; the country surpassed the continent by an even greater margin in the magnitude of the "unexploited profits of its mountains and rivers," and its tea, silk, and other sundry goods attracted countless foreign merchants who aimed to "cash in on the vast wealth of the central lands."[6]

If more than a few people accepted the Shanghai view of the Qing empire's resource abundance and agrarian productivity during the heyday of imperialist globalization, historians have been more inclined to peer at the nineteenth century through the lens of the Anhui view, with its emphasis on overpopulation and ecological exhaustion. There is little doubt that many elements of this view, cogently encapsulated in Wang Shiduo's analysis, accurately reflected patterns of environmental change during the rule of the Qing dynasty in China (1644–1912). By the turn of the nineteenth century, the population of the empire had reached over three hundred million, and it surged in the following half-century, climbing to well over four hundred million by 1850.[7] Such remarkable demographic growth put exceptional pressure on lands and waters, forests and grasslands, and plant and animal populations within and even well beyond the frontiers of imperial territory. Officials and literati could not help but serve as eyewitnesses to astonishing patterns of environmental destruction and unsustainable growth, leaving a rich archive of evidence that historians have begun to explore.[8] In some provinces of China, the need for arable land spurred mountainside deforestation and the reclamation of land from lakes and rivers, creating engineered landscapes highly vulnerable to siltation and flooding.[9] Competition over access to common-pool resources such as coastal fisheries and shorelines intensified, prompting litigation, sparking altercations, and resulting in resource scarcity.[10] As wealthy consumers in cities like Beijing and Guangzhou demanded ever-increasing quantities of rare, wild products from forests, mountains, rivers, and oceans, certain populations of plants, animals, and fungi were decimated.[11] In some areas, deforestation was so extensive and energy shortages so acute that farmers had no choice but to burn valuable fertilizers such as animal dung to cook their food.[12] In sum, environmental degradation was so rampant by the nineteenth century that some historians have concluded that it was a period of "environmental decline" or "environmental crisis" in China.[13]

Given the substantial amount of evidence pointing to an ecological crisis, it may seem puzzling that the Shanghai view existed at all. Indeed, even people like Feng Guifen, who articulated this point of view with great clarity, were not immune from worrying about overpopulation, land scarcity, and the social tensions they engendered.[14] Yet the idea that the Qing empire possessed a cornucopia of unexploited land and mineral resources and enjoyed a bounty of lucrative agricultural commodities was neither an expression of willful ignorance nor an attitude particularly unique to people in Shanghai. Instead, it was a shared response to a confluence of unprecedented crises that threatened the very social and political foundations of the country at a time of accelerating global economic integration. These crises pushed Chinese elites to develop a newfound appreciation not just for mainstays of commercial agriculture like tea and silk but also for the untapped natural wealth of the entire Qing empire, whose outer territories extended far beyond the provinces of China. In the second half of the nineteenth century, more and more Chinese gazed upon those territories with anticipation, recognizing their potential for development, and although some never relinquished their anxieties about overpopulation, many gradually came to regard China's hundreds of millions of people not as a liability but rather as an asset in the struggle to exploit the frontiers. Paradoxically, as the century of crisis wore on, concerns about resource scarcity gradually gave way to a sense of resource abundance.

Few people shared more in this sensibility or had more power to act on it than Zuo Zongtang. Born in 1812 and drawn into government service four decades later when rebels attacked his native Hunan province, Zuo eventually became one of the most prominent statesmen of the late nineteenth century as he served in far-flung regions of the empire. Over the course of his life, Zuo gained a keen awareness of his country's resource wealth and its potential for development, shrewdly viewing land and other resources as tools of imperial power. "China has a vast territory and abundant resources, and its products are inexhaustible," he once wrote to the Qing government's foreign ministry in Beijing. He believed that commodities like tea, silk, cotton, and rhubarb could be exported to international markets in unlimited quantities to aid in the country's enrichment.[15] He also learned to see the empire's resource potential in spatial terms. From his perspective, frontier regions held enormous areas of uncultivated soil that could be transformed into private wealth and government revenues. To this day, Zuo remains best known for his role in orchestrating campaigns to suppress rebel movements in the southeast and northwest regions of China and then masterminding the reconquest of the empire's western borderland, Xinjiang, after the region had fallen outside the ambit of Qing control. Yet, although he is remembered for his military prowess, he was never concerned with territorial control only in a strategic sense. By following Zuo through the nineteenth century and across the empire, this book reveals how resource development became a central feature of the struggle to revive Qing power during an age of extraordinary crisis—a struggle in which he played a principal role.

Zuo belonged to a pivotal generation of leaders who lived through the most tumultuous period of history since the middle of the seventeenth century, when the Manchu rulers of the Qing conquered the provinces of China. Starting in the early nineteenth century, Qing state and society were confronted by what William Rowe has called "a perfect storm" of social and political problems.[16] Such problems, including population growth, ecological degradation, opium consumption, landlessness, wealth inequality, and government corruption, escalated gradually and unevenly across the empire's provinces and territories, exacerbating social tensions and giving rise to acute episodes of tax resistance, popular unrest, and other troubles. By the middle of the century, these troubles had reached a tipping point, sparking territorial crises of startling breadth and severity. The Taiping

Figure 0.1 Zuo Zongtang, left, with Prince Chun, father of the Guangxu emperor. Photograph ca. 1881. Courtesy of the Alinari Archives.

Rebellion (1851–64), the insurgency that drove Wang Shiduo and Feng Guifen from their homes and propelled Zuo Zongtang into government service, engulfed provinces up and down the Yangzi River, killing tens of millions of people and utterly destroying some of the country's most productive agricultural communities. The Muslim Rebellions (1862–78) then subverted government rule throughout the empire's northwest, throwing Shaanxi and Gansu provinces into turmoil and severing Xinjiang from the rest of the country. Meanwhile, the Qing state was buffeted by serious external threats to its sovereignty. Britain and other foreign powers attacked the empire on multiple occasions and compelled its diplomats to sign numerous treaties, which opened up Chinese ports to foreign commerce, undermined the state's tariff autonomy, and granted a host of extraterritorial privileges to citizens of other countries. In the 1850s, Russia began to use treaty negotiations to force the Qing to cede land on its northeastern and northwestern frontiers in Manchuria and Xinjiang. To top things off, these crises collectively plunged the state into deep financial distress, hampering its ability to pay for the ballooning costs of defense while continuing to fund all of the other functions of government.

In response to such crises, Qing officials initiated changes in the underlying principles and core practices of imperial statecraft. Within the Chinese provinces, longstanding political dogma mandated that rulers "nourish the people" (*yang min*), which meant sustaining people's lives and livelihoods by providing access to food and farmland through policies for famine relief and land reclamation. Yet when the territorial and fiscal troubles of the mid-nineteenth century seemed to imperil the existence of the dynasty, leaders gradually abandoned their "commitment to social reproduction," as Kenneth Pomeranz has written, and started to prioritize the creation of a more robust state characterized by "wealth and power" (*fuqiang*) that would be capable not just of quelling domestic social unrest but also of surviving in an increasingly competitive international landscape.[17] This new priority focused the state's attention above all on protecting territory from internal and external dangers. To achieve this goal, government revenues were diverted away from customary projects conducted in the interest of public welfare, such as stocking granaries and maintaining dikes along the Yellow River, and instead were allocated for a range of strategic initiatives. The new statecraft found its most visible expression in the rise of new institutions designed to enhance the state's capacity in the realms of defense, diplomacy, finance, and industry.[18] In part because of the significant threat posed by seaborne empires, many of these institutions were built in China's eastern coastal provinces, creating a spatial pattern of government spending and state building that endured into the early decades of the twentieth century.

The crises of the nineteenth century also held major implications for Qing statecraft far beyond China's eastern littoral. The Manchus presided over a vast multiethnic empire stretching from the subtropical island of

Taiwan to the arid deserts and snow-capped mountains of Turkestan in Central Asia, and they employed a diversity of administrative systems and customs to govern the native inhabitants of these largely non-Chinese borderlands.[19] For a variety of reasons, the state sought to protect the livelihoods of some groups of indigenous people by preserving the ecological basis of their subsistence. In practice, this usually meant prohibiting Chinese settlers from colonizing frontier regions and trying to prevent them from overexploiting animal and plant populations or clearing grasslands and forests to make way for agriculture.[20] Such prohibitions were only partially successful, and they became harder to enforce as the Chinese population grew, commercialization expanded, and migrants to the frontiers increasingly chose to flout the law to take advantage of land, mineral, botanical, and animal resources. But when those areas came under external threat and the state's fiscal troubles multiplied, Qing leaders gradually abandoned rules prohibiting Chinese settlement. In these circumstances, they no longer worried as much that farmers, merchants, miners, lumberjacks, and other migrants would menace the native inhabitants of the borderlands or destroy the environments that sustained their lives. Instead, they began to place a higher value on Chinese settlers as agents of development and as bulwarks against encroachment by foreign empires. This reversal in policy happened at different times in different frontier regions, but by the final years of the century, there were no longer any regions off limits to Chinese colonization.

Meanwhile, as demographic growth in the provinces of China roused anxieties about social instability, officials and literati grew more conscious of the need to foster agriculture and promote rural development. In the early nineteenth century, when Zuo Zongtang was just beginning to pursue his education to prepare for a career in government service, elites in his home province were actively engaged in studying and propagating knowledge about techniques and technologies for land and water management. Zuo himself developed a passion for learning about agriculture. Over time, he acquired a substantial understanding of ways to improve farm productivity and thereby increase the utilization of what he and his contemporaries called the "natural profits of heaven and earth" (*tiandi ziran zhi li*), or sometimes simply the "profits of nature" (*ziran zhi li*). Zuo's interest in agriculture was shared fairly widely among other Qing scholars, who assumed that helping people make use of the earth's resources was a core responsibility of any respectable official.

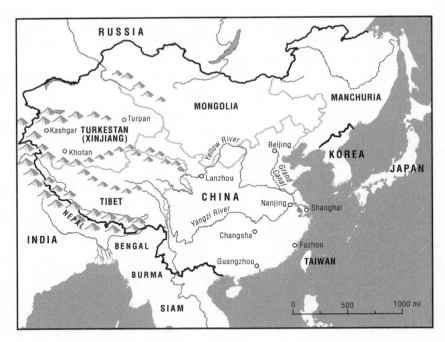

Map 0.1 The Qing empire in the early nineteenth century. Map by Erin Greb.

At the same time, Chinese elites were gradually developing a deeper awareness of the Qing empire's outer territories and their resources. This awareness arose largely from reading new scholarship about the geographies, histories, and peoples of borderland regions that had been produced in the wake of their incorporation into the empire in the seventeenth and eighteenth centuries.[21] By the late 1820s, when Zuo Zongtang commenced his studies of geography, he could draw upon a considerable collection of published materials about the Qing territories, enabling him to glean certain insights about their environments and economies, including their agricultural products and other resource commodities. Like other literati of his day, Zuo grew interested in learning about Xinjiang. The Qing court was just then in the process of rescinding the prohibition on Chinese colonization in the southern part of the territory, the homeland of hundreds of thousands of Turkic Muslims, the ancestors of today's Uyghurs. The things that Zuo read and the people he talked with shaped his impression of the territory as a sparsely populated but resource-rich region on the doorstep of his own homeland, one that had the potential to ease problems arising from demographic growth in the provinces. At the frontier, abundance appeared to be scarcity by another name.[22]

Zuo Zongtang entered into the ranks of officialdom several decades later, at a time when the Qing empire was imperiled by military crises and the institutional and spatial dynamics of the new statecraft were just beginning to take shape in the coastal provinces. Zuo played a significant role in the now-familiar history of this era, working to establish a naval yard for the construction of warships outfitted with new technology in coastal Fujian province in the mid-1860s.[23] But that is only part of the story. By moving beyond the empire's coastlines and toward its inland frontiers, it is possible to uncover another side of the late nineteenth-century statecraft: the concerted drive to develop agriculture and foster natural resource production across the Qing territories. From the time of his first high-ranking commission in 1862, Zuo collaborated with a wide array of people to carry out development projects in the name of stabilizing territory, generating revenue, and fostering wealth. Such projects arose in the aftermath of warfare, and they often began with the twin goals of providing relief to refugees and stimulating postwar reconstruction. But they quickly grew to encompass the broader aim of improving agriculture and other industries through the allocation of capital, knowledge, and technology to rural households. In the northwest, where Zuo was reappointed in the late 1860s, development projects became more elaborate and more attuned to current economic realities. Farmers were given various forms of state assistance and were encouraged to cultivate cash crops, including cereal grains, cotton, and mulberry. Such efforts reflected not just the massive demand for food generated by the presence of Qing armies but also the potential opportunities afforded by markets for textile fibers, the lifeblood of the domestic and global economies. The most substantial development projects were undertaken in Xinjiang. After the reconquest of the territory in 1877, officials wasted little time in carrying out measures to expand agrarian production, build hydraulic infrastructure, and promote sericulture in Turkestani communities, seeking to boost the region's output of commodities at a moment when it enjoyed substantial commercial connections to other regions of Central Asia.

These projects reveal how Qing leaders sought to capitalize on the country's natural resources by establishing new institutions to coordinate the work of land development. From the 1850s onward, provincial leaders set up a bevy of bureaus to implement policy initiatives at the provincial and district levels.[24] These agencies proliferated in number and variety in subsequent decades: one tally identified over fifty kinds of bureaus handling matters ranging from military logistics to public welfare.[25] While those with strategic functions received the lion's share of provincial funding, officials also allocated money to bureaus dealing with natural resources. In the aftermath of war, Zuo Zongtang created bureaus for postwar reconstruction and land reclamation, charging them with the tasks of recruiting settlers to cultivate abandoned land and providing people with capital loans and technical assistance. Such bureaus also generated new knowledge. Like state authorities in other parts of the world, bureau personnel employed tools of measurement and quantification to make the earth and its resources known, legible, and governable.[26] They surveyed and mapped lands and waterways, collating information about property size and productivity so that provincial officials could assess land taxes, verify land claims, and distribute unclaimed soil to migrants. Their activities did not yield knowledge about the natural world with the same degree of numerical precision as surveying work carried out with new statistical techniques in other parts of the world.[27] Nonetheless, they did produce useful data about lands and waterways, especially in regions where records had been destroyed or lost. Although many bureaus did not outlast the imperial court's repeated calls for financial austerity in the second half of the 1880s, they were significant for being among the most substantive manifestations of the state's commitment to natural resource development prior to the wave of institution building during the period of the "New Policy" (*xinzheng*) reforms at the turn of the twentieth century.[28]

Everyday agrarian technologies featured prominently in late Qing projects for rural development. Drawing upon customary tactics for promoting agriculture, Zuo and his deputies printed and distributed concise farming handbooks to local authorities, gentry, and literate farmers, seeking to propagate knowledge about techniques and tools for crop production through what Francesca Bray has called "mobile forms of authoritative natural knowledge that could be applied anywhere in the empire."[29] Along with such knowledge, officials allocated to villages and rural households a variety of physical tools and organisms that were chosen to facilitate land reclamation and boost agricultural output. While heavy, bulky tools such as plows and plow animals were usually procured locally, officials often went out of their way to purchase seeds, eggs, and saplings from distant provinces, knowing that certain regional agricultures in China had developed particular landraces with the potential to raise farm productivity considerably. Late nineteenth-century projects thus witnessed the dissemination of various kinds of cotton, rice, and vegetable seeds as well as mulberry seedlings and silkworm eggs to communities in Gansu and Xinjiang, creating patterns of the movement of farming technology that connected economies in eastern China to sites of rural development in the Qing northwest.[30]

Despite the important role they played in the empire's economy and politics, everyday agrarian technologies have rarely been incorporated into narratives of Chinese history in the late nineteenth century. Many narratives of this period focus instead on the transmission of Western science and technology to China, one part of the now well-worn story of the global diffusion of European capitalism and China's transition to modernity.[31] There is little doubt that foreign knowledge in fields such as mechanics and geology, as well as a host of related technologies, eventually exerted a powerful influence upon the dynamics of intellectual, economic, and political change in China.[32] Indeed, foreign knowledge and technology began to play an influential role in some resource development projects in this period. In the late 1870s, Zuo Zongtang purchased German-manufactured machines and shipped them to Gansu for experimental projects in mining, dredging, and textile weaving with the intention of stimulating postwar reconstruction.[33] Yet in narrating the embrace of foreign science and technology in nineteenth-century China, historians have tended to lose sight of the social and ecological complexities of Qing geography, inadvertently transforming the empire into a two-dimensional and primarily coastal frontier for the expansion of Europe. This approach has obscured the fact that Chinese knowledge and technology related to industries such as agriculture, sericulture, and mining circulated within the bounds of imperial territory, and sometimes even beyond them, through official and nonofficial channels in the late nineteenth century.[34] If historians often have neglected such patterns of circulation, it is not because agriculture was unimportant to the Qing or global economies, but perhaps because they have turned their attention elsewhere, toward newer, larger, or noisier things like steam engines that seemed to revolutionize people's relationships with the natural world and with each other.[35]

Most of the technologies in the following story catalyzed no such revolutionary changes, but they sometimes brought people and environments together in new configurations. Late nineteenth-century development projects took place alongside the emergence of a new territorialism in the Qing borderlands in which Han Chinese officials came to wield an increasing degree of authority over non-Chinese communities. After the reconquest of Xinjiang, Chinese elites were appointed to govern Turkestani communities for the first time, one sign of the erosion of the administrative and legal pluralism that had characterized Qing rule in earlier periods.[36] Meanwhile, Zuo Zongtang became the leading advocate for a plan to establish a provincial system of governance in Xinjiang—the clearest manifestation of the desire to shore up the empire's territorial power in Central Asia by erasing the administrative distinctions between the western frontiers and the eastern provinces. But while old distinctions were being eroded, new ones were being formed. When officials carried out projects to develop hydraulic infrastructure or improve sericulture production, they created numerous sites for Chinese-Turkestani collaboration, entangling people, technologies, and nonhuman nature in new patterns of interaction. On a day-to-day basis, officials managed such projects with an ethos of practicality and technological pluralism, employing both imported Chinese and local Turkestani technologies and shifting tactics as the situation required. Yet sites of interaction that emerged around environmental resources inevitably became hierarchical spaces, reflecting and shaping the forces of the new territorialism. Interactions produced tensions and, at certain moments, sparked resistance among Turkestani farmers and workers, demonstrating that the process of development was never as straightforward as Chinese elites purported it to be.

The dynamics of development in Xinjiang serve as a useful reminder that Qing China remained a colonial empire in the final decades of the nineteenth century. Even as Chinese society was subjected to colonial violence by Britain and other imperial powers and was influenced by quotidian forms of colonialism in the treaty ports, the late Qing state practiced a certain brand of colonialism in its own internal frontiers.[37] This brand no doubt shared some traits with patterns of Chinese colonial settlement in earlier centuries. Indeed, late Qing elites were fond of evoking references dating back to the Han period (206 BCE–220 CE), describing the recruitment of farmers and merchants to Xinjiang and other borderlands as "moving people to solidify the frontiers" (*yimin shibian*).[38] Yet it would be misleading to take such references at face value or to conclude that Chinese, inland colonialism was "old" whereas foreign, coastal colonialism was "new." Instead, it is better to regard nineteenth-century colonialisms as distinct but contemporaneous manifestations of the intensifying struggle for territory during the "golden age of resource-based development," when the growth of natural resource industries and waves of commercialization pushed development into new frontiers and drove the global economy to a new level of integration.[39] In large territorial states and settler societies, people rushed to open up remaining unclaimed lands in the internal peripheries and turn them into farmland or rangeland supplying cash crops and animal products to domestic and international markets.[40] In colonial empires, administrators took a stronger role in the development of rural economies, investing in agriculture, infrastructure, and institutions to improve production and spur growth.[41] In the Qing empire, the policies and patterns of agrarian development in borderland territories reflected certain elements of both of these trends. It is thus reasonable to conclude that even though such policies and patterns emerged out of a confluence of crises unique to Qing China, they were part of a broader dynamic of colonial development that was evident in many regions of the world in that era.[42]

The following story of crisis and colonial development would be incomplete without acknowledging that one of the strongest influences on Zuo Zongtang and the society around him was the environment itself. In China, the nineteenth century was riddled with natural disasters. Many began with unexpected fluctuations in weather patterns, which created the conditions for floods and droughts, and were then exacerbated by the financial and organizational weakness of the Qing state.[43] The deadliest disaster came late in the century. The lack of rain across a handful of northern provinces for several years in a row gave rise to an intense and sustained drought, leaving farmers in the lurch and eventually killing millions in what came to be known as the North China Famine (1876–79). Because of decisions made by Qing officials, this famine did not significantly draw resources away from projects in Gansu and Xinjiang. But such a terrible disaster must have reminded even staunch resource optimists, who looked out across the imperial territories and saw their potential for development, that the patterns of the heavens were beyond the control of people and that abrupt changes in the environment easily had the power to wreak havoc in the human world. Of course, the nonhuman world has never been an inanimate, stable setting for the unfolding of human history. Rather, it is a dynamic entity characterized as much by disorder as by the perceptible rhythms of the days and the seasons.[44] People of Zuo Zongtang's generation knew all too well how disasters could quickly interrupt such rhythms, revealing the limitations of their own power. Zuo himself learned these lessons early in his life, just as he set out to gain knowledge about a subject on the minds of many: how to improve the exploitation of the earth.

CHAPTER 1

Agriculture in an Era of Crisis

S ometime in the 1820s, Zuo Zongtang cracked opened the pages of a book and read about the lands and rivers of his birthplace. Born in Xiangyin county in northern Hunan province in 1812, Zuo was one of six children from "a family of moderate means but with scholarly traditions."[1] Like his two older brothers and other boys from educated families, he studied classical texts and their commentaries from an early age to prepare for the civil service examinations sponsored by the imperial government. His academic horizons grew over the years, and by the time Zuo was a teenager, he had become an avid reader of works in other fields of scholarship.[2] The book he now held in his hands, the *Gazetteer of Xiangyin County (Xiangyin xianzhi)*, was one such work. Its editors had gone to the trouble of interviewing Zuo's father, a local schoolteacher, along with other Xiangyin natives to gather information about the county as they readied it for publication.[3] Given his father's ties to the project, the book must have held some fascination for Zuo, whose family had moved from Xiangyin to Changsha, the provincial capital, when he was still a young child. Flipping through its pages, Zuo could learn much about his native place and its physical environments, including its hills and bamboo groves, extensive waterways, and ubiquitous rice paddies. As he perused its contents, the young scholar may have paused to glance at the images in the second chapter: a set of maps of Xiangyin and illustrations of scenes from around the county. One image captured geese flying over clumps of reeds and

Figure 1.1 Geese on sandbanks along a river. From *Xiangyin xianzhi* (Gazetteer of Xiangyin county), 1823. Courtesy of Toyo Bunko (The Oriental Library).

standing on sandbanks along a river. Although alive with the movement of the birds, the scene was printed on the page in stunning stillness, as if the geese were frozen in time. Such imagery may have given readers the impression that Xiangyin's environments were immutable except for the cycling of the seasons and the motion of waterfowl. Notes accompanying the text of the gazetteer offered a similar message: "The towering of the hills and the flow of the rivers has not changed throughout the ages."[4]

Yet the idea that the environments of northern Hunan were immutable could not have been further from the truth. Since Zuo's ancestors had migrated into the region during the era of the Southern Song dynasty (1127–1279), the province's lands and waters had undergone tremendous change.[5] In fact, for centuries migrant families who moved to Hunan in search of new farmland were the main anthropogenic drivers of ecological change in the region. The pace of change fluctuated over time in relation to demographic expansion, warfare, and commercialization. In the sixteenth century and again in the eighteenth century, Hunan experienced strong in-migration and local population growth, a sustained increase in arable land, and the gradual transformation of its valleys, hillsides, forests, and lakes. To the northwest of Xiangyin, people reclaimed land from the once-enormous Dongting Lake, enclosing sections of lake bed behind dikes to create paddies for the cultivation of rice, the province's most important cash crop. Over time, the surface area of the lake shrunk considerably, leaving the region and its rivers at greater risk of flooding.[6] On dry ground, people opened up more land for grain and gradually deforested the hillsides, planting tea and fruit trees or harvesting bamboo and other forest products, thus boosting the rate at which soil eroded down into the rivers. By the early nineteenth century, poor peasants who went looking for land were stripping vegetation from more remote mountainsides to make way for maize, sweet potato, and other subsistence crops.[7] Agriculture had spread to all corners of the province, expanding even to "mountain tops and marginal lands" and leaving little of the landscape untouched.[8] This, too, was something that Zuo may have learned from his reading, belying the image of a serene and static natural environment.

Perhaps the most striking lesson of all was just how suddenly environments could change. In the 1830s, as Zuo embarked upon the third decade of his life, Hunan province and Xiangyin county experienced repeated bouts of disaster brought on by unexpected changes in the weather. In that decade alone, Xiangyin recorded significant flooding in four separate years along the Xiang River, which flowed northward past the county seat. The rising waters inflicted serious damage upon the area's dikes. These floods were interrupted in 1835 by the arrival of a debilitating drought and a plague of locusts, which together decimated Hunan's precious rice harvest and left farmers and townsfolk to suffer and die of starvation and disease.[9] However local these episodes of acute crisis may have seemed to people at the time, they were not reserved for Hunan alone. Indeed, the weather fluctuations underlying disasters like these were manifestations of larger disturbances in global climate patterns, which were likely catalyzed to a certain extent by volcanic eruptions whose emissions of particulate matter into the atmosphere induced a measurable cooling of temperatures worldwide.[10] In this period, regions around the world, from sub-Saharan Africa to the Japanese archipelago, suffered from drought and famine.[11]

In the Qing empire, this period of climatic turbulence and natural disaster exacerbated a variety of social and economic problems that had been building for some time and helped to push Chinese society into a period of economic lassitude known as the Daoguang Depression.[12] From the late eighteenth century onward, population growth, environmental

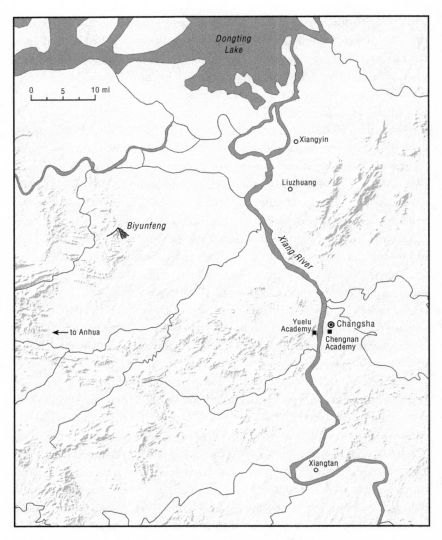

Map 1.1 Northern Hunan in the nineteenth century. Map by Erin Greb.

degradation, economic inequality, and declining financial reserves in Beijing all took a toll on social stability. During the reign of the Daoguang emperor (1821–50), long-distance commercial exchanges slowed and prices for agricultural commodities in many parts of the empire declined.[13] Farmers faced mounting hardship, especially because the value of their cash crops fell while the price of silver, the officially sanctioned medium for the

payment of land taxes, rose at an increasingly accelerated rate.[14] This combination of unsettling economic forces and disasters rattled the urban and
rural poor, enlarging the ranks of the unemployed, increasing the incidence of vagrancy, and gradually leading to acts of antigovernment resistance in Hunan and other provinces.[15]

These crises were troubling enough on their own. But for Zuo Zongtang, they coincided with a period of intense personal frustration. By the
time he turned twenty, he had managed to pass the provincial examination in Hunan, thus earning the title of "recommended man" (*juren*). This
afforded him the privilege of sitting for the metropolitan examination in
Beijing, the final stage of the empire's civil examination system. But in the
1830s, Zuo failed to pass this test on three separate occasions, leaving him
without the "presented scholar" (*jinshi*) title that would have assured him
a coveted position in the imperial bureaucracy. Although this type of failure was in fact very common among educated men who aspired to obtain
jobs in government service, it nonetheless presented a maddeningly stub-
born obstacle to Zuo's intended career trajectory.[16] In 1837, after his second
failure and in need of money, Zuo began to give lectures at a local school.
Several years later, after his hopes for passing the exam had been all but
extinguished, he took up work as a private tutor.[17]

Amid this conjunction of crises and personal failures, Zuo was determined to devote his attention to an array of scholarly subjects loosely
grouped together under the appellation "practical learning" (*shixue*).[18] As
the translation of the name implies, practical learning revolved around
the study of fields of useful knowledge that could be applied in real-life
settings to solve concrete problems. The intellectual climate of early
nineteenth-century Hunan incubated interest in this kind of scholarship,
fostering a desire among many literati to use their academic studies to help
solve society's myriad troubles. In this milieu, Zuo's budding interest in
practical learning blossomed into a deeper engagement with the study of
agronomy. It is no coincidence that Zuo chose to explore a field of knowledge that, at its core, grappled with how people could take advantage of
the earth's resources. Weather patterns were a perennial cause for concern
among farmers, but the fluctuations of the 1830s stood out for the number
and severity of the disasters they caused. The growing uncertainties of life
in this period must have made knowledge about the natural world and how
to exploit it seem especially valuable. After his examination failures, Zuo's
family came to rely on income from farming and land rents, and thus his

interest in agronomy was also personal. Even so, he maintained the pretense of conducting research so that he could share his knowledge with other farmers and thereby contribute to the state-sanctioned mission of improving agriculture.

There was much that Zuo gained through his studies of agriculture. His extensive readings certainly imbued him with the core agrarian ideology of the Qing state, which viewed agriculture and particularly family farming as the proper socioeconomic foundation for society. But his studies went much further than mere political dogma. They introduced him to the rich heritage of Chinese agronomy, giving him a broad understanding of various forms of agrarian technology, past and present, and they opened his eyes to the dilemmas of formulating agricultural policy. They also broadened the spatial horizons of his research, guiding him out into the fields to gain first-hand knowledge of farming practices. Moving between the studio and the fields outside, he accumulated experience and expertise and gained direct insight into the potential for agrarian knowledge to help farmers make the most of the resources around them.

The rise of practical learning was strongly correlated with the occurrence and experience of crisis. When Hunanese scholars of the early nineteenth century sought useful knowledge to help them tackle the social, environmental, and political problems of their day, they found some of their greatest inspiration in the works of scholars of the seventeenth century who themselves had endured an era of profound crisis, one that was represented most visibly and violently by the Qing conquest of Ming China in 1644. Many forces contributed to the decline of the Ming dynasty (1368–1644), from factional conflict and financial troubles at the imperial court to the weakening of its military and the rise of Manchu power in Northeast Asia. Research has revealed an even more fundamental force of destabilization: the cooling of the global climate in the early and middle decades of the century. This period of cooling, the so-called Little Ice Age, witnessed a decline in average temperatures around the world, with devastating consequences for agricultural productivity and political stability in many places.[19] From the 1610s to the 1640s, Chinese society experienced lower-than-average temperatures, repeated episodes of flooding and drought, smaller annual harvests, and outbreaks of contagious disease.[20] The turmoil that arose from these crises motivated some late Ming literati to devote themselves to scholarship. While taking refuge in their studies, these scholars sought to acquire useful knowledge that seemed to offer solutions for the troubles around them. This trend continued after 1644, as those who had survived the Manchu conquest carried out research in various subjects, sometimes hoping to understand what had gone wrong with Ming society and at other times merely looking for ideas to aid in the recovery process. The written works that resulted from their efforts constituted a significant body of new scholarship and offered a model for later generations who aimed to use what they had learned to tackle real-world problems.[21]

Practical learning in seventeenth-century China developed alongside another scholastic movement, "evidential learning" (*kaozheng xue*). This movement was in part a backlash to a predominant mode of intellectual inquiry among neo-Confucian scholars of the Song and Ming dynasties who employed inductive logic to grasp the moral principles underlying human affairs and worldly phenomena. By contrast, literati who embraced the practices of evidential learning employed research methods grounded in textual empiricism and championed the use of evidence to draw conclusions in a variety of fields of knowledge.[22] The most prominent evidential scholar of the seventeenth century, Gu Yanwu, was reputed for his practice of making sure to "scrutinize every fact thoroughly and confirm it with supporting evidence."[23] This commitment to empiricism also led people like Gu to consult ancient versions of key texts so that they could avoid the sort of mistakes in transcription and interpretation that had been committed by earlier generations of scholars.[24] By the eighteenth century, evidential learning had gained wider purchase among literati, who increasingly applied its methods of research to subjects such as mathematics, geography, and medicine.[25]

Scholars of the lower Yangzi River region had long occupied a central place in Chinese intellectual life, outnumbering literati in other regions and dominating scholastic movements like practical learning and evidential learning. But in the late eighteenth and early nineteenth centuries, communities of educated elites in other parts of the Qing empire were gaining notoriety for their vibrancy and their distinctive approaches to learning. In this period, scholars in Hunan began to stand out for their eclecticism and activist spirit. They embraced moral philosophy and the study of principles, accepted the value of empiricism while rejecting the pedantry of philology, and above all advanced the cause of practical learning in the service of statecraft (*jingshi*).[26] The growing vitality of Hunanese scholarship owed much to eighteenth-century changes in educational policy in Beijing as well as to the patronage of Chen Hongmou, who twice served as governor of Hunan in the 1750s and 1760s. Chen reinvigorated Changsha's Yuelu Academy and its sister school, the Chengnan Academy, by allocating funding, boosting enrollments, and reorienting curricula toward knowledge that could prepare young men for careers in public service.[27] Teachers and students in Changsha embraced this revival and its emphasis on practical learning. Luo Dian, the headmaster of the Yuelu Academy from 1782 to 1808, sought to train students using a range of pedagogical methods, from rigorous studies of classic texts to experiential learning outside the classroom. Luo organized field trips into the western hills behind the academy, which became a "hands-on venue for the study of flora and folk customs" and "an informal context for discussion of the classics and contemporary affairs." He used such outings as a way to instill in his students an appreciation of the value of personal observation as a means for gaining knowledge about the world.[28] By the early decades of the nineteenth century, such a broad and diversified approach to learning had become a hallmark of education at Changsha's elite academies.

As Zuo Zongtang grew up in Changsha, he must have acquired a sense for the varieties of scholarship in vogue among Hunanese literati. But it was not until his late teenage years that he started to explore practical learning and to establish formal connections with the province's academic elite. Zuo's entrance into this world began with books, and perhaps no source was more influential in the development of his knowledge about matters related to statecraft than the *Compilation of Statecraft Essays of the Imperial Dynasty (Huangchao jingshi wenbian)*, published in 1827. Modeled upon a similar compilation printed in the last years of the Ming dynasty, this anthology brought together several thousand essays by Ming and Qing scholars covering a broad array of topics, from administrative concerns like revenue collection and personnel management to matters of economic and environmental significance, such as irrigation control and farming techniques.[29] It was the brainchild of He Changling, a Hunan native and a Yuelu Academy alumnus. In undertaking this project, he hoped to inspire support for political reforms and bureaucratic action which he thought necessary to ameliorate the empire's social and political conditions, and he tapped a fellow provincial, Wei Yuan, to oversee the work of editing the compilation.[30] By the time Zuo made He's acquaintance in 1830, the young scholar already had begun to read this collection of essays, and its voluminous contents no doubt served as fodder for their discussions. The following year, Zuo enrolled in the Chengnan Academy, where he attended lectures by He Changling and his younger brother, He Xiling. The He brothers subsequently became Zuo's mentors, loaning him books from their personal libraries, advising him on his studies, and corresponding with him in later years.[31]

As Zuo continued to study for the metropolitan examination, his academic interests expanded. He no doubt spent much time preparing his interpretations of the classics, but his knowledge about subjects of practical learning also grew. By 1838 he had acquired a substantial understanding of agricultural scholarship. This is evident because copies of his exam essays have been preserved, and several of them broach the subject of agriculture. The essays show what could be expected of a young scholar struggling to gain a spot in the bureaucracy: Zuo had assimilated the orthodox views and language of Chinese statecraft from the texts that he studied. "Agriculture and sericulture," he wrote in one essay, "are the tools which support life and the source of great profit in the world. For the state they are an inexhaustible storehouse."[32] Such views held that the production of grain crops and textile fibers was of paramount importance because they were the main source of material sustenance for imperial subjects and the main source of revenue for the government. As such, the paired practices of farming and weaving were considered to be indispensable to Chinese statecraft and, as Zuo wrote, the basis for "nourishing the people."[33]

Given the centrality of agriculture to state ideology, it is no surprise that Zuo also included in his essays some acknowledgement that promoting agriculture among the populace was one of the chief responsibilities of officials. In the Qing period, emperors and officials alike tried to encourage people to engage in agriculture, sericulture, and other forms of rural production. Sometimes they issued official exhortations to industriousness and frugality, aiming to educate people about the material and moral benefits of productive work. This method of encouragement was exemplified by the Kangxi emperor's *Sacred Edict* (*Shengyu*) of 1670, which stressed the importance of agriculture and sericulture and the imperative of having imperial subjects fulfill their tax obligations to the state.[34] At other times, emperors and officials called upon families to uphold the propriety and prosperity of the household by having men labor in the fields and women work within the home to tend silkworms and reel silk, a gendered division of labor that had long been a centerpiece of statecraft thought.[35] Certainly, the encouragement of agriculture was not limited to rhetoric. The

Qing state often invested money and organizational capacity in the cause, sponsoring campaigns in which officials granted awards and offered tax breaks to farmers for opening up land for cultivation or raising the productivity of land already under the plow. Such campaigns first commenced in the very earliest years of the Qing period, as the new rulers sought to accelerate the pace of agrarian reconstruction after the disasters of the mid-seventeenth century, and they became increasingly common in the eighteenth century, as elites worried that the empire's growing population would exceed its existing supplies of food and clothing without concerted efforts to expand farmland.[36]

Imperial officials also promoted agriculture by providing assistance to rural residents in the form of knowledge, technology, and capital. Agrarian technologies came in a variety of forms.[37] They could be implements like plows or looms, organisms like cotton seeds or mulberry trees, or practices such as intercropping and fertilization. For literate farmers and officials, agricultural treatises were particularly valuable tools for learning about and propagating knowledge of such technologies. Treatises about agriculture were by no means new in Zuo's age. Textual records about agriculture and its technologies have a long pedigree dating back to the early periods of Chinese history, and all imperial governments enacted certain policies to stimulate agriculture in some way, including through the publication and circulation of texts.[38] But the output of written works about agriculture surged in the period from the sixteenth to the nineteenth centuries, a trend driven by growing interest in agronomy, greater attention to the monetary value of commercial crops, and the falling cost of book printing. By the end of the Qing period, new agricultural treatises from the preceding three centuries had come to outnumber by a significant margin treatises from all earlier eras combined. The corpus of agricultural treatises was also influenced by the increasing specialization and regionalization of knowledge, as some authors composed entire volumes about particular crops and others focused on farming in specific provinces or regions of the empire.[39] Not all of the new treatises entered into wide circulation, but those that did became important tools of edification, enlightening their readers about how to increase and improve the production of food grains, textile fibers, and other valuable farm commodities.

During the years that he traveled to Beijing for the exams, Zuo was in no position to influence agricultural policy or technology in Hunan, as he held no official post and owned no land. Nonetheless, he made a point to learn about the technical side of agriculture. One of his essays for the examinations demonstrates that, by the late 1830s, he had acquired a basic understanding of the genealogy of Chinese agrarian knowledge, if not a comprehensive mastery of farming technology. In this essay, Zuo enumerated and commented upon ten texts spanning much of the recorded history of Chinese agronomy. He began with the *Lesser Annuary of the Xia* (*Xia xiao zheng*), a calendrical record of celestial, phenological, and agrarian phenomena dating to the Zhou period (1045–256 BCE), and concluded with the magnus opus of late Ming scholar Xu Guangqi, the *Complete Treatise on Agricultural Administration* (*Nongzheng quanshu*). Such a collection of works not only encompassed knowledge from different historical eras but also illuminated various areas of expertise about how to make the best use of soil, plants, and water for production. When discussing three treatises from the Yuan dynasty (1271–1368), for example, Zuo praised them for their insights into the proper growing conditions for certain plants and the proper plants for certain soils and environments, or what he called the "suitability of the soils and the nature of things." His knowledge of textual sources also covered works in related fields of scholarship, including materia medica.[40]

Among all of the texts that he read, Zuo reserved special praise for Xu Guangqi's scholarly masterpiece. The book had its origins in the early seventeenth century, during a period of repeated natural disasters. In 1608, while Xu was at home in southern Jiangsu province to observe a period of mourning following the death of his father, the region endured a bout of serious flooding. By then Xu was already an established scholar with a record of government service and considerable knowledge of astronomy, mathematics, and hydrology. As a matter of principle, Xu believed that expanding agricultural production was the best way to increase wealth in a society under duress.[41] When confronted by the disaster, he seems to have become more interested in researching agriculture. He scoured written works for relevant information and conducted experiments on cultivation techniques and crops like the sweet potato. By the time of his death in 1633, he had consulted well over two hundred sources. The result of his efforts was a text with an almost encyclopedic coverage of topics ranging from irrigation and farming tools to animal husbandry and famine relief.[42] Xu's treatise was published posthumously by a group of late Ming scholars who saw its potential value for helping to rescue Chinese society in troubled times.[43] After its initial publication, it remained out of print for two centuries, until 1836, when He Changling took the initiative to republish the work as part of an effort to galvanize interest in agricultural technology among farmers in Guizhou, where he was then serving in high office.[44] It is unclear when Zuo examined the work for the first time, but by 1838 he had read enough of it to confess his reverence for Xu's painstaking research methods and his work's broad coverage of myriad agricultural topics.[45]

As his readings in agricultural scholarship expanded, one thing that Zuo learned was the existence of regional styles of agriculture. Decades later, he recalled having "enjoyed studying and probing into the various books about northern agriculture and southern agriculture."[46] While the distinctions between farming in different parts of China no doubt reflected regional discrepancies in social practices and environmental conditions, agricultural treatises themselves played a role in fostering the idea that there were northern and southern versions of agriculture. At least as early as the sixth century, when Jia Sixie wrote his *Essential Techniques for the Common People* (*Qimin yaoshu*), Chinese agronomists were employing geographical categories to describe variations in crops, cultivation patterns, irrigation systems, and the like. Elite consciousness of these regional characteristics solidified over the centuries, as population centers shifted, agriculture expanded, and the corpus of agricultural scholarship developed. Wang Zhen, a native of Shandong who served in office in southern provinces in the Yuan period, carried out a "systematic and conscientious effort to contrast northern and southern agricultural technology" in his work, simply titled *Agricultural Treatise* (*Nongshu*), adding his imprimatur on the preexisting practice of categorizing agricultural tools and tecnhiques by region.[47] By the Qing period, the regionalization of agrarian scholarship had advanced considerably, with authors paying greater attention to local environments and practices beyond the north-south binary. In early eighteenth-century Hunan, for example, provincial native Li Jinxing contributed to this literature by writing a slim volume that reflected the prominence of riziculture in the hilly terrain of his native place, located in the southern part of the province.[48] While there is no indication that Zuo read Li's work, he was aware of the regional nature of agricultural knowledge and seemed to grasp the value of learning about agrarian practices in different parts of the empire.

Another lesson Zuo learned was that textual sources of knowledge about agriculture had certain epistemic limitations. Treatises could illuminate many aspects of farming, and people had much to gain by reading them. But there were some things about agriculture that were "difficult to speak about," Zuo wrote, and thus hard to record in writing.[49] This presented a quandary to officials, who often relied upon textual sources of knowledge to do their jobs. The Qing system of rotating appointments meant that high-ranking officials were regularly transferred from post to post, often in different provinces, because so-called laws of avoidance prohibited them from holding office in their native provinces, within five hundred *li* of their homes, or in provinces inhabited by close relatives.[50] In principle, these regulations precluded conflicts of interest, reduced opportunities for corruption, and forestalled provincialism in the ranks of the bureaucracy. But it also meant that magistrates, prefects, governors, and governors-general often were unfamiliar with the social and ecological conditions of the regions to which they were assigned. "Those who govern a locale are not the people accustomed to its soil," Zuo noted. As for knowing about "the fertility of the soil, the timing of the seasons, the location of water sources, the suitability of plants to soils, and the efficacy of tools, they certainly cannot match the people of the land, who have pondered them for a long time and who know about them in great detail."[51] In other words, officials who had to rely upon written texts for insights about agriculture would never be able to match the accumulated wisdom of the local people. This conundrum was significant because it created a contradiction with potentially large implications for agricultural policy: officials who possessed an inferior knowledge of local environments had the power to formulate agricultural policies and promote certain technologies, while local residents who were deeply familiar with the land had limited power to influence policies.

As Zuo explained in his examination essay, the proper response to this problem was to make sure that officials overcame the limitations of their own knowledge by seeking information from alternative sources. They could gain an experiential awareness of environmental conditions by personally traveling through the countryside and calling on farmers to share their expertise about crops and planting methods.[52] In his emphasis on the benefits of seeking advice from local farmers, Zuo reiterated a principle of natural knowledge dating back at least to the Spring and Autumn period (770–481 BCE), which recognized the value of information from experts and local informants who possessed a hands-on knowledge of the world. Confucius famously advised one of his students to seek knowledge from "old farmers" and "old gardeners" if he wanted to learn about agriculture and horticulture.[53] Meanwhile, Zuo's recommendation that officials learn about places through sensory perception and observation reflected another longstanding tendency among elites to place value on personal experience as a source of knowledge. Certainly by the late Ming period, but probably at least by the Song dynasty and perhaps much earlier, literati were emphasizing the usefulness of experience and observation as modes of inquiry.[54] The recognition of the need to supplement bookish learning with local and experiential sources of knowledge gained wide acceptance, influencing not just late Ming scholars in fields such as agriculture and geography but also their intellectual heirs in later eras.[55]

After dealing with such questions, Zuo came to the conclusion that official campaigns for agricultural development had to be tailored to local ecological and economic conditions, even if that meant deviating from the best or most profitable practices employed elsewhere. Officials should enact policies based upon climate and soil characteristics, he wrote. In principle, this meant that officials in different parts of the empire would employ a diverse range of strategies and technologies to improve production in the areas they governed. To illustrate his argument, Zuo offered a hypothetical case involving irrigation policies in the empire's southeast and northwest. Because the southeast enjoyed a natural abundance of water but the northwest was naturally arid and had soils prone to erosion, officials "need not force the northwest all to be paddy fields or the southeast all to be a vast plain of dry land." Acknowledging the connection between environments and social customs, Zuo determined that officials "need not force the people of the southeast to eat wheat or the people of the northwest to eat rice." He extended a similar logic to the question of crop varieties. Although sericulture occupied a prime place in the empire's economy and ideology, the exam candidate admitted that a host of nongrain plants, from jujubes and chestnuts to cotton and ramie, could be valuable crops in certain regions and should not be removed automatically to accommodate the cultivation of mulberry trees and the raising of silkworms.[56] Thus, by his rationale, officials could help maximize the material benefits derived from agriculture by preserving some degree of ecological and cultural diversity across the imperial territories.

The 1838 examination turned out to be a disappointment for Zuo. It was his third attempt to win the "presented scholar" degree, and his failure left him feeling dejected. He had had enough of Beijing, he wrote, and he would "not again walk through the vanity fair and compete with a group of juveniles to be a mere piece of rejected fruit by the roadside."[57] This failure narrowed his chances for career advancement, at least along the route he had planned to take. Although he later considered obtaining the office of county magistrate through outright purchase and even contributed some money to secure the post, teaching became his primary vocation in the following years.[58] But teaching was not his only pursuit. While giving up on his quest for examination success, Zuo remained committed to carrying on the family lineage by creating opportunities for subsequent generations of Zuo men to achieve career success via the examination system. To make this possible, he opted for a household strategy called "plowing and reading" (*gengdu*), which meant trying to pursue his family's prosperity through agriculture and academics simultaneously. This strategy revolved around using the household's investments in land and its income from rents and agricultural production to support the education of young men in the family. They would be expected to strive for a top degree in the imperial examinations to achieve a position in the bureaucracy, which could bring income, privilege, and prestige to the family.

Zuo characterized the dual pursuits of farming and studying as a family tradition.[59] But the tradition was hardly unique to his family. In fact, it was a commonplace strategy among the tens of thousands of families who had aspirations for using the examination system as a pathway of upward social mobility. One of the leading exponents of this strategy, seventeenth-century scholar Zhang Ying, characterized permanent property in land as the single most important vehicle for maintaining a family's wealth and social standing over the long term. In his short treatise *Remarks on Real Estate* (*Hengchan suoyan*), Zhang wrote that even tiny parcels of land could be made to yield income. He counseled readers to capitalize on their investments by choosing diligent tenants and immersing themselves in the technical details of agriculture—including learning how to plant, fertilize, and irrigate farmland—to maximize productivity.[60] It is possible that Zuo may have read the abbreviated version of Zhang's treatise that appeared in the *Compilation of Statecraft Essays*.[61] Yet, regardless of the source of his inspiration, Zuo had started to view the acquisition of property as his best bet for supporting the next generation of scholars in the family. At the time of his marriage to Zhou Yiduan in 1832, he could not afford to buy property, leaving the couple with no choice but to reside with her family.[62] But by the early 1840s, with money that he had earned from teaching, Zuo made an effort to purchase his own tract of land in northern Hunan.

Zuo's desire to acquire farmland was magnified by the outbreak of an unforeseen political crisis. In 1839, the dispute between the Qing government and foreign merchants over the opium trade in southern China erupted into war, plunging the empire into serious turmoil and causing great consternation. Amid reports of British violence along the coasts, Zuo wrote to friends and teachers expressing his fears and his determination to find a safe haven far away from everything that was happening. "Current events are gradually becoming worse," he explained to He Xiling in 1841, filling him with trepidation and leading him to "consider choosing a distant, secluded place where no human traces have reached, buying ten-plus *mu* of land, and personally farming there."[63] A year later, he lamented that "since I cannot plunge into the sea to perish, the only thing to do is to purchase a mountain and go into hiding."[64] His plan to acquire a hideout in the hills and live in seclusion to weather the ongoing crisis was hardly an original idea. Some scholars of the late Ming period who lived through the Manchu conquest of their country had retreated from cities to the countryside to avoid the worst of the violence and to find places where they could carry on with scholarship relatively undisturbed by the political turmoil around them. Perhaps inspired by their example, Zuo began to investigate available properties in the vicinity of Xiangyin, including a secluded, mountainous place with fertile land called Biyunfeng, where people of the late Ming had reportedly gone to "hide from the world."[65] In 1843, Zuo finally settled on a piece of property. Using the savings from his work as a teacher, he purchased seventy *mu* of land at a spot called Liujiachong in the Xiangyin countryside. The following year, he moved his family to this new homestead, giving it the name Liuzhuang, meaning "Willow Manor."[66]

Despite his claims about retreating from the world, Zuo's prospects for household success through landownership depended upon the countryside's connections to markets far and wide. Indeed, it was the commercialization of rural life and the growth of networks of exchange for agricultural commodities that had long made "plowing and reading" a useful strategy for households with aspirations for social mobility.[67] By the early nineteenth century, Hunan was well connected to markets throughout the Qing realm. The province was crisscrossed by routes used by shippers and porters to move a panoply of agricultural commodities and precious merchandise. Up and down the Xiang River, boats conveyed rice, tobacco, tea, bamboo, rosin, paper, parasols, eggs, fruit, and medicinal materials.[68] Hunan's largest export commodity was rice, and merchants shipped load after load down the Yangzi River to large urban markets in Jiangnan, the region south of the river along its lower reaches. Merchants from afar also flocked to Hunan, where they sold felts, furs, and carpets from the northwestern provinces, silks from Jiangnan, and various wares from other regions, including pickles, processed tobacco, alcohol, medicinal materials, fans, and ocean products.[69]

Although Zuo sometimes made known his aversion to the hubbub of big cities like Changsha, it was impossible for him to avoid the influence of urban markets on agriculture or deny the appeal of earning an income from farming.[70] Market demand influenced the way he viewed the possibilities for land use. During his search for property, he imagined how an available parcel of land in a place called Qingshan could be exploited for the production of subsistence and cash crops, providing his family with firewood for cooking and potatoes and yams for sustenance while also yielding returns on mulberry, bamboo, and sheep.[71] Commercial opportunities also influenced his household's decisions about agriculture. Starting in 1840, Zuo worked for eight years in the city of Anhua as a private tutor to the son of Tao Shu, a deceased Qing official. Located in the hills of central Hunan, Anhua and its surrounding area had long been known for its cultivation of tea. Production surged in the eighteenth century as the demand for tea increased, stimulated by the growth of domestic consumption and the expansion of the border tea trade in Xinjiang.[72] Zuo's presence in Anhua opened his eyes to the strong profit-making potential of tea farming and gave him an understanding of how other crops like palm, paulownia, plum, and bamboo brought cash into the local economy.[73] This knowledge inspired him to try growing tea at Liuzhuang in the mid-1840s, and he was delighted by the results, which showed that the income from tea alone could suffice to cover the taxes that he owed on his property. Given the successful outcome of his trials with tea, he was eager to take advantage of his land for the production of tea, bamboo, mulberry, and other cash crops.[74]

Zuo's interest in agriculture in these years was driven by the need to provide for his family, which grew to include his wife, a concubine, four daughters, and two sons by the late 1840s. Yet, after 1838, it also reflected wider ambitions. Before leaving the imperial capital to return to Hunan in the spring of that year, the twenty-something patronized the city's bookshops and decided to purchase a large number of agricultural treatises.[75] His acquisition of these works signaled his growing desire to research subjects of practical value and "abandon ornamental phrases" in favor of "useful studies," as his mentor He Xiling put it.[76] It also demonstrated his resolve to learn more about agricultural technology with the intention of leaving his own mark on agrarian scholarship. In the spirit of practical learning and evidential research, and likely influenced by the example of meticulous investigation set by Xu Guangqi, Zuo planned to examine the treatises, submit their contents to trials in the fields, and thereby carry out "on-the-ground testing." He then intended to take the results of his experiments and "compose them into a book for instruction in agriculture and horticulture."[77]

One of Zuo's earliest forays in experimentation focused on sericulture. In 1839, he obtained a thousand mulberry saplings and planted them where he then resided, with his wife's family in the vicinity of Xiangtan, to learn how to cultivate the trees and to test the profitability of silk production.[78] As he and his family grew mulberry trees and raised silkworms, Zuo developed a routine of pairing the hands-on experience of tending the organisms with the scholastic practice of reading extensively about how to rear them. He consulted Xu Guangqi's treatise, scouring the text for methods that he could test in the hope of improving his trees' production of mulberry leaves, which were fed to the silkworms. While he was away in Anhua, he was delighted to learn that his household had produced over twenty thousand silkworm cocoons in the spring of 1840, a result that allowed him to get a glimpse of what economic benefits might come from pursuing sericulture further.[79] Yet, at least in letters to family, he maintained that he had loftier objectives than making money. As he told one of his brothers-in-law, he intended to accumulate knowledge about mulberries and silkworms through reading and experience so that he could educate other farmers. As an aspiring official still without an official post, he thought that helping the community to profit from sericulture could be "our great meritorious and virtuous deed."[80]

In the following years, Zuo's curiosity about agricultural technology came to focus on a particular cropping pattern, the plot farming method (*qutian fa*), sometimes called the pit farming method. To carry out plot farming, farmers divided one *mu* of land into thousands of small squares and then cultivated the squares in various patterns, concentrating their labor on particular sections of soil, intensifying their day-to-day management of the crops, and economizing on the input of seeds, water, and fertilizer. Like other scholars, Zuo was probably attracted to plot farming because of its professed potential to boost productivity relative to average cropping methods. Some proponents claimed that yields from soil cultivated with methods of plot farming could reach as high as thirty *dan* or more of grain per *mu*—an astounding figure when compared with the roughly three *dan* of rice that an average *mu* of paddy land in Jiangnan was said to produce in good years.[81] Zuo also may have been motivated to study plot farming for its purported ability to serve as a measure of famine prevention. Agronomists wrote that fields cultivated using this method could produce decent harvests even in years of little or no rain, an alluring claim at a time of unusually disruptive weather events.

Zuo must have known about plot farming well before 1838, when he returned to Hunan with a load of books on agriculture. In the Qing period, plot farming was the subject of a great deal of attention from scholars. Their

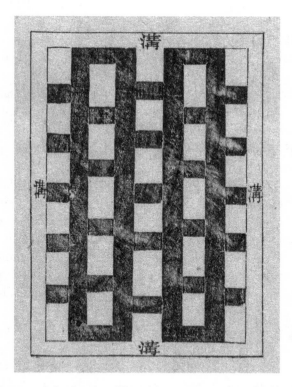

Figure 1.2 Diagram of plot farming. The white spaces are planted with rice, the black spaces are left uncultivated, and the entire area is surrounded by irrigation ditches. From Pan Zengyi, *Kenong quzhong fa tu* (Illustration of the method of plot farming for teaching farmers), 1834. Courtesy of Harvard-Yenching Library.

enduring fascination with this technology was certainly related to its potential for improving agricultural productivity. But as a topic of research, plot farming also seemed to be tailor-made for the intellectual climate of the era. Learning about it combined the opportunity to conduct extensive textual research with the prospect of acquiring useful knowledge with immediate practical benefit. Scholars who examined the pages of major treatises in the canon of Chinese agronomy discovered that many of them discussed plot farming and its historical origins, which dated back at least to the era of the Western Han (206 BCE–8 CE), when the method appeared in the textual record for the first time.[82] The standard-bearer of early nineteenth-century statecraft, He Changling, also played a role in fostering interest in plot farming, having chosen to include three essays about it in the *Compilation of Statecraft Essays*.[83] Later, when he served as governor of Guizhou, He compiled a short tract to educate the province's poor farmers about the method.[84]

Zuo is likely to have read all of the works on plot farming in the statecraft compilation, including an essay by seventeenth-century scholar Lu Shiyi.[85] Born in Jiangnan in 1611, Lu developed an interest in agricultural technology in the aftermath of the Manchu conquest of his homeland. In 1644, he sought refuge from the violence by retreating to the countryside, and it was there that he began to research cultivation methods even though he admitted to being physically weak and ignorant of farming tools.[86] As he studied agriculture and took a more active role in supervising cultivation by tenant farmers on the twenty *mu* of land he owned, Lu became curious to know more about plot farming and to learn why such a "marvelous method" was not in wider use. After speaking with farmers near his hometown, he concluded that a combination of factors, such as the characteristics of local soils and people's reservations about the amount of labor required to build and tend the plots, prevented them from using the method more regularly.[87] Still not satisfied, he hatched a plan to conduct trials of plot farming to gain first-hand knowledge of its productivity and its limitations.[88] The results of the experiment, carried out in seven small plots next to the house of a friend, were a disappointment; harvests taken from the plots were smaller than those from normal fields. But Lu interpreted the results as an indication that the experiment had been tainted by improper seeding, foul manure, and other issues, not as an indictment of plot farming in general.[89] Perhaps more important, the results of the trial were omitted from the version of Lu's essay that appeared in the *Compilation of Statecraft*

Essays, with the likely effect that many nineteenth-century scholars received a less blemished view of the method and a more optimistic impression of its potential to boost yields.

The most outspoken advocate of plot farming in Zuo Zongtang's own day was probably Pan Zengyi, a native of the Jiangsu province city of Suzhou. The holder of a "recommended man" degree, Pan grumbled that farmers in his area suffered from a myopia for "petty profits." In his view, their desire to make money drove them to employ certain farming techniques that diminished soil quality and crop productivity.[90] Beginning in 1828, Pan set out to convince farmers of the efficacy of plot farming for rice production, hoping to show that it could improve annual yields and enrich soil quality at the same time.[91] Believing that farmers would overcome their hesitation to adopt the method if they could see it in practice, Pan set up demonstration gardens around the city where he conducted trials and modeled plot farming for any farmers who cared to come and take a look. In addition, he handed out awards to farmers who obtained the largest harvests with plot farming, and he devised a set of "handy guidelines" about the method for distribution to locals.[92] Several years later, he printed an illustrated leaflet containing terse month-by-month instructions for how to put plot farming into practice.[93] He also compiled a short treatise based upon his experience of promoting agriculture in Suzhou. After its publication in 1834, the treatise caught the attention of literati in other provinces, including Zuo Zongtang, who asked one of his mentors to help him acquire a copy.[94]

Zuo's appetite for agricultural research and his fascination with plot farming grew in the 1840s as his hopes of a career in officialdom seemed to fade. Writing to He Xiling, he expressed his desire to leave his teaching job in Anhua, return home, and rent over ten *mu* of land so that he could "test out the ancient method of plot farming" and promote its use among farmers.[95] A few years later, after he moved to Liuzhuang, he used his own property for field trials and came to regard the practice of experiential research as a pillar of his identity as a rural scholar. "Every time I return from Anhua," he wrote in 1844, "I supervise and attend to cultivation, taking what I research on an everyday basis and testing it out. I spend my days going through the fields and call myself the Farmer on the Xiang River."[96] His commitment to studying "ancient farming methods that are useful in the present" also reflected an expectation that he could teach what he had learned to tenant farmers and hired laborers to improve their productivity.

Yet he found that disseminating such technology through discussions with farmers was not as easy as other scholars had made it seem. The people whom he taught were unable to implement the method of plot farming with complete success.[97]

Despite such letdowns, Zuo used his research and his experiential knowledge as a springboard for writing his own treatises. Sometime after 1838, he composed a short tract on plot farming with the intention of publicizing it to farmers.[98] In the preface to the work, Zuo championed the method, presenting it as an ideal technique to improve rural productivity and create abundance throughout the empire, especially in the face of environmental adversities such as droughts and insect plagues. He touted its numerous benefits, including the method's ability to help farmers conserve water and soil fertility, and he claimed that it could lead to increases in harvest yields of tenfold or more. Echoing Pan Zengyi, he worried about the short-sightedness, complacency, and ignorance of farmers, but maintained that, once they were able to learn the real facts about plot farming, they would consider it a useful strategy of cultivation.[99] Aside from writing this tract, Zuo also worked on a treatise with a more general focus. Entitled the *Agricultural Treatise from the Pavilion of Pucun (Pucun ge nongshu)*, the work contained over ten chapters on various aspects of farming.[100] It is impossible to know exactly how the contexts of the treatise may have reflected his particular interests in agrarian technology and his outlook on land use, as the work is no longer extant. But it seems to have been a culminating product of more than a decade of study, and Zuo was certainly proud of his work, hoping naively that it would someday reach a wide audience as an "essential book for the world."[101]

No amount of research, whether in agriculture or other subjects, could have fully prepared anyone for the weather events and disasters that battered Hunan in the late 1840s. From late 1846 to early 1847, the northern part of the province endured months of intense drought.[102] Then, in 1848, unusually heavy rainfall caused devastating flooding and major crop losses.[103] In some areas of Xiangyin, the waters rose above six meters, swamping embankments and damaging an untold number of homes.[104] At Liuzhuang, located a mere ten *li* from the Xiang River, fields were inundated, grains molded, and everyone in Zuo's family fell ill.[105] Flooding worsened the following year, when nearly all counties in the province suffered from standing water. Houses and dikes collapsed, market transactions had to be conducted by boat in some places, contagion spread quickly, and countless people died.[106] Cities and rural areas across Hunan were filled with refugees, and groups numbering in the thousands roved around looking for victuals.[107] The provincial government tried to ameliorate the severity of the disaster by setting up soup kitchens to feed the hungry.[108] Zuo's family also participated in relief efforts by collecting donations of grain and money from rich households, offering meals to people who happened to pass by the family homestead, and helping to set up a facility to formulate medicine for the sick.[109] But such activities could do only so much to reduce the hardship, which touched nearly everyone in the province, elites and commoners alike.

These floods seem to have curtailed Zuo's research in agriculture, probably because high waters made it virtually impossible to carry out experimental fieldwork and diverted his attention from textual studies to more pressing matters. But, by that point, Zuo had become quite familiar with farming practices and technologies. He liked to believe that this knowledge distinguished him from many of his contemporaries, whom he chided for their stodgy scholasticism and their neglect of practical learning.[110] Perhaps the most basic thing he learned, however, was something he shared with many others in a diachronic community of literati stretching back to the late Ming period: the importance of figuring out how to exploit the earth to its fullest potential. Officials and scholars working in the statecraft tradition felt a deep sense of responsibility to help people "exhaustively use the resources of the land," as Peter Perdue has written.[111] They regularly invoked concepts like the "profits of the land" (dili) in discussions of policy and technology and professed their dedication to the idea that making the most of the world's resources through agriculture and other industries was essential to sustaining the social fabric.[112] Zuo embraced the discourse and logic of natural resource exploitation without hesitation. At times, his attention to such questions was no doubt personal. Writing about Liuzhuang in 1846, he stated his intention to cultivate and harvest tea and bamboo as a means to "exhaust the profits of the land," a reflection of his financial interests as a rural landowner.[113] Even so, there is reason to believe that he also assimilated the concerns and commitments of practical learning and statecraft scholarship, including their emphasis on studying and promoting agriculture for the benefit of public welfare and the imperial state.

This way of thinking about natural resources had the effect of making Qing elites more observant of the world around them. They were sensitive to the problems of abundance and scarcity and more perceptive of the discrepancies between existing and potential levels of agricultural production based upon their appraisals of environments and local customs. Especially in times of crisis, they took note of places where lands and other resources appeared to be underutilized. Indeed, insofar as agriculture relies upon the existence of land, its promotion was not just technological, but also territorial. As Zuo came to learn, the idea of using agriculture to ease some of the most daunting challenges facing the Qing state in the nineteenth century was a spatial question that implicated even the outer reaches of the empire.

CHAPTER II

Geography in a Growing Empire

On an early January evening in 1850, just weeks before the Chinese New Year, Zuo Zongtang boarded a boat on the Xiang River where it flowed past the city of Changsha. Then employed as a teacher in the city, Zuo had become a well-known figure among Hunanese elites through family ties and patronage networks that connected him with scholars and officials far and wide.[1] The previous year, a fellow provincial had recommended his name to Lin Zexu, one of the most prominent statesmen of his time. Lin's lengthy resume of service to the imperial government included his role as imperial commissioner in charge of enforcing the prohibition on the opium trade in southern China when tensions with the British catapulted the two countries into war in 1839.[2] Now, as Lin was passing through Changsha, having just completed a different term in office, Zuo took the opportunity to meet and talk with him in person. The two must have felt a certain rapport, for their conversation lasted late into the night.[3] They may have discussed Lin's tense dealings with the British and his efforts to eradicate opium smuggling. But, years later, Zuo would recall another element of their exchange: the elder statesman's insights about agrarian development in Xinjiang.

Lin was no stranger to the empire's western borderland. In 1840, he had been dismissed from office for his inability to resolve the military crisis over opium, and he was later punished with a sentence of exile in Xinjiang. After reaching the territory in late 1842, he was called upon to assist with a number of government matters, including the supervision of rural development. Under the leadership of Bu-yan-tai, the Manchu general who governed Xinjiang in the early 1840s, Lin participated in campaigns to build irrigation systems and reclaim land from the deserts, mobilizing the labor of Qing troops in an effort that added hundreds of thousands of *mu* of farmland to the region's agrarian landscape. In 1844, acting under the emperor's direction, Bu-yan-tai dispatched Lin on a mission to the oasis communities of southern Xinjiang, where he and a different Manchu minister carried out extensive surveys of lands and waterways. Their goal was to count recently reclaimed farmland and search for wasteland that could be brought under cultivation in the future.[4] Traveling across the region for the better part of a year, Lin gained extensive firsthand knowledge of its environments and resources, enabling him to visualize the possibilities for the further growth of agriculture and other industries.[5]

When he met with Zuo Zongtang in Changsha, Lin recounted his experiences in Xinjiang, telling the younger scholar about oasis agriculture and explaining strategies for exploiting the region's soil and water resources. From his perspective, no strategy was more essential than colonization. He advised Zuo that, without an active policy of colonial settlement in Xinjiang, the "profits of the land will not be exhausted, with the result that fertile areas will be unable to prosper and become strong."[6] An expert in riziculture, Lin also suggested that the expansion of rice cultivation in southern Xinjiang could be the key to its development, apparently worrying little about the ecological obstacles to carrying out such a plan.[7] He counseled Zuo that if the territory's farming settlements built more extensive hydraulic infrastructure in the fashion of wealthy cities like Suzhou and Songjiang in Jiangsu province, using what they had built to irrigate rice paddies, the "fine profits" resulting from such work would match the material rewards of rice farming in southeastern China, the empire's most productive agricultural region.[8]

Lin's comments left a deep impression on Zuo, one that he would remember for decades, perhaps because they diverged from certain mainstream perspectives on Xinjiang among Chinese elites in the early nineteenth century. From a narrowly financial point of view, some worried that the Qing state was squandering its monetary resources to pay for the maintenance of imperial dominion in Xinjiang.[9] Such worries persisted as the annual costs of supporting military deployments in the territory increased.

The amount of money sent to the territory reached close to one million taels of silver by the 1820s and jumped to over four million taels—or roughly one-tenth of total annual government revenues—in the 1840s.[10] Beyond these financial concerns, many harbored a cultural aversion to Xinjiang, regarding it as little more than a distant, alien frontier that was arid and desolate and thus possessed no appreciable value for their country. Indeed, the Qing government recognized this aversion and exploited it, sending common criminals and disgraced officials such as Lin to serve sentences of exile there. Because the territory was so far removed from China and because some exiles were never permitted to return home, this punishment was considered to be "second only to execution" in its degree of severity.[11] This must have only increased the sense of foreboding that many Chinese elites felt when they thought about the region.

Despite the salience of such perspectives, Zuo Zongtang was inclined to view the borderland through a different lens. By reading books and essays about Xinjiang produced in the decades after Qing armies conquered the territory in the 1750s, he not only gained a basic familiarity with the region and its geography; he also learned about its natural resources, especially its seemingly limitless abundance of open land. He came to consider such resources as useful tools in the struggle to relieve social tensions in the empire's populous eastern and southern provinces, the areas that scholars collectively called the "innerland" (*neidi*). In these decades, Qing leaders were confronted by a host of problems. They had to deal with the costly matter of maintaining embankments along the Yellow River and the Grand Canal and respond to disastrous floods caused by their failure, as happened in 1824.[12] But Zuo Zongtang and other literati seemed to regard overpopulation and its myriad consequences as perhaps the most disturbing dilemma of all. They were particularly concerned about the phenomenon of land scarcity, which threatened to lead to food shortages, rend the social fabric, and undermine political stability. As they became more familiar with Xinjiang, however, they were increasingly inclined to see its lands and resources as offering a colonial solution to China's demographic plight. Echoing emperors and officials of the eighteenth century, they thought that troubles related to robust population growth and land scarcity could be managed, if not entirely solved, by encouraging people from the provinces to migrate to the western borderland, where they could take up farming and settle down permanently. This way of thinking caused Zuo Zongtang and other Chinese elites to grow accustomed to seeing Xinjiang not as a forsaken frontier but as a place of potential development whose fate was increasingly intertwined with the fortunes of Chinese colonists.

For a young scholar growing up in Hunan, the acquisition of knowledge about the geography of the empire began with books and maps. Around the year 1829, Zuo Zongtang purchased several large treatises on historical geography written by late Ming literati Gu Yanwu and Gu Zuyu.[13] He was soon enthralled in studying them. He spent entire days scouring their contents for information about topography and military strategy, filling blank volumes with notes as he went along.[14] Employing methods of research that were prevalent in his day, he consulted multiple sources of evidence to validate or reject claims he found in the texts. Over time, he developed a practice of using what he had learned through reading to draw and revise maps of the empire and its various regions. He also turned to his wife for assistance, relying upon her knowledge and her labor to analyze geography and draft cartographic images on paper.[15]

Over time, Zuo's research grew to encompass sources that belonged to a more recent body of scholarship that focused on the empire's northern and western borderlands. Produced in the wake of the empire's territorial expansion, this scholarship was driven partly by the demand for new knowledge about places that were beyond the ken of most Manchu, Mongol, and Chinese officials and often poorly documented in previous writings. It grew especially in the decades after the conquest of Xinjiang, as the Qing court sponsored projects to gather information about the territory, its peoples, and their languages and histories. Research about the borderlands also flourished through the efforts of individual officials and scholars, who carried out textual studies, conducted personal observations, and employed other methods of investigation to produce a corpus on new information that reached the hands of scholars across China.[16]

Within this body of scholarship, the source that most influenced Zuo's conception of Xinjiang was the voluminous *Illustrated Gazetteer of the Western Regions (Xiyu tuzhi).*[17] This gazetteer, commissioned by the Qianlong emperor in 1755, was completed only after many years of textual research and on-site observations carried out by Qing officials in the newly conquered territory.[18] Although Zuo Zongtang left few notes indicating how this text influenced his thinking, what he gleaned from it was almost certainly shaped by patterns of information that typified the genre of the gazetteer. As compendia of knowledge about particular places and regions, gazetteers offered many insights about local geography, history, and society to those who read them.[19] Gazetteers compiled in the Qing period usually contained one or more sections comprised of details about local topographical features and environmental conditions, such as the locations and characteristics of rivers and mountains. They also often included annotated lists of local products ranging from domesticated and wild varieties of plants and animals to minerals and manufactured goods. In short, these texts offered snapshots of local geography and shed some light on how material culture intersected with local ecological conditions.[20]

One of the first things Zuo may have learned about Xinjiang from reading gazetteers was the centrality of the region's lofty mountains to its physical geography. Running through the territory and encircling the Zunghar Basin in the north and the Tarim Basin in the south, Xinjiang's mountains were its premiere landmarks, helping Qing officials to orient themselves in an unfamiliar terrain. These mountains have also played a crucial role in shaping the territory's climate. By blocking the movement of precipitation-bearing clouds, they have fostered the conditions for intense aridity in certain places. This is especially true of the Tarim Basin and its central physical feature, the Taklamakan Desert, which receives only minimal amounts of rainfall every year.[21] But the mountains themselves generally receive larger amounts of precipitation. Certain parts of the Tianshan Mountains accumulate enough moisture to support large areas of alpine woodlands and grasslands. For this reason, the mountains have served as an essential source of water for organisms inhabiting the region. Flowing down out of the mountains, waters from melting snow and glaciers have long enabled plants, animals, and humans to colonize the dry, sandy soils of the basins.

Gazetteers also revealed that Xinjiang possessed an abundance of wildlife, a wide range of vegetation, and lots of minerals. Like similar works of scholarship, the *Illustrated Gazetteer of the Western Regions* cataloged the territory's resources, making it easy for readers to appreciate the full scope of its natural wealth even when the local names for flora, fauna, and minerals were derived from Turkic, Mongol, or other languages that were incomprehensible to nearly all Chinese elites in the provinces. Zuo could read about Xinjiang's grain crops, vegetables, fruits, melons, trees, grasses, flowers, birds, mammals, fish, insects, and reptiles, as well as its minerals, precious metals, salts, and gemstones. The most noteworthy products were the ones

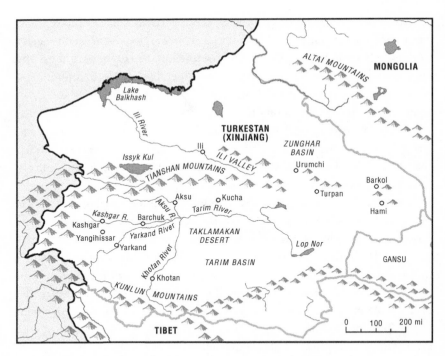

Map 2.1 Xinjiang in the early nineteenth century. Map by Erin Greb.

that differentiated the territory from the empire's other regions. Qi-shi-yi, a Manchu official who authored an account of Xinjiang, described the wild and curious things that could be harvested, hunted, or seen in its deserts, mountains, rivers, and lakes. There were groves of poplars and oleasters in the oases, herds of wild horses in the deserts, flocks of wild sheep in the forests, and snow lotuses growing on its mountain slopes.[22] Other products earned mention and even renown for being so unique or so highly valued that they became items of tribute shipped back to the court in Beijing. These included fruits like sweet melons and seedless grapes from Hami and Turpan, as well as jade stones gathered by the thousands of pounds from the foothills and riverbeds near Khotan.[23]

As he read gazetteers and other accounts of Xinjiang, Zuo also had the chance to glean information about the region's human geography. The largest and, by some measures, the most politically significant human communities in the territory were located in the oasis cities and farming settlements of eastern and southern Xinjiang. Populated by Turkic Muslims who maintained ties and shared cultural, linguistic, and religious affinities with Turkic and Islamic communities in other parts of Asia, the oases of the Tarim Basin constituted what Qing leaders called the empire's "Muslim borderland" (*Huijiang*). In this region, irrigated agriculture occupied the heart of the economy. Tens of thousands of households who inhabited the oases drew their sustenance and wealth primarily from cultivating staple grains like wheat and maize as well as horticulture and textile crops such as tree fruits and cotton. Others relied upon weaving, mining, hunting, or animal husbandry for a certain portion of their livelihoods. Because Turkestanis drew much of their livelihoods from agriculture and other sedentary occupations, they were considered to be more akin to people in the Chinese provinces than some of the native inhabitants of other Qing borderlands who were pastoralists or hunters. As the authors of one work wrote, compared with groups of nonsedentary Kyrgyz who inhabited certain parts of Xinjiang, Turkestanis "practice agriculture to exhaust the profits of the land," and thus were more capable of taking advantage of the resources around them.[24]

The human geography of northern Xinjiang was markedly different. Before the mid-eighteenth century, the region had been under the control of a confederation of Mongols, the Zunghars, who became engaged in a series of military clashes with Qing leaders. While they themselves were pastoralists, they relied upon the labor of Turkestanis from the Tarim Basin and a multiethnic group of war captives to develop their economic and military capacities through agriculture, mining, commerce, and manufacturing.[25] During the Qing conquest of the territory, which was launched to put an end to the Zunghar polity, the human population of the region north of the Tianshan Mountains was decimated, although later claims that the Zunghars had been completely annihilated were exaggerated.[26] Even so, the victory allowed Beijing to take possession of a massive and sparsely populated region comprising the forests and pastures of the Tianshan and the extensive scrub lands and deserts to their north. Sources like the *Illustrated Gazetteer of the Western Regions* celebrated this acquisition and purveyed the idea that the region contained a bounty of unexploited resources: because the Zunghars had practiced not sedentary agriculture but animal husbandry, they had failed to capitalize on the region's soils, plants, and water, leaving a great many "leftover profits" (*yili*) for future colonists to exploit.[27]

Soon after the conquest, Qing leaders began to facilitate colonization in areas north of the Tianshan, seeking to create a more substantial economic foundation for their dominion. In these areas, a mixture of Manchu, Mongol, and Han troops, merchants and farmers from the provinces, and exiled convicts built irrigation systems and transformed grassland, scrubland, and desert into fields of wheat, barley, millet, and market vegetables. One important site of colonial development was Ili. Located in a river valley between two chains of mountains, the city of Ili served as the base of operations for Xinjiang's military governor, who oversaw various construction and development projects. In the process of establishing military colonies, officials and Qing troops tapped nearby rivers to irrigate new farmland. In addition, some six thousand households of Turkic Muslim farmers were recruited from southern Xinjiang and resettled in the valley, expanding the amount of arable land and boosting local grain production.[28] Some newcomers ventured into the mountains, exploiting seams of coal and iron to manufacture farming tools or chopping down trees to sate the demand for wood from the city's construction industry.[29] The region was also inhabited by an abundance of wildlife, including rabbits, pheasants, wolves, wild sheep, boar, gazelles, fish, and otters, some of which undoubtedly ended up in the stomachs of settlers.[30]

Meanwhile, the area around the city of Urumchi flourished as a hub of colonial agriculture and commerce, attracting tens of thousands of people from the Chinese provinces who viewed Xinjiang as an opportunity to make money or find work. Like Ili, Urumchi sat along important trade routes in close proximity to natural resources. Colonists in the area exploited nearby sources of coal and timber and harvested vegetation and wildlife from the mountains to sell in the city.[31] But, for settlers, the area's main attraction was its rivers and open land. For roughly the first quarter-century after the conquest, the Qing state offered subsidies to Chinese migrants willing to undertake the long journey to Urumchi.[32] Upon arrival, they received grants of land along with loans for tools, seeds, housing, and other expenses. Merchants also got involved in agricultural development, hiring laborers to farm the land they owned or renting plots to grow vegetables and other nonstaples that could fetch good money in urban markets.[33] By the turn of the nineteenth century, nearly 1.25 million *mu* of land had been brought under cultivation and the population of Urumchi and neighboring settlements extending eastward to Barkol had reached over 150,000 people.[34]

The expansion of colonial agriculture did not proceed without prompting questions about soil fertility. In the beginning, Qing leaders were confident that the lands of northern Xinjiang were highly fertile. Some attributed the soil's fecundity to its prior use as pastureland: in "old nomadic areas, fertilized cultivation is obtained from nature, and this is the reason why annual harvests are so abundant."[35] But farming soon depleted the land's nutrients, requiring settlers to find ways to keep their soils rich. In the Chinese provinces, where population densities were typically much higher, farmers customarily applied human and animal manures in combination with a range of other fertilizers to sustain soil fertility year after year.[36] In northern Xinjiang, however, low population density meant that there simply were not enough people or farm animals to sustain the type of intensive agriculture found in eastern and southern China. Indeed, as early as 1759, imperial officials recognized that farming in the Zunghar Basin differed from agriculture in the provinces to the extent that human manures were not available in the same quantities.[37] Colonists soon resorted to techniques like crop rotation and fallowing, sometimes for up to seven years in a row, giving soil time to recover nutrients through natural processes.[38] Fallowing and other practices of extensive cultivation, in turn, necessitated larger allotments of land. In part for this reason, government authorities granted approximately thirty *mu* of land to each household of military and civilian settlers.[39]

Despite questions about the maintenance of soil fertility, the system of colonial agriculture in northern Xinjiang appears to have functioned well enough to meet one of the state's key goals: sustaining an adequate supply of food for Qing troops. Average grain yields across the region varied significantly, but, in some places, harvests were far in excess of what the state could use. At the end of the eighteenth century, agriculture in Ili was so productive that food was going to waste. In 1799, the Ili general Bao-ning memorialized to Beijing to suggest that, because government stocks of grain were rotting in the warehouses, some troops working the fields should be demobilized and transferred to other duties.[40] Other northern cities reported similar grain surpluses around the same time.[41]

What rich agricultural harvests could not do was sustain or pay for Qing rule in Xinjiang by themselves. Aside from developing farming and mining enterprises in the north, officials relied on the populous cities of the Tarim Basin and their surrounding oases to furnish much-needed supplies. While they imposed certain taxes on Kashgar and Yarkand, they also collected a variety of material goods from across the oases, redistributing such items to government personnel or selling them to raise revenue. These items included grains, cooking oil, woven and raw cotton, saltpeter and sulfur for the production of gunpowder, and copper for the casting of coins.[42] In addition, the state levied duties on Kazakh and Kyrgyz herders, taking a fraction of their herds of cows, horses, and sheep as payment.[43] But Xinjiang's natural resource commodities were insufficient to keep the machinery of the military government functioning smoothly. To supplement local revenues, the state annually shipped thousands of bolts of silk cloth from the imperial silk workshops of Jiangnan to officials near the frontier, where they were traded along with other Chinese manufactures to Kazakhs in exchange for livestock.[44] Beijing also supplied annual financial subsidies to Xinjiang, sending silver via Gansu to pay for salaries and support the roughly forty thousand Qing troops who were stationed in the territory by the early nineteenth century.[45]

When Zuo Zongtang was still an adolescent, a small group of Chinese scholars in Beijing began to write about Xinjiang in a way that brought new attention to the territory. The city had long been a place of interaction among bureaucrats, expectant officials, and examination candidates, and it served as a natural meeting ground for like-minded literati who shared a penchant for scholarship about the western borderland. One of the most outspoken people to emerge from this group was Gong Zizhen. A native of Zhejiang province with a reputation for poor handwriting, Gong purchased an office within the Grand Secretariat after having failed to obtain a government post through the examination system.[46] Like others in his circle of interest, Gong sought to learn from Xu Song, a native of the capital who had served a sentence of exile in Xinjiang and had accumulated a wealth of knowledge through research and personal experience during his seven years there.[47] But even before he began to consult Xu and his writings, Gong had already thought deeply about Xinjiang and its future within the empire. In 1820, he wrote an essay in which he advanced the idea that the emperor should establish a provincial system of government in Xinjiang, with a new set of administrative districts and civil offices modeled upon the Chinese provinces. His proposal soon gained notoriety, and Gong was henceforth widely regarded as the first person to advocate for transforming the imperial territory into a province.

Although Gong's essay ostensibly focused on the administrative reorganization of Xinjiang, its underlying message revolved around the territory's natural resources. In his view, the region was a valuable possession because it held a great deal of open land that could be exploited for the benefit of Chinese people in the provinces. Like other early nineteenth-century analysts, Gong could not deny the existence of earnest concerns about the costs incurred by the imperial treasury in governing the region. But he railed against "moronic scholars with superficial views and ignoramuses from the countryside" who believed that annual outlays of silver amounted to "exhausting the center to manage the frontier."[48] Believing that financial calculations alone were not sufficient to grasp Xinjiang's importance, Gong offered an analysis in which he articulated its value by revealing how it could help to mitigate troubling social phenomena in the provinces.

Gong was deeply alarmed by the empire's prodigious population growth and the troubles it caused. "These days in China," he wrote, "the population is growing more numerous, circumstances are increasingly distressful, and the Yellow River is steadily more prone to disaster."[49] Gong, who was then in his late twenties, traced the rise of such problems to the long reign of the Qianlong emperor, who had presided over a so-called "prosperous age" of extraordinary demographic expansion and imperial conquest from the 1730s to the 1790s. Despite its reputation as a period of unparalleled power and affluence for state and society, it was also an era of growing tensions.[50] Writing a quarter of a century after the end of Qianlong's reign, Gong identified numerous drawbacks to the growth and prosperity that were visible in his own time. He fretted that as many as 50 or 60 percent of all people did not belong to any of the four customary social categories—scholars, farmers, artisans, and merchants—and therefore contributed nothing of value to society or the economy. People had become "accustomed to extravagant waste" and developed an insouciance for honest work. Excessive wealth gave rise to all types of social deviance, including opium smoking, the practice of heterodoxy, and vagrancy. As common people abandoned farm work for other pursuits, their fortunes declined. "In general, rich households have become poor households," he observed, "and poor households have become starving ones."[51] Paradoxically, the great wealth of the Qianlong era had created the conditions for great poverty.

Gong's gloomy assessment of Qing society was rooted in two assumptions about political economy. The first assumption was that the emergence of large numbers of people who appeared to contribute nothing useful to the economy but survived off the country's accumulated wealth was a sign of grave social imbalance. Such imbalance contravened several principles of statecraft outlined in classic works of Chinese political philosophy. These works advised rulers that the path to prosperity lay in making sure that producers outnumbered consumers and that production increased while consumption was restrained through frugal behavior.[52] The second assumption was that in order to increase the number of producers, people needed to have access to land, the most essential means of production in agriculture and the resource at the heart of the empire's agrarian economy. For Gong, the burgeoning ranks of China's landless population were among the clearest indications that society was coming undone.[53]

Gong's expression of concern about demographic growth, land shortages, and the contradictions of prosperity in China, though tied to his unprecedented call for provincial governance in Xinjiang, were altogether familiar to those who read his work. In fact, similar concerns had been voiced for more than a century. In the eighteenth century, emperors and scholars alike made regular, even hackneyed, comments about the number of people in China increasing on a daily basis. But behind such comments were real fears that the swelling population would outstrip the supply of arable land, leading to the even more distressing prospect of food scarcity. As early as 1709, the Kangxi emperor indicated his apprehension of this prospect, worrying that "although the population increases, farmland certainly has not increased" and wondering how many households could be fed by harvests obtained from the produce of a single household.[54] In the following decades, Kangxi's two successors conveyed similar misgivings about disparate rates of growth for the country's population and farmland. Data from the Qing period suggests that such fears were not unfounded. According to one calculation, the amount of arable land per capita declined from nearly four *mu* per person in the mid-eighteenth century to less than two *mu* per person by the 1830s.[55] Although such figures are only approximations, historians generally agree that the population of Qing China was growing faster than its supply of farmland in this period. While there is evidence to suggest that innovations in land use increased agricultural productivity by a modest amount during the Qing period, they did little to quell persistent anxieties about overpopulation and the looming threat of food scarcity.[56]

In the eighteenth century, the Qing emperors tried to tackle the population problem through campaigns to promote land reclamation. Policies encouraging people to open up new farmland received special emphasis during the thirteen-year reign of the Yongzheng emperor. In 1723, his first year on the throne, the emperor offered periods of tax remission of between six and ten years to farmers who were willing to develop fresh land for cultivation. He also mandated that local officials take charge of efforts to urge land reclamation among people in their districts.[57] Although the Qianlong emperor subsequently pursued a more moderate approach to policy-making, he also implemented plans that led to the exploitation of new soil. In 1740, he authorized tax exemptions for Chinese and non-Chinese civilians who agreed to cultivate "the fragments of land that can be opened up in the border provinces and the innerland," including "mountain tops and remote places" containing untold expanses of earth which could be pressed into service for the production of grain.[58]

High-ranking officials and literati also grew anxious about the imbalance between population and land resources. Chen Hongmou, the governor of Shaanxi province in 1744, revealed his apprehensions in a letter to another official. "Even if shorelines and mountain cliffs all were to become people's productive property," he admitted, "I still worry that a limited amount of land is not sufficient to nourish a growing populace."[59] Chen responded to the crisis in the same manner as the emperors, strongly encouraging people to engage in land reclamation activities. In Shaanxi and other provinces, he enacted plans to expand farm acreage and build waterworks for irrigation and flood control.[60] Chen recognized that opening up new soil for farming was not a perfect solution, as it pushed the frontiers of arable land into hilly, arid, and marginal terrains that were less fertile or less easily irrigated and thus usually less productive than existing farmland. While there was still much unused land on "mountainsides and shorelines" in the late 1740s, such places often had inferior soils, which required farmers to practice fallowing for durations of one or two years so that the soil could regain its fertility.[61] Even so, Chen and other leaders continued to view land reclamation as their best course of action in the face of incessant population growth.

After Xinjiang was incorporated into the empire in the 1750s, the Qianlong emperor began treating the territory as part of the solution for China's population problem. At the time, he was greatly perturbed by patterns of internal migration. Farmers from Shandong and other northern provinces were migrating to the northeast, into Manchuria, to escape poverty or natural disasters. By doing this, they were flouting the prohibition on settlement in the Manchu homeland that had been put in place to preserve the ecology and social stability of the region. Although Xinjiang was much further away, the emperor quickly decided that it should become a site of settlement for such migrants. In 1760, he decreed that "poor people without property" from Gansu should be encouraged to resettle in northern Xinjiang, and the next year the imperial government began to sponsor the migration of poor farmers to the far west.[62] In 1776, the emperor ordered provincial leaders to notify their subjects that the "fine profits of nature" awaited them in Xinjiang, perhaps hoping to help prospective migrants overcome their prejudicial assumptions about the frontier being a barren land.[63] Before the state formally ended its financial support for westward migration in the 1780s, over ten thousand households from Gansu had moved to the territory with the government's assistance.[64] Thereafter, although subventions for frontier settlement declined, the movement of people from the provinces continued with Beijing's blessing.

Despite these measures, anxiety about population growth only intensified as the century wore on, prompting scholars to write about the topic. The most famous analysis of China's demographic woes was produced by Hong Liangji. In 1793, Hong wrote an essay pointing to worrying signs of a crisis. Chinese families were growing faster and becoming larger, outstripping the availability of land and food resources needed to support them. Meanwhile, rising levels of inequality left the poor especially vulnerable to the forces of nature. Hong acknowledged that disasters periodically reduced China's population, but he believed that families and politicians could be proactive in confronting the problem of land scarcity by engaging in certain activities, especially land reclamation and frontier colonization. "The countryside should have no unused land and the people no leftover energy. Transplant people to reside in newly opened places in the borderlands," he advised.[65] In an ironic twist, Hong himself had an opportunity to gain firsthand knowledge of the colonial process at work in Xinjiang. In 1799, following his impeachment for political malfeasance, he was exiled to Ili. Though he spent only a few months there before being recalled to Beijing, he grew more knowledgeable about the territory, its resources, and their potential to be exploited by Chinese colonists.[66]

Two decades later, when Gong Zizhen composed his essay about Xinjiang, he followed in the footsteps of his eighteenth-century predecessors not only in worrying about the problems of population growth and land scarcity but also in seeing the western borderland as an opportunity to resolve them. Describing frontier migration as a process of spatial rebalancing, Gong argued that officials should follow the "way of increasing and decreasing," taking people from the crowded provinces and moving them to the frontier to abate population pressures. He suggested they focus on recruiting poor folk, opium cultivators, bannermen, and the like for resettlement in Xinjiang, where such people could claim unoccupied lands, begin to cultivate them, and become permanent residents of the territory. In this manner, "people from the innerland who have no property" would become "people with property on the western frontier," and the undeveloped terrain of the Zunghar Basin would be transformed into productive agricultural soil. His plan required significant capital investment from the Qing government, but Gong was confident that it was bound to pay off in the future.[67] Colonization would ensure that more of the territory's soils were fully used, he later wrote, allowing China's population to be appropriately rebalanced.[68]

Although Gong was the most visible proponent of such policies in the 1820s, he was not alone in considering Xinjiang a prime target for Chinese settlement. Wei Yuan, a fellow statecraft scholar and enthusiast of frontier research, authored his own essay portraying the borderland as a valuable asset for China.[69] "Some say the land is vast but useless," he wrote, referring to critics of the empire's expenditures in Xinjiang. Such people believed that spending hundreds of thousands of silver taels annually to prop up imperial rule in a distant land meant "squandering the center to manage the frontier" and "incurring losses without gains." Statements like these rankled Wei because they seemed to reveal a stunning lack of awareness about the region's natural wealth. Critics were inclined to "begrudge a tiny trickle of expenses" but were "ignorant of oceans of profit." In reality, he wrote, the borderland possessed a vibrant economy with great opportunities for making money: "Cattle, sheep, wheat flour, fruits, and vegetables are cheap. Irrigated agriculture and the trade in felts and furs are profitable. Gold mining flourishes. Corvée duties and taxes are light and decreasing. And they are all ten times more so than in the innerland."[70]

While such opportunities for profit may have been enough by themselves to counter critics' claims, Wei argued that Xinjiang's real value lay in its potential to help solve China's population dilemma. "The country has grown densely populous. China is completely full of people. Only Xinjiang has few people but a vast amount of land," he asserted. Echoing the language of balancing population and resources that appeared in Gong's essay, the Hunan native wrote that Qing leaders should focus on "taking from what is excessive and adding to what is deficient" by moving people out of the provinces and sending them to the west. In essence, colonizing Xinjiang would be a way of saving Chinese society from its own excesses and inequalities.[71] Indeed, the region seemed so well suited to serving this function that Wei suggested that its very existence as an appendage of his own country had been ordained by a higher power: "Heaven left a vast, undeveloped wasteland to act as the outlet for the fluctuations of the prosperous era."[72] By referring to Xinjiang as an "outlet" (weilü), an allusion drawn from the seminal Daoist text *Zhuangzi*, Wei seemed to portray China's population as an undulating body of water whose massive size required a point of drainage in order to maintain balance amid ongoing change.[73] It was for this reason that the empire needed to maintain control over the territory and its people.

At some point during his studies of geography, Zuo Zongtang came across the essays of Gong Zizhen and Wei Yuan and perused them for insights about the relationship between China and Xinjiang. He likely found them in the *Compilation of Statecraft Essays*, where they appeared alongside other pieces of writing under the subject category of frontier defense.[74] Over time, Zuo developed a certain reverence for their commitment to statecraft.[75] Indeed, it did not take long for their writings to sway his thinking. Their influence on him was already evident by 1833, when Zuo first traveled to Beijing. During his time away from Hunan, he composed a set of ruminations in poetic form in which he briefly remarked upon Xinjiang. Although he was familiar with mainstream Chinese perspectives on the territory and repeated banal tropes that drew attention to its desert environments, he was also clearly interested in what the two men had written. Alluding to Gong's proposal, Zuo suggested that Xinjiang might be transformed into a province at some point in the future, calling it a "plan for another day." He was less hesitant about embracing Wei's point of view. At a time when many people in the provinces were facing hardship in trying to make a living, he was convinced that the far western reaches of the empire appeared to provide an "outlet" for all of the "fluctuations" in China.[76] By referring to Xinjiang in this fashion, Zuo demonstrated his adherence not just to the statecraft ideas of outspoken literati, but also to a vision of the borderland as an indispensable site of colonial development for his own country.

By the early 1830s, the Qing state's development policies in Xinjiang were starting to undergo substantial change owing to recent events in the Tarim Basin. In the summer of 1826, a descendant of a famous Sufi Muslim lineage led a coalition of fighters from Kokand, which lay beyond the empire's western frontier, to southern Xinjiang, where they attacked garrisons guarded by Manchu troops. With the assistance of local Turkestani leaders, the fighters gained control of the cities of Kashgar, Yangihissar, Yarkand, and Khotan and held them for a number of months before fresh contingents of Qing troops arrived and managed to oust them. Then, in 1830, another descendant of the same lineage participated in a similar expedition to Kashgar and succeeded in holding the city for several months until Qing forces retook it.[77] While such episodes did not result in permanent territorial losses for the empire, they did cost the government dearly in silver and manpower. They also provoked a great deal of consternation at court, leading the Daoguang emperor to dispatch special envoys to conduct assessments and recommend policy reforms with the aim of eradicating the root causes of the troubles and preventing future crises.

One of the most significant proposals put forth in the wake of these wars was the removal of restrictions on Chinese settlement in the oases of southern Xinjiang, the homeland of tens of thousands of Turkestani families. From the time of the conquest up through the early decades of the nineteenth century, the court had limited the scope of colonization to the lands of northern Xinjiang, believing that permanent residence by Chinese in the Tarim Basin was bound to spawn tensions that would break along ethnic lines and trigger disputes that could snowball into larger emergencies. While Chinese merchants had been permitted to conduct trading missions in the southern oases and to reside for long periods of time among the local population, their families had been forbidden from accompanying them.[78] But after the latest military troubles, Qing ministers concluded that the state could benefit from authorizing Chinese colonization while also enlarging its military presence. By increasing the number of non-Muslims in the Tarim oases, they expected not only to generate more local tax revenues but also to create a group of people whose presence would act as a bulwark against future episodes of unrest.[79] Wu-long-a, a Manchu minister stationed in Kashgar, argued that by allowing Chinese to relocate permanently to southern Xinjiang with their families and settle alongside Qing troops, "soldiers and civilians will grow more numerous with time and Muslim power will gradually weaken," meaning that Turkestanis "will never again dare to sprout other ambitions."[80]

Others saw colonization as a means to augment the region's pool of labor, spur development, and substantiate Qing claims to the territory's unexploited resources. Shen Yao, a scholar in Xu Song's circle of literati, expressed concern that the existence of what appeared to be unused lands and waters would attract the unwelcome attention of foreigners and ultimately precipitate challenges to Qing authority in the region. For this reason, he suggested that Turkestani households be resettled on unoccupied soil to advance the cause of land reclamation, and "if they are not sufficiently numerous, recruit civilians [from the provinces] who have no land, are strong and healthy, and are willing to migrate far away to go to farming sites" in southern Xinjiang.[81]

Following a stream of recommendations, the Daoguang emperor overturned the ban on Chinese colonization in the Tarim oases. In 1831, he authorized people from the provinces to migrate with their families to Daheyan, one of the first sites targeted for settlement.[82] Located in Kashgar's eastern environs, the area reportedly consisted of a huge expanse of land stretching across more than a million *mu*, some of it adjacent to the Kashgar River and strewn with the ruins of irrigation canals built in an earlier era, when the Zunghars ruled the territory.[83] One of the main objectives of development planning was to make sure that such a large expanse of potentially productive soil did not go to waste. As one report stated, officials had to ensure that the "profits of the land are not abandoned," meaning that land should be completely converted to farmland as quickly as possible and then taxed to help underwrite the costs of maintaining Qing garrisons in the region.[84]

In overturning the ban, the emperor was not repudiating the established practice of relying upon local people to coordinate and carry out land reclamation activities. Indeed, while Chinese investors and several hundred Chinese households participated in projects to expand agriculture around Kashgar in the early 1830s, the main protagonists were Turkestani farmers and investors, including the Muslim governor of Kashgar, who put up some of the capital needed to pay for tools and seeds and who supervised the construction of irrigation canals.[85] On one hand, local people's involvement

Figure 2.1 Southern Xinjiang as viewed from the north. From Song-yun, ed., *Qinding Xinjiang shilüe* (Imperially commissioned summary of knowledge about Xinjiang), 1821. Courtesy of Cornell University Library.

in a Qing land reclamation scheme such as this one simply reflected a tradition of collaboration between Turkestanis and imperial officials in matters of natural resource exploitation that had emerged since the time of the conquest.[86] On the other hand, it reflected officials' attempt to use development projects to manage the growing ranks of the landless poor in the oases, who were increasingly visible and, for officials, increasingly worrisome. In 1813, in a striking echo of anxieties aired by his counterparts in the Chinese provinces, the Ili general Song-yun had reported troubling signs that strong population growth was leading to landlessness and indigence among Muslim households in Kashgar.[87] The state's primary response to this problem, just as in China, was to engage those households in land reclamation schemes with the aim of reducing indolence, poverty, and related social problems. In 1833, the emperor enacted such measures in Kucha, approving the allocation of over fifty thousand *mu* of land and granting a three-year tax holiday to "poor Muslims without property" to foster agriculture and economic activity in the area.[88]

Although eager to promote the expansion of cultivated lands, Daoguang had initially vacillated on the decision to throw open the Tarim Basin to settlers from the provinces.[89] He remained apprehensive that Chinese colonization might lead to the encroachment of property held by Turkestani farmers, sparking altercations between outsiders and locals. Some Chinese elites harbored similar doubts. As Xu Song once wrote to Shen Yao, "Muslims cultivate the places in Xinjiang that have water. It would be impermissible to seize their profits, so colonization (*tuntian*) will not be easy."[90] In this view, colonial development was a double-edged sword. It facilitated the exploitation of nature and promised to create new revenues for the state, but it also threatened to cause turmoil stemming from disputes over land, water, and other resources. In the late 1820s, officials had conducted wide-ranging property surveys in the Tarim Basin, seeking to sort out claims to farmland and waterways, partly to guard against the pitfalls of haphazard colonization. They used the information they gleaned from these surveys to reassure the emperor that development projects would not impinge upon local people's properties or livelihoods and therefore were unlikely to inspire serious opposition.[91] But such assurances did not ease Daoguang's worries, and he remained suspicious that plans for land reclamation near Kashgar could end up facilitating the expropriation of Turkestanis' lands or the usurpation of their claims to water resources at the hands of Chinese settlers. By 1834, his trepidation had driven him to reverse course on his earlier decision to permit Chinese colonization in Daheyan. He authorized the voluntary retreat of Chinese farmers from the area and the reallocation of their lands to Muslim farmers and merchants.[92] Nonetheless, the court continued to allow colonization at other sites in the Tarim Basin.

Not all Chinese households opted to leave the Kashgar oasis. But hundreds did, and some ended up in Barchuk, another site of state-sponsored settlement. Situated over one hundred miles to the northeast, Barchuk occupied a strategic location on the main route between cities on the northern side of the Taklamakan Desert. In addition, the surrounding region stood out for its environmental characteristics. Travelers who passed through Barchuk noticed its abundance of water, its fish, and its reeds, especially during the summer season, when snowmelt from the mountains raised the level of nearby rivers and inundated low-lying lands.[93] The region also boasted arid jungles and a profusion of wild animals. Even decades after the drive for colonization had begun, travelers remarked upon the tall grasses lining the rivers and the poplar forests that provided habitat for tigers, deer, pheasants, and other creatures.[94] From the vantage point of Qing officials, Barchuk's most important characteristics were its close proximity to huge expanses of uncultivated land and its ample supply of water. In addition, unlike colonial sites closer to Kashgar, which sat adjacent to existing villages and thus were seen as having the potential to incite interethnic violence, land in Barchuk was reportedly far removed from existing Muslim villages and its settlement was considered to have no risk of leading to unrest.[95]

The colonization of Barchuk began formally in 1832, when a Mongol minister in Yarkand, Bi-chang, oversaw the construction of a new fortified settlement on the southern side of the Kashgar River using funds drawn from the imperial treasury.[96] This settlement, known as Maralbashi, served as a garrison for a new contingent of Qing troops.[97] As with some other state-backed development projects in Xinjiang, officials tapped the services of a former official who had been sent into exile, Zhou Tingfen, to supervise land reclamation in the vicinity of Barchuk. Zhou had gained experience on similar projects closer to Kashgar, facilitating the participation of wealthy Chinese merchants who invested capital to erect embankments along the river, construct irrigation canals and sluice gates, and allocate grants of seeds, tools, oxen, food, and housing to arriving colonists.[98] In Barchuk, he recruited an array of Chinese settlers, including families who had tried homesteading in Kashgar and colonists who had come from Urumchi or directly from the provinces. Under his leadership, the colony built dams and branch canals along certain sections of the Kashgar and Yarkand rivers. Within a few years, the total population had climbed above three hundred households, with start-up funds for the venture coming from donations made by Zhou and other moneyed individuals.[99]

The colony at Barchuk endured in the following years, though not without encountering certain obstacles to its growth and experiencing some turnover in its population. The earliest settlers may have benefited greatly from the exploitation of virgin soils, producing bumper crops in the first several seasons.[100] But this success was difficult to sustain. Reports indicate that the drive to expand arable land eventually pushed cultivation into areas of poor soil, diminishing the returns on money and labor invested in its reclamation. Officials struggled to maintain dikes along rivers that ran for dozens of miles through sparsely populated terrain. Facing difficulties, some colonists chose to abandon Barchuk after just a few years, reducing the population by a certain margin. Even so, Qing leaders recognized the value of the location for asserting their power in the Tarim Basin, and they continued to allocate capital and mobilize workers to monitor and refurbish the river dikes, sustaining the infrastructure needed to keep the settler community supplied with water.[101] Such measures seem to have been effective in keeping the colony alive. Little more than a dozen years after the founding of the settlement, Barchuk was still inhabited by more than two hundred civilian households farming over twenty-four thousand *mu* of land, all taxed at a low rate to incentivize newcomers to join the colony.[102]

By the time Lin Zexu embarked on his roving survey of southern Xinjiang in 1845, new sites of land reclamation by Turkestanis and Chinese in the Tarim Basin had enjoyed over a decade of public and private sponsorship.[103] Lin and his surveying partner, Manchu minister Quan-qing, eventually tallied over six hundred thousand *mu* of fresh farmland.[104] Their tally suggests that recent development initiatives had indeed brought a large area of soil under cultivation in the oases, increasing Xinjiang's total acreage by roughly 10 to 20 percent.[105] But that was only half the story. They also came across huge expanses of land with no sign of human activity, corroborating information contained in earlier reports to Beijing about the existence of hundreds of thousands of *mu* in the Tarim oases that could be turned into farmland for the production of food and fiber crops.[106] In essence, the message was that the borderland territory still held much promise for agricultural development. It was a message that Lin Zexu impressed upon Zuo Zongtang when the two met in Changsha five years later, and one that continued to resonate with Zuo for decades afterwards.

Yet Lin may have made farming in Xinjiang sound easier than it was in practice. By the early nineteenth century, Qing officials had accrued a substantial amount of experience with agriculture in the region, and they were highly aware of the numerous constraints on its development. Some of the most significant constraints were environmental in nature. In certain places, the characteristics of the earth—too alkaline, too barren, too sandy, and so on—thwarted the aims of planners and farmers. In others, there simply were no readily accessible sources of water. Topographic conditions could also complicate reclamation efforts. In areas where rivers and streams caused erosion or carved gullies through the landscape, leaving their waters coursing through beds sitting meters below the level of the surrounding land, there was no easy solution for irrigation.[107] Climate and weather also presented certain challenges. Unusual changes in temperatures or patterns of precipitation could easily harm farm productivity. Such changes had the potential to disrupt annual hydrological cycles in which winter snows accumulated in the mountains, springtime thaws gave birth to alpine streams, and waves of summer heat accelerated the flow of water down into the lowland oases. When this cycle was disturbed, farmers were forced to delay planting or reduce the quantity of water they distributed to their fields, often significantly diminishing the size of their harvests.[108]

The other major constraint on agricultural development that worried Qing officials was the supply of labor. Those who bore some responsibility for overseeing land reclamation often expressed frustration that they were unable to make use of all of the available land resources. They traced the cause back to the small size of Xinjiang's population and the vast distance separating it from the densely populous parts of China, which made it a remote destination for most people in the provinces. Writing about Barchuk in 1836, the Ili general Te-yi-shun-bao reported that "wide-open lands that have not been reclaimed are extremely plentiful," but "labor power is insufficient." He determined that, for poor migrants from the provinces, undertaking a journey to the Tarim Basin was simply too expensive, if not too cumbersome, and many ended up traveling westward only as far as Urumchi.[109] Certainly, officials did not dismiss the value of Turkestani labor. But even with robust demographic growth in southern Xinjiang, Muslim households could not always be recruited in sufficient numbers to fully populate new settlements, especially when they were located far away from the major oases.[110] The new policies for colonization that were enacted in the 1830s suggest that Qing leaders, while being quite willing to see Turkestani people enlisted in the service of agricultural development, came to believe that the only real recourse for solving labor scarcity in Xinjiang was to draw upon the Chinese population. For this reason, policies not only removed restrictions on permanent Chinese settlement in the southern oases, but also dangled enticements to potential colonists and to wealthy individuals who agreed to fund them.[111]

By the 1840s, the idea that Xinjiang urgently required Chinese labor for its development was becoming more prominent in official and scholarly discourse. This suggests that an important shift in thinking and policy-making was underway. In the decades after the conquest of the territory, emperors and Chinese scholars had envisioned the soils of the Zunghar Basin as an essential resource for helping to alleviate social and ecological pressures that were intensifying in the Chinese provinces. From their perspective, the borderland served as a spatial outlet for China's immense population, allowing people to find land and pursue the hope of a better life while reducing the potential for turmoil in the provinces. But after the 1820s, when a series of raids in southern Xinjiang revealed vulnerabilities in the empire's defenses, the court began to prioritize colonization and agrarian development in the Tarim Basin in the service of enhanced security. In this view, it was Xinjiang that now urgently demanded labor, and it was the Chinese provinces that would be tapped to fulfill that demand. Although this way of viewing the relationship between Xinjiang and China represented a certain change in the logic of Qing imperialism, it only served to reaffirm important assumptions at the heart of the older view: that the western frontier possessed land and other resources in great abundance, and that its future was inseparable from the provinces and the people of China.

CHAPTER III

Reclaiming the Land

J
ust a few years after meeting with Lin Zexu in Changsha, Zuo Zongtang returned to the provincial capital for a rendezvous of a different
sort. Now about forty years old, he was summoned to the city to
attend to a matter of great urgency. In the summer of 1852, tens of thousands of followers of the Taiping Heavenly Kingdom had entered Hunan
from the southwest, seeking to strengthen their movement by expanding
into new territory and increasing their numbers. The Taipings, a group
energized as much by their material needs as by their anti–Manchu ideology, found the province to be fertile ground for recruitment. The natural
disasters of the late 1840s had created an environment of insecurity among
the growing ranks of Hunan's poor, unemployed, and itinerant folk, and
some people found cause for hope by throwing in their lot with the rebels.[1] The situation intensified in September, when Taiping leaders rallied
their partisans, now numbering over one hundred thousand, to besiege
Changsha.[2] As soon as Zuo heard the news, he fled with members of his
family to a prearranged hideout in eastern Xiangyin.[3] But the governor of
Hunan, who was in charge of organizing a response to the crisis, contacted
Zuo to request his prompt assistance. He had gotten word of Zuo's extensive knowledge of military history and strategy, and, in the midst of the
siege, the governor decided to call upon him for help in formulating plans
and handling logistics to defend the city.[4] Zuo thus found himself back in

the provincial capital in October 1852, this time in the employ of the governor. It was his first break into government service.

The rise of the Taiping Rebellion created a territorial crisis of unprecedented magnitude for the Qing state and initiated a period of civil warfare lasting nearly three decades. Although the siege of Changsha ended after several months, Taiping forces continued to attract supporters and expand their power throughout the provinces located along the middle and lower reaches of the Yangzi River. The central government's standing armies, weak and disorganized in some places, were unable to vanquish the rebels on their own, and the task of defeating them eventually fell to a handful of armies from Hunan and neighboring provinces that were raised precisely for that purpose.[5] Fighting between these new provincial armies and their Taiping adversaries dragged on through late 1864, when loyalist troops finally managed to disperse the rebels. But by that point, violence had erupted in other parts of the empire. In 1862, enmity between Han Chinese and Hui Muslims in Shaanxi sparked a disastrous period of interethnic violence and warfare that engulfed the province and soon spread to neighboring Gansu.[6] Two years later, the Turkic Muslim inhabitants of the Tarim Basin oases rose in revolt against the Qing, toppling the edifice of imperial power in Xinjiang and putting nearly the entire northwest beyond the reach of Beijing.[7] Rebellious movements in other parts of the empire also broke out in these decades.[8]

This period of civil warfare marked a watershed in the fiscal history of the Qing state. By the time Taiping forces entered Hunan, the imperial government had been plagued by financial problems for quite some time. Poor economic conditions, bad weather, opium consumption, and the increasing incidence of acts of tax resistance hindered the ability of provincial authorities to meet their quotas for tax collection and tax remittance. In the 1840s, a number of provinces fell short of their targets, and reserves at the Board of Revenue shrank.[9] After 1853, when Taiping forces moved into the Yangzi River basin and occupied parts of Jiangsu and Zhejiang provinces, the fiscal fortunes of the Qing state took a nosedive. Those two provinces typically accounted for around one-quarter of all government income from the land tax, which was by far the empire's most important source of revenue.[10] As receipts from the land tax plunged, Qing officials found it impossible to fulfill all of the state's financial obligations. The rich and populous eastern provinces, which had long subsidized imperial rule in the outer territories, quickly found themselves unable to remit money to regions like Xinjiang, and the flow of silver to the western borderland dwindled to a mere trickle.[11] In response to these fiscal challenges, officials across the empire hastily enacted a range of measures to try to revive the flow of money into government coffers. They raised funds by selling titles and offices, soliciting contributions from wealthy elites, and issuing new paper and metallic coin currencies.[12] The most consequential measure was the imposition of a new commercial tax (*lijin*) upon a wide range of domestic goods, such as cotton and tea. First employed in Jiangsu province in 1853, this tax became an essential source of money to finance salaries, equipment, and provisions for the new provincial armies. It soon spread to other provinces and territories, and within several decades it had superseded the land tax to become the single largest source of income for the Qing government.[13]

Although commercial taxes proved to be transformative for the financial capacity of the Qing state in the long run, it would be misguided to think that imperial leaders simply abandoned their longstanding interest in using agriculture and other industries as vehicles for generating revenue. In fact, the crises of the mid-nineteenth century intensified their drive to make the most of the empire's natural resources. Beginning in the 1850s, some officials called for programs of resource development with the explicit goal of alleviating the state's financial troubles. Such calls initially focused on what officials believed were unexploited or underexploited resources in regions far beyond the geographical scope of the Taiping war, where the loss of subsidies from the provinces placed considerable stress on officials and institutions involved in territorial administration. In both Xinjiang and Manchuria, areas that previously had served as pasture for animals were targeted for land reclamation. Other resources, such as forests and mines, were also incorporated into development plans.[14] In Manchuria, these calls eventually translated into major changes in Qing policy. After 1860, the court gradually rescinded longstanding restrictions on Chinese settlement in the northeast. The decision to throw open the region to migrants from the provinces no doubt reflected concerns about recent Russian advances and acquisitions of territory in the Amur River region.[15] Yet, in the financial circumstances of the times, the state's decision to promote colonial agriculture also revealed the exigency of raising money for a depleted imperial treasury.

Calls for land reclamation reached a crescendo in the 1860s as officials in the provinces refocused their attention on an emergent frontier: the extensive wilds that flourished in the wake of civil warfare. The violence of those who rose in revolt and the Qing loyalists who fought against them wreaked havoc in many urban and rural communities, leaving a trail of death and devastation whose traces remained visible in the landscape for decades afterward. Buildings were turned to rubble, towns and farmlands were abandoned, and people perished in enormous numbers. Indeed, the Taiping war led to the deaths of some twenty or thirty million people, and in the three decades after 1850, the empire's human population may have declined by as many as seventy million.[16] Such tremendous demographic contraction caused a remarkable downturn in agricultural production, first in the Yangzi River provinces and later in the northwest. As the human population dwindled, undomesticated plants and animals recolonized territory for themselves, rewilding former farmlands and turning them into what Qing observers simply called "wasteland." These were places defined by desolation, bareness, the lack of cultivation, and the absence of humans.[17] The sudden, explosive growth of wasteland in the mid-nineteenth century was unwelcome news for a government whose financial system and political ideology, at least in the Chinese provinces, depended heavily upon agriculture. As one official wrote: "Where there is land, there is wealth. The income from taxes on farmland are the country's natural profits. If lands are left abandoned and ungoverned, financial resources will go to waste. For this reason, the reclamation of wasteland is a matter of first priority."[18] In the face of the proliferation of wasteland, Qing leaders quickly rallied to the cause of land reclamation. In 1862, the imperial court endorsed a plan to have leaders in all war-torn provinces recruit refugees to their districts, assist them in opening up abandoned tracts of soil, and then gradually reimpose the land tax on the recovered acreage.[19] Officials throughout the empire soon allocated scarce funding and drafted regulations for land resettlement at the provincial and district levels, signaling their commitment to join the campaign to develop postwar wastes into productive agricultural land.

Zuo Zongtang's first experience with overseeing agricultural policy began right when enthusiasm for land reclamation surged. In 1862, after serving as an advisor to provincial officials in the 1850s and then leading his own army for over a year, he was appointed governor of Zhejiang province. As he transitioned into the role of high-ranking civil servant, he quickly became enmeshed in the politics of land use. Amid widespread human death and the reappearance of wild lands, Zuo and other officials in Zhejiang enacted policies to attract refugees and settlers to the soil with a raft of incentives, from tax abatements to offers of start-up capital and equipment. His administration also established government bureaus to handle reconstruction in districts across the province, endowing them with the authority to supervise and coordinate policies on land use at the local level. Several years later, when Beijing reappointed Zuo as governor-general of Shaanxi and Gansu provinces during the Muslim uprisings, he carried his experiences of agrarian development with him, taking what he had learned in Zhejiang and adapting it to Gansu. These two provinces were distinguished sharply by their ecological, economic, and social characteristics, and certain policies in Gansu, such as the forced resettlement of Hui Muslims, had no analog in Zhejiang. But, on a basic level, Zuo's strategies for agrarian development in the two provinces were quite similar and reflected the urgency of using the labor of war survivors—humans and nonhuman animals alike—to exploit the environmental resources around them for the sake of the stability and fiscal health of the empire.

The Taiping Rebellion was no doubt a social movement of great proportions, but it was also an environmental event on a massive scale. The war between Taiping and Qing forces unleashed waves of destruction, savagely disfiguring urban and rural landscapes and overturning the balance between populations of flora and fauna.[20] The violence that engulfed the Yangzi River provinces starting in 1853 decimated the region's human inhabitants, leaving nonhumans to flourish in their absence. This was especially visible to observers in Jiangnan. Accounts from foreign and Chinese travelers testify to the extreme levels of destruction and extensive loss of human life in this region. In some places, the ground was littered with death. As one witness reported, "bleached skeletons, skulls, or partially decayed dead bodies . . . literally cover the ground for miles." Along one stretch of rural highway, he wrote, "the ground is literally white, like snow, with skulls and bones."[21] Cities such as Zhenjiang, a junction for commerce and transportation at the intersection of the Yangzi and the Grand Canal, were thoroughly destroyed by the violence. Travelers who passed through the city in the late 1850s and early 1860s found it largely deserted, its streets empty and its buildings demolished and covered in a profusion of weedy vegetation.[22] Outside of major urban areas, eyewitnesses observed additional evidence of

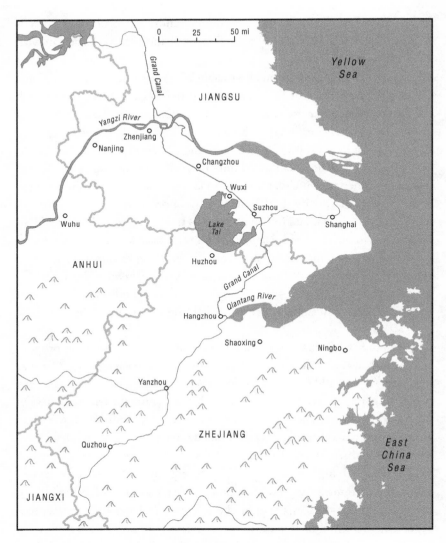

Map 3.1 Jiangnan in the nineteenth century. Map by Erin Greb.

devastation. One of the telltale signs of war's mark on the landscape was the widespread absence of tree cover, often a result of people's desperate search for fuel as they sought to survive.[23]

As humans retreated from the landscape, other creatures thrived. Europeans in China, who seemed to share a penchant for hunting game with rifles, paid particular attention to the varieties of wildlife that found space to prosper in people's absence. A British captain who was on a voyage up the Yangzi from Shanghai observed around Zhenjiang that "the whole surrounding country, having been for years overrun alternately by Rebels and Imperialists, who had effaced all traces of cultivation, was rapidly regaining a state of nature, and was most favourable for sporting purposes."[24] Warfare left the land teeming with animals such as pheasants, quail, rooks, jackdaws, ducks, hare, hogs, musk deer, and other small game.[25] Sometimes the profusion of wildlife was a sign that animals were taking advantage not just of humans' absence but of their recent deaths. Yu Zhi, a native of the city of Wuxi, published an illustrated pamphlet at the war's end depicting a scene of pigs and dogs devouring human carcasses.[26] Other animals, including larger predators, also took advantage of chaos in the human world. Starting in the 1860s and continuing for several decades, reports came out periodically of wolves and tigers prowling around Jiangsu and Zhejiang provinces hunting their human prey along country roads or on the outskirts of towns and cities.[27] The prevalence of such reports suggests that the Taiping war initiated a period in which the loss of animal habitat from farmland development was reversed and the availability of human flesh increased, allowing some animal species to flourish for many years afterward.[28]

As the human population dwindled and total farmland acreage plummeted, land that had once been used for agriculture quickly grew more wild. Domesticated cultivars were soon displaced by other varieties of plants. Travelers who made their way between Shanghai and Nanjing across the fertile soils of southern Jiangsu readily noticed the change in scenery. In the spring of 1861, a British missionary observed that, near Wuxi, "lands lie untilled for half-a-mile on each side" of the road and "long grass has taken the place of rice and other crops."[29] Others took the sight of unkempt grasses as an unmistakable sign that people had disappeared from the land. A scholar traveling from Shanghai, Mao Xianglin, wrote that the countryside in those parts was simply "overgrown plains without any traces of people."[30] In some places, grasses and other wild vegetation grew uninhibited for years. Wandering through a river valley in central Zhejiang in 1871, the German geologist Ferdinand von Richthofen observed that "fields in the valley, as well as the terraced rice ground on the hillsides, are covered with a wild growth of grass, no other plants being apparently able to thrive on the exhausted soil." Surrounded by once productive farmland, he came to grips with the root of the problem: the lack of people and domesticated

Figure 3.1 Human bodies being eaten by dogs and swine. From Jiyun shanren (Yu Zhi), *Jiangnan tielei tu* (Illustrations to draw tears from iron in Jiangnan). Courtesy of Princeton University Library.

animals to work and fertilize the soil. The area of uncultivated ground was vast, leading Richthofen to surmise that the "decrease of the productive power of the ransacked provinces, and the amount of taxes by which their exchequer is diminished, must be very large."[31]

Nearly a decade earlier, when Zuo Zongtang entered Zhejiang in early 1862, the extent of the devastation quickly became apparent to him. Advancing across some of its most heavily damaged districts with his army, he was horrified by what he saw. "The rich soils of Zhejiang province have been completely occupied by the rebels," he wrote in May of that year. Fields had gone to waste, houses were burnt down, and there were "refugees, men and women, sleeping out in the open and victims of starvation all along the roads."[32] That summer, he claimed that Taiping forces had ravaged rural areas "right when farmers were transplanting seedlings and reaping rice. The old grains were plundered and the new grains were not harvested." In Quzhou, a district in the southwest of the province, Zuo came across a small number of survivors who appeared to be "starving and tired in the extreme. None had color in their faces. In the worst cases, some just shriveled up and died." He inspected destroyed buildings strewn with "putrid flesh and skeletons" in which "diseased vapors" wafted through the air.[33] In March 1863, after his troops had captured the city of Shaoxing, he painted a dire portrait of the surrounding countryside at a time when farmers normally would be hard at work sowing their crops. "Farmland has become wasteland," he wrote, "and there are white bones and yellow grass as far as the eye can see." Almost all farming tools had been destroyed, and he estimated that less than 1 percent of all draft animals remained alive. Unable to purchase grains, beans, or seeds, survivors scavenged in "barren farm plots and abandoned vegetable gardens, picking wild greens for food." When they could search no more for lack of light, "they snuggle up and lay their heads under cracking and crumbling walls, using pieces of earth to sleep."[34]

The problems of the living were compounded by the loss of the dead and departed. Like its neighboring provinces, Zhejiang was heavily depopulated by the Taiping war. Indeed, estimates suggest that the province's prewar population of thirty million people may have declined by over 50 percent.[35] Although depopulation affected both urban and rural areas, population losses were not evenly distributed across the province. Western and northern districts bore the brunt of the violence and destruction.

Approximations from the 1860s and 1870s, which were based upon impressionistic observations and hearsay, put the proportion of survivors in some of the hardest hit regions at just 2 or 3 percent of prewar totals.[36] Zuo Zongtang estimated that several districts in the western part of the province, including Quzhou and Yanzhou, had a survival rate of around 5 percent.[37] Such figures may seem hyperbolically low, and demographic historian Cao Shuji has questioned their veracity.[38] Nonetheless, estimates from other districts seem to validate the basic impression that population losses in some areas were shockingly high and much greater than the rate of roughly 50 percent for the province as a whole.[39]

As governor of Zhejiang, Zuo responded to the devastation around him by first attempting to stem population losses. Soon after military forces under his command occupied a district, they were ordered to carry out disaster-relief measures and provide aid to the living using the types of tactics that were detailed in the extensive literature on famine relief that existed in Qing times.[40] "At the beginning of having recovered each city," he wrote, "I direct officials and gentry to cook congee, distribute rice, produce medicinal pills, give out warm clothing, and bury the dead bodies."[41] His army doled out gruel to survivors from stocks of grain confiscated from captured rebels or taken from military provisions. To replenish the stocks, he procured additional grain from neighboring Jiangxi province and had it shipped by boat and cart and then by human porters across the mountains of southwestern Zhejiang.[42] Zuo deemed these to be only stopgap measures, and they may not have accomplished much beyond simply keeping people alive. Some officials reported witnessing destitution among survivors even after they had received food aid.[43]

During the winter of 1862–63, the governor began to implement more formal measures for reconstruction. For centuries, temperate and water-rich Zhejiang had enjoyed a core position in the empire's economy, being a major producer of commodities such as silk, cotton, and tea.[44] Zuo aimed to use government-financed development projects to spur the regrowth of agriculture, textiles, and other industries. These measures were codified in a set of twelve regulations that was distributed to local officials for circulation and posting throughout the province.[45] The regulations mandated that each district establish welfare bureaus (*tongshan ju*) headed by local gentry, who were to take a leading role in organizing relief.[46] The twelve articles also stipulated that the bureaus undertake charitable activities, reorganize and regulate local finances to raise money, and enforce prohibitions against activities deemed harmful to public order.[47] Although the bureaus were charged with the responsibility of providing aid to refugee women, children, and the poor, they were more than charitable organizations. They carried out work-for-welfare programs and economic stimulus measures designed to revive Zhejiang's industries, especially in the once-vibrant north, where textiles had long held a commanding place in the economy. Yang Changjun, a Hunan native who served in local government posts in Zhejiang in the early 1860s, worked with Zuo to devise and execute plans to "purchase copper, tin, iron, lead, and tea" and "hire women to pick tea, paying them in rice and using the tea as provisions" for the military.[48] The bureaus also employed women in the production of silk. Regulations stipulated that they "take in and provide support for women," but the bureaus actually exploited women's knowledge and labor power by having them reel thread and weave cloth in a putting-out arrangement and then selling the finished products to raise revenue.[49]

Agriculture quickly became one focus of reconstruction policy in Zhejiang. As much as three-quarters of all farmland had fallen out of cultivation, according to Zuo's calculation.[50] Such figures were deeply concerning not only because they indicated heavy population losses, but also because they augured shortages of foodstuffs and reduced tax revenues at a time when the costs of military mobilization were ballooning. Within the first year of his arrival in the province, Zuo had taken steps to prioritize land reclamation. Hoping to stave off further losses of labor power, he forbade the slaughter of farm cattle, which people used for plowing and other labor-intensive activities.[51] Local officials also began to establish bureaus of reconstruction (shanhou ju) and taxation (qingfu ju) staffed with personnel who conducted walking surveys of fields, processed land claims, assessed taxes, and promoted farming. They enacted commonplace measures of agrarian development, such as offering capital loans to farmers and distributing cattle, seeds, and agricultural tools to people in rural communities.[52] Given the extent of the destruction in Zhejiang, Zuo felt he had little choice but to send deputies to purchase tens of thousands of liters of seed and thousands of farm cattle from Jiangxi and Anhui, where regulations for land reclamation contained provisions for state-funded stockyards to raise draft animals.[53] Once such materials were brought back to Zhejiang, they were distributed to refugees via reconstruction bureaus in Quzhou, Yanzhou, and other districts to help them return to farming as quickly as possible.[54]

Figure 3.2 Agricultural reconstruction in Jiangnan. From Jiyun shanren (Yu Zhi), *Jiang-nan tielei tu* (Illustrations to draw tears from iron in Jiangnan). Courtesy of Princeton University Library.

In the following years, Qing officials worked to codify regulations for the reclamation of wastelands. Like their counterparts in other provinces who formulated concise guidelines for agrarian reconstruction in the early 1860s, Zhejiang's leaders devised protocols to systematize and streamline what could be a complicated process, especially when disputes over land ownership arose.[55] In 1866, around the time that Zuo was informed by the imperial court that he would be sent to the northwest, the new Zhejiang governor, Ma Xinyi, issued an eight-point set of regulations to govern the process of land reclamation.[56] In some ways, the new regulations merely reflected existing practices, calling for the allocation of oxen, seeds, and tools to farmers, who were required to repay these interest-free loans within three years. But they also sought to impress upon magistrates the importance of surveying land to determine the locations and sizes of landholdings, identify which wastelands had owners and which ones lacked them, and calculate taxes on the various types of properties. Local officials were also ordered to clarify property claims in places where people "gathered firewood, siphoned spring water, or cultivated garden vegetables" and where confusion over boundary lines and usage rights had the potential to spark disagreements between claimants and end up in litigation.[57]

Agricultural policy in this era also aimed to solve perhaps the most basic obstacle to development: the scarcity of human labor. After the war, officials regarded Zhejiang as simply having too few farmers to return all wasteland to cultivation. Zuo Zongtang viewed "farmers from neighboring provinces" as the antidote, and he hoped that the standing offer of free land and capital inputs would be enough to entice migrants to move to Zhejiang, settle down, and contribute to population growth.[58] Ma Xinyi, for his part, instructed his deputies to recruit anyone who would be willing to cultivate land regardless of their origins. Yet in practice, most recruits to agriculture in the 1860s came from areas within Zhejiang that had escaped the worst of the violence. Even though Ma maintained a tepid attitude toward people from Zhejiang's coastal regions, considering them to be uncouth troublemakers, he cloaked his agricultural policy in imperial ideology, asserting that the "court makes divisions between land but does not distinguish between people."[59] The pervasive scarcity of farm labor made it almost impossible for officials to exclude people based on their origins or identities, and leaders searched for whomever they could find, even those living on the margins of society. In 1866, the magistrate of Yanzhou recommended that officials target "shack people" (pengmin) for recruitment.[60] The ancestors of the shack people, who were named for their flimsy hillside abodes, had migrated into the highlands in the preceding centuries as population growth reduced the availability of land in the valleys and commercialization increased the profitability of upland farming. As they settled on mountainsides in Zhejiang and neighboring provinces, they made their livelihoods by cultivating cash crops such as lumber, tobacco, and indigo, and subsistence crops like maize. Because mountainside farming caused deforestation, erosion, and soil exhaustion, shack people were often blamed for ecological degradation and social instability in upland regions.[61] But their social and ecological marginality afforded them a significant measure of protection during the Taiping war, and their communities emerged from the crisis relatively unscathed. The plan to recruit them to open up wastelands in Zhejiang's river valleys was a testament to how fully the war had reversed earlier demographic trends in the lowlands and how desperate officials were to bring land back under the plow.

Although it may have appeared simple on paper, agrarian development was never straightforward in practice. One difficulty was the perpetual scarcity of funding. Zuo Zongtang set up bureaus to levy commercial taxes and dispatched subordinates to Shanghai to solicit contributions from provincial elites who had fled to the city to escape the war, but he grew frustrated when some rich merchants rebuffed his requests for money.[62] Without sufficient funding, officials had to cut back on the number of reconstruction projects they carried out and reduce the amount of capital they could allocate to farmers. Climate conditions presented another major challenge. In the 1860s, erratic weather disrupted agricultural cycles just as communities seemed to be emerging from the mayhem of the war. In June 1864, many areas of central Zhejiang were inundated with heavy rains that lasted for days on end and unleashed a cascade of flooding in the valleys. These floods damaged crops and destroyed houses, bridges, reservoirs, and dikes.[63] Other parts of Zhejiang suffered through serious droughts.[64] Such disasters reduced or wiped out harvests in some places and gave rise to epidemics of infectious disease that killed hundreds of people per day.[65] They not only inflicted physical damage on infrastructure that was necessary for agriculture but also further reduced available funding, as the governor felt compelled to reduce taxes to ease the burden on Zhejiang's battered residents.[66]

The environmental repercussions of civil warfare extended far beyond the lower Yangzi River provinces. Less than five years after becoming the governor of Zhejiang, Zuo Zongtang received a new commission to serve as governor-general of Shaanxi and Gansu provinces and take charge of the government's response to the Muslim uprisings. When Zuo finally arrived in Gansu in the summer of 1869, trailing Qing battalions as they marched westward, he saw firsthand the vast destruction that had resulted from the fighting. From his headquarters near the city of Pingliang, the governor-general estimated that the "miserable plight of Gansu is similar to conditions in Yanzhou, Zhejiang, but [here] the infertile wastes are larger, and not one in a hundred people has survived."[67] Describing the scene in the eastern part of the province, he wrote: "the place is a weedy wasteland and people are few and far between. Yellow sands and white bones fill one's view. It does not resemble a scene from our human world."[68]

The intense devastation and loss of human life in Gansu spread westward along with the fighting until early 1874, when Qing troops completed what was sometimes a brutal campaign of suppression against their Hui adversaries. The few foreign travelers who ventured through Gansu in the 1870s were shocked by what they saw. While traveling with a small

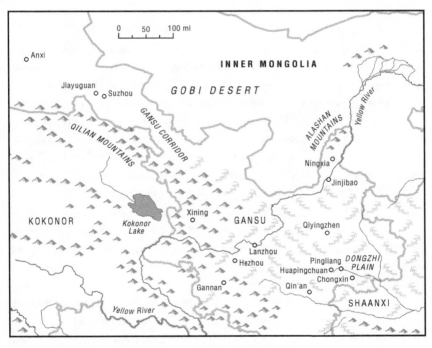

Map 3.2 Gansu in the nineteenth century. Map by Erin Greb.

RECLAIMING THE LAND [77]

contingent of fellow Russian explorers, Pavel Piasetskii repeatedly encountered the abandoned remains of former settlements after entering the province from the east in the spring of 1875. "All the villages we came across were burnt to the ground," he observed, "the walls of the fruit-gardens destroyed, and the trees were nothing but withered trunks. No living soul was to be seen in these ruins."[69] Before reaching the city of Lanzhou, the provincial capital, he tallied two full weeks of going past "heaps of abandoned ruins" where the "few inhabitants seemed most wretched," and he noted that, aside from "a few strips of land producing wheat and peas, sown by the soldiers of the local garrison, the fields remained uncultivated."[70] In late summer, after having passed through Jiayuguan at the western terminus of the Great Wall, his party reached Anxi, nearly emptied of its former residents: "Nothing remained of this big town but a heap of stones, fragments of walls, and ruined temples." Apart from "a few aged inhabitants" who managed to subsist amid the wreckage, "nothing was to be seen but an abundance of grass."[71] The ruins of Anxi and neighboring towns in the deserts of western Gansu stunned other observers as well, leaving them with a sense of how terrible the war must have been.[72]

While the war caused a precipitous decline in Gansu's human population, it created room for nonhuman species to flourish. Qing officials were quick to notice the growth of undomesticated grasses, brambles, and other wild vegetation, which colonized plots of farmland and claimed space for themselves in the ruins of former towns. In eastern Gansu, across a region known as the Dongzhi Plain, Zuo noted that "cities and countrysides are deserted wastes and grasses extend endlessly."[73] In the district of Chongxin, agricultural fields were reclaimed by the wilds: "Brush in the flatlands grew to be several feet tall and it was like entering a land without people."[74] Meanwhile, foreign visitors took note of the profusion of wildlife. Indeed, like their British counterparts in the Yangzi River basin, Russian and German explorers in Gansu were delighted to find that there were many animals they could shoot, including numerous bird species, such as ducks, geese, snipe, pigeons, ravens, pheasants, and vultures, and lots of other game, like foxes, deer, chamois, rabbits, gazelle, and antelope.[75] In the Alashan Mountains, located to the northwest of Ningxia, populations of animals flourished and "forests untouched by the woodman's axe grew luxuriantly" before the onset of postwar recovery.[76] In sum, undomesticated plants and wild animals prospered greatly in the deadliest years of the conflict.

Figure 3.3 Ruins in Anxi, Gansu. Photograph by Adolf-Nikolai Erazmovich Boiar-skii, 1875. Courtesy of the National Library of Brazil.

Wolves were one of the primary beneficiaries of human death and vul-nerability.[77] Their numbers seemed to grow significantly in this period. Indeed, the abundance of wolves became apparent to Zuo not long after he entered Gansu.[78] In places ruined by warfare, he later reported, "shrubs and grasses grew into forest, the calls of wolves echoed throughout the countryside, and people stopped traveling the roads."[79] Amid the destruc-tion, wolf attacks on people, donkeys, pigs, and other prey increased. Wolves also became more temeritous in their hunt, boldly advancing from roadways into villages and even into people's houses. In the late 1860s, packs of wolves comprised of several dozen animals readily attacked people in Chongxin, picking one human target out of a group and then going in for the kill. Records suggest that so many victims perished in these attacks that wolves grew plump off the flesh of humans.[80] Some attacks were so fierce and so brazen that local elites decided to record them in gazetteers. According to one narrative of an attack near the city of Suzhou in western Gansu, three battalions of Qing troops were set upon by an enormous pack of wolves, first numbering over a hundred but then multiplying into the thousands. Confronted by their lupine assailants on a rural highway, the troops managed to fend off the attack only after taking hold of their rifles and engaging in battle for a number of hours.[81] People quickly learned to travel with rifles to prepare themselves in the event of an attack.[82] Officials responded to the escalation of wolf attacks by offering bounties paid in cash to people who tracked and killed the animals.[83]

The war in Gansu dragged on until 1874. By the time it was over, the province had lost a huge number of people to violence, disease, starvation, and migration. Estimates suggest that the war may have reduced the population by as much as 75 percent, leaving it with between three and five million people by the mid-1870s.[84] Losses were especially steep in the eastern and northwestern parts of Gansu, as well as in cities and towns along the imperial highway that ran through the province. Around Pingliang, for example, the population declined by nearly 90 percent, transforming an area that previously had been inhabited by over two million people to a place with just a few hundred thousand.[85] Given such high rates of depopulation, it is little wonder that Zuo lamented the existence of "empty cities" and others described certain parts of postwar Gansu simply as "land without people."[86]

Initially, it was not depopulation but the ethnic composition and distribution of the remaining population in Gansu that most worried the governor-general. Among the survivors of the war were millions of Hui Muslims. Most of them were native to Gansu, where communities of Muslims had become acculturated to a Chinese-speaking society over the course of many generations.[87] Tens of thousands of others were Hui from Shaanxi province who had been displaced by violence or embroiled in the fighting. In deciding how to incorporate Muslims into postwar agricultural policy, Zuo Zongtang was eager to exude an air of impartiality. He tried to reassure people that what mattered was not one's identity but one's willingness to obey imperial authority. He even acknowledged that Han people bore some culpability for starting the conflict that led to the war.[88] But in practice, his policies were influenced by a certain prejudice against Hui people based on a conviction about their proclivity for lawlessness. "Hui by nature are like dogs and sheep," he once wrote to Beijing, adding that "I worry they will secretly gang up and expand" their influence.[89] Concerned about the long-term stability of Qing rule in Gansu, Zuo formulated a policy of removal and forced resettlement for any Hui who had been caught up in the conflict. After carrying out sieges on Muslim strongholds, Qing troops forced Hui to surrender their weapons and their horses. Hui who submitted to imperial authority were then sent under armed escort, thousands at a time trudging along rural highways, to new sites of settlement in the hinterlands of the province. In some cases, captured Hui asked to be allowed to return to their hometowns. But Zuo denied their requests, arguing that because they had become entangled in the war, they showed no signs of possessing a "love of their native land." He also expressed fear that the return of Hui to their native places could spark smoldering animosities with Han people and lead to new rounds of violence.[90]

The policy of forced resettlement was crafted to allow the state to take advantage of Muslims' labor while minimizing the risk they posed to imperial rule. Zuo stipulated that potential sites of resettlement were required to be in remote areas away from cities, located at some distance from major roadways, and segregated from Han communities. In many cases, he asked magistrates of districts targeted for Hui resettlement to conduct land surveys and search for areas of unclaimed and unoccupied wasteland possessing nearby water sources that could be divvied up easily into individual properties. For example, in 1871 government personnel carried out rural land surveys in the district of Guyuan, where they identified a suitable area of fertile soil with nearby sources of water, supplies of firewood, and even some dilapidated cave dwellings that could be refurbished to serve as people's homes.[91] The plan was then to send a group of Hui under guard to that location, enroll them in local population registers, give them door placards noting their status as law-abiding people, supply them with parcels of land, farming tools, plow animals, and seeds of wheat, sorghum, buckwheat, and millet, and order them to "exhaust their labor on cultivation and land reclamation."[92] After a period of several years, they would be required to pay the land tax and could sell any surplus grain they produced on the open market. To keep people engaged in agriculture, regulations stipulated that resettled Hui were not allowed to travel away from their new homes, even temporarily, without the permission of local officials, who possessed the authority to grant or deny travel documents. In addition, small detachments of Qing troops were often stationed nearby to enforce compliance.[93] In the early 1870s, Zuo Zongtang and other officials in Gansu applied the policy of forced resettlement to more than one hundred thousand Hui, including at least sixty thousand who were natives of Shaanxi.[94] While most were moved to eastern districts of the province, some were resettled in northern districts that sat along the Yellow River.

The actual experience of forced resettlement must have been far more arduous for Hui people than protocols and regulations made it seem. Consider the history of resettlement at a place called Huapingchuan, located in the mountains of eastern Gansu about one hundred *li* from Pingliang. Starting in 1870 when Qing forces captured Jinjibao, a fortified Muslim stronghold in the north of the province, officials sent a stream of more than ten thousand Muslims, most of whom were "old, weak, weary, or sick," on a days-long southward march to reach the site.[95] According to official records, arriving Hui were given food aid until the first harvest and granted plow animals, seeds, materials for housing, and individual parcels of land totaling over sixty thousand *mu* along with tax abatements for a period of half a dozen years.[96] Officials also erected government buildings and set up two checkpoints staffed with foot soldiers and cavalry to monitor the area's inhabitants.[97] From the state's perspective, Huapingchuan was an ideal location for resettlement because of its abundance of land and its remoteness from major transportation routes. But Hui soon learned of the hardship that awaited them. "When we first arrived," one resident later recalled, "there was little cultivated land but much wasteland in Huaping. It was very difficult to open up the mountain wastes and wild forests. There was not enough grain to eat."[98] Some people had no choice but to grow crops in the poor soils they were given and haul heavy loads of water from low-lying rivers to irrigate fields in the hills.[99] Others recalled being threatened by wolves and snakes in the forests or enduring the hardship of agricultural labor without the assistance of draft animals. But people found ways to survive despite the hardship. Many continued farming. A small number managed to circumvent the restrictions on travel and move away permanently. Others resorted to finding lines of business that permitted them to leave temporarily, such as collecting firewood from the forests and selling it in Pingliang and other cities.[100]

Meanwhile, Hui people sometimes faced vociferous antipathy from communities of Han people, who worried that Muslims posed a threat to their livelihoods. In 1870, Chinese gentry from Pingliang submitted a request to the governor-general asking that Muslims be resettled in "distant locations" where they would have little opportunity to encroach on Han-owned real estate, including the properties of Han owners who had not yet returned to reclaim them after the war.[101] Three years later, a group of Han from the district of Qin'an drew up a petition expressing their vehement objection to a plan to resettle more Hui in their district. They argued that such outsiders were prone to criminality, and besides that the region had no more space for Muslims—even though an official tally counted only about three thousand Hui at one site that was estimated to be able to accommodate ten thousand.[102] Han people teamed up to voice their animosity toward Hui settlement even in cases where the state seemed to have no direct role in facilitating their movement into a region. In 1878, a group of Han townsfolk from Qiyingzhen, in Gansu's northern countryside, jointly sponsored the carving of a stele commemorating their cooperation in an effort to eject Hui from the area. The stele recorded how, prior to the war, Hui had visited the town as day traders but had never resided there. But after the uprising, "farmland was completely occupied by Hui people and when peace came Han people had no land to till." They thus appealed to the governor-general, who came to the conclusion after some investigation that Hui should not be permitted to live or own farmland within ten *li* of the town. Muslim residents were subsequently expelled, and Han people chose to enshrine their victory in stone.[103]

Certainly, communities of Han received more than just legal support from the Qing state in the postwar years. In the 1870s, Zuo Zongtang carried out a broad program of agrarian development in Gansu, aimed at both Han and Hui communities, which provided government assistance and capital to farmers. By one estimate, the war had disrupted agriculture on 60 to 70 percent of farmland in the river plains, and even more on dry land at higher elevations.[104] The state had an interest in seeing such land return to cultivation as quickly as possible, because if more grain was produced locally and made available for purchase, officials could reduce the great sums of money spent on costly overland transportation to supply Qing armies with food. As in Zhejiang, Zuo's first instinct was to sustain the lives of survivors and thereby keep labor in the province. He allocated money for food and other aid, sometimes even buying winter clothing for tens of thousands of refugees who sauntered along rural highways in the expectation that he could "retain these disaster-afflicted people to exhaust their energy on land reclamation."[105] At the same time, officials worked to establish reconstruction bureaus in Pingliang, Lanzhou, Jinjibao, Suzhou, Hezhou, and other cities to carry out agrarian development projects.[106] The bureaus took on a variety of responsibilities, from conducting land surveys to allocating capital to farmers in the form of seeds, tools, and plow animals. Bureau officials generally treated these materials as loans, and farmers were required to repay an amount equivalent to their value after the first harvest, often through in-kind payments of grain and seed.[107] The bureaus also distributed land to settlers. The amount of land given to individuals and families probably varied by location; one set of regulations called for ten *mu* of land to be assigned to each able-bodied male.[108] In places where no reconstruction bureaus were established, district magistrates, local gentry, or officials working in military procurement bureaus, which had been set up to support the government's war effort, shouldered the burden of promoting land reclamation through similar policies.[109]

Many Han farmers, and probably many Hui as well, benefited from the state's distribution of plow animals. Privately owned stocks of ungulates had dwindled during the war, becoming casualties of violence or human hunger in the leanest years.[110] Qing leaders knew how essential animals were to plowing and other farm tasks, and they worked quickly to get animals back into the hands of cultivators. Zuo sometimes authorized subordinates to spend government funds to purchase animals for distribution to refugees. But the state also acquired animals during the war, confiscating the living property of Hui people whom they captured. In certain cases, Qing officials permitted Hui who had surrendered to keep their cows, mules, and donkeys if they were to be used for agriculture, but they dispossessed them of all horses, knowing that such animals could be used for warfare.[111] State confiscations of Hui property yielded large numbers of animals. In Hezhou, a Muslim stronghold southwest of Lanzhou, the Qing state obtained nearly four thousand horses in this fashion.[112] Over the course of the war years, officials probably confiscated tens of thousands of animals from Hui people. After they became state property, some horses were sent to Qing battalions for military deployment or to government-run post stations for use in the empire's communication system.[113] Thousands of others ended up as the property of farming households and were made to labor in the fields. The state also redistributed cows, mules, donkeys, and even some camels to settlers so that they could be put to work in the service of farmland development.[114]

Qing troops became another significant source of agrarian labor in Gansu. As different battalions were garrisoned across the province in the wake of the fighting, they contributed to a wide range of nonmilitary projects, especially the rebuilding of government offices, city walls, bridges, schools, irrigation facilities, and other infrastructure.[115] These soldiers, many of whom were Han from southern provinces, also spent time plowing soil and growing food to increase local supplies of grains and vegetables for their own consumption.[116] Zuo was fond of suggesting that his troops did the most arduous work of reclaiming land from the wilderness—rooting out grasses and bushes, chopping down trees, plowing land that had not been plowed for years, and digging irrigation ditches—and thus prepared the ground for the return of civilians.[117] But soldiers themselves also sometimes became permanent cultivators. Many were demobilized, given land, and asked to farm year-round, contributing a portion of their harvests to the government and being allowed to sell any surplus on the open market.[118]

While trying to accelerate the pace of land reclamation, Zuo acknowledged that the long-term growth of agriculture in Gansu would require the recruitment of much larger numbers of settlers from other provinces. Starting in 1874, as Qing troops wrapped up offensive operations in the

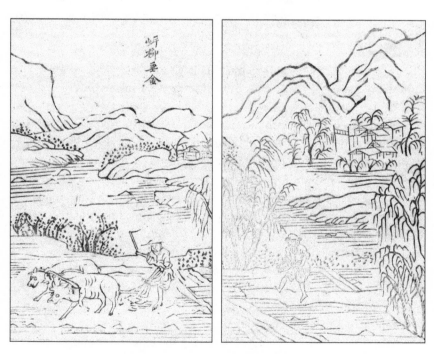

Figure 3.4 Farmers in eastern Gansu. From *Fuqiang xian xuzhi* (Updated gazetteer of Fuqiang county), 1872. Courtesy of Harvard-Yenching Library.

province, the governor-general had lower-level officials conduct thorough cadastral surveys to determine which parcels of land remained unclaimed and open for settlement.[119] The next year, he devised more formal and detailed regulations for collecting taxes and rents on the properties of homesteaders based upon soil quality, terrain conditions, and cultivation status.[120] In 1877, in what was perhaps his most enterprising move to make Gansu an attractive place for settlers and investors from other provinces, Zuo proposed to allow outsiders to enroll in local population registers on an accelerated schedule. Statutory norms dictated that people who migrated to a different province had to wait twenty years before enrolling in the registers, but under Zuo's plan, migrants who agreed to pay high tax rates on their new land could enroll almost immediately. The benefit for them would be that the young men in their families could quickly register for the imperial examinations in Gansu, where competition was less intense than in other provinces.[121] Yet, like the proposal in Zhejiang to incorporate "shack people" into land reclamation programs, Zuo's plan to lure outsiders to Gansu with the promise of a quick reward is more significant for what it says about his desperation to recruit people to cultivate wasteland and pay taxes than for what it may have accomplished in terms of creating additional farmland acreage. After nearly a decade in the northwest and over a decade of experience with agricultural development policy, the governor-general struggled to boost rates of land settlement in the province.

In the middle decades of the nineteenth century, the resurgence of wild spaces in the provinces of China marked a significant reversal in patterns of population growth and agricultural expansion that had been sustained for two centuries. Coming at a time of financial crisis for the Qing state, the emergence of these new internal frontiers prompted Qing officials to target them for development. Yet, aside from the forced resettlement of tens of thousands of Hui who were compelled to engage in farmwork, policies for land reclamation often employed enticements that cost the state money and succeeded only gradually in reversing the contraction of agriculture. In fact, in the provinces most damaged by the mid-century wars, recovery was often quite slow. When Zuo Zongtang first arrived in Zhejiang, he estimated that complete rehabilitation would require at least two or three decades.[122] Officials in the province were still reporting the existence of millions of *mu* of abandoned and idle wasteland in the 1880s, but the pace of development quickened as new waves of migrants arrived from northern Jiangsu and provinces further up the Yangzi River such as Hubei and Hunan.[123] Meanwhile, the process of reconstruction in Gansu was even more protracted. Official figures suggest that nearly 30 percent of the province's total prewar acreage remained out of cultivation as of 1887.[124] If one takes population as a proxy for recovery, the process lasted nearly a century: Gansu's population did not reach prewar levels until the middle of the twentieth century.[125]

For the Qing empire as a whole, the decline of the human population and the growth of wilderness were merely temporary setbacks. The empire's total farmland acreage surpassed the prewar benchmark by the 1890s, and its population likely had exceeded prewar levels by the first decade of the twentieth century.[126] It may be true that, for several decades, patterns of migration within the empire were thrown into reverse, as the lower Yangzi River provinces—formerly among the most densely populated regions of China—began to absorb settlers from upriver provinces and more distant peripheries.[127] Given this historic reversal, it may seem reasonable to expect that officials and literati shifted their attention away from Xinjiang and other imperial borderlands. Zuo Zongtang and others who led the fight against insurgents and who engaged in reconstruction activities no doubt temporarily refocused their energy on redeveloping the new frontiers of wasteland that emerged in the provinces. But patterns of population growth and decline were highly geographically uneven, with some regions emerging from the war heavily damaged and others remaining relatively intact. Overall, most of the Chinese provinces continued to be densely populous. In this situation, some people still looked to the empire's borderland territories to find new land and new economic opportunities.

CHAPTER IV

Promoting Profitable Crops

In September 1873, Zuo Zongtang departed from Lanzhou and headed to the northwest, riding for several weeks so that he could oversee military operations at Suzhou. Two months later, the city's surrender to Qing troops marked the end of the last major battle in the government's war to recapture Gansu from Muslim insurgents. But as the war for territory was wrapping up, another struggle was unfolding across the province's agricultural landscapes. Waged not with rifles and cannon but with hoes and plants, the struggle revolved around the cash crops at the heart of the rural economy. Provincial authorities had learned that some farmers were growing opium poppies, slicing open their seed pods, and harvesting the latex inside them to make opium. As the governor-general realized the scope of the problem, he zealously embraced efforts to eliminate the cultivation of poppies, regularly issuing pronouncements banning the plant and ordering deputies to conduct search-and-destroy missions to stifle its propagation. The struggle against opium poppy was not simply a campaign of suppression, however. It was accompanied by plans for rural development that aimed to wean households off their habit of planting poppies by teaching them about other crops that could provide alternative sources of income. Taking account of Gansu's economic and ecological conditions, Zuo chose to promote cotton to challenge the increasing prominence of the opium poppy in local agriculture, hoping the fiber crop could steal land away from its vilified rival. For this reason, he was delighted when he came across fields laden with white bolls of cotton ripening in the early autumn air as he passed through dusty farming towns on his way to Suzhou.[1]

Gansu was perhaps an unlikely battleground for a contest between opium poppies and cotton. Landlocked and months away from port cities like Shanghai and Guangzhou, the province seemed to exist beyond the fringes of the seaborne and riverine trading networks that had enabled these two flowering plants to become such potent forces of political and economic change in the nineteenth-century world.[2] Like some other inland peripheries of the Qing empire, Gansu did not enjoy access to cheap, waterborne modes of transportation. This raised costs significantly for all but the most local goods, circumscribing what types of natural resource commodities and cash crops could be produced and marketed profitably to other provinces.[3] Nonetheless, Gansu was deeply integrated into domestic networks of commercial exchange, functioning as a corridor for people and merchandise moving between far-flung imperial territories. The province funneled goods from Xinjiang and the largely pastoral economies of the Tibetan plateau and the Mongolian steppe into China's eastern and southern provinces while moving Chinese manufactures to the empire's northern and western borderlands. Gansu itself was also a significant producer of primary products, in large part because its great ecological diversity sustained a range of industries, including farming, herding, foraging, forestry, and mining. Its foragers and farmers gathered and cultivated plants such as rhubarb, goji berries, and, most famously, water-pipe tobacco, harvesting and processing these botanical goods in upland and rural areas and delivering them to markets in Lanzhou, where they were transported onward to larger and richer cities in the east or to border towns to enter into the frontier trade.[4]

The campaigns to eradicate opium poppy and promote cotton in Gansu effectuated a new level of state intervention in agriculture and the rural economy. Qing officials had always taken an interest in encouraging the cultivation of food crops, which were instrumental to guaranteeing subsistence and achieving the political mandate of "nourishing the people." They also had long proscribed practices that were seen as detrimental to people's livelihoods and the environments that supported them, such as land reclamation in the Mongol grasslands, mountainside farming in the Yangzi River provinces, and tobacco and maize cultivation in prohibited areas.[5] In postwar Gansu, the disciplinary and developmental sides of agricultural policy became more tightly and transparently intertwined as Zuo

Zongtang and his deputies tried to force farmers to abandon one cash crop and embrace another. On one hand, the surveillance of agriculture and rural areas intensified as provincial authorities mandated more frequent patrols of the countryside, imposed strict penalties on poppy farmers, and penalized dilatory officials who failed to enforce the ban on opium cultivation. On the other hand, authorities reached out to rural folk with seeds, technical training, and practical advice about cotton farming, seeking to assist them in adopting and improving their production of a crop that was seen as fundamental to both household welfare and the imperial economy. In short, by closely combining the use of punitive measures with the dissemination of agricultural technology, officials in postwar Gansu forged a distinctive approach to the problem of rural development.

Imperial officials may have wielded a significant amount of state power in establishing and enforcing agricultural policies and prohibitions. But they had much less power to prevent the economic and environmental volatility that became a hallmark of the nineteenth century. Such volatility resulted from a confluence of domestic and international forces. While China's mid-century civil wars devastated agricultural lands in many provinces, unpredictable weather unleashed flooding in some regions and induced deadly droughts in others. At the same time, warfare and weather in other parts of the world exerted their own modest influence on the changing dynamics of the Qing economy, a result of the increasing integration of global commodity markets. The volatility produced by all of these forces registered most clearly in the wildly fluctuating prices of agricultural commodities in the 1860s and 1870s. While it is not always easy to pinpoint the exact cause of such fluctuations, which varied in intensity and duration depending upon location, the price mechanism strongly affected the dynamics of agrarian change in this period, altering patterns of consumption and production in unforeseen ways and creating new incentives and disincentives for farmers to cultivate particular crops. Neither officials nor farmers could understand fully why prices for cotton and opium rose and fell so precipitously in these years. Yet, perhaps more than anything else, it was the combination of these forces and the volatility they caused that determined the course of the battle between opium poppies and cotton in Gansu.

Few species in the plant kingdom had a larger influence on the course of nineteenth-century history than the opium poppy. Before the nineteenth century, however, the plant had only a modest presence in Chinese society and agriculture. Since the Tang dynasty (618–907), people had been cultivating the herb for a variety of purposes.[6] In the Ming period, some farmers grew poppies for the beauty of their blossoms and for their inner substances, which people ingested as a medicine and an aphrodisiac, but the plant never attained the status of a major crop.[7] It was only in the eighteenth century that the plant's economic and political significance was gradually transformed by a combination of domestic and international forces. As the recreational practice of opium smoking expanded among China's upper classes, British traders shipped larger and larger quantities of Indian opium to the southern coast around Guangzhou, where they exchanged the narcotic for silver and valuable Chinese merchandise. Despite Qing prohibitions on the drug's sale and consumption, the illicit trade in opium surged in the early nineteenth century, feeding a growing pool of addicts and casual users. While the opium trade eventually brought the Qing and British empires to blows, it also boosted the poppy plant's agricultural significance within China. Indeed, by the 1820s Chinese farmers had caught on to the lucrative nature of the trade and were growing opium poppies widely in the empire's southern coastal provinces, creating a domestic supply of raw materials to manufacture the popular drug.[8] The Qing government banned opium cultivation starting in the 1830s, issuing a slew of regulatory measures designed to stifle its domestic production.[9] But in part because Chinese opium was notably cheaper than imported varieties, the spread of poppy farming made the narcotic available to a much wider range of users across all social classes. Farmers planted more poppies, allowing the crop to colonize ever larger areas of soil, and it soon spread throughout the empire's inland provinces and territories.

In Gansu, where the opium poppy had been cultivated as a medicinal herb for many centuries, the plant became a major cash crop starting in the 1840s and 1850s.[10] Farmers embraced the poppy for its profitability and versatility. They opted to grow it primarily for the money that could be made by harvesting and selling its latex. Some also found uses for other parts of the plant, pressing its seeds for oil or burning its stalks as a fuel. Officials, for their part, often tacitly permitted people to grow the poppies because the revenues they generated filled growing gaps in local government budgets.[11] As farmers devoted more land to poppy production, the plant's colorful blossoms proliferated across rural areas, creating what must have been a visually stunning and increasingly common sight. But, as some people recognized, the poppy's pretty flowers obscured an ugly truth about the harm they caused. According to one local gazetteer, in the 1850s opium "smokers became more numerous by the day, and those who grew it also multiplied. Because the profits were substantial and the work easy, and there was no need for fertile soil, people pursued [poppy farming] like ducks." Although it seemed to represent a windfall for rural households, opium agriculture took a heavy toll on many families. Some farmers picked up the habit of smoking the drug, and, as the practice spread to their wives and children, the crop became a persistent source of poverty and illness.[12]

After he arrived in Gansu in late 1869, Zuo Zongtang quickly made the decision to outlaw opium poppies. The governor-general had several reasons for detesting opium. He presumed that it fueled social unrest, telling his sons in a letter that Taiping rebels and Muslim insurgents had been "brewed with this poison."[13] He also criticized the cultivation of opium poppies for encroaching on the production of grain crops, echoing a concern that had been circulating among Qing elites since the 1830s. Because he believed opium poppies had a tendency to occupy fertile soils that farmers would otherwise use to produce cereals, he worried that poppy farming was gradually eroding the foundation of the country's subsistence. Employing a polarized language tied to visions of agrarian orthodoxy, Zuo lambasted greedy farmers who chased after quick profits by choosing to plant "evil grasses" (e'hui) rather than "good grains" (jiahe) and thereby endangered the food supply that served as the bedrock of the empire's moral and material order. Moreover, insofar as grain supplies were essential to the ability of Qing troops to continue to campaign westward, the ban on opium poppies also constituted an attempt to preserve local sources of provisions for his armies.[14] Given the fact that warfare and population decline were the primary causes of the downturn in agricultural production in Gansu, blaming opium farming for any reduction in the supply of foodstuffs may appear to have been misguided. Yet evidence from other provinces suggests that by the 1860s poppies indeed were starting to take land away from crops like rice as their cultivation spread from peripheral patches of soil to primary cropland.[15]

Within a few months of his arrival, Zuo had issued an order outlawing the production of opium poppies, hoping to suppress its cultivation and make headway toward the goal of wiping out consumption of the drug. Because he wanted to communicate the ban directly to residents of the province, he wrote the order entirely in rhyming, four-character phrases to make it easy for people to read and commit to memory. The short decree forbade farmers from growing poppies and instead urged them to sow grains and vegetables to ensure the availability of local supplies of food and satisfy the common welfare. Seeking to mobilize public sentiment by vilifying the plant and its production, the order attributed the practice of poppy farming not just to the pursuit of illicit profits but to the "treacherous plots of foreign countries" that "harm our Chinese customs." The prohibition emphasized that all farmers were forbidden from growing opium poppies and all local elites were responsible for helping to exterminate the plant from their communities.[16] First distributed to post houses and village schools, the order was reposted and recirculated multiple times in urban and rural areas in the following years to remind people of their duty to resist the temptation to plant the herb on their properties.[17]

To enforce the ban, officials carried out surveillance activities in rural areas and monitored what farmers were doing with their lands. Although these activities subjected Gansu's agriculture to a new level of state scrutiny, they were not entirely novel. Since the 1830s, imperial leaders had devised a range of regulatory measures for rural surveillance, aiming to uncover any signs of poppy cultivation. In 1839, for example, Beijing called upon provincial authorities to carry out inspection tours of the countryside twice a year to verify that farmers were not secretly growing opium poppies nor renting their land to outsiders for the production of the flowering crop. Provincial officials also were urged to employ the existing system of household registration and community security to enforce compliance with the ban.[18] In postwar Gansu, the responsibility for keeping a close watch over agriculture fell to civil officials and soldiers, who worked together to conduct investigations and enforce the law in rural areas. Prefects, magistrates, and other local authorities accompanied troops and light cavalry on inspection tours to search for signs of poppy cultivation as many as several times every month.[19] Tan Jixun, a Hunan native who served as a surveillance commissioner in Gansu in the 1870s, issued declarations reminding people of the ban on poppy farming and then accompanied village elders on surveillance missions. Zuo Zongtang also was said to have participated in some rural inspection activities.[20]

Farmers who violated the ban on poppy cultivation faced a range of potential punishments. In the simplest cases, officials forced farmers to plow up their crops, ensuring that the plants were destroyed before they departed.[21] In more serious cases, authorities acted on their power to confiscate farmland, sequestering the properties until their owners vowed to grow only cereal crops or state-approved cash crops.[22] In neighboring Shaanxi province, there is evidence that governor Tan Zhonglin, who communicated regularly with Zuo Zongtang during his tenure in Gansu, paired the confiscation of property with the physically tiring and demeaning punishment of having to wear the cangue, a wooden yoke worn around the neck, so that opium farmers suffered in multiple ways and could serve as a public warning to other rural folk about the dangers of illicit agriculture.[23]

Enforcing the ban on poppies was much easier in principle than in practice. Zuo expressed confidence that regular surveillance and enforcement would succeed in putting an end to the production of the crop. Unlike opium smoking, he wrote, farming had to be done in broad daylight over a period of months, making the practice much more visible and easier to catch.[24] "From the planting of the seeds, the emergence of the sprouts, the opening of the flowers, and the fructification to the cutting of the pods and the taking of the fluid, a great deal of time is required," he explained. "In these circumstances it is difficult to conceal with any certainty."[25] As local authorities discovered, however, finding opium poppies was not so simple. Gansu's rural residents resorted to using a variety of tricks to thwart the prying eyes of the state and prevent the detection of their crops. One of the most common methods of obfuscation was to grow poppies in places that were difficult for officials to see. The edaphic and topographic conditions of the province offered much help in this regard. In Gansu's eastern districts, the thick deposits of loess that cover the surface of the earth, forming part of China's Loess Plateau, are extremely susceptible to erosion by wind and water, largely a result of long-term patterns of human activity that denuded the region of its vegetation.[26] Over time, erosion carved gullies into the land, producing a highly uneven landscape marked by a combination of high hills, table land, and deep ravines. Some opium farmers tried using this landscape to their advantage. To evade detection, they sowed their crops up on remote hillsides or down in invisible ravines, almost guaranteeing that only the most assiduous inspectors would have any possibility of discovering their poppies. Other farmers made the riskier choice of trying to hide poppies in plain sight, sowing the plants among beans and wheat and using these crops as camouflage. While the colorful blossoms of the poppies may have alerted officials to the existence of opium in certain cases, the practice of intercropping must have succeeded in many

Figure 4.1 Terrain in the loess region of central Gansu. From Ludwig Lóczy, "Geologie," 1893. Courtesy of the Ernst Mayr Library, Museum of Comparative Zoology, Harvard University.

other cases, since it proved to be a common tactic for hiding opium from the state.[27]

Not all farmers relied solely on methods of passive resistance, however. Sometimes they chose to shield their opium poppies from the eyes and arms of the state using acts of physical obstruction and violence, seeking to ward off inspectors or prevent them from destroying their precious crops. There were reports of rural residents joining forces to confront government authorities when they came through the countryside. Such people "often gathered in groups to hinder inspections" when officials approached their fields with shovels to root out poppy plants.[28] In Shaanxi, those who were responsible for conducting rural surveillance and enforcing the ban sometimes encountered the resistance of what one official called "conniving women." Such women strongly defied the authorities, deciding to relent and pull out their opium plants only after being harshly reprimanded.[29]

Zuo Zongtang viewed opium suppression as a crucial step in the process of rebuilding Gansu's economy after the war, even if it sometimes provoked opposition. But it became clear to him, after several years of monitoring for evidence of poppy farming, that not only had the problem gotten worse, the process of reconstruction itself was partially to blame. Zuo was inclined to absolve most of the region's Hui Muslims of culpability, believing that they largely avoided the drug and its herbal source because they saw them as contrary to the maintenance of religious discipline.[30] Instead, when he surveyed the situation, he discerned a relationship between the settlers who had drifted into Gansu after the war and the spread of illicit agriculture. Although incoming migrants were essential for reviving agrarian production in areas abounding in wasteland, it turned out that a certain proportion of them had contravened the governor-general's policy by deciding to grow poppies. "Recruits for land reclamation gradually became more numerous," Zuo later wrote of certain areas in Gansu, "and the clandestine propagation of opium poppy turned out to be several times greater than in the past."[31] Other Qing frontiers experienced similar surges in opium cultivation in the late nineteenth century, a result of the demographic convulsions and wartime dislocations that allowed refugees and migrant farmers to find open land in unfamiliar and remote terrain.[32] Such a phenomenon indicates that, while some viewed the empire's sparsely populated borderlands as places to take refuge from social turmoil or natural disasters, others saw them as opportunities to get rich.

If there was one thing that Zuo Zongtang found unpalatable about life in nineteenth-century China, it was the way in which people had internalized the desire for money, making it the basis for their approach to dealing with the human world around them. He once described the problem in a letter to a colleague: "In recent times, people's hearts have been completely corroded by the word 'profit.' It is really difficult for them to free their minds of it."[33] This expression of dismay no doubt reflected how deeply his Hunanese education had influenced his way of thinking. Decrying the corrupting power of profit to warp human ethics was an age-old exercise with roots in Confucian thought. Yet for Zuo, the idea of profit also seemed freshly relevant for comprehending why farmers in Gansu had decided to cultivate such an odious herb as the opium poppy. "Ignorant people lack knowledge and lust after large profits, and thereupon take fertile earth suitable for grain and sow it with opium poppies," he wrote.[34] His criticism was not a blanket condemnation of people's longing for material well-being, nor a denunciation of the desire to maximize the exploitation of natural resources. Instead, it was a rebuke of the practice of acting solely on the basis of financial gain in an era when almost everything seemed to have a price.

Despite his misgivings about people's pursuit of profit, Zuo did not discount the importance of the idea of profit when devising agricultural policy. In fact, like other nineteenth-century elites, he recognized the value of analyzing political and economic matters through the prism of profit, and he viewed the profit motive as a powerful device for manipulating farmers' behavior.[35] "When ignorant people greedily grow the opium poppy, if they are greedy only for its profits, then profits shall be used to mobilize them," he proclaimed.[36] He believed farmers could be enticed to act in accordance with the larger political and economic objectives of the Qing state if they were offered the proper guidance. He thus devised a plan for ridding Gansu of opium: "If one wants to prohibit the cultivation of opium poppies, one must first think of a kind [of plant] that can trump its profits. Thereafter people will be aware that opium poppies are not so profitable, and then greed can gradually fill in."[37] In other words, to eliminate poppy farming in the province, one merely had to select a profitable replacement cash crop and notify farmers, whose desire for pecuniary gain would automatically lead them to cultivate it without requiring the state to resort to more coercive or punitive measures.

When the governor-general chose cotton to compete with opium poppy in Gansu, he must have been aware of the fluctuations in the market for cotton in recent years. Just a decade earlier, the Taiping war had wreaked havoc across some of the most productive farmland in the empire, constricting the domestic supply of cotton from Jiangnan. Meanwhile, the outbreak of civil war in the United States caused major turbulence in global cotton markets.[38] The war temporarily severed the massive flow of cotton from the southern states to Britain, sending textile manufacturers in Manchester and Liverpool scrambling to secure new sources of raw material from other countries. Imports of raw cotton from India, Brazil, and Egypt surged, and suppliers even began to buy cotton in China for manufacturing in Britain.[39] In a short period of time, the price of cotton skyrocketed worldwide. There is evidence that prices for cotton jumped in China, too. In Sichuan province, for example, cotton prices were reported to have risen by nearly 300 percent between 1861 and 1866.[40] It remains unclear what proportion of this increase can be attributed to global events rather than to the Taiping war. Whatever the cause, no region seemed to be immune from the upswing in cotton prices.

Higher prices quickly catalyzed a bonanza of cotton farming around the globe, with investors and farmers racing to expand acreage of the cash crop in the expectation of reaping outsized profits. Chinese farmers in some parts of the empire were not immune to the epidemic of cotton fever. Reports produced by commissioners at the Imperial Maritime Customs Service, the Qing government agency responsible for collecting customs duties at China's international ports, suggest that farmers in coastal provinces sought to take advantage of the robust market by expanding the amount of land devoted to the fiber crop.[41] The lure of high returns on cotton agriculture was strongly felt in Zhejiang, where the price reportedly climbed by more than 300 percent in 1860 alone.[42] While Chinese farmers in eastern Zhejiang busily rebuilt and extended irrigation canals to increase their output of cotton, foreigners took an interest in the region's potential for becoming a new producer of foreign cotton varieties, which tended to have a longer staple than Chinese varieties and therefore were better suited to machine manufacturing. In 1866, the Cotton Supply Association, a British trade and manufacturers' organization, attempted to carry out experiments with Egyptian cotton in Zhejiang, sending around one hundred pounds of seed to the province in hopes of creating new supplies of the Egyptian variety.[43] In the same year, a certain amount of American cotton seed was dispatched to Shanghai for test cultivation in local soils.[44]

For areas with a strong tradition of cotton agriculture such as Zhejiang, where farmers possessed the necessary knowledge and infrastructure to capitalize on market demand, the surge in prices had the potential to bring a windfall of profits. But for regions of the country which were not self-sufficient in cotton and had to rely upon imports for raw and woven fibers, market instability could cause significant hardship. In 1866, Zuo Zongtang was stationed in Fujian province, where he was overseeing reconstruction efforts after the end of the Taiping war two years earlier. In the region around the city of Fuzhou, the provincial capital, he found that although rural households grew cash crops like longans, lychees, tea, and sugarcane, they produced little cotton, hemp, or other fiber crops, leaving them vulnerable to fluctuations in the price of textile commodities at a time when many could ill afford to pay for clothing.[45] Because Fujian was not self-sufficient in food or fiber crops, many people had no choice but to bear the elevated costs of cotton and rice.[46] Zuo resolved to try to ameliorate people's vulnerability to market volatility and spur the development of local textile production by investing resources in cotton and mulberry agriculture. He established a state-funded mulberry and cotton bureau (*sangmian ju*) in Fuzhou, creating a place where farmers could learn about techniques for growing and processing the two plants.[47] He also imported cotton seed from other provinces for distribution to farmers in the region, and he encouraged the cultivation of cotton on farmland that was not already engaged in the production of cereal crops.[48]

Three years later, Zuo began to diagnose similar problems in Gansu. He determined that residents of the province suffered from low incomes and severe wartime deprivation, some lacking even basic clothing. Moreover, they appeared to rely on imports of cotton from neighboring provinces, making them susceptible to fluctuations in the commodity's price. Owing to meager local production, many households had to purchase cotton hauled in by pack animal from Sichuan, Shaanxi, and Hubei to obtain a sufficient supply for household use. Others were simply unable to pay for imported cottons. In addition, unlike consumers in the region around Fuzhou, Gansu's residents had to shoulder the additional burden of high transportation costs.[49] In communicating such problems to Beijing, the governor-general often resorted to using the formulaic language of Chinese statecraft, pointing out the need to nurture the well-being of the common people, recognizing the difficulties that they faced in trying to obtain clothing, and proposing to assist them through concerted government action. Yet his remarks about encouraging a profitable alternative to opium poppies suggest that his plans for cotton in Gansu were shaped as much by the notion that people could take advantage of the market for their own financial gain as they were by the idea that people needed the state's assistance to protect them from the market. In other words, the scarcity of cotton in Gansu was not merely a detriment to public welfare. It was also a chance for farmers to make a better living.

Almost as soon as Zuo initiated a policy of encouraging farmers to grow cotton in Gansu, people started to raise questions about the plant's ability to flourish in the region. Rural residents and local officials alike expressed skepticism that Gansu possessed the proper environmental conditions for cotton's propagation. Some pointed to the deficient "nature of the soil" or claimed that "local conditions are unsuitable," believing that the region simply was not hospitable to its cultivation.[50] Others worried about Gansu's climate and the length of its growing season, which many observers agreed was shorter than in other provinces.[51] Zuo himself had to admit that the local climate adversely influenced agricultural productivity because it had colder weather and shorter summers than eastern parts of the empire.

Gansu's "land leans toward the northwest, warm air is scarce, and cultivation is naturally inferior to the southeast," he concluded.[52] Phenological comparisons seemed to validate such impressions. In the spring of 1871, he had heard that Shaanxi's "fields of wheat are dewy and lustrous and grain glistens throughout the countryside," but to the west in Gansu, "the curling buds still have not fully developed, snow and rain frequently soak them, and the splendors of spring are still withheld."[53]

Zuo was not unaware of the need to ensure that plants were afforded conditions hospitable to their growth. Back in the 1830s, when he first studied agronomy, he had learned to be conscientious of land and soil characteristics and climate and weather patterns, understanding that crops flourished best when the environments around them suited their natural qualities. But he was unconvinced by skeptics of cotton's ability to be grown in Gansu. The province enjoyed the four seasons, with "winter and summer naturally coming one after another" just like other parts of the country, he wrote, "so it is certainly untenable that every location is unsuitable" for cotton. Citing textual evidence from ancient sources to make the case that geographic proximity was an indicator of ecological resemblance, he argued that because eastern Gansu abutted western Shaanxi, the two provinces were bound to enjoy roughly equivalent climates and growing conditions, suggesting that farmers in Gansu could grow cotton just as well as their counterparts in Shaanxi. In addition, he believed that the characteristics of the cotton plant conferred upon it the advantage of being adaptable to a wide variety of locations. By its nature, cotton "likes dryness and hates moisture and is suited to cultivation on hillsides and in sand," he explained. The plant could thrive even in inferior soils, he believed, so it would be unlikely to encroach on farmland devoted to the production of grain crops.[54] Over time, he devised a standard reply to his skeptics in which he reiterated cotton's need simply for warm, dry land: "All rich, warm areas facing the sun that can be planted with opium poppies are suitable for growing cotton."[55] From this perspective, the fact that cotton and opium thrived in similar ecological conditions made cotton a fitting substitute for the drug plant.

To combat misunderstandings about the environmental obstacles to cotton agriculture, Zuo reached into the agronomist's toolkit, adopting a strategy that combined the acts of observation, persuasion, and experimentation. He described the work of convincing farmers to grow cotton as a systematic, step-by-step procedure in which the objective was to demonstrate the process and the rewards of cultivating the crop. Officials were ordered to conduct investigations of local soils and learn about planting methods and seed varieties before calling together village elders to educate them on the benefits of cotton farming. Such activities then led to a period of trial cultivation, the most essential step in the process. During trials, farmers were given the opportunity to see for themselves the tools and techniques involved in production and to recognize how they stood to gain from planting cotton. Trial cultivation was intended to be both heuristic and persuasive, a culmination of the state's argument for cotton that was embodied in the act of raising the plants and seeing their produce. Zuo expected that trials would convince some people to give cotton a try, which could then generate further excitement about the crop. "After one or two years," he surmised, "there will gradually be some profit and the common people will pursue it like a flock of ducks."[56]

As he prepared to sponsor trials of cotton farming in Gansu, Zuo drew inspiration from a long tradition of agricultural experimentation and field testing. He regarded the act of testing as an essential technique for learning about the world, one which had begun with the mythical progenitors of Chinese agriculture in the very earliest days of farming.[57] But he did not need to evoke the legendary past to find relevant examples of people relying upon field testing to improve agriculture. He could look to the example of late Ming scholar Xu Guangqi, who had conducted experiments with the sweet potato, a plant native to the Americas that was new to China in the sixteenth century. Xu sought to show that the leafy tuber could easily be grown more widely if people were informed of the best techniques for its cultivation.[58] Zuo could also seek inspiration in the work of one of his former mentors, He Changling. When he served as governor of Guizhou province during the Opium War, He promoted cotton farming as an alternative to poppy cultivation. In addition to distributing cotton seed procured in Hubei and Henan provinces and dispatching local officials to the villages to teach people about cultivating cotton, He also set up demonstration gardens near the provincial capital to show interested farmers how they themselves could grow the crop and reap its rewards.[59] Some people had criticized the decision to encourage cotton farming, claiming that Guizhou's environment was not appropriate for the crop. But after seeing how well the experimental cotton had matured, he felt vindicated, concluding that "we can do away with the longstanding saying that 'the soil is not suitable.'"[60]

Taking such examples as models for agrarian research and education, Zuo Zongtang issued a directive in 1871 to all districts in Gansu to grow rice, mulberry, and cotton on an experimental basis. The directive served to formalize some of the rural development activities that officials were already starting to undertake at the local level in districts that had been retaken by Qing forces. It also reflected the basic presumption that the province possessed an array of opportunities to increase the production of agricultural commodities, and that the only thing standing in the way of people taking advantage of them was their lack of knowledge. As Zuo advised prefects and magistrates to provide development assistance to rural communities, he reminded them that "the profits of nature merely await people to take them."[61]

One of the main objectives of the new initiative was to improve agriculture by disseminating better seed varieties. This was evident in plans unveiled by Zuo to enhance the production of food grains in the province. Gansu's farmers grew cereal and oil crops such as wheat, barley, millet, maize, and sesame, but when their plants matured, they turned out to have "short tassels of grain, single shoots, and small granules." Each *mu* of land reportedly yielded just over one hundred catties (*jin*) of grain, significantly less than good harvests from paddy land in eastern provinces.[62] Such low productivity made it very difficult for rural households to accumulate surpluses which could be sold at market, leaving Zuo to wonder how they managed to survive without an income. The governor-general thus called for field trials of "southern rice" in hopes that local farmers could be convinced to adopt new, more productive seed varieties. He himself had overseen experiments with rice cultivation in Pingliang in 1870. But the crops turned out poorly because the late-ripening rice seeds used in the experiments did not mature at the right time. His hopes dashed, Zuo was considering giving up on the idea of rice farming in Gansu when he heard from the district magistrate that a new trial had been carried out successfully, producing around four hundred catties of grain per *mu*. This result reassured him that rice cultivation could be profitable in eastern Gansu as long as farmers sowed quick-ripening varieties of rice seed—harvested sixty to seventy days after planting—in areas with access to ample supplies of water.[63]

The initiative also aimed to improve cotton agriculture and industry through a multifaceted development approach involving everything from seeds to textile education. By the time Zuo issued the 1871 directive, cotton had already begun to receive some attention from officials and village gentry, who conducted trials of its cultivation and distributed seeds to rural residents.[64] Others proceeded to establish bureaus where people could be trained in the arts of textile manufacturing, a reflection of the acknowledgement that simply raising the output of raw cotton would do only so much to improve rural livelihoods. Two magistrates in eastern Gansu garnered recognition for working energetically to improve cotton farming and textile weaving in these ways. After acquiring cotton seeds from other provinces, they reportedly set up a nursery, grew cotton seedlings, and then distributed the plants to households in their districts. They also set up bureaus for textile education, gathering spindles and looms and hiring female teachers to offer instruction in weaving to enhance productivity and raise the quality of the finished fabrics.[65] The promotion of cotton also occurred in less formal settings. Sometimes it happened when government ministers journeyed into the countryside for official business and had the chance to speak directly with rural people. Zuo himself engaged in such conversations. On his way to Suzhou in late 1873, he met with town residents whenever he stopped to rest. These impromptu meetings gave him the opportunity to tout the benefits of cotton and persuade people that growing it was just as profitable as opium poppy.[66]

Yet the power of these face-to-face interactions was limited by their relative infrequency. To engage a wider audience in learning about cotton, Zuo resorted to printing and disseminating informational pamphlets about cotton varieties and propagation methods. In early 1874, he ordered two texts to be published and circulated among officials and elites throughout Gansu and Shaanxi.[67] The first, the *Ten Essentials for Growing Cotton* (*Zhong mian shi yao*), was likely to have been a short how-to guide for cotton agriculture, perhaps offering basic tips for farmers who had never tried cultivating the crop.[68] The second text, the *Treatise on Cotton* (*Mian shu*), offered explanations of fifteen topics related to the technical aspects of cotton agriculture and industry, from seed selection and planting to methods for ginning, spinning, and weaving cotton fibers. At just twelve double-sided pages, this booklet served as a quick reference guide for local authorities and cotton farming households.[69]

The *Treatise on Cotton* reveals how the state's attempts to transmit technical information to officials and farmers were based upon assumptions about the geographic mobility of agricultural knowledge and technology. Originally published in late 1866 by the provincial government office in

Fujian, the booklet seems to have been written for use in conjunction with Zuo Zongtang's efforts to promote cotton farming in that province. Although the booklet itself was new, its contents were neither new nor tailored to the social and environmental characteristics of Fujian. The information that it contained was compiled from a small handful of cotton treatises and agronomy handbooks published in the seventeenth and eighteenth centuries, some depicting various scenes of cotton-production activities.[70] In drawing together knowledge from various sources and repackaging it for circulation in new places, the *Treatise on Cotton* epitomized the objectives of state-sponsored agricultural publications as Francesca Bray has described them: "To produce comprehensive, mobile knowledge that could successfully be transferred through the medium of print, across the vast spaces of the empire, and translated into local action."[71] Certainly, this does not mean that the information it contained was free of geographical bias. Nineteenth-century cotton technologies bore the traces of their historical and geographical contexts of development, and those traces sometimes were revealed in the booklet's passages. For example, many cotton seed varieties were named after the regions in which they had evolved through centuries of human selection: there were Hubei seeds, North China seeds, and Zhejiang seeds. Weaving technologies were also marked by their association with particular places. The best weaving tools were said to come from Songjiang, near Shanghai.[72] Such remarks not only reflected the technical dominance of certain regions of the empire, but also the regionally specific nature of essential agricultural inputs like seeds. Yet the booklet's compilation, publication, and circulation suggests that the information it contained was intended for use in any region, regardless of local conditions. It is for this reason that Zuo Zongtang ordered another printing of the booklet eight years after its first print run, this time planning to distribute it to people in the northwest.

In the second half of the 1870s, the cotton promotion scheme expanded across Gansu and Shaanxi. Copies of the reprint edition of the *Treatise on Cotton* reached the district of Dali in eastern Shaanxi, where farmers gradually increased the area of land sown with cotton.[73] The state's efforts also led to an upturn in cotton production in western Gansu.[74] In the region around Suzhou, officials distributed copies of both booklets and disseminated "several hundred thousand catties of cotton seeds" purchased from other provinces. Although poor soil quality reportedly limited the viability of cotton in Suzhou, cotton farming grew significantly in several neighboring

Figure 4.2 Weeding fields of cotton. From Dong Gao et al., *Qinding shouyi guangxun* (Imperially commissioned teachings on the provision of clothing), 1808. Courtesy of Columbia University Library.

towns, with up to 30 percent of households in one area growing the crop and supplying local families with textile fibers after years of wartime dearth.[75] Efforts to promote cotton extended even into Xinjiang. In 1878, officials in the Turpan oasis received two hundred copies of the *Ten Essentials for Growing Cotton* for distribution to area gentry and farmers so that they could emulate the methods contained within it.[76]

In the mid-1870s, cotton agriculture seemed to be gaining momentum in some parts of Gansu. The governor-general was therefore quite dismayed to find that poppies appeared to be flourishing in other areas. By the late 1870s, the most productive opium farming region was Ningxia. Centered upon a vast plain astride the Yellow River as it flows northeast through Gansu toward Inner Mongolia, Ningxia and its residents enjoyed the benefit of having access to an abundance of fertile land and irrigation water. Zuo learned, however, that farmers were exploiting such natural endowments to grow more than just food and fiber crops. He discovered the magnitude of the region's poppy problem by chance after the start of the North China Famine, which decimated agriculture in Shaanxi and neighboring provinces starting in 1876.[77] The following year, requests were made to procure grain from Ningxia to assist with famine relief. Government reports of decent harvests in the area in the preceding years suggested that its granaries possessed sizable stockpiles that could be used to supply relief to famine-stricken provinces. But the order to allocate Ningxia grain exposed the startling truth that the region actually held only meager stores of grain.[78] Zuo quickly became suspicious that opium cultivation was one of the causes of Ningxia's grain shortage. He ordered an investigation that soon uncovered the widespread practice of poppy cultivation in the region. Indeed, Ningxia seemed to be growing more poppies and manufacturing more opium than the rest of Gansu combined.[79] Farmers in districts up and down the Yellow River were planting the crop liberally, helping poppies to colonize "distant countryside, backwaters, and places that officials have a hard time reaching." Some were not even bothering to hide the crop or disguise their poppy fields.[80]

Viewed from an economic perspective, it is not difficult to see why Ningxia's residents would have chosen to flout the prohibition on opium. The domestic market for the narcotic was growing prodigiously in the late nineteenth century as an increasing number of day laborers and peasants availed themselves of the lower prices of Chinese opium, which was regarded as less potent than foreign varieties.[81] Opium farmers responded to rising demand by increasing production. Some rural households cultivated poppies for personal and local use, but many grew the crop for export to other provinces, as much of the demand originated from beyond Gansu's borders. Chinese consumers, for their part, seem to have favored opium from Gansu, which enjoyed a reputation for being superior to all other domestic varieties of the drug. Because of this, Gansu opium fetched higher prices than other domestic varieties in markets across China.[82] When combined with information on the productivity of poppy farming in Ningxia, data on prices for Gansu opium suggests that rural households could earn handsome sums of money cultivating poppies and processing even small amounts of opium.[83] In sum, the business of illicit agriculture was simply too lucrative for many farmers to pass up.

But the profitability of opium was not just a function of the long-term growth in consumer demand. The natural and agricultural disasters underlying the North China Famine likely also played a role, albeit indirectly through the price mechanism, in enticing Ningxia's farmers to grow more poppies. Foreign and Chinese observers contended that opium was one cause of the crisis, often partially blaming its severity on the expansion of opium farming and the consequent contraction of grain agriculture in Shaanxi and nearby provinces.[84] When rains failed across these areas of northern China, the ensuing drought hindered the production of many agricultural goods, including opium. The acute damage inflicted upon rural economies in drought-stricken regions forced some treaty port cities to increase imports of the drug from India, which was itself mired in a succession of droughts, and probably contributed to the upturn in opium prices across China.[85] This upturn registered strongly in markets in Gansu, where the cost of the drug reportedly jumped by 500 to 600 percent in 1877.[86] While this was no doubt unwelcome news to opium smokers, many of whom were forced to consume less of the drug or settle for inferior varieties, for farmers it must have been a tantalizing inducement to plant more of the flowering crop. The result of this turn of events seems to have been that more farmers in Gansu jumped into poppy cultivation to capitalize on the commodity's incredibly high prices.

Zuo, for his part, blamed the surge in opium cultivation on neither weather nor markets but on local authorities. To his great chagrin, opium production in Ningxia seemed to be a result of the poor performance of prefects and magistrates, who failed in their duty to enforce the ban on poppies. In fact, since the early 1870s, Zuo had discovered numerous cases in which officials willfully neglected their obligation to carry out rural surveillance. In 1871, there were reports of low-level government functionaries in the southern district of Gannan manipulating the prohibition on opium poppies to their financial advantage. They were said to have done nothing to prevent people from sowing seeds of the poppy early in the growing season. Then, when the plants were about to ripen, they suddenly sprang into action to enforce the ban. Yet instead of obliging people to destroy their poppy fields, they leveraged their administrative power to extract bribes from farmers, leaving those who paid up to go about their business.[87] Elsewhere, district officials imposed fines on opium farmers and simply permitted them to continue their work, allowing the plants to reach maturity. In other cases, local authorities submitted reports to Lanzhou falsely claiming to have purged opium from their districts.[88] When attention turned to Ningxia, it was revealed that some officials had neglected to conduct surveillance altogether or had chosen to collude with growers to evade punishment. Zuo lambasted one official, Ningxia prefect Li Zongbin, for relying on the excuse that it was impossible to clear the entire region of opium poppies because the crop had grown so prevalent that its cultivation had essentially become a local custom.[89] Incensed by their dereliction of duty, Zuo disciplined the prefect and several others for not thoroughly investigating or punishing agrarian scofflaws. He had them removed from their posts and mandated that their replacements diligently monitor the countryside to hunt for poppies.[90]

Despite his zealous insistence on enforcing the ban, the governor-general could not deny that some officials had chosen to quietly tolerate opium production in their districts because the crop had become an indispensable boon to household incomes and government revenues. "There are those who say," Zuo wrote, "that to eradicate opium poppy would mean depriving the people of their source of profit and making the collection of the land tax even more troublesome."[91] Some local authorities worried that prosecuting rural residents for cultivating opium poppies could easily provoke a violent backlash at a time when Gansu was still recovering from more than a decade of warfare. Others were reluctant to meddle with a cash crop that had given farmers a new source of income and had allowed them to more easily fulfill their tax obligations to the state.[92] Such cases suggest that the prohibition policy had failed to prevent opium poppies from taking root in the economies of certain parts of rural Gansu.

Although it contravened provincial policy, this kind of tacit legalization of poppy farming through taxation was not an aberration from the larger dynamics of the expansion of China's opium economy. Indeed, it was but one manifestation of the highly conflicted and incoherent nature of the Qing state's approach to governing opium in the nineteenth century. Back in the 1830s, when imports of Indian opium escalated sharply, the Daoguang emperor had solicited ideas from his ministers for how to tackle the empire's drug problem. Some officials had counseled a more permissive approach to domestic production, arguing that native opium could benefit the empire's economy by becoming a replacement for more expensive foreign opium and thereby staunch the outflow of silver that resulted from Chinese merchants using large sums of money to pay for imported opium. They believed that native opium was less addictive and less damaging to human health than foreign opium because it was less potent than Indian, Persian, or Turkish varieties. But the emperor was persuaded to take a hard line against both foreign and domestic narcotics, setting the tone for strict prohibitions against poppy cultivation and opium smoking in the following decades. Zuo and a number of other provincial leaders tried to uphold the prohibition, justifying their vehemence with various arguments. Yet not all Qing statesmen held the same position or complied with the ban to the same degree. In the second half of the nineteenth century, an increasing number of high-ranking officials came to appreciate the perverse value of Chinese opium. After the import trade in foreign opium was legalized formally in 1858, officials in Yunnan and other western provinces started to collect taxes on domestic opium even though its cultivation, production, and consumption remained illegal in the eyes of the central government.[93] Other officials viewed domestic opium through the lens of state power, seeing it as a strategic tool in the fight against Indian opium and foreign influence. High-ranking minister Li Hongzhang held the opinion that allowing Qing subjects to produce opium would not only benefit the empire economically, but also give the imperial government the leverage to outlaw foreign opium at a later date. In 1874, he worked with ministers in Beijing to successfully lobby the court to ease its restrictions on the cultivation of poppies in China.[94]

Eventually, Zuo Zongtang also relaxed his position on native opium after years of trying to combat poppy farming in rural areas. In 1881, less than a year after leaving his post as governor-general in Gansu, he sent a memorial to Beijing calling on the central government to raise taxes on foreign and domestic opium. In his memorial, he conceded that it would be impossible to maintain an effective ban on opium production without a coherent and integrated policy for the entire empire. But what seemed to worry him even more were the problems caused by fluctuations in the price of the narcotic. The price of Gansu opium had skyrocketed in 1877. But just two years later it tumbled, falling to just half its peak price.[95] Meanwhile, he heard that the price of foreign opium had dropped by over 25 percent.[96] Such figures were concerning because he believed they created the conditions in which opium consumption would rise and the country's drug addiction would worsen. Given the circumstances, he concluded that the best way to counteract the effects of declining prices was to inflate the cost of opium by imposing higher taxes on the drug. He therefore urged the court to increase the combined rate for customs duties and transit taxes on foreign opium to 150 silver taels per chest of the drug and increase levies on domestic opium by an equal proportion. His goal was to put opium financially out of reach of more Chinese consumers, constrict the demand for both foreign and domestic supplies, and ultimately reach a point where the Qing state could effectively outlaw the drug altogether.[97] In 1885, Beijing amended its agreement with Britain regarding tariffs on the drug, bringing combined duties on imported opium up to 110 taels per picul.[98]

Qing leaders viewed the plan to raise opium taxes as the next stage in the empire's fight against the drug's importation, domestic production, and abuse. Zuo Zongtang called his idea for higher tariffs a "prohibition without a prohibition," seeing it as a means to curtail the rate of opium use and lay the groundwork for a more comprehensive ban on the substance in the future.[99] His vision turned out to be untenable. Farmers in Gansu interpreted Zuo's departure from the province and the new taxation policy as concessions that the former strategy of criminalizing poppy farming had failed and as signs that they now were allowed to cultivate the cash crop unmolested by the threat of punishment.[100] Evidence suggests that opium agriculture quite literally bloomed in Gansu in the following years. As one foreign visitor described the landscape: "Now, in the months of March and April, one sees only poppies in a white and red profusion of blossoms on the extensive fields of the valley plain in Lanzhou."[101] The cultivation of poppies expanded quickly in other provinces as well, and, after the 1870s, the amount of opium produced in the Qing empire surpassed the quantity imported from India by increasingly large margins.[102]

Meanwhile, after several years of state investment in agricultural outreach, the expansion of cotton farming in Gansu seems to have stalled. This outcome likely had as much to do with challenging market conditions as with any particular obstacles to the policy of teaching farmers about cotton. For one thing, the price volatility that was a hallmark of markets for cotton in the 1860s continued. Globally, the earlier surge in cotton prices was followed by a significant decline in prices.[103] Falling prices in turn jolted rural communities in many parts of the world, revealing how the advancing integration of domestic and foreign markets made peasants increasingly vulnerable to forces beyond their control.[104] In Gansu, farmers almost certainly felt the pain of declining prices. Sparse data suggests that the price of cotton in the province may have dropped by as much as 60 percent between 1874 and 1878.[105] While it is impossible to determine the exact cause of this decline, it likely had the effect of dampening farmers' enthusiasm for growing cotton beyond the immediate needs of their households. Qing officials did not relinquish the goal of developing cotton agriculture in Gansu, and efforts to spread knowledge about farming and weaving techniques continued intermittently in subsequent decades.[106] Even so, it was difficult for them to counteract the dynamic conjunction of economic and environmental forces that gave longtime residents and new settlers in Gansu much more incentive to plant opium poppies.

CHAPTER V

Water in a Fertile Frontier

I n the middle of March 1875, Zuo Zongtang received an urgent message from the capital.[1] The document, sent by horse courier to Lanzhou at top speed, raised serious questions regarding the country's strategic predicament. For several months, officials had been engaged in a contentious debate over military priorities and defense spending. A surprise Japanese expedition to the island of Taiwan almost a year earlier had caught them off guard, stoking fears about the frailty of the Qing state's coastal defenses and prompting calls for greater investment in naval training and shipbuilding to bolster its military capabilities along the eastern littoral.[2] But while some officials viewed seaborne countries like Japan as the primary threat to the security of the empire, others identified Russia and its actions along the empire's inland boundaries as the main menace.[3] Events of the foregoing decades had given them cause to worry. In the early 1860s, Russian diplomats had outmaneuvered their Qing counterparts in a series of negotiations and surveys to clarify the borders between the two empires in Central Asia, resulting in sizable territorial losses for the Qing side.[4] Then, in 1871, years after unrest had sundered the foundations of imperial rule in Xinjiang, Russian soldiers occupied over a thousand square miles of land in the Ili Valley, land that the Qing still considered part of its domain.[5] For these reasons, some officials encouraged strong military action in eastern Turkestan to shore up their empire's territorial claims in the region. Beijing thus presented Zuo with the question of whether to halt further military action in the northwest and divert money to the cause of coastal defense, or press ahead with campaigns in a bid to recapture the land and people in the erstwhile borderland.

Historians have remembered this debate for what it reveals about the contentious nature of Qing military policy in the 1870s.[6] But the debate also shows that there was more than territorial security at stake in the decision about whether to reconquer Xinjiang. While observers agreed on the crisis of imperial finances, they differed sharply in their perceptions of the area's natural wealth and its potential for development. In December 1874, Li Hongzhang, then grand secretary and governor-general of Zhili province, submitted a memorial urging the court to focus on the coastlines and abandon the idea of controlling Turkestan.[7] Comparing the region to a "leaky wine vessel" that annually siphoned millions of silver taels away from the treasury, Li argued that Xinjiang held neither strategic importance nor material value. To his mind, it was nothing more than "several thousand *li* of empty land" that had been "vainly acquired."[8] Li's characterization of the territory did not go unchallenged, however. Several months

Map 5.1 Xinjiang in the late nineteenth century. Map by Erin Greb.

later, when Zuo Zongtang prepared his response to Beijing's inquiry, he set forth a vision of Xinjiang that emphasized its resource abundance, which made it an alluring possession to outside powers. Zuo believed the Russians had been drawn to Ili for precisely this reason: they had "looked with envy upon its rich soil and sweet springs, its broad river plain, and its abundance of products," and they had decided to take advantage of the political turmoil to "seize its wealth to enrich themselves."[9] But, as Zuo argued, if the Qing state had a chance to reassert its power, it could exploit those resources for its own benefit. Although large parts of Xinjiang were nothing more than arid desert, there were certain areas north and south of the Tianshan that collectively formed what he called a "fertile borderland" (*yujiang*) of rich, irrigated soils and oases that produced a plenitude of goods. Echoing arguments made decades earlier about the cost savings that resulted from establishing a more westerly defensive posture, Zuo proposed that if the government pushed its line of control far enough to the west to reincorporate those resource-rich areas into the imperial territories and worked to develop them, it would be able to glean their bounty and govern the entire region on more solid financial footing far into the future.[10]

As the chief architect of Qing military policy in the northwest, Zuo Zongtang had a distinct interest in the outcome of the debate. But his perception of Xinjiang's prospects for development was far from unique. Since the early nineteenth century, explorers, scientists, and military men from Russia, Britain, and other European empires had traversed the region in a small but growing stream of visitors.[11] These men were participants in the so-called Great Game, a competition for territory and strategic advantage across Central Asia driven partially by the worldwide colonial race to exploit the earth for its material wealth. When they explored Xinjiang, some were quick to see opportunities for the expansion of agriculture. After a cohort of travelers from British India visited a handful of Tarim Basin cities in 1873, several of the British officers on the trip determined that "a much wider area might be settled and brought under cultivation" in the Kashgar oasis if the circumstances were ripe for the extension of irrigation systems.[12] Another member of the same expedition traveled further north and reported that the "country round Maralbashi is well watered, and the soil rich, and seems only to want population."[13] Three years later, when Russian military colonel Aleksei Kuropatkin visited the Tarim Basin, he found himself contemplating similar thoughts. On the journey from Kashgar to Korla, he saw "vast tracts of crumbling sands" and large patches of soil ruined by salinization. But in a region that was "in the highest degree dry," where farming required the diligent management of rivers, streams, canals, and groundwaters, he found no lack of water for development. "There is water in Kashgaria sufficient to irrigate a considerably larger tract of country than is now in use," he observed. From his perspective, the main thing that constrained the region's growth was not its aridity but its scarcity of labor: "The sparseness of the population of Kashgaria is the principal cause for the relatively small portion of land now under cultivation, whilst the amount of land that is suited to irrigation and cultivation is not small, and might be taken up by a considerably larger number of inhabitants."[14]

By the time of Kuropatkin's sojourn in the Tarim Basin, Qing forces were already on the march, capturing towns and cities near the Tianshan Mountains in a war to resurrect imperial power in Xinjiang. When the court granted its permission for these campaigns to proceed in May 1875, it put an end to the debate over the empire's military priorities and endowed Zuo with new authority to govern the borderland.[15] The decision satisfied those who saw the domination of eastern Turkestan as essential to the empire's survival. However, it only served to further complicate its financial woes. From 1874 to 1877, yearly expenses for the western campaigns

Figure 5.1 Kashgar and the surrounding landscape. From Robert Shaw, *Visits to High Tartary, Yarkand, and Kashghar (Formerly Chinese Tartary), and Return Journey over the Karakoram Pass*, 1871. Courtesy of Harvard University Botany Libraries.

reached above eight million taels of silver, estimated to be approximately one-sixth of all annual government revenues.[16] It also revealed the callous calculus of late Qing imperialism. While millions perished from hunger in the North China Famine, officials funneled staggering amounts of money to the military, all in hopes of securing control over a colonial territory.[17]

As the war brought Xinjiang into the empire once again, Chinese leaders took a hands-on approach to managing its environments and economies. In the late 1870s, Zuo Zongtang was not shy about reminding the court what the region had to offer in terms of material wealth. His reports to the capital were sprinkled with references to the natural fecundity of lands on both sides of the Tianshan, and he hailed their capacity for producing rich harvests as measured by fabulous harvest-to-seed ratios.[18] He touted the existence of populous and wealthy cities in the oases, the surprisingly low cost of food and clothing in local markets, and the extraordinary variety of merchandise they offered, including "medicinal materials, pelts, Turpan cotton, Khotan jade, and gold, copper, lead, and iron from Kucha."[19] Yet, from his perspective, there was much more to be done to develop the territory. In January 1878, he promised Beijing that "Xinjiang's sources of profit can be opened up."[20] In making this claim, Zuo was playing upon the phrase "opening up springs and restricting the outflow" (kaiyuan jieliu). In political discourse, this phrase referred to the idea of striking a healthy balance between incoming revenues and outgoing expenditures when it came to managing government finances.[21] Participants in the debate over military priorities several years earlier had invoked this phrase repeatedly to highlight the urgency of creating new sources of revenue for the imperial treasury. While the Qing state had a number of options for raising revenues, many regarded the expansion of natural resource production as the most expedient one. Li Hanzhang, the governor-general of Hunan and Hubei, had gone so far as to argue that, "at present, the only way to increase funding is to prioritize the profits that come from nature."[22] He and others called for the expansion of tea and silk production, the exploitation of organic and nonorganic minerals, and the use of steam-powered machinery in farming, weaving, and mining enterprises.[23] Such ideas resonated with Zuo Zongtang and other officials in the northwest. In the aftermath of Xinjiang's reconquest, they initiated reconstruction and development projects to increase the amount of arable land under cultivation, bring that land onto the tax rolls, and improve farm productivity, all in the hopes of making the territory yield more revenues for the state.[24]

While officials spoke metaphorically about "opening up springs" to create new streams of government income, they also worked literally to tap into Xinjiang's water sources. Of all the environmental conditions that shaped colonial development in the region in the late nineteenth century, none was more critical than its aridity. In this regard, the situation was little different from earlier periods, when harnessing water for irrigation was a perennial concern among officials at every level of the administrative hierarchy.[25] By the 1870s, the newest cohort of Qing leaders in Xinjiang had learned this lesson well, having read gazetteers, histories, and other works of geographical scholarship or having spoken with former exiles to the frontier, as Zuo had done with Lin Zexu years earlier. In 1878, Zuo reminded one of his top military commanders, Liu Jintang, that the paucity of rainfall in the territory stretching from western Gansu out past the Tianshan range meant that farmers had no choice but to rely on alpine snowmelt and groundwater to irrigate their crops of grains, vegetables, fruits, and cotton. Such conditions made it incumbent upon Liu and other deputies to manage sources of water with great diligence. "Those who control the northwest should prioritize water resources," Zuo advised, "and those who develop water resources should start with irrigation canals."[26] It is unlikely that Liu needed much convincing, as he had acquired ample direct knowledge of the region's arid landscapes during the military campaigns. In any case, Liu acted in accordance with Zuo's advice in the years following the reconquest, devoting considerable amounts of money and manpower to the repair and expansion of embankments, canals, and other physical structures that facilitated the exploitation of Xinjiang's water resources.

The expansion of hydraulic infrastructure following the reconquest of Xinjiang is significant not just because it was a core concern of those who oversaw reconstruction and development, but also because it reveals how attempts to control water gave rise to multiple entanglements between people and environments. States have always been engaged with natural environments in an incessant, dynamic exchange in which the concentration and dispersion of political power, changes in technology, the fluctuations and cycles of the earth, and other factors shaped the lives of states, environments, and their inhabitants.[27] But entanglements also materialize on a more basic level. They are embodied in the very structures that people have built to constrain, channel, siphon, or accumulate water, such as embankments, dikes, spillways, and conduits. In the Qing empire, these forms of infrastructure, which were created and maintained by both state and nonstate actors, were simultaneously natural and human systems and were always prone to change.[28] There were many things about these hybrid systems that people could never completely control, including the characteristics of the soil contained within them. Yet such things shaped the history of water control in Xinjiang just as much as human activity, limiting where people could build certain types of waterways and influencing how the state and local society became enmeshed in the politics of water management.

State-sponsored efforts to take advantage of Xinjiang's lands and waters began soon after Qing leaders launched their war of reconquest. Officials were initially motivated by the need to supply their armies with food in a cost-effective manner as troops advanced further into the territory. Unless officials found a way to procure grain locally, they had no choice but to expend enormous amounts of money transporting provisions across treacherously dry terrain from Gansu or Inner Mongolia.[29] But securing local sources of grain was not easy. When commander Zhang Yao entered the Hami oasis from the east with thousands of troops in late 1874, he found it was inhabited by just one or two thousand residents, a mere one-tenth of its original population.[30] Much farmland sat abandoned and little food was for sale. To solve this problem, Zhang led his soldiers to plow soil and cultivate it themselves. They purchased tools, seeds, and any available plow animals and set to work, farming the land and restoring old water channels or building new ones to irrigate their crops.[31] In 1875, they managed to open up some twenty thousand *mu* of land. But it turned out that the garrison farms yielded only enough grain to feed the troops for two months that year.[32] After hearing the disappointing news, Zuo Zongtang ordered Zhang to use financial incentives to raise productivity, reasoning that soldiers would invest more time and energy in agriculture if they were paid top prices for their harvests.[33] Similar incentives were extended to civilian farmers. In 1875, the Qing commander in Gucheng, a town on the north side of the Tianshan, offered to purchase grain from rural households at more than double the price of the previous year. For officials, grain acquired in this fashion was a bargain. Even at inflated prices, it was between four and seven times cheaper than grain imported from the east.[34]

Leaders also promoted agrarian development by providing material assistance directly to civilian farmers. As armies moved across northern Xinjiang, Gucheng was chosen as the location for a new head bureau of land

Figure 5.2 A view of Gucheng, Xinjiang. Photograph by Adolf-Nikolai Erazmovich Boiarskii, 1875. Courtesy of the National Library of Brazil.

reclamation (*tunken zongju*), one of the leading regional institutions for agriculture in the late 1870s. The bureau provided a range of services to civilian settlers and was responsible for distributing seeds, tools, plow animals, and parcels of land to them.[35] In the late summer of 1876, after Qing forces recaptured Urumchi and its hinterlands, the state launched similar programs there. Turmoil and warfare had decimated the formerly thriving commercial hub, reducing the population to perhaps sixty thousand people and leaving housing in ruins and tools destroyed.[36] To reverse Urumchi's demographic and economic decline, officials promised land and capital to returning refugees and new settlers. In the first several years, they spent more than one hundred thousand taels of silver on oxen and seeds for farmers in Urumchi and Gucheng.[37] They also revived local iron production and set up a small factory to manufacture plows and spades, aiming to fulfill the needs of the region's development by smelting iron implements locally.[38] These efforts, though constrained by certain obstacles, seemed to pay off: the regional price of grain plummeted across northern Xinjiang as towns experienced a jump in registered farming households.[39] By early

1878, because sufficient quantities of grain could be procured locally, long-distance grain transports were suspended and transport stations were shuttered, saving the imperial treasury a great deal of money.[40]

Meanwhile, as the war of reconquest expanded across southern Xinjiang, Qing leaders set up additional government institutions to foster agrarian development.[41] By 1878, there were over a dozen reconstruction bureaus scattered throughout the territory.[42] Although an assortment of other state institutions—military supply bureaus, fuel and fodder bureaus, taxation bureaus, neighborhood security bureaus, schools, sericulture bureaus, and smallpox vaccination bureaus—were also established, the reconstruction bureaus occupied a central place in the new institutional landscape. Staffed by a bureau chief, clerks, security guards, and translators proficient in Chinese and the local Turkic language, the reconstruction bureaus quickly assumed a multitude of administrative and juridical functions, coordinating the Qing state's approach to postwar governance and development policy.[43] They facilitated official communications between cities, presided over legal disputes, carried out educational programs, oversaw the collection of the land tax, and provided logistical and financial support for projects in agriculture and water control. For these reasons, reconstruction bureaus were among the most important institutions of imperial rule in Xinjiang between 1877 and 1884, when they were rebranded and incorporated into local government offices.[44]

Reconstruction activities got underway soon after the war's conclusion. For bureau officials, one of the first orders of business was carrying out comprehensive surveys of rural land and landownership to produce reliable data about farmlands, vineyards, and orchards so that they could accurately calculate the land tax. Such surveys had not been conducted in some oases since the late 1820s, meaning that a significant portion of arable land that had been reclaimed in the previous decades remained invisible to the state.[45] The turmoil of the preceding years, which in many places led to the almost wholesale destruction of population and land registers and the widespread displacement of locals inhabitants, made it all but impossible to gather the relevant information in other ways. So officials dispatched functionaries into the countryside to measure and evaluate properties and record the names and ethnicities of their owners.[46] Zuo Zongtang, who remained in Gansu and oversaw Xinjiang's reconstruction from afar, expected the new data to include details about land quality so that the territory's tax system could be regularized and brought into line with common

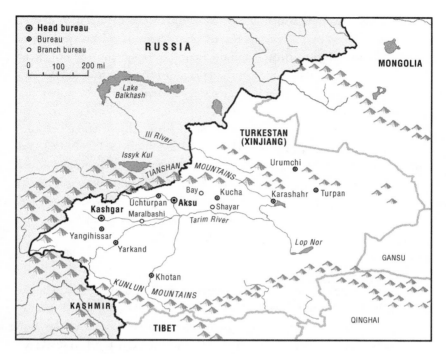

Map 5.2 Reconstruction bureaus in Xinjiang, ca. 1882. Map by Erin Greb.

practices in the Chinese provinces, where land size and soil quality, rather than harvest volume or family size, constituted the basis for the government's assessment.[47] Perhaps because some surveyors were unfamiliar with local geography and environmental conditions, the process dragged on for several years, and officials eventually decided to simplify the numerical scale used for grading land quality to expedite the process.[48] But once surveyors finally completed their work, reconstruction bureau staff utilized the data to compile new property registers, issue new deeds to property owners, and reimpose the land tax.[49]

Land surveys were indispensable to state extraction, allowing officials to take a portion of the harvest in a systematic fashion. But they were much more than simply vehicles for the collection of tax data. Surveys enabled Qing officials to intensify their supervision of Xinjiang's myriad resources, including its waterways. When they traveled through the countryside accompanied by translators, agents of the state had the opportunity to observe the lay of the land, discover where waters flowed and pooled, and talk with people about local practices and environmental conditions. Bureau officials could assess the availability of water and monitor waterways in their jurisdictions, keeping tabs on the locations and volumes of streams, rivers, canals, and lakes as they shifted and fluctuated over the course of the year. They relied upon local headmen in the villages to conduct walking surveys, look for broken-down waterways or clogged canals, estimate how much land they might irrigate, and report their findings to the local government office.[50] Based on information gathered during their inspection tours, they drew maps of rivers and canals, calculated the amount of labor needed to carry out repairs on older canals and embankments, and determined which materials should be used to build new ones.[51] Officials not employed by the reconstruction bureaus also participated in surveying water resources in Xinjiang's oases. In 1880, Chen Baoshan, a former official from Zheji-ang appointed to act as an inspector general of the reconstruction process, gathered information about waterways in Turpan to assess how much land they irrigated and how many repairs they required.[52]

In certain cases, major hydraulic problems became apparent even before officials had a chance to conduct surveys. In October 1877, just months before Qing armies completed their march through the southern oases, they were halted near the city of Karashahr by water from the Kaidu River. Normally, the river flowed southeast out of the Tianshan Mountains, past the city and its nearby farmlands, and into Lake Bosten. But when troops entered the area, they found it completely submerged.[53] Reports later sug-gested that forces allied with one of the leaders of the anti-imperial insur-gency had sabotaged the area's riparian embankments, unleashing a torrent of water in an attempt to thwart the advance of Qing troops.[54] Whatever its cause, the flooding was disastrous. Floodwaters covered an enormous area estimated to be over 100 *li* wide and reached as high as several meters above the ground. The disaster also inundated Karashahr, swamping the city in several feet of water and destroying its houses, office buildings, and other structures. Military scouts had no choice but to ride an extra 120 *li* to locate a suitable detour so that the army could circumvent the flooding. Officials were later dispatched to the city to establish a reconstruction bureau, drain the floodwaters, repair the embankments, and provide aid to flood victims and war refugees.[55]

Once the war was over, field surveys revealed that years of neglect had undermined the structural integrity of much of Xinjiang's hydraulic infra-structure, weakening levees designed to keep waters within their established courses. In the Tarim Basin, the area around Maralbashi was particularly devastated by the untamed flow of water. Local farmers had long benefited from the area's natural aquatic abundance, a result of its low-lying topography and its location at the confluence of rivers flowing northward out of the Kashgar and Yarkand oases. But political turmoil since the 1860s had prevented people from dredging the Kashgar River or repairing its dikes. As silt and logjams accumulated in the riverbed, the river widened and overran its banks in numerous places, unleashing great volumes of water into the surrounding countryside and turning the area into a massive flood zone. Inspectors identified four major breaches and ten sandbars along the river in the vicinity of Maralbashi. But the floodwaters were not contained to that area alone. They extended beyond the town for hundreds of *li* up the Kashgar River, ruining houses and rest stations, covering farmland, and impeding travel in certain places.[56]

Officials responded to such instances of flooding and infrastructure damage by organizing labor parties to rehabilitate the rivers and canals whose waters were essential to the success of agriculture in the oases. They mobilized teams of Qing troops to dredge sandbanks and remove other obstructions, fill breaches in the dikes, and reinforce embankments by making them thicker and taller. Soldiers restored the Kashgar River near Maralbashi in this fashion, forcing the water back into its main course and making it useful for irrigation once again. At other places, they fixed ruptures in the riverbanks and built new canals branching off from the river's primary channel to reduce its velocity and siphon water to irrigate nearby farmland.[57] Almost all of Xinjiang's major oases experienced some type of hydraulic construction in this period as workers renovated river embankments and refurbished state- and community-owned canals on both sides of the Tianshan.[58] In some districts, special officials were appointed to oversee matters relating to water control and irrigation.[59]

Over time, the work on infrastructure transitioned from repair to maintenance and development, a process that continued for years after the war.[60] Qing troops remained a major source of labor for water projects. A report from 1891 indicates that they fashioned jetties out of huge timbers, mud, and stones to shore up some forty *li* of embankments along the Aksu River, and they built dikes and well over a hundred canals along the northern and southern banks of the Kashgar River in a phase of hydraulic development that consumed in excess of 1.9 million man-days of labor.[61]

Although Qing officials coordinated work on river dikes and canals across Xinjiang, they held no monopoly on water in the territory. They oversaw hydraulic projects of a particularly urgent, large, or costly nature, such as those carried out to mitigate flooding near Maralbashi. But at the local level, property owners and tenant farmers regularly committed their own money and labor to maintain small-scale but often intricate infrastructure for irrigation. Russian colonel Nikolai Przhevalskii witnessed an impressive attentiveness to water among the Turkestani inhabitants of Niya and Keriya when he passed through the southern Tarim Basin in 1885. Farmers in these two oases had created elaborate canal networks that "ramify like the veins and arteries in the animal organism, and fertilise every plot of arable land." Fed by water diverted from nearby rivers, "these water channels cross and recross one another in the oasis, now flowing side by side, only at different levels, now coursing through wooden troughs placed one over the other, and again pouring over the flat roofs of the hovels in the same troughs." No patch of ground was left untouched by the meticulous management of water: "Every hovel, every garden and enclosure, nay, every big tree if it stand alone, has its separate water supply turned on or off as occasion requires."[62] The entire hydraulic system of the village was overseen by a designated supervisor and was governed by rules about how and when water would be allocated to members of the community.[63]

The Qing state usually did not intervene in such arrangements on a day-to-day basis, leaving the matter of local water usage in the village up to its inhabitants and the local headmen who governed them. Likely for this reason, Chinese agents of the imperial state in Xinjiang rarely wrote about community water systems, even though they were vital to the prosperity of oasis agriculture. Yet the imperative to maintain river dikes, canals, and the larger components of the territory's hydraulic infrastructure compelled officials to turn to Turkestani communities to furnish labor for some projects. In most regions, this required officials to work through local elites to recruit and manage Turkestani workers. Since the eighteenth century, Beijing had granted official recognition, land, and tax exemptions to a class of local elites, the begs, in return for their collaboration in ruling the Tarim Basin oases.[64] Begs held considerable responsibility for governing various affairs at the village level, including the allocation of water rights.[65] Starting with the outbreak of unrest in the 1860s, however, the power of the begs declined and some lost their lands in several cycles of expropriation.[66] In principle, by the late 1870s begs no longer wielded authority over civilian households, and Zuo Zongtang expressly forbade them from exploiting other Turkestanis, something for which they had gained a notorious reputation.[67] Yet, in practice, while their status was downgraded to some-thing akin to local gentry in the Chinese provinces, some of them contin-ued to play a significant role in Xinjiang's public life, serving as interme-diaries between the group of mostly Chinese bureaucrats who now ruled the oases and the large population of primarily Turkestanis who inhabited them.[68] Thus, when reconstruction bureau officials needed civilians to help with hydraulic repairs and upkeep, they notified these headmen, who in turn recruited skilled and unskilled workers from their communities on an ad hoc basis to join the work crews. Sources indicate that these civilian Turkic Muslim workers, compensated by the state with wages or rations, contributed at least half of the labor on certain hydraulic projects, and some-times much more.[69] It would have been impossible for the Qing state to accomplish so much without their labor.

In other situations, Turkestanis sought help from imperial officials to resolve quarrels over water. In November 1880, for example, four longtime residents of Shahezi, a village in the Turpan oasis, brought a legal com-plaint to the attention of Qing authorities involving hydraulic infrastruc-ture in their village. The men—Yu-su-pu, He-si-man, Mao-sha-er, and Ai-ling-ba-hai—testified that they had spent over twenty taels of their own money to construct a weir across a creek to collect irrigation water for their farmland. But then two miscreants, A-bu-du-re-yi-mu and Ga-si-er, had come along and sabotaged the weir, destroying their investment and let-ting the water run loose across nearby yards and fields. The four plaintiffs therefore requested that the local government force the two suspects to repair the weir. The outcome of the case remains unclear, but it is instruc-tive nonetheless for what it reveals about hydraulic development in post-war Xinjiang. It shows that, while Qing officials tried to manage large-scale infrastructure across the territory, nonstate actors of relatively modest means built infrastructure on a much smaller scale to increase their capac-ity to exploit local waterways for agriculture. The case also indicates that Turkestanis sometimes were quite willing to entangle themselves in the machinery of the Qing legal system to safeguard their investments in tech-nology that allowed them to control a most precious resource.[70]

In the Turpan oasis, state and private efforts to build infrastructure for irri-gation focused on a particular type of subterranean conduit, the karez.[71] Like wells, karez allow people to exploit groundwater resources, but their primary shafts run underground, not vertically to the surface, and their design and construction reflect the particular topographic and environmental conditions in the Turpan Depression. They use the force of gravity, exploiting the natural downward slope of terrain surrounding the oasis on its northern side, to convey water to the earth's surface. A karez is comprised of a main tunnel, which runs laterally for several miles underground, and numerous vertical boreholes linking the tunnel to the surface, which allow for ventilation and maintenance access. The tunnel is constructed so that its gradient is more gradual than the incline of the earth's surface and the water table below it. As the top end of the tunnel sits below the level of the water table, the karez naturally accumulates water, channels it downward through the tunnel, and pours the water into a canal or catchment basin at the point where the tunnel reaches the surface. Although karez lose some water to seepage, they have been valued by Turpan's farmers for their ability to provide a constant supply of water in an area of extreme aridity.[72]

Historians have debated when and how karez first came into use in Turpan, but there is compelling evidence that it was not until the nineteenth century, during a period of robust agrarian development, that the technology greatly proliferated in the oasis.[73] More than anything else, it was the surging market for raw cotton that underwrote the expansion of karez across the oasis, enticing wealthy landlords and merchants to hire workmen to do the arduous and sometimes deadly work of excavating the tunnels.[74] In 1845, during his inspection tour of farmland and waterways in Xinjiang, Lin Zexu had been shocked to discover "earthen pits" conveying water underground in an "unimaginable" fashion to irrigate fields that produced immense quantities of cotton in Yargul, on the western side of the Turpan oasis.[75] By the early 1850s, farmers in the oasis were selling an estimated two to three million catties of cotton per year to merchants from the Chinese provinces, Mongolia, and western Turkestan.[76] As market forces motivated people to increase the amount of land devoted to cotton production, they searched for new sources of water to reclaim land from the deserts. Building karez was an expedient option, but not everyone could afford them. The price of constructing a single karez, estimated to be about one thousand strings of copper cash in the mid-1880s, was well beyond the means of most rural households. Yet cotton farming was not just a household enterprise. Wealthy investors also got involved, pouring capital into farmland and hiring skilled and unskilled workers to excavate karez, which could each irrigate an estimated two hundred to three hundred *mu* of soil.[77]

The prospects for turning a profit on cotton farming in Turpan were large enough that they attracted many Chinese investors, who flocked to the oasis to set up shops and lease land and karez from Turkestani owners or purchase their own land and build their own karez.[78] For example, one man migrated from his native Shanxi province to Turpan in the 1850s, concluded an agreement with a local property-owner, Zi-ya-bu-dong, to rent one karez for forty years at the price of two thousand silver taels, and then hired another man, A-bu-se-min, to manage the entire farming operation.[79] While sources do not reveal how many Chinese investors built their own karez in Turpan, the influx of capital from the provinces surely contributed to the surge in karez construction in the decades prior to the 1864 uprising.[80]

But years of upheaval and warfare had resulted in the deterioration of the karez and the commercial economy that had bankrolled their development. After Qing forces invaded Turpan in the spring of 1877, officials surveyed the oasis and found much of its population gone and dozens of karez dried up.[81] The preceding period of turmoil no doubt had traumatized many people in the oasis, regardless of their ethnicity. The anti-imperial revolt was particularly deadly for Han Chinese in Turpan.[82] Amid the political chaos, some Turkestanis felt empowered to enact retribution against their Chinese creditors, repossessing karez, vineyards, farmlands, and other productive assets they had rented out to them or expropriating properties that had belonged to Chinese investors and farming households.[83] What hurt Turpan's cotton economy and its subterranean water infrastructure the most, however, was probably the decline in the commodity trade between Turpan and the Chinese provinces during the years when long-distance travel across the entire northwest became much more dangerous and difficult. Certainly, not all oases in Xinjiang suffered the same demise. Kashgar's agricultural economy seems to have profited in the aftermath of the uprising insofar as more opportunities opened up to sell raw cotton to buyers from Russian Turkestan.[84] But at least in Turpan, cotton production dwindled and farmers neglected the karez and other waterways, allowing them to crumble and run dry.

In response to the crisis of hydraulic infrastructure, officials mobilized soldiers and civilians to repair old karez and build new ones. They allocated government funding for karez on public and private lands, knowing that water was the key to reviving agriculture across the oasis. In 1878, after having dispatched military personnel to conduct a survey of karez to determine their location and condition, Zuo Zongtang ordered local officials to prioritize the repair of karez that were easy to fix while postponing work on more challenging projects. He did this reportedly to ease the burden of labor on Qing troops, who often had to do construction work in cases where residents lacked the money or manpower to carry out the work themselves.[85] By 1880, soldiers and civilians had managed to repair and construct karez in 185 locations.[86] The process of rebuilding continued in the following years. In the summer of 1884, headmen in Turpan were asked to carry out surveys of karez in their local areas to assess how many karez there were, how much land they could irrigate, and how much money and labor would be required to renovate them. In this way, authorities identified nearly a dozen karez in need of repair, with the work on each costing between fifty and two hundred taels of silver.[87]

The reconstruction bureau in Turpan employed additional measures to expedite hydraulic development in the area. For one thing, it offered loans to civilians who wanted to refurbish their karez.[88] Chinese officials assumed that most Turkestanis were too poor to fix up the waterways without government assistance.[89] Although some wealthy Turkic Muslims did have enough capital on their own to repair karez that had deteriorated or dried up without state aid, in practice the Qing state provided loans to both Turkic and Chinese property owners.[90] In the summer of 1880, a group of four Han merchants who operated three karez irrigating over eight hundred *mu* of farmland notified the authorities that their karez were blocked up. Since they claimed to have no capital to pay for the repairs, they applied for in-kind loans of sorghum and wheat so that they could hire laborers to do the work. Officials decided to offer them 40 percent of the total amount of grain they requested, which came to twenty-eight *dan*, and mandated that the merchants repay the same amount after the autumn harvest.[91] Several years later, the reconstruction bureau received a flurry of requests for loans after a spell of unusual weather involving high winds and heavy rains damaged numerous karez in the area. In one case, a man named A-sheng-mu successfully appealed to officials for millet to finance the dredging of his karez.[92] Landowners also approached local government offices for money to repair their hydraulic assets. One Chinese merchant requested a loan of five hundred taels to hire workmen and buy lumber, seeking capital to refurbish an abandoned karez on land adjacent to his own in the hopes of restarting the flow of water to bring several hundred *mu* of soil into productive use.[93] In other cases, well-heeled individuals who owned several karez and village leaders who sought loans on behalf of poor country folk were able to obtain assistance from the local government for karez restoration.[94]

As the work on karez construction proceeded, Qing officials began to hatch plans for spreading the technology to other parts of Xinjiang to serve the cause of agrarian development beyond the immediate vicinity of Turpan. For example, in the village of Chiktam, located to the east of Turpan, soldiers spent more than forty days in 1886 digging tunnels and shafts, earning themselves special dispensations of meat and alcohol. When the new karez were completed, the lands that they irrigated were offered to three Turkestanis of some financial means who paid for their own seeds, tools, and plow animals and then cultivated millet on a trial basis to assay the quality and productivity of the soil.[95]

But the technology of the karez was not as geographically portable as officials hoped it would be, a lesson they learned through trial and error. Five years earlier, in 1881, Liu Jintang had concocted a plan to build karez in the Hami oasis to speed up the pace of land reclamation in a place still struggling to regain its economic footing after the war. Liu seems to have simply assumed that Hami could replicate the success of Turpan in utilizing karez for farmland development. Part of his rationale revolved around the topographic similarities between the two oases. Because both sat at the base of the mountains, he reasoned, karez would function the same in both locations. Liu also had confidence in his plan because he believed in the ingenuity and adroitness of the craftsmen who built karez for a living. He described these engineers as being able to "know the locations of mountain springs through estimation," and he resolved to send a group of them to Hami to teach its local inhabitants the arts of subterranean hydraulics. Within less than a week of Liu first conceiving of the idea, eighteen craftsmen and two foremen—all Turkestanis recruited by local headmen in the Turpan oasis—were on their way to Hami, where they were expected to stay for about a month.[96] For all of the ambition and money invested in their mission, however, their work yielded few successes. Liu later blamed this unsatisfactory outcome on the fact that "there are some things that people do not have the power to overcome."[97] What exactly had gone wrong?

When people traveled across Xinjiang in the nineteenth century, there was much for them to see, from its bustling urban bazaars to its boundless deserts. No matter their origin, one thing they could not help but notice as they trekked between the territory's cities and its vast open spaces was the natural condition of the earth beneath their feet. Members of the 1873 British expedition discovered soils in Kashgar to be "mostly sandy and charged with salts" and learned that the earth in Turpan was "similar to that of Kashghar, but more gravelly."[98] Three years later, when Nikolai Przhevalskii was on a journey to explore the waters of Lop Nor in the eastern Tarim Basin, he plodded across "an undulating plain covered with a pebbly or gravelly soil" and later happened upon places where the "loose, saline, clayey soil pulverized instantly."[99] Qing officials tended to use pithier language, but their descriptions of soils in the territory were more or less the same. Gong-tang, a Manchu who was installed as a military official in Urumchi after the war of reconquest, characterized Xinjiang's land simply as "sandy and alkaline."[100] Having resided in the borderland for nearly five years, Liu Jintang was able to compose his own concise description in 1881. "On the Muslim frontier," he wrote, "land is either sandy or alkaline. It is naturally light and prone to drifting, gathering and dispersing with much frequency."[101]

Aside from water itself, nothing was more important to hydraulic infrastructure in the nineteenth century than soil. Embodied in such infrastructure was the human desire to dictate how and where water flows. That goal was unattainable without the scrupulous manipulation of dirt by moving, excavating, dredging, piling, compacting, or reinforcing it. Yet the very nature of the earth in Xinjiang meant that such manipulation was hard to sustain in the face of flowing waters. Recent research has shown that the arid soils and desert sands that cover much of the territory in its lower altitudes exhibit several characteristics in their interactions with water, chief among them their susceptibility to erosion.[102] This characteristic was not lost on nineteenth-century observers. British officer Henry Trotter witnessed how easily water reshaped land in the countryside south of Kashgar. Surveying the area's irrigation canals, he concluded that they were changing constantly as water passed through them. "I have often seen one canal . . . eating its way rapidly through the soft soil into another one," he reported. Elsewhere, he determined that "the saline nature of the soil causes breaks down [sic] and consequent leakage," diminishing the structural integrity of the canals within the span of a single year.[103] Trotter also noticed another problem with the soil: its permeability, which allowed water to seep underground and escape human designs. On outings into barren foothills on the edges of the Tarim Basin, he discovered "thirsty gravelly soil" that "swallowed up" rivers and absorbed water "that would otherwise profitably be employed in irrigation."[104]

The characteristics of the earth in eastern Turkestan may have been little more than a curiosity for Russian and British explorers. But for inhabitants of the region and the officials who governed them, soil proved to be a considerable challenge. The twin problems of erosion and permeability loomed over hydraulic engineering in the territory, shaping how people tried to exploit water and limiting what they could do to control it. After trials with karez in Hami ended in failure, Liu Jintang determined that the characteristics of the soil were the primary cause. The Turpan oasis, he wrote, possessed soils that were "firm and compact," meaning that water could "accumulate and flow through the solid banks" of the underground tunnels "without causing worry about erosion or sedimentation."[105] Such soils clearly met the engineering requirements of the karez. But when he dispatched craftsmen to replicate the technology in Hami, he found out that edaphic conditions there were different from those in Turpan, a discovery that served to repudiate his claim that the oases were both suited for karez by virtue of their similar topographies. Before the trials, Liu had attributed the failure of earlier attempts to dig water channels in Hami to people's lack of skill in the arts of excavation.[106] However, it turned out that even skilled artisans from Turpan could not overcome environmental obstacles to the construction of karez elsewhere. Some of the new karez tunnels yielded no water while others caved in as soon as they were constructed. In the end, Liu wrote off the failure as a result of the "limitations of the terrain."[107]

To be sure, officials and craftsmen were not entirely helpless in the face of such limitations. In certain cases, they adopted technology to cope with soil characteristics that plagued the efficiency of hydraulic infrastructure at the surface. Even before Liu Jintang orchestrated trials with karez, Qing officials knew that Hami's soils were prone to seepage, and they tried to employ technical measures to mitigate the problem. In 1875, as Qing troops dug canals to accompany the expansion of farmland in the oasis, they made use of a particular construction material in combination with soil and stones to prevent unnecessary losses of water. Imitating an existing local practice, they lined the canals with strips of felt, using the manufactured animal-hair textiles as an inner lining in an attempt to limit the amount of water that seeped through the sides and bottoms of the waterways and into groundwater.[108] Felt liners were not a complicated technology, but getting them to Hami was anything but simple. To obtain the material, Zuo Zongtang sent special orders to functionaries in three locations in Gansu reputed for their production of animal-hair textiles, mandating that they manufacture ten thousand strips of felt and forward them to Hami via the chain of supply bureaus that existed during the war.[109] After 1875, hydraulic engineers in other parts of Xinjiang continued the practice of building canals with felt, and they paired the textile with other materials like timbers and tree branches to conserve as much water as possible for agriculture.[110] Some later abandoned the use of felt, having learned that it was not a good material for projects involving water. At one canal near Urumchi, people switched to using wooden troughs to convey water after discovering that felt fibers deteriorated rather quickly when submerged.[111]

The greatest difficulties with soil and water occurred along Xinjiang's largest rivers. Like other waterways, these rivers constituted important parts of the territory's hydraulic infrastructure, entangling human intention and nonhuman nature in their very material forms, even if they underwent only a modest degree of human manipulation. They also had a stronger tendency to run wild, driven by fluctuations that people could not control. The major rivers of the Tarim Basin were influenced especially by large seasonal variations in water volume and velocity. Because the rivers are fed primarily by snowmelt and glacial meltwater from the Tianshan and Kunlun mountains, they usually swell during the hotter months and dwindle during the cooler months, with some rivers discharging as much as 80 percent of their total annual flow in the warmest six months of the year.[112] In the past, these annual summertime surges brought an abundance of water down into the lowlands, where it nourished fields of wheat, cotton, and other crops on lands reclaimed from the desert, making the Tarim oases rich producers of agricultural goods. These surges, characterized by large volumes of fast-moving water, also inflicted major wear and tear on embankments built of soil, stones, and wood. But given the state's commitment to agricultural development—and the fact that these rivers were often the main sources of water for irrigation canals in southern Xinjiang's oasis settlements—leaders had little choice but to try to maintain the embankments despite the money and human energy they consumed.

The history of the Yarkand River and its branch canals in the 1880s illustrates how the combination of soils prone to erosion and seasonal fluctuations in water volume led to failures of infrastructure and mired the Qing state in a reiterative struggle to keep irrigation waters flowing. In 1881, military commanders and soldiers were directed to build embankments along more than 240 *li* of the river and construct sluiceways in strategic places to channel water to nearby fields. In addition, they reconfigured a winding section of the riverbed to enervate the force of the flowing water, reducing its capacity to inflict damage. Yet, because the "nature of the soil was loose and unstable," as Liu Jintang reported, the new construction crumbled in multiple locations within the span of a year. The river breached its dikes again in 1885, prompting another round of infrastructure building. This time, workers carefully dredged a newly created channel and repaired holes in the dikes with stone and timber reinforcements. Not long after the project reached completion, the river again burst through its banks, sending dozens of streams of water flowing into the desert and cutting off irrigation to a different area of cropland. This triggered yet another round of repairs to the river's dikes to stanch the flow of wasted water and redirect it toward farmland.[113]

While this situation induced officials to engage in what may have seemed like Sisyphean efforts to manage the unpredictable interactions of water and soil, it also drew the state into a deeper entanglement with the inhabitants of the Tarim Basin oases. The most important resource that officials deployed to repair hydraulic infrastructure was labor, and the volatile nature of the Yarkand River demanded more maintenance work than Qing troops alone could complete. Indeed, the "nature of the water" combined with the contours of the riverbed meant that "labor and expenditures are endless."[114] While the government paid for repairs to the river's dikes, nearby cities were required to furnish the corvée laborers necessary to complete the work. In 1885, after the river burst through its banks, officials gathered men from Yarkand, Khotan, Kashgar, and Yangihissar and dispatched them to fix the levees. The existing documentary record says sparingly little about such workers, but it is reasonable to assume that most of them were Turkic Muslims recruited within their communities by local headmen. The record does indicate, however, that they became unhappy with their labor obligations, as environmental conditions and the power of the state conspired to keep them locked in a pattern of work from which they had no simple escape. In light of the demands placed upon them, officials enacted a new policy in 1887 to distribute the burden of the corvée duty more evenly across the population. It mandated that village leaders select workmen based on the number of households in the village. In fact, the new policy only signified the deepening reliance of the Qing state on Turkestani workmen within the larger crisis of water control. According to the new system, workers were dispatched every year in the first month of spring to inspect the dikes and repair them section by section. While the workload may have been less onerous in an average year, the system brought agents of the state, workers, and the river into contact with greater frequency. Because the river demanded constant attention, the government continued to call upon Turkestani workmen year after year.[115] In this sense, the Qing state's domination of the territory and the exploitation of its natural resources was enacted through the everyday politics of controlling local people and their labor power.

Sometimes it was not the difficulty of controlling water but the inability to find any water at all that hindered development goals. In certain areas of Xinjiang, water scarcity placed limits on the extension of agriculture that were not so easily overcome. Karez dried up, new well shafts struck no water, and summer meltwaters failed to materialize, all of which made farming simply impossible at specific times and places.[116] Far from forcing leaders to rethink their approach to development, however, these complications only seemed to engender new efforts to locate sources of water and exploit them more fully. In 1879, Gong-tang twice performed rain-making ceremonies, seeking to trigger precipitation and show soldiers and civilians that he was discharging his official duties with sincerity.[117] When no rains fell, he opted for a familiar tactic: investing greater amounts of labor and money to dig deeper and farther, expanding wells and irrigation canals to tap into the region's hydraulic resources, however distant from homes or fields they happened to be.[118]

Yet it was the scarcity of labor, not the scarcity of water, that remained the chief worry among Qing leaders committed to Xinjiang's development. This issue had taken center stage in discussions of the territory's political future starting in 1877, when Beijing asked Zuo Zongtang to devise a comprehensive plan for governing the borderland. In response to this request and on four subsequent occasions from 1878 to 1882, Zuo recommended that the court establish a new province in Xinjiang, echoing the plan for provincial rule first articulated by Gong Zizhen over fifty years earlier.[119] Zuo's initial proposal was received by Beijing with some doubt about whether the region was sufficiently populous to generate enough tax revenue to fund the bevy of official positions required in a provincial administrative system.[120] Beyond the Qing court, opponents of the proposal shared similar concerns.[121] One of the most vocal critics, Li Yunlin, viewed the borderland as having too few Chinese farming households to sustain provincial rule.[122] Li's analysis demonstrates just how crucial ethnic distinction was to his understanding of the problem. He not only denied the possibility that Turkic Muslims or Mongols were suitable subjects for a provincial government; he also called for the rapid mobilization of Qing troops and their families, along with Han civilians from northwest Gansu, to settle on the northern side of the Tianshan, believing that the region's Mongol inhabitants were "unable to exhaust the profits of the land" on their own.[123] Others were less concerned by the ethnic composition of the population but expressed similar worries about the region's diminutive demographic size. Tan Zhonglin believed that Turkestanis could be incorporated into a Chinese system of rule, provided they were given more Chinese language training and education. After all, he wrote, the "turban-wearing Muslims are also people," using a common Chinese term of designation for Turkestanis. "Although a distinct ethnic group (*zulei*), they must all naturally have a love of land and home." Even so, Tan stressed that there simply were not enough people in Xinjiang to support a full provincial system, the villages and cities of the Tarim Basin being quite small by Chinese standards, so he suggested the creation of a pared-down system with fewer administrators to reduce costs.[124]

In 1884, after seven years of debate, the imperial court approved a new system of civil offices and administrative jurisdictions for Xinjiang, authorizing the creation of the empire's newest province.[125] Historians have recognized the pivotal nature of this decision, for it was one sign of the Qing empire's departure away from a pattern of imperial rule in which Manchu and Mongol officials held most of the highest offices in Xinjiang and Turkic leaders wielded considerable authority over local matters. Han officials from eastern and southern China now began to hold preeminent authority in most parts of the territory and assert greater influence over day-to-day affairs.[126] Yet the creation of the province did little to alter Xinjiang's demographics in the short term and thus did nothing to allay leaders' concerns about the problem of labor scarcity or its impact on development. Alluding to the situation, Liu Jintang wrote in 1886 that, "on the whole, Xinjiang suffers not from poverty but from paucity," a condition measured in people and households.[127] Statistics on land-holding in certain parts of the territory seemed to affirm his assessment. As of 1887, around three-quarters of all farmland in northern Xinjiang remained uncultivated, according to one estimate.[128] The persistence of large expanses of unclaimed and apparently unused land a full decade after the war of reconquest was one reason why Wei Guangtao, Xinjiang's first provincial treasurer, devised a set of regulations to facilitate colonization. The regulations identified three groups of potential settlers: recent migrants to the province, including Qing soldiers, camp followers, and merchants; Turkestani households, especially impoverished ones, from the Tarim Basin; and underemployed people from Gansu, Sichuan, Shaanxi, and other Chinese provinces. Aiming to stimulate interest in settlement in the region, provincial officials offered allotments of sixty *mu* of land and a package of start-up capital and materials valued at over seventy taels to every team of two settlers who arrived looking for a new beginning.[129]

It is difficult to determine how such regulations influenced patterns of colonization, but evidence suggests that the final decades of the Qing period witnessed significant farmland development in Xinjiang. The most heavily depopulated northern and eastern regions of the province attracted settlers in modest numbers.[130] The southern oases, by contrast, rebounded after the war and then grew steadily, mainly through natural increases in population, pushing the total number of people in the province to around 1.3 million by the late 1880s and above 2 million two decades later.[131] Meanwhile, the amount of farmland grew markedly, a result of a flurry of land reclamation activity and closer government scrutiny of the countryside, bringing Xinjiang's total arable land to between nine and twelve million *mu*.[132] It remains unclear what proportion of irrigated farmland in these decades was indeed newly reclaimed rather than simply being newly revealed to the state via land surveys. Yet regardless of their prior use or their actual productivity, Xinjiang's reported farmlands were hailed by Qing officials both as a sign of postwar recovery and development and as an essential resource to assist in funding their control of the region.

Growth did not come without environmental costs. By the late 1880s, some observers began to perceive the underside of state and private efforts to exploit Xinjiang's lands and waters. Russian naturalist Grigorii Grumm-Grzhimailo, who traveled through the Turpan Depression in 1889, interpreted changes in the landscape as signs that people were laying waste to the very resources that had allowed them to prosper in such an arid place. South of the city, at the lowest point in the depression, an area of marshland had been stripped of its reeds, "remorselessly cut down for fuel," and was now at greater risk of desertification. In his view, the remaining pockets of vegetation and the animals that lived in them were threatened by demographic growth and the endless exploitation of groundwater. Indeed, local residents were "ever burrowing beneath the surface to find water" and were utilizing the "land so thoroughly as not to leave a drop of moisture in it." In this "marvellous struggle between nature and man," the naturalist deduced that people were ultimately harming themselves by extracting so much water out of the ground, provoking nature to take revenge and creating the conditions for their own demise.[133] His analysis no doubt was articulated in the language of European science, echoing a tradition of deciphering the connections between human patterns of land use, the destruction of vegetation, and the desiccation of the environment.[134] At the same time, it was also a testament to the existence of ecological damage and the emerging specter of man-made water scarcity that Qing officials in Xinjiang, in their drive to achieve colonial development, were only just beginning to recognize.[135]

CHAPTER VI

Sericulture in a Colonial Borderland

T he reconquest of Xinjiang in 1877 was a major territorial victory for the Qing state, but not an unreserved one. At the end of the war, Russian troops remained in the Ili Valley. As representatives of the two empires discussed a resolution to the situation, Russian negotiators tried to bargain for the right to establish consulates in cities across Xinjiang.[1] Meanwhile, Russian explorers traipsed through the Zunghar and Tarim Basins conducting geographical and scientific surveys, and merchants from western Turkestan gradually returned to the oasis bazaars, buying and selling cotton, livestock, and other goods. Wary of Russian expansionism, Zuo Zongtang kept track of the official negotiations over the fate of Ili while monitoring Xinjiang's commercial landscape. In the spring of 1880, he expressed concern that the borderland's paltry production of silk made the empire more vulnerable to Russian designs. "Russians and various border peoples purchase silk in Xinjiang," he reported, but because the borderland could not supply enough material to satisfy their needs, they sought to travel deep inside Qing territory to acquire silk cloth from places like Sichuan. In his view, this situation constituted a security threat, although one that could be managed through economic development. If Xinjiang's oases were to improve and increase their output of raw and woven silk, Russian merchants would have no reason to expand their commercial networks across the northwest. He thus wrote to Beijing outlining his plans to develop sericulture in Xinjiang, arguing that if silk production flourished, "the other parties will obtain their profits, while we, for our part, can apply techniques for their control."[2] Paradoxically, then, Zuo aimed to increase the territorial power of the Qing state in Xinjiang by more deeply integrating the region into the international silk economy.

The governor-general had reason to be optimistic about the future of sericulture. In the second half of the nineteenth century, the external market for Chinese silk was growing prodigiously.[3] Indeed, in the fifty years after 1840, exports of raw silk increased 1000 percent, consuming between 30 and 40 percent of all domestic production.[4] The surge in foreign demand partially reflected the spread of pébrine, a parasitic disease of the silkworm, in countries of the Mediterranean region, forcing major producers like France and Britain to turn to East Asia to secure new sources of material for their own silk industries.[5] Although Jiangnan sustained extensive damage in the Taiping war, it quickly regained its place as the empire's most productive region for sericulture, supplying raw and processed fibers via Shanghai to the expanding world market, including new buyers on the Pacific coast of North America. The market was so strong that by the 1870s outspoken elites believed that selling Chinese silk to foreigners was one of the most expedient means to enrich and empower the country.[6]

Zuo Zongtang's rationale for a program of sericulture development was not just about territorial power or financial enrichment, however. It was also rooted in ideas about the deficiency and improvement of Xinjiang's human population. Zuo envisioned the project as a way to train the native inhabitants of the territory to more fully exploit the resources around them. From his perspective, aside from some Turkestanis in the Khotan oasis who had a certain degree of knowledge about the techniques for raising silkworms and reeling silk, people in Xinjiang were woefully ignorant of sericulture despite having access to the most essential means of production: mulberry trees and silkworms. The borderland was regarded as being particularly well stocked with mulberry trees. One tally of the mulberry population in the oases south of the Tianshan, carried out during the land surveys of the late 1870s, showed that the region possessed at least eight hundred thousand of the trees.[7] Zuo interpreted this information as an indication that the primary obstacle to the expansion of silk production in Xinjiang was not environmental but human. Believing that if the region "has mulberry trees then it must be suited to silkworms," he deemed the absence of sericulture in many of the oases not just a missed opportunity, but a misuse of resources.[8] Echoing a common rhetoric of colonizers worldwide, who often looked down upon their colonial subjects for their purported lack of technology and their waste of resources, Zuo decried the ignorance of the native inhabitants of Xinjiang's oasis communities, where mulberry trees grew in great abundance: "Heaven produces magnificent profits, and people simply abandon them. A pity indeed!"[9]

Starting in 1879, Qing leaders embarked upon a major program to improve sericulture in Xinjiang. They hired technical experts from eastern China to train Turkestanis in all aspects of silk production, from the cultivation of mulberry trees to the weaving of finished cloth. In many ways, the program was not unlike other postwar efforts to spread sericulture technology and knowledge to Chinese subjects in the provinces.[10] Yet Zuo's plan for Xinjiang was distinct insofar as he invoked territorial security as a justification for sericulture development. The distinctiveness was further underscored by the particular dynamics of colonial rule in Xinjiang, in which late nineteenth-century officials often regarded Turkestanis with a sense of suspicion and held them culpable for the violence and political turmoil of the preceding years. The imperial court betrayed a similar sensibility and seemed to support the idea of inculcating Turkic Muslims with Chinese knowledge to make them more productive and more easily governed subjects, at one point heralding the transformation of the "inveterate habits of the ignorant Muslims of Xinjiang."[11] The promotion of Chinese education had begun soon after 1877, as the provisional government in postwar Xinjiang established scores of schools to train Turkestani men in Chinese language and political philosophy with the goal of creating a cohort of people who could act as translators and facilitate imperial rule among the area's non–Chinese inhabitants.[12] But the use of instruction as a tool of colonial governance was not confined to the realm of language and bookish learning. As the sericulture development project demonstrates, the process of educating the native inhabitants of the oases extended into the realm of technology for natural resource exploitation.

The promotion of sericulture was a human endeavor carried out to achieve political aims. Yet people were by no means the only entities shaping the social and ecological dynamics of silk production in late nineteenth-century Xinjiang. To fully appreciate the political ecology of development, it is necessary to examine the roles of nonhuman entities and their physical forms in structuring relationships between people and places. Historians have assembled a rich collection of examples to illustrate how nonhuman organisms influenced patterns of colonialism and imperialism, often by facilitating or thwarting the extension of power by one society over another.[13] In taking stock of the influence of animals, plants, fungi, and viruses in social relations, it must be remembered that nonhuman organisms were not merely historical actors. Like people, they themselves were also products of history, embodying both the outcome of eons of evolution as well as the particular evolutionary and nonevolutionary changes that they underwent because of human activity.[14] The two organisms at the heart of sericulture coevolved long before humans began to domesticate them, with the silkworm developing the ability to digest chemicals in the leaves of the mulberry tree that most other insects cannot stomach.[15] Populations of these species continued to evolve after people in China first appropriated their labors for making silk, changing over many generations as people selected certain specimens for propagation because of the physical traits they possessed. In addition, mulberry trees were subjected to certain forms of physical manipulation to increase their productivity. Over time, these organisms came to embody the knowledge and practice of silk production, becoming "biological artifacts shaped by humans to serve human ends."[16] The physical forms of these organisms were not the same in all populations throughout the Qing empire, however. Their differences reflected their long-term adaptation to specific environments and the divergent histories of sericulture in the empire's various territories. As officials discovered, mulberry trees and silkworms in Xinjiang possessed traits that seemed to distinguish them from their counterparts in eastern China. Such distinctions not only inspired them to try to transform populations of these organisms in Xinjiang to support the goal of sericulture improvement. They also revealed tensions between Chinese administrators and the Turkestani inhabitants of the southern oases regarding a fundamental question of human survival: How can people best make use of the earth's plants and animals to sustain their lives and livelihoods?

Back in the middle of the eighteenth century, when Qing officials who governed Xinjiang thought about silk, their minds usually turned to shipments of woven fabric from China. Manufactured in the workshops of Jiangnan and sent to the borderland on an annual basis, Chinese silks constituted an essential item of exchange with Kazakh traders at the frontier, paying for the acquisition of livestock and other goods needed to sustain contingents of Qing troops garrisoned in the region.[17] Silks from the eastern provinces played a crucial role in financing imperial dominion, but they were not the only silks in Xinjiang. Some inhabitants of the southern oases also produced raw and processed silk, selling their wares to nearby customers for local use or to long-distance merchants for export to other parts of Central Asia. Residents of the Khotan oasis were particularly well known for their sericulture. The silk carpets, silk fabrics, silk-cotton weaves, and silkworm cocoons they produced garnered recognition from travelers and sojourners in Xinjiang throughout the first century of Qing rule.[18]

In the nineteenth century, the silk industry in Khotan and other southern cities fluctuated with the times. The industry seems to have enjoyed the benefits of an expanding external market for silk, especially after the start of the Taiping war, which cut off shipments of silk fabrics from the east. Turkestani producers took advantage of the constricted supply of Chinese silks and the growing demand for silk among buyers from Russian Turkestan and British India, increasing exports of cocoons and thread to both regions. With the demise of Qing power in Turkestan in 1864, Khotanese sericulture experienced a period of turbulence. The oasis suffered from depopulation, consumer appetites for some luxury items dwindled, and political turmoil stifled exports for several years.[19] But the native industry received encouragement from the independent regime of Yaqub Beg, which ruled parts of the territory from 1865 to 1877, and it rebounded, becoming once again a valuable source of income for oasis residents who raised silkworms, reeled silk, and wove various types of textiles for regional consumption.[20] The export market also quickly returned. Silks from Khotan were purchased at the market in Yarkand by traveling merchants, who shipped them to Andijan and Kokand in western Turkestan, to Leh in northern India, and to Lhasa in Tibet. Even damaged cocoons and silk refuse found a place in the international trade, being bought and sent to Vernyi for processing into paper.[21] By the mid-1870s, Khotan was exporting tens of thousands of pounds of cocoons to Russian Turkestan and British India on an annual basis, and raw and woven silk together accounted for about 6 percent of the total value of exports from Kashgar to Russian territory.[22]

The burgeoning sericulture industry in the Tarim Basin was primarily a cottage industry. One member of the 1873 British expedition to the region, Edward Chapman, observed the practices and temporal rhythms of silk production in Turkestani households in Khotan and judged them to be similar to what might be found in Chinese households in the eastern provinces. Starting in early April, members of the household brought silk-worm eggs out of winter storage, where they had been preserved since the previous year. To incubate the eggs and induce hatching, men and women carried them around for up to a week, tucking them into their clothing and warming them with their own body heat. Once the eggs began to hatch, their human caretakers spread the tiny worms out on piles of mulberry leaves harvested from nearby trees. Over a period of roughly forty days, the silkworms feasted on leaves, molted several times, and grew large before reaching the point where they were ready to spin their cocoons. In July, after the cocoons had been spun, people reeled the silk by putting the cocoons into cauldrons of scalding hot water, teasing apart their individual fibers, and bringing a small number of threads together to be turned onto a reel.[23] Members of the family then used the silk thread to weave cloth on looms at home. While most of the work was done within the household, Chapman and his fellow travelers also came across some evidence of commercialization and specialization, especially in the latter stages of the production process. Quite a few households sold their cocoons to export traders or reeling workshops, where local merchants or investors from Russian Turkestan employed craftsmen to operate reels and looms for the manufacture of thread and cloth.[24]

Figure 6.1 Silk reeling in Yarkand. Photograph by Edward Chapman, ca. 1874. Courtesy of the Getty Research Institute, Los Angeles (2017.R.16).

Despite the renown of Khotan's silk industry, observers from outside of Turkestan were quick to offer critical appraisals of the quality of its products.[25] Their attention to quality largely reflected the increasing importance of quality control as international commercial competition in commodity markets intensified and as mechanization slowly began to reshape how silk threads and fabrics were manufactured worldwide. British and Russian travelers identified a number of different flaws in local silk manufactures in the Tarim Basin. Aleksei Kuropatkin reckoned that cocoons from Khotan were "coarser . . . weaker and inferior altogether" compared with cocoons from the city of Fergana in western Turkestan.[26] Chapman praised Turkestanis for their diligence in breeding silkworms, but he sharply criticized their techniques for reeling silk fibers from the cocoons. They had "no idea of sorting the cocoons before reeling," he explained, nor counting how many strands they brought together on the reel.[27] As a result, Khotan silks lacked "uniformity in the thread," convincing him that the city's "manufactured silk is valueless as an article of export."[28] Robert Shaw, a British secretary stationed in the northern Indian region of Ladakh, reported that inspectors in London had received a sample of silk from Khotan and had deemed it "excellent material, but utterly spoilt in the winding" because too many threads were wound together to produce the skein.[29]

As Qing officials contemplated the prospects for sericulture development in Xinjiang, they too discerned certain problems with the existing industry based upon their knowledge of products from eastern China. In early 1880, Zuo Zongtang described silks from southern Xinjiang as being "stiff" and "dark" in color, disparaging them for their poor texture and lackluster appearance. He concluded that local silk fabrics were simply "far inferior" to silks from the Chinese provinces.[30] He and other leaders identified a variety of reasons for the deficiencies of silk manufactures from Khotan and neighboring oases. One reason was the nature of silkworms in Turkestan. In comparison to silkworms from eastern China, silkworms hatched from eggs in southern Xinjiang reportedly took over ten days longer to mature, grew to have larger heads and bodies, and spun cocoons that were thinner and yellower. These characteristics diminished their productivity: according to one estimate, each catty of cocoons from Khotan yielded up to half an ounce less silk than Chinese silkworms. Silkworms from the Tarim Basin oases were also said to be prone to congregating when they spun their cocoons. As a result, they produced many dupions—enlarged cocoons spun jointly by more than one silkworm—which increased the coarseness of the skein and the cloth woven from their fibers.[31]

From the perspective of Qing officials, another reason for the poor quality of Xinjiang's cocoons and silks was human error. Some faulted Turkestanis for their failure to raise silkworms in a manner that attended to the creatures' needs, preferences, and aversions. This critique was rooted in the idea that successful sericulture required people to "nurture silkworms" (*yang can*), to provide a level of care that was deeper and more encompassing than simply making sure they completed their short life cycles.[32] One way of doing this was to maintain a hospitable ambient environment for them. Guidelines contained in Chinese sericulture treatises counseled people to monitor the temperature, humidity, noise level, and brightness in places where silkworms were raised, and to avoid exposing them to aromas, vapors, or airs that were believed to harm their *qi* and diminish their productivity.[33] In the eyes of officials, such rules were almost totally unknown among Turkestanis, who seemed to betray a startling lack of awareness about how to coax the small insects to spin their finest silk in copious quantities. According to one report, local people not only failed to protect their silkworms from wind and cold, thus leaving them vulnerable to harm caused by fluctuations in temperature; they also neglected to create the type of sanitary conditions that were ideal for maximizing their productivity. People in Xinjiang "keep no taboos. The rooms in which the silkworms are kept, the leaves which are fed to the silkworms, and the people who raise the silkworms are all unclean."[34] Such an indictment suggested that the lifestyles of Turkestanis themselves were partially to blame for the low quality of their native silks.

Evidence suggests that authorities were misguided in their belief that Turkestani households paid no attention to such issues. Chapman did find some glaring instances of disregard for maintaining the proper ambient conditions for silkworms. There was "no regulation of the temperature in which the worm has passed its life," he wrote, and thus apparently little appreciation of the influence of climate on the productivity of the insects or the quality of their silk.[35] But he also observed numerous practices indicating that Turkestanis were highly aware of the need to coddle their tiny charges. Silk producers in Khotan raised silkworms in a separate room of the house, segregating them from most members of the family and preventing them from coming into contact with "tobacco, snuff, onions, and garlic." They also forbade pregnant or menstruating women from handling the worms and turned responsibility for their care over to elder women. People exercised great diligence even when incubating the eggs with their body heat, making sure to avoid members of the opposite sex during that period of time.[36]

Even if Qing leaders had been aware of such practices among Turkestani households, they would not have been satisfied that they were sufficient to nurture silkworms. At a basic level, the act of nurturing required the provision of sustenance. In the long tradition of Chinese medicine, the process of "nurturing life" (*yang sheng*) entailed fostering vitality in human bodies through a variety of physical practices, including the practice of following certain dietary regimens.[37] In Chinese political philosophy, the emperor and officials were required to "nourish the people," a mandate that could be fulfilled only if imperial subjects never went hungry.[38] In Chinese sericulture, nurturing silkworms meant not just treating the insects with special care, but also feeding them ample quantities of nutritious leaves from the mulberry tree. It was also for this reason that Zuo Zongtang and other officials judged Turkestani sericulture to be deficient. In what might be called an alimentary understanding of silk quality, they presumed that the mediocre visual and tangible characteristics of native silk were partially a result of the substandard quality of the food that was fed to the silkworms. This presumption then led them to think more deeply about the source of that food: the region's mulberry trees.

Elites in eastern parts of Qing China had known about the mulberry trees of Xinjiang since the middle of the eighteenth century, when officials began to catalog new knowledge about the region and its animal and plant life. Although their descriptions varied, what Qing gazetteers and travel reports seemed to agree upon was the notion that inhabitants of the Tarim Basin almost universally exploited the mulberry tree as a fruit tree. The *Illustrated Gazetteer of the Western Regions* classified mulberry trees among the domesticated and wild vegetation of southern Xinjiang, noting that the "mulberry fruit is really large and has a deep flavor. It is called *yuzhuma* and can be stored as food."[39] Another gazetteer compiled not long after the conquest recorded the existence of a great abundance of mulberry trees in the Tarim Basin and described their use. Four or five times a year, local people harvested black, white, red, and purple mulberries up to an inch (*cun*) long, consuming the "sweet and very juicy" fruits as food, drying them for later consumption, or extracting their juices to make wine.[40]

Some Turkestani families were said to pick a few bushels of ripe mulberries every summer, ferment the extracted liquids to produce wine, and then enjoy drinking the wine together in evening sessions under the canopies of trees.[41] Later sources contained similar information, noting that people harvested the small, sweet morsels for food or turned their juices into a beverage.[42] But there were other uses of the mulberry tree that had nothing to do with the fruit. People stripped the tree of its bark to make paper. They hewed its trunks and branches, turning the wood into a construction material. And, in certain places, people harvested the leaves to feed silkworms.[43] In sum, Turkestanis approached the mulberry tree as a multifaceted resource, utilizing its many parts and products as they saw fit.

The versatility of the mulberry tree must have been an advantage to oasis residents. Perhaps some even cherished the many benefits it provided. But the tree's diverse uses, and in particular its cultivation as a source of fruit, irked Zuo Zongtang. From his perspective, Turkestanis were exploiting their mulberry trees in ways that failed to maximize their potential to serve the goals of sericulture. "Local people only harvest mulberries as a food or consider them a medicinal material," he explained to Beijing, "so the profits of sericulture and silk textiles are not widespread."[44] Liu Jintang later concurred, writing that "Muslims only know about eating mulberries. They do not know about cultivating leaves and feeding silkworms" and thus were missing out on the "profits of cocoons" (jianli).[45] These two leaders plainly assumed that mulberry trees were best employed in the service of feeding silkworms, not people, and that eating the fruit but not harvesting the leaves constituted a waste of resources.

Their criticisms went further, suggesting that, even in cases where Turkestanis used mulberry trees for sericulture, the physical form of the trees themselves harmed the quality of the silk. In Zuo's view, Xinjiang's existing silk producers relied upon a supply of leaves from a population of "wild mulberry trees" (shengsang).[46] This posed a problem for the sericulture industry because, in his understanding, there was a strong correlation between the morphological characteristics of the tree, the quality of its leaves, and the productivity of the silkworm, a correlation that was illuminated by the human manipulation of plants through the practice of grafting. Grafting scions from certain types of mulberry trees onto the rootstock of others had the potential to create organisms that produced a greater quantity of more nourishing leaves. Such leaves were said to improve the quantity, color, and tensile strength of the silk fibers spun by the silkworms that ate them.[47] As Zuo explained, "If you feed the leaves of un-grafted mulberry trees to silkworms, the cocoons will not be plump and their threads will be stiff, their color will be dark, and only local pongees and Muslim brocades can be woven" from the resulting silk. But if people chose to "feed silkworms using grafted mulberry trees, the cocoons will be plump, the silk will be lustrous and strong, and the profits garnered from the silk will be quite large."[48] In other words, if people went to the trouble of modifying their mulberry trees, they could do much to improve the productivity of their silkworms and the quality of the silk they spun.

Zuo was mistaken in seeing the region's mulberry trees as untouched specimens of nature. Turkestanis did not refrain from practicing certain forms of botanical manipulation. It may have been true that such practices remained limited in regard to silk production in the late nineteenth century. Chapman had observed households in Khotan cultivating, pruning, and taking cuttings from one species of mulberry tree for use in sericulture, but the trees still grew to "a considerable height," convincing him that they in fact received "but little attention."[49] Three years earlier, members of another British expedition who traveled through the smaller oasis of Sanju, at the foot of the Kunlun Mountains, had found that, "except on one occasion," mulberry trees "did not bear the marks of having been lopped for feeding silkworms."[50] But the absence of visible signs of manipulation did not mean that oasis residents had never taken action to change mulberry trees to suit their needs. Fruit tree horticulture was practiced widely, and the abundance of evidence showing that Turkestanis harvested mulberries for consumption or wine-making suggests that they had played a role in the domestication of mulberry trees for their fruits, altering the physical characteristics of the population over a long period of time through the acts of selection and cultivation.

Qing leaders disregarded the value of mulberry trees laden with fruit. Because they were intent on pursuing sericulture development in the oases, the condition of the existing population of mulberry trees in Xinjiang was for them a summons to action. In 1880, Zuo proposed that the hundreds of thousands of mulberry trees already growing in the Tarim Basin region could be made useful by grafting new branches onto their old trunks, turning the existing stock into a vast collection of botanical devices for producing nourishing leaves to feed silkworms.[51] He recognized, though, that one of the consequences of prioritizing the production of leaves in this manner would be the diminution in the number and size of the mulberry fruits. On grafted mulberry trees, "the fruits are small but the veins of liquid are flourishing and the leaves are plump, round, and thick," making them an ideal source of food for silkworms.[52] The upshot of this plan seemed to be that Turkestanis would need to reconceptualize their mulberry trees more narrowly as organisms designed to nurture insects rather than as plants offering fruits and a variety of other resources to them.

As Zuo Zongtang imagined the future of sericulture in Xinjiang, he adopted a blueprint for development modeled upon the silk industry of northern Zhejiang. He was especially drawn to the example set by producers in the area around the city of Huzhou, whose efficiency and quality control earned them a reputation for being the best in the empire.[53] In the nineteenth century, households in Huzhou thrived by raising silkworms and reeling silk using labor within the family and then selling the thread to licensed silk traders, who furnished it to workshops and factories for the weaving of silk fabrics. Although some households supplied their own inputs, many others relied upon the region's commercial economy to obtain them, purchasing mulberry saplings, silkworm eggs, and extra leaves from firms that specialized in such items.[54]

The fabulous reputation of sericulture in Huzhou partially resulted from the productivity of the organisms that served the industry. Nothing was more emblematic of the area's advanced technical development than the eponymous Huzhou mulberry tree (*Husang*). This type of tree was characterized by the growth of large, round, and moist leaves and brittle branches, making it an excellent and easily exploitable source of food for silkworms.[55] Far from being a native species of the region, however, the Huzhou mulberry tree was the product of anthropogenic change. Over many centuries, people selected trees for propagation based upon traits such as profuse leafage, gradually transforming the population of mulberries in the region into what appeared to be a distinct variety. Their form became inseparable from the function they served, and by the Qing period people had come to associate Huzhou mulberry trees with the region's vibrant silk economy, viewing them as the most useful cultivar for sericulture.

Aside from inducing evolutionary changes in the mulberry population by selecting for various traits, people also made nonevolutionary changes by physically manipulating the trunks and branches of the trees. As early as the Northern Song period (960–1127), farmers in Huzhou had started to increase the quality and quantity of leaves produced by the mulberry tree

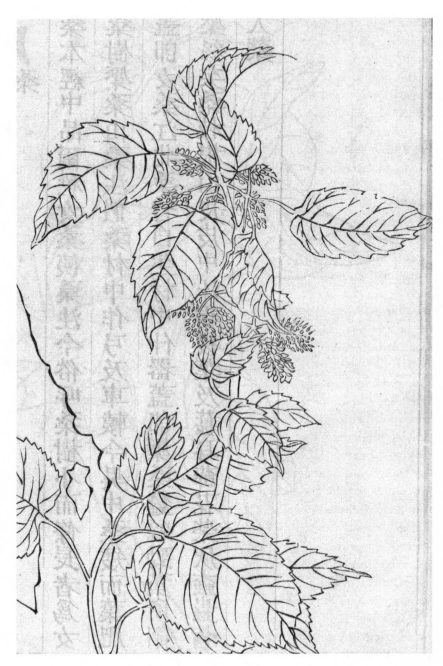

Figure 6.2 Mulberry tree. From Wu Qijin, *Zhiwu mingshi tukao* (Illustrated study of the names and facts of plants), 1848. Courtesy of the Harvard University Botany Libraries.

through grafting, a practice that became more common in the thirteenth and fourteenth centuries.[56] In later eras, technical manuals for Huzhou sericulture described grafting as an essential technique for improving the production of mulberry leaves. Grafted trees were commonly comprised of parts from two kinds of trees with different morphological characteristics. The first, the rustic mulberry (*yesang*), had a stout trunk and branches covered with frail, pointy leaves and numerous mulberry fruits. The second, the house mulberry (*jiasang*), had branches that produced just a few large mulberry fruits but many large, lush leaves. Because silk producers had little use for the fruits, people in northern Zhejiang got into the habit of taking the tender branches from the house mulberry and grafting them onto the sturdy trunk of the rustic mulberry, creating an amalgamated organism capable of producing food for silkworms in a more efficient manner.[57]

Mulberry cultivators in Huzhou also practiced the art of pruning, cutting off shoots and branches to configure the plants in ways that best served their interests. They pruned their trees for two main reasons: to induce them to produce greater volumes of nutrient-rich leaves and to allow the leaves to be harvested more easily.[58] In the Ming period, people learned to prune the longer branches of the trees after silkworms had been raised for the year, forcing the plants to send nutrients to younger branches and yield a larger supply of tender leaves the following season.[59] As the art of pruning became more sophisticated, farmers learned to prune their trees on an annual basis, removing certain branches, leaving others, and gradually modifying the trees so that their growing limbs reached upward and culminated in what were described as fists of leaves. Such trees were covered in thick layers of foliage. They were also short, reaching no more than two meters tall.[60] At this height, many people could easily reach their branches to gather leaves without resorting to the use of tall ladders. The petite stature of the pruned tree was such a common sight in Zhejiang that it was recognized by Wu Qijun, a noted nineteenth-century scholar of botanical knowledge, as a characteristic feature of mulberry trees in Jiangnan.[61]

Huzhou was also famous for the quality and productivity of its silkworm varieties. Prior to the Ming period, most sericulture households saved silkworm eggs from year to year, selecting the best specimens from the annual brood of cocoons and allowing the moths to emerge, mate, and lay eggs. Patterns of egg production gradually changed, however, as the art of breeding became more refined and commercialization opened up new opportunities for businesses to specialize in the production and sale of silkworm

一桑之大利總以十年爲期五年後漸次斫成拳式每
到正月拳上斫枝不可斫長只斫分許只要有葉眼
爲是枝大疤包來年更茂小民不知其法將枝本斫
長其葉必壞如斫手得法養桑十年斫枝斫條一株
可得葉數十斤育蠶利倍蓰有曰十歲之兒不能養
老有十數畝之桑十年後可以養老誠非謾語

一拳桑葉茂難免偷扯亦可斫下飼蠶樹小切忌斫剝
一嫩枝樹大本足且在拳上斫之無妨葉眼再長謂之
微條來年之葉仍茂所謂斧頭自有一倍桑是也
一交冬後霜桑葉多收潔淨者曬乾入臼杵末收入罈
內來年育蠶蠶大眠時遇雨葉潮風吹未乾者用乾

桑葉末摻在葉上拌之其葉卻乾飽蠶無患
一栽桑將根理直覆土築實斫去上條只斫二寸栽在
春冬萌芽時只斫一芽深秋肥者長成五六尺高冬
令又斫去上條離地一尺五寸如此樣
來春頂上又斫兩芽長成雙條冬令又斫去如此樣
清明出芽頂上又各斫兩芽冬又

春芽又如前法斫之冬令又斫成八頭如此樣
斫如此樣

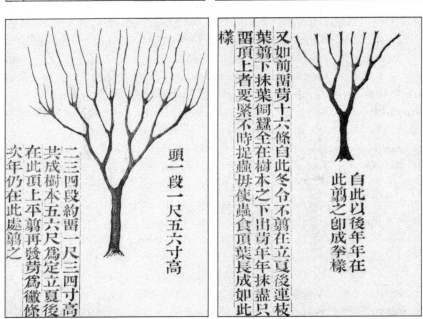

自此以後年年在
此斫之卽成拳樣

又如前法斫十六條自此冬令不斫在立夏後連枝
葉斫下抹葉飼蠶全在樹本之下出芽年年抹盡只
斫頂上者要緊不時捉蟲毋使蟲食頂葉長成如此
樣

頭一段一尺五六寸高

二三四段約斫一尺三四寸高
共成樹本五六尺爲定立夏後
在此頂上平斫再發芽爲微條
次年仍在此處斫之

Figure 6.3 Instructions for pruning mulberry trees. From Shen Bingcheng, *Cansang jiyao* (Collected essentials of sericulture), 1871. Courtesy of Toyo Bunko (The Oriental Library).

eggs. Around the turn of the seventeenth century, the practice of breeding specific varieties of silkworms became more prevalent in northern Zhejiang. Breeders created strains of silkworms possessing a range of advantages. Some were valued for their ability to produce copious amounts of silk even in adverse conditions. Other strains achieved notoriety for the fineness of their pure white fibers. Still others were bred to mature quickly, eat fewer leaves, and spin cocoons that were easy to unravel, thus reducing the costs of production and making sericulture more profitable. By the nineteenth century, sericulture egg specialists in the Huzhou region had developed dozens of varieties of silkworms, many of which found buyers from other districts and provinces.[62]

The visibility of Huzhou sericulture grew in the decades after the Taiping war, as officials in the provinces enacted measures to accelerate the pace of postwar reconstruction and take advantage of the expanding international market for silk by promoting sericulture.[63] Consider the experience of Shen Bingcheng, a native of northern Zhejiang. In 1869, Shen moved to the southern banks of the Yangzi River near the city of Zhenjiang to take up an official post. When he arrived, he found many of the area's towns in poor condition, a lingering result of wartime devastation.[64] Stocks of mulberry trees throughout the region had been decimated by the war.[65] Hoping to improve the local economy, Shen decided to promote silk production using Huzhou as a model, in large part because he understood its potential to generate revenue for rural households and the state.[66] He consulted with local elders, gathered monetary contributions, and dispatched subordinates to his home prefecture to purchase over two hundred thousand mulberry saplings and hire workers skilled in their cultivation. Shen also ordered them to buy silkworm eggs and invite sericulture experts from Huzhou to travel throughout the region to share their expertise with local people. In Zhenjiang and the surrounding countryside, he revived older sericulture bureaus (*cansang ju*) and established new ones, creating places where arborists could experiment with mulberry trees, teach farmers about grafting and pruning, and distribute Huzhou saplings. Meanwhile, craftsmen trained people how to care for silkworms and reel the thread from their cocoons.[67] From Shen's perspective, such measures promised to replicate the productivity of Huzhou's silk industry and foster economic vitality.

Huzhou gained further recognition through the publication and circulation of sericulture handbooks. The decades after the Taiping war witnessed an outpouring of scholarship on the technology and economics of silk production. From the 1860s to the 1880s, scholars wrote over a dozen new treatises and reprinted many older texts on the subject, seeking to expand people's understanding of the leading techniques for cultivating mulberry trees and raising silkworms.[68] Among these treatises were some which focused specifically on practices in Huzhou. Inspired by his experiences in Zhenjiang, Shen Bingcheng himself compiled such a book. First published in 1871, his *Collected Essentials of Sericulture* (*Cansang jiyao*) covered a wide range of topics, from identifying different mulberry varieties to handling silkworms.[69] The book exposed scholars and officials in many provinces to the technological prowess of Huzhou in matters of sericulture, and it became a standard reference for information about silk production in the last decades of the nineteenth century. Yet, as Shen strongly believed, knowledge alone was insufficient to replicate the vibrancy of Huzhou's industry in another region of the empire. Anyone who wanted to reproduce the successes of northern Zhejiang sericulture would need to mobilize an entire assemblage of tools, texts, resources, organisms, and people.

In 1879, Zuo Zongtang adopted the Huzhou model for a program of sericulture development in the oases of Turkestan, hoping to "spread the profits of Zhejiang into Xinjiang," as he later told the court.[70] Perhaps inspired by his reading of Shen Bingcheng's sericulture treatise, Zuo hired a Zhejiang province native, Zhu Yingtao, to spearhead the program.[71] Zhu worked with Zuo's longtime procurement agent, Hu Guangyong, to engage the services of sixty skilled craftsmen who specialized in various aspects of silk production and send them from northern Zhejiang to the far west, where they were slated to train Turkestani apprentices in the craft of sericulture. Although many potential recruits were reportedly hesitant about relocating to such a distant frontier, dozens were eventually hired, and by early 1880 they were traveling through Gansu on their way to Xinjiang.[72] When they reached the territory, they were split into smaller groups and dispatched to newly established sericulture bureaus located in a handful of oasis cities.[73] Eventually there were eleven such bureaus distributed across eastern and southern Xinjiang, including a head bureau in Aksu, each staffed by functionaries, scribes, guards, and translators.[74] They served as the primary locations where salaried Chinese sericulture experts interacted with their Turkestani apprentices, who generally were paid a daily stipend for their work.[75]

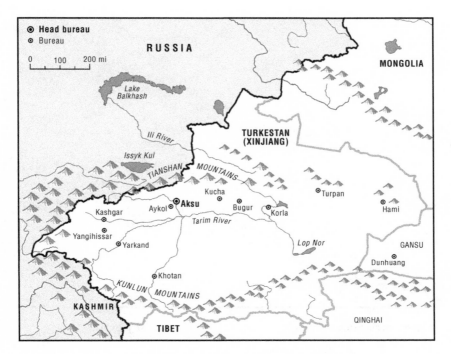

Map 6.1 Sericulture bureaus in Xinjiang, ca. 1883. Map by Erin Greb.

The history of sericulture development in the Turpan oasis suggests that state-sponsored efforts to spread knowledge of silk technologies in Turkestani communities grew quickly and expanded beyond the scope of Zuo Zongtang's initial plans. After twelve Zhejiang craftsmen arrived in the city in April 1880, officials posted announcements about the opening of the new sericulture bureau in villages throughout the oasis, some even tens of miles away from the city, calling upon people to sign up for training regardless of their ethnic background.[76] Meanwhile, the bureau's chief manager, Huang Xianyi, coordinated with Turkestani headmen to encourage all households in the oasis to begin raising silkworms.[77] The project soon expanded into the surrounding area as local officials established subbranch bureaus in half a dozen towns and farming communities, which were ordered to shoulder some of the cost of the new operations.[78] In addition, Turkestani carpenters were commissioned to construct some of the wooden tools employed in the bureaus, including reeling wheels and mulberry tree ladders.[79]

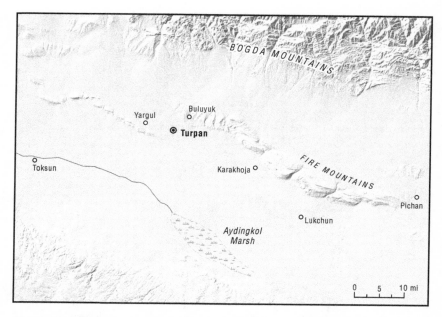

Map 6.2 Sericulture bureaus in the Turpan oasis, ca. 1882. Map by Erin Greb.

While the apprentices commenced their training under the tutelage of their teachers in the bureaus, officials worked to disseminate start-up capital to local households. Among inputs for sericulture, nothing was more essential than the eggs of the silkworm. Because the quality of local silkworm cocoons was considered to be substandard, Zuo ordered his deputies to purchase eggs in Zhejiang and ship them to Xinjiang. Silkworm eggs were easily acquired in the markets around Huzhou, sold on special sheets of paper or cloth each carrying tens of thousands of tiny eggs.[80] One shipment, dispatched to the borderland in 1880, contained nearly four hundred egg sheets packed neatly into four crates and was accompanied by two silkworm experts who bathed and dried the eggs in the sun as required during the long journey.[81] Initially, the quantity of eggs in such shipments was sufficient to meet the needs of the project in the Turpan oasis. But the length and arduous nature of overland travel, combined with the rapid increase in the number of households raising silkworms, led to an egg shortage in 1882.[82] The bureau chief thus had no choice but to procure local silkworm eggs and distribute them to rural households along with a small number of remaining Zhejiang egg sheets.[83]

Officials helped rural households acquire other tools as well, realizing that the paucity of proper equipment created a variety of production problems. Liu Jintang attributed the roughness and weakness of silks from Khotan to the prevalence of dupions in the supply of cocoons. He blamed the high incidence of dupions on the fact that, when silkworms were ready to spin their fibers, people placed the insects on tree branches laid out on the ground rather than on bundles of straw, a practice that allowed the worms to tangle together.[84] In Turpan, poor households reportedly lacked even basic tools like pruning blades for mulberry trees or wooden racks to keep silkworms off the ground during the period when they fed and molted. They were said to make do without such items, putting newly hatched silkworms on planks of wood or straw mats on the ground and feeding them rough leaves still attached to large branches. The bureau chief believed such practices harmed the creatures by exposing them to moisture, stunting their growth, allowing them to become diseased, or turning them into prey for sparrows and mice. To fix these problems in the production process, he offered financial assistance to families so that they could purchase sericulture tools on the condition that they repay their loans following the harvest of the cocoons.[85]

Sericulture bureaus also reached out to rural households indirectly through the dissemination of new sources of information. Perhaps inspired by the flurry of sericulture publications that circulated in eastern China, Qing officials printed a thirty-page bilingual Chinese-Chaghatay manual, *On Raising Silkworms* (*Yu can shuo; Pila baqadurghan bajani*), in Hami in 1881. Dozens of copies of the text were distributed the same year to Turkestani headmen in the farming villages of the Turpan oasis. These headmen were then expected to edify members of their own communities regarding the various techniques it discussed.[86]

A more substantial pattern of engagement between the state and Turkestani communities emerged after sericulture bureaus started sending extension agents into the villages. In 1882, fifteen Turkestani technicians were sent "down to the countryside to provide instruction" to local households in the Turpan oasis, teaching them how to handle silkworms and how to improve the quality of the cocoons they spun. Unlike Chinese officials and craftsmen in Xinjiang, who were not expected to learn to speak the local language, these young men were capable of communicating fluently with the Turkic-speaking residents of the region, greatly facilitating the spread of information. These agents were selected from the group of apprentices who had completed their technical training in the bureaus, and they were paid a monthly stipend during sericulture's busy season.[87] Officials also hired an exceptionally knowledgeable and skilled apprentice, a man in his early thirties named Tie-mu-er, to supervise the agents and their work in the villages.[88] In the following years, the extension program expanded to keep pace with the number of households involved in the production of cocoons. In 1884, the Turpan sericulture bureau employed seventy-three extension agents chosen from a larger pool of candidates who had passed an examination, and the next year it hired over a hundred such agents.[89] Sericulture extension work was also carried out in other oases south of the Tianshan.[90]

As the program developed, extension agents served as the main link between rural households that produced silkworm cocoons and the state-run sericulture bureaus that consumed them. Each agent dealt with twenty to thirty households and, aside from advising them on production techniques, each was responsible for ensuring that the required materials moved between the households and the bureaus. Every spring, agents distributed local and Chinese varieties of silkworm eggs to the families under their purview.[91] At the end of the silkworm rearing season, they returned to purchase the cocoons that had been spun. Acting on behalf of the sericulture bureaus, the agents paid set prices for yellow cocoons, white cocoons, and dupions, sometimes taking a small share of the total output as part of their compensation.[92] After the cocoons were gathered and sent to the bureaus, Chinese craftsmen used them as practice materials for their apprentices, training them how to unwind the cocoon fibers in cauldrons of hot water, reel the silk strands into thread, and weave the thread into cloth.

Outside of the bureaus and rural households, much of the state's effort to promote sericulture focused on the growth and transformation of Xinjiang's mulberry population. Based on his assessment of the unimproved nature of trees in the region, Zuo Zongtang ordered his operatives to acquire mulberry saplings in the region around Huzhou and ship them to the oases of Turkestan. Like silkworm eggs, young mulberries were readily available in markets in northern Zhejiang.[93] Roped together in bundles of about fifty saplings, the trees were transported by boat and cart to their final destinations, with attendants irrigating them periodically to keep them alive.[94] Starting in 1879, at least two shipments totaling several hundred thousand saplings were sent from Huzhou to Xinjiang: one via the

Yangzi River to Hankou and then on roads through Hubei, Shaanxi, and Gansu, and another by ship to Tianjin and then across Mongolian territory.[95] Preserving the trees' vitality during the long, arduous trek proved difficult. Some ended up in Lanzhou, Suzhou, and other Gansu cities, where officials decided to plant thousands of withering mulberry trees that were not expected to survive the remainder of the journey, believing that they might be exploited for seeds and cuttings to support future initiatives in sericulture.[96] Many others reportedly arrived in the borderland in a languished condition, with "wrinkled bark and shriveled flesh," and had to be nursed back to health or discarded.[97]

Zuo Zongtang's original vision had been to modify Xinjiang's existing stock of mulberry trees through grafting, taking organisms laden with fruit and turning them into efficient producers of leaves. But even before officials could attempt to do this, they learned how protective Turkestanis were of their trees. Liu Jintang discovered that the act of harvesting leaves from people's trees sparked protestation. In the spring of 1881, as the sericulture bureaus set to work raising silkworms in the first full year of production, officials dispatched workers into the surrounding countryside to gather leaves to feed them. Specialists from Zhejiang had determined that, despite earlier reports to the contrary, some mulberry trees in the oases yielded "large, juicy, and thick" leaves suitable for the insects.[98] However, the decision to harvest leaves from mulberry trees in the villages quickly provoked the anger of local residents. They worried that plucking foliage from the branches harmed the trees and their precious fruits, depriving them of their customary right to exploit the trees to feed themselves.[99] Because workers from the bureaus apparently attempted to collect leaves without compensating the trees' owners, the harvests also constituted an unexpected form of state exaction, causing further infuriation. Liu, who acknowledged the local penchant for eating mulberry fruits and hoped to head off bigger troubles, suggested that bureau officials place a limit on such harvests.[100] As a stopgap measure, he proposed that they compensate people for taking their mulberry leaves and hire special leaf pickers who could exercise greater discretion when gathering the greenery, packing it into crates, and shipping the crates to the bureaus by pack animal.[101]

With troubles brewing over leaf harvesting, officials decided to pursue a more permanent solution by establishing a separate population of trees whose leaves would be reserved for sericulture. Liu Jintang ordered local leaders to earmark "many *mu* of government land" adjacent to the bureaus for the cultivation of mulberry trees, telling them to use leaves harvested from those trees so that "in the future it will be possible to not take mulberry leaves from amongst the people and thus to prevent disturbances."[102] These mulberry yards were expected to double as nurseries, where saplings could be reared and mulberry seeds gathered for distribution to civilian households in surrounding areas.[103]

Beyond simply increasing the total number of mulberry trees in Xinjiang, the plantations also served as proving grounds for the manipulation of the trees to enhance their productivity for sericulture. Liu Jintang, following Zuo Zongtang's lead, aimed to reshape the region's mulberry population to foster the development of its silk economy. He argued that, because leaf quality was of the utmost importance, local people should "imitate the methods of the innerland, pruning and grafting" branches so that "the trees are not large, the fruits are not plentiful, and their essence is entirely emitted in the leaves," making them a nourishing source of food for silkworms. He also seemed to recognize the politically contentious nature of any activity that threatened to usurp the authority of Turkestanis to decide for themselves how to use their trees. Because only the new stock of mulberry trees was slated to undergo manipulation through grafting and pruning, at least initially, Liu tried to reassure other officials that "Muslims' practice of eating mulberries" would not be impeded.[104]

Officials also attempted to augment Xinjiang's mulberry resources by promoting cultivation of the trees in rural areas. Beginning in 1881, Liu Jintang called upon local leaders in each oasis to depute authority to one or two begs who would bear the responsibility for coordinating tree-planting activities with headmen in the villages. He also dispensed technical advice, telling such people when to transplant the trees, how much space to leave between them, how to care for their roots, and how to water them—the kinds of practical information recorded in text and imagery in sericulture manuals of the late nineteenth century. As the campaign got underway, Turkestani leaders mobilized local residents to transplant mulberry saplings and "small mulberry trees from the open countryside" to areas close to the villages, where they could conveniently serve the needs of household producers of cocoons.[105] The results of the campaign, reported annually by local headmen and village elders, were hardly trivial. In the first year alone, civilian workers and Qing troops planted over fifty thousand mulberry trees in locations throughout the Turpan oasis.[106] In subsequent years, tens of thousands of additional trees were transplanted into

Figure 6.4 Transplanting mulberry trees. From Wei Jie, *Cansang tushuo* (Illustrated guide to sericulture), 1895. Courtesy of Columbia University Library.

the villages and countless quantities of mulberry seeds were distributed to farmers.[107]

Despite Liu Jintang's claim that no harm would come to people for choosing how to exploit their trees as they saw fit, the campaign for sericulture development continued to inflame tensions over mulberry resources. In the spring of 1882, a village elder in Toksun, an agricultural community to the west of Turpan, determined that there simply were not enough mulberry leaves to nourish all of the silkworms then being raised by local households. The elder, Ma Taihe, also expressed frustration that some mulberry tree owners had prevented other people from picking their leaves. Given these circumstances, Ma argued that members of sericulture households should be allowed to gather leaves regardless of who owned them, and he suggested that any cases of resistance to leaf harvesting should be assigned to local authorities for adjudication and punishment.[108]

The state's strong support for sericulture caused additional headaches for local residents. At some point in the 1880s, officials imposed a ban on chopping down mulberry trees with the aim of preserving them for the silk industry. The ban frustrated some people because it seemed to deprive them of the opportunity to exploit the trees for their wood. In 1887, three Turkestani men complained to officials in Turpan for this reason. As business partners, the three jointly owned a karez which was now in need of repairs. Under normal circumstances, the men harvested several varieties of trees, including mulberry, elm, and willow, hewed their wood into timbers, and installed the timbers as support beams to reinforce the internal structure of the karez. They were especially fond of using mulberry lumber for such repairs because the material was said to be capable of withstanding the moist subterranean conditions of the karez without rotting for two or three decades, nearly ten times as long as other types of timber. In the face of the government's ban, they grew worried that, without access to mulberry wood, either their karez would collapse or they would have to waste time and labor replacing structural support beams more frequently with timbers of inferior quality. The men thus petitioned Qing authorities for special permission to chop down mulberry trees, promising to plant new ones to take the place of those they killed. In response to their petition, officials decided to permit them to harvest mulberry wood on the condition that they plant ten new trees for every one they cut down. This condition subsequently became the rule governing requests to fell mulberry trees in the oasis.[109] The case suggests that, even when local people sought to exploit mulberry trees to develop irrigation infrastructure, Xinjiang's leaders persisted in using the legal power of the state to protect and encourage the growth of one of the sericulture industry's key resources.

Sericulture spread rapidly in Xinjiang in the 1880s, bringing an increasing number of Turkestani households into the silk economy of the late nineteenth century. Despite the tensions surrounding mulberry trees, many people opted to participate in the state's development project, likely attracted to the prospect of earning a new source of income. In 1882, around 140 households in Turpan raised silkworms for their cocoons. Just five years later, over 3700 households were involved in the production of cocoons, constituting an astounding 35 to 45 percent of all households in the oasis.[110] The total output of silk from the oasis also rose swiftly, increasing by more than 1000 percent in just three years to reach over thirty thousand ounces of yellow and white silk thread by 1885.[111] Without reliable data, it is impossible to determine if other oases experienced similar increases in household silk production. The existing evidence also does not reveal to what extent bureaucratic training for Turkestani apprentices and extension work in the villages resolved problems related to quality control. But Zuo Zongtang, who was deeply invested in the notion of spreading Chinese sericulture to the borderland, hardly waited before deciding to laud the development program as a success. Happy to act as a booster, he declared just a year into the project that woven silk manufactured at the bureau in Aksu was "white and resilient and no different from [silk produced in] the central lands."[112] He also hoped to spread awareness of Xinjiang's growing industry among officials and merchants in other parts of the empire, so he forwarded samples of finished silk to Beijing and Shanghai.[113]

As silk production expanded, the state gradually reduced its financial stake in the project. Indeed, by late 1882, sericulture chief Zhu Yingtao was already telling officials to slash the number of managers and craftsmen employed at the bureaus.[114] In the following two years, many bureaus went through a process of downsizing, laying off their most expensive salaried staff while retaining some craftsmen, apprentices, and translators. Although a few sericulture experts from Zhejiang decided to stay in Xinjiang indefinitely, most returned home in these years, leaving much responsibility for technical education in the hands of Turkestani craftsmen.[115] Meanwhile, activities in the remaining bureaus gradually shifted to focus more on education in the techniques of weaving. In early 1885, ten Turkestani craftsmen who specialized in cloth production were dispatched from Aksu to Turpan, where they set up shop in the local sericulture bureau and started to train nearly two dozen apprentices, all recruited from local Turkestani households. Bringing tools and looms with them, these craftsmen taught their students how to operate the different types of looms and how to weave silk cloth in a variety of patterns, including striped gauzes, figured pongees, Khotan pongees, Huzhou crepes, and fine brocades.[116]

Merchants began to play a more prominent role in Xinjiang's silk industry in these years. Officials welcomed their involvement, believing that, if they gradually privatized the industry, they could improve market efficiency, lower prices, reduce government costs, and foreclose opportunities for graft.[117] In Turpan, Turkestani businessmen were recruited to invest in the industry by establishing firms and storefronts dealing in silk. By 1884, silk firms were starting to conduct business directly with rural households, dispensing silkworm eggs at the beginning of the rearing season and later returning to purchase cocoons.[118] Merchants also gradually took over the enterprise of silk weaving. In 1886, officials transformed the government-run weaving workshop into a semiprivate venture capitalized with money from a tiny cohort of Turkestani shareholders whose wealth and status derived partly from their political connections to the Qing state.[119] Within a few years, many of the functions formerly carried out by the sericulture bureau in Turpan had been taken over by merchants and were no longer directly controlled by Chinese officials.[120]

The privatization of sericulture in Xinjiang coincided with an empire-wide push to reduce government expenditures. Since the 1870s, scholars and officials had voiced fears that the high costs of reconstruction and development were bloating provincial budgets, sapping the strength of the imperial treasury, and drawing funds away from more urgent priorities. Critics looked upon the bureaus that had proliferated since the Taiping war with a combination of apprehension and ire, believing that many served no justifiable purpose and calling for their dissolution.[121] These concerns led to government action in late 1884 when, in the middle of the Sino-French War, Beijing issued a directive to all provinces to reduce expenses.[122] Liu Jintang heeded the directive by terminating six sericulture bureaus and cutting back on salaried personnel.[123] The Qing court relayed similar orders to the provinces in 1885 and 1890, mandating that authorities raise revenues and cut costs through measures such as consolidating and downsizing the bureaus.[124] Given the weak financial circumstances of the imperial government, it is hardly surprising that many of Xinjiang's postwar bureaus did not survive the repeated calls for austerity. By 1890, the provincial government had greatly reduced its involvement in the day-to-day management of the remaining sericulture bureaus and had trimmed expenses on other development projects.[125]

Although events on China's eastern shores certainly helped to catalyze the gradual termination of the sericulture development project after just ten years, they were not the only cause. Labor troubles in Xinjiang also may have contributed to its demise, driving Qing officials to throw up their hands in exasperation. In May 1889, an administrator anxiously reported that sericulture extension agents at the Turpan bureau had suddenly demanded extra compensation for their work. Perhaps even more troubling, the dozens of young Turkestani men who worked in the bureau processing cocoons into thread and cloth had begun to harbor "minds of dissent" (*yixin*), leading them to engage in sabotage and undertake other acts of resistance against their employer. "If they don't intentionally ruin the looms and textiles, then they'll sabotage the cocoons and silk threads," he wrote. Given the ongoing financial deficits, he and his superiors decided that it would be best to cease production, sell off the remaining cocoons to recoup some money, and shutter the bureau to prevent further occasions for unrest.[126]

The fate of the sericulture development project may appear to lend credence to the long-familiar story of the weakness and decline of the Qing state in the final decades of the nineteenth century. But the significance of the project lies neither in its eventual demise nor in its ephemeral success. Instead, it lies in the novel patterns of cooperation and conflict between Chinese and Turkestanis that emerged inside the sericulture bureaus and out in the villages. When Zhejiang craftsmen were sent to the oases with the aim of training local people in the practices of silk production, they established a precedent for technical education in Xinjiang in which Chinese craftsmen assumed the state-sponsored role of the purveyors of technical expertise while Turkestanis were hired to act as the recipients of that expertise, in turn becoming extension agents who propagated their knowledge in rural areas or master craftsmen who taught their own cohorts of students. Zuo Zongtang's decision to create the bureaus and staff them with people from eastern China not only underscores the growing influence of Chinese officials and government personnel in Xinjiang after the 1870s; it also shows how technology and the propagation of expertise for exploiting nature became a more explicit tool in their struggle to control territory and people in Central Asia.

The dynamics of these intrahuman interactions can be fully appreciated only by considering the world beyond humans. No components of that world were more crucial for sericulture than silkworms and mulberry trees. These creatures sat astride the "illusory boundary" between nature and technology, partially embodying the designs of their human handlers and partially escaping them.[127] They were quite visibly different from the steamships and telegraph wires that were coming to transform patterns of exchange between Qing China and the rest of the world in the final decades of the nineteenth century. Nonetheless, sericulture's plants and animals were also technological entities, and their deployment brought people together in new ways. At certain moments, divergent views on what mulberry trees should be used for made the trees themselves a point of tension within a larger field of social relations. Such tensions may not have threatened to undo Qing power in the borderland. But they were serious enough to worry high-ranking officials, who left behind a trail of documents revealing just how much nonhuman organisms could shape the politics of colonial development.

Conclusion

I n early 1884, Zuo Zongtang found himself in the midst of another crisis. Several years earlier, he had been recalled to Beijing for an audience at court. This summons spelled the end of his career in the Qing northwest, though he continued to monitor developments in Xinjiang from afar. Now, in his latest position as the governor-general of Jiangsu, Anhui, and Jiangxi provinces, he was confronted by a new round of disasters. Heavy rains were leading to frequent flooding in certain districts of northern Anhui and Jiangsu. Water inundated fields, destroyed crops, and sent families scrambling to find food.[1] As life became treacherous, people had little choice but to seek refuge on dry ground. There were now tens of thousands of people trudging to the south, heading toward the Yangzi River valley in search of relief. Alerted to their existence, Zuo ordered the construction of aid stations to offer them food and assistance and engaged with other officials in a discussion about the best means to prevent similar disasters in the future.[2]

By that point in his life, Zuo was no stranger to crises in rural areas or their impact on the country.[3] Back in the early decades of the nineteenth century, he had lived through a period of intensely bad weather featuring repeated bouts of flooding and several major droughts. He had witnessed the precarious conditions in which poor peasants were forced to make hard decisions about how to keep themselves alive. Such conditions were not unique to Hunan, of course. Across China, a significant segment of the population suffered in one way or another from a combination of harsh weather, economic volatility, social inequality, and scarcities of land and other resources driven partly by unprecedented demographic growth. In the middle of the century, when foreign empires began to attack the Qing state and millions of people took up arms in revolt, the problems of the imperial government greatly escalated, diminishing its capacity and also, in certain cases, its willingness to mobilize resources to help people survive through the worst of the country's environmental woes. In fact, the refugees of 1884 may very well have been a manifestation of this troubling situation. Following the Yellow River's dramatic avulsion three decades earlier and the long-term deterioration of infrastructure for water control, the entire North China region and its people had become more vulnerable to intensifying patterns of ecological instability.[4]

Yet while a multitude of crises may have reduced the state's capacity in some important respects, it also increased the determination among a certain segment of the ruling elite to take better advantage of what they perceived to be the empire's considerable abundance of natural resources and their potential for development. The mounting social and ecological pressures within the Chinese provinces, which were visible in the eighteenth century and quite obvious in the early nineteenth century, prompted literati to devote greater attention to the question of their resolution. Statecraft scholars were at the forefront of this movement, and they identified both technological and colonial methods for easing such pressures. Some scholars took great interest in the knowledge of nature and its utilization. They studied how to squeeze more "profits" from the earth through the meticulous management of soils, waters, plants, and animals, seeing increases in productivity as key. Other scholars were inspired by new knowledge about imperial geography and the Qing borderlands. They articulated the value of Xinjiang as a space of growth for people in the provinces, suggesting that untapped resources on the frontiers were essential to solving China's problems. Taken together, these strands of thinking suggest that the country's internal dynamics were fostering not just the conditions in which natural disasters and ecological degradation became more prevalent, but a new level of consciousness regarding the prospects for a more intensive and extensive exploitation of the natural world.

Following the wars of the mid-nineteenth century, the drive for natural resource development was manifest most clearly in state-financed projects to expand and improve agriculture and sericulture and the bureaucratic institutions that were established to support them. Although such projects were closely intertwined with the imperative to promote postwar reconstruction, their goals transcended the mere achievement of postwar recovery. Zuo Zongtang aimed to foster vibrant rural industries with the capacity to produce surpluses that could be sold at market, increasing people's incomes while reducing the costs of supplying his armies with food and other materials. He also justified these projects in other ways. He expected that they would lead to increases in total farmland acreage and invigorate rural economies, eventually boosting tax revenues and helping to ease the state's financial distress. No less important was his belief that colonization and natural resource development would enhance the empire's control of its borderlands.

By the final decades of the nineteenth century, building territorial power had become the main justification for policies of colonial development in frontier regions. In the summer of 1885, just months before his death, Zuo articulated a plan for shoring up Qing claims to Taiwan, which had been subjected to bombardment and blockade by French forces over the course of the preceding year.[5] With thoughts of Xinjiang still fresh in his mind, the ailing septuagenarian called upon the court to convert the beleaguered island into a province, speed up its economic development through government planning and investment, and suppress its indigenous communities. "If policies to pacify the aborigines can be carried out earnestly and the profits of nature do not continue to be wasted," he proposed, then Taiwan could quickly become a populous territory that was less costly to govern and more securely tethered to the mainland.[6] He also urged officials to pay attention to Taiwanese agriculture, noting the island's promise for boosting the production of sugar and other commodities.[7]

Plans for development were enacted in the following years under the leadership of the island's first governor, Liu Mingchuan. The governor brought a large amount of farmland under taxation through cadastral surveys, established land reclamation bureaus to promote agriculture, built telegraph and railway lines, and invested in Taiwan's coal industry, hoping to tap into the island's resource wealth to facilitate Qing rule.[8] Meanwhile, Liu carried out numerous campaigns against Taiwan's indigenous inhabitants and set up schools to educate them into a Chinese-speaking world. Recognizing the gravity of what had transpired in the northwest provinces in the recent past, he justified these activities with the argument that "unless we pacify them, we will have worries as large as the Muslim rebellions in

Shaanxi and Gansu."[9] In other words, the specter of chaos became a warrant for enacting punitive and pedagogic policies toward the island's native peoples with the aim of securing their compliance and opening up space for tea, camphor, and other cash crops.

The pursuit of colonial development, whether in Taiwan or Xinjiang, shows how deeply Chinese elites had come to accept the idea that the preservation of their empire required the transformation of its borderlands into replicas of Chinese territory. They also saw a certain Chinese future in them. When Taiwan was formally granted provincial status in 1887, it was a sign that the process of administrative reform that had taken place in Xinjiang three years earlier had become a template for asserting authority in frontier regions. It would not be the last time: a similar process was enacted two decades later, when Manchuria was divided into three new provinces.[10] These episodes of provincialization were perhaps the most cogent political expressions of the will to maintain power over outlying territories despite the internal and external pressures that threatened to pry them out of the hands of the imperial government. But, to a large extent, they were also expressions of a belief in the potential of such regions to be exploited for their resources. The creation of new provinces was premised on the assumption that their Chinese-speaking populations would grow and their agriculture, mining, and other industries would be developed, all of which would serve to enlarge the tax base enough to pay for all of the administrative costs that came along with provincial rule. By this logic, colonial development was bound to accompany provincialization, gradually changing the borderlands to become more like the provinces of China and making the "frontiers and hinterlands indivisible," as Zuo had written.[11]

Yet, in practice, the success of colonial development was far from certain. Plans for development faced a variety of obstacles, especially the state's financial weakness and people's animosity toward them. In Gansu, the process of land reclamation dragged on for decades, slowed by extensive wartime depopulation and persistent funding shortages. Campaigns to prohibit the cultivation of opium poppies and replace them with cotton also ran into trouble, largely because farmers and district officials resisted attempts to eradicate a crop that could yield heady profits and boost local tax revenues. In Xinjiang, development projects produced some notable changes in the region's economic and ecological landscape. Qing officials allocated substantial labor and capital to refurbish old irrigation channels and build new hydraulic infrastructure. As a result of state and nonstate efforts, the extension of waterways led to significant growth in the amount of farmland, although maintaining embankments along certain rivers proved to be an ongoing challenge. Meanwhile, efforts to improve sericulture in Turkestani communities led to a burst of activity around cocoon production and silk spinning. They also generated tensions of the sort that worried imperial officials, ones that seemed to have the potential to spark unrest or cause wider territorial instability. Ultimately, though, it was financial austerity imposed by Beijing that made these projects unsustainable. After the mid-1880s, Xinjiang's provincial leaders felt as if they had no choice but to rein in spending and curtail the government's role in the sericulture industry. Other borderlands also experienced financial belt-tightening. In Taiwan, a vigorous period of investment in agriculture, transportation, and mining was followed by a sharp withdrawal of funding in the early 1890s.[12] Despite the grand designs of Qing leaders, inconsistent support for development projects was one of the main reasons why their impact on people and environments was geographically uneven and sometimes impermanent.

Meanwhile, Chinese elites persisted in seeing frontier colonization as an essential strategy for dealing with demographic and financial problems in China. In fact, the idea that Xinjiang could serve as an outlet for growth never really disappeared. Back in 1876, scholar Zhang Peilun had asserted that the imperial government could save a great deal of money by sending the large population of Manchu bannermen who resided in the capital to Xinjiang for permanent resettlement.[13] Borrowing language from Wei Yuan, he indicated that the borderland essentially existed for China's use: "Isn't it the case that Heaven intentionally left a fallow land, an area of barren frontier, to serve as the fluctuating outlet for the central plains?"[14] Other elites were prepared to offer a resounding "yes" to this question. In 1883, as the idea of turning Xinjiang into a province was still being discussed, imperial censor Hong Liangpin wrote that Heaven "left a vast, undeveloped wilderness to be China's outlet" (*Zhongguo weilü*), choosing to mention the native inhabitants of the territory only to criticize their misdeeds. He then proposed that officials should recruit "surplus people from the innerland," especially those who were inclined to migrate to Southeast Asia or more distant destinations looking for work, and send them to Xinjiang, where they could work in agriculture. Hong championed this policy as a way to mitigate overpopulation in the east, accelerate the pace of colonial development, and offset the costs of Qing rule on the frontier.[15]

Similar ideas held sway among a cohort of literati who were committed to seeing the Qing court enact deeper political reforms. Zheng Guanying, whose *Words of Warning to a Prosperous Age* (*Shengshi weiyan*) gained widespread notoriety in the 1890s, emphasized the urgency of stimulating the growth of colonial agriculture. In an essay on land reclamation, he argued that, while the inner provinces were crammed with people who could barely subsist on the food they produced, the northwest possessed an untold supply of unused resources but remained sparsely populated and thus practically "empty" (*kongxu*). Given this imbalance, Zheng proposed that the government recruit unemployed and landless people to move to the frontiers, where they could open up deserts, grasslands, and forests for agriculture.[16] Another reformist scholar, Chen Chi, also worried about the unbalanced distribution of land and labor within the country. After more than two centuries of demographic growth, he observed, China's central provinces suffered repeatedly from disasters. Seeking better lives, people joined rebel movements or sought passage on ships to sail across the oceans. But Chen found cause for hope in Xinjiang. As he explained, settlers there managed to produce rich harvests from extremely fertile soil, and there was an enormous area of land still unclaimed owing to the region's small population. He thus advocated for "combining the overflowing and the empty" and "evening out the inner and the outer" by sending civilians to the far west, where they could draw wealth from the soil through agriculture.[17]

These proposals, which invoked colonial solutions for the pitfalls of growth, were not without parallels in other empires. While they no doubt reflected a particular Qing discourse on population resettlement that dated back to the eighteenth century, they also echoed a conceit shared widely among nineteenth-century advocates of colonization the world over, who looked to frontiers—whether in the American West, North Africa, the Antipodes, or Siberia—to serve as "outlets" or "safety valves" for the intensifying contradictions of growth or worrying concentrations of capital and labor.[18] However, as the decades passed, such parallels were gradually overshadowed by rising disparities between the Qing empire and its imperial rivals. Industrialization in the Atlantic world fueled new patterns of imperialism by European states, helping to produce historically unprecedented variations in wealth and power that became prime manifestations of the "great divergence" between societies around the globe.[19] Through force and diplomacy, European states turned the Qing empire itself into a certain kind of colonial frontier for their development, reaping large profits from the opium trade, helping themselves to China's rich collection of botanical resources, or exploiting Chinese workers in natural resource industries across the Pacific and Indian Ocean worlds. It was not until the early twentieth century that intellectuals would try to theorize exactly what kind of colonial space China was becoming for foreign capital and for the system of capitalism that seemed to be emanating from Europe.[20] By then, though, Chinese elites were already well aware that the economic and military might of other empires had grown enough to eclipse the power of their own country, whose stature in the global economy had shrunk considerably compared with a century earlier.[21]

As the Qing empire's place in the global order changed, so did the relations between the Chinese provinces and the borderlands surrounding them. The outcome of the Sino-Japanese War of 1894–95 was a watershed in this conjoined history. The stunning defeat of the Qing state and the conditions of its surrender simultaneously diminished the geographic horizons of Chinese colonial development and generated an even stronger desire among elites to assert authority over other frontiers. The main territorial casualty of the war—the loss of Taiwan to Japan—extinguished the possibility for further Chinese-led development on the island colony. At the same time, the huge indemnity imposed on the Qing state by Japan made it even more difficult for leaders to bankroll colonial projects in Xinjiang and other peripheries.[22] Yet the defeat also sparked a reckoning among Chinese elites about the urgency of salvaging the territories of the Manchu-led empire to serve as the geographical foundation for a renewed Chinese state. In the following years, as the government launched a bevy of political and institutional reforms in Beijing, elites reaffirmed their commitment to the idea of keeping colonial territories within the empire for the benefit of their own homeland.

One indication of this commitment was the adoption of a new language to describe Chinese colonialism. At the turn of the twentieth century, while foreign commercial interests were scrambling to secure concessions for railway and mining rights in China, Chinese advocates of political reform were studying the dynamics of the new imperialism then spreading around the world.[23] One of the earliest serious treatments of imperialism came from the hand of Liang Qichao. A classically trained scholar, Liang had gone into exile in Japan in 1898 at a moment when certain members of the Qing court moved to silence discussion of reform. During his time abroad, he traveled around the world and gained a new perspective on global affairs. Liang soon learned to think of modern imperialism as an outgrowth of nationalist sentiment that empowered people and governments to expand into new territory. In 1902, he defined "national imperialism" as a process whereby the "strength of a citizenry, having filled up the interior, is bound to overflow into the exterior. Thereupon they anxiously seek to extend authority over other lands, which they consider their own outlet."[24] While Liang's definition underscored the spatial patterns of the new imperialism, other authors emphasized the connections between expansionism and natural resources. Imperialism, one author explained, was an expression of the fact that "uncivilized people lack the ability to develop sources of wealth from the land, so civilized people must do it for them."[25] Such analyses spelled out the linkages among nationalism, imperial violence, and the exploitation of the natural world, creating a pool of critical knowledge that inspired Chinese intellectuals as they elaborated more trenchant critiques of imperialism and capitalism in the following decades.

While some intellectuals were defining patterns of behavior that seemed unique to their imperial adversaries, others were looking to draw attention to parallels in the practices of colonialism. Perhaps inspired by a growing sense of nationalism, some began to view their empire's own colonial territories as Chinese instantiations of a global pattern. Some compared the place of Xinjiang in the Qing empire to the places of Hokkaido and Taiwan in the Japanese empire and the Philippines in the American empire, while acknowledging that each colony was shaped by a specific national brand of colonialism reflecting the characteristics, policies, and customs of natural resource exploitation of the colonizing country.[26] Other authors used the analogies of Japanese imperialism in Taiwan and British imperialism in India to justify spending large amounts of money to control Xinjiang.[27] Elites raised similar comparisons when talking about Mongolia and eastern Tibet, pointing to the examples of Australia, Madagascar, and western North America to suggest that Chinese colonialism was not so different from its European and American counterparts.[28] These comparisons suggest that, as elites laid claim to the lands and resources of the entire Qing empire as part of their national patrimony, they were seeking not just to legitimize Chinese rule in regions inhabited primarily by non-Chinese people but also to demonstrate that China, too, had its own colonial territories, a sign that their country had the determination and wherewithal to survive in a competitive world.

Chinese discourses about the inhabitants of the borderlands also grew more critical. In this period, discussions of Xinjiang's Turkic Muslims often drew attention to their perceived cultural deficiencies. At a time when ideas of racial hierarchy permeated global politics and Westerners regularly depicted Chinese as backward and ill-equipped to maintain their sovereignty, Chinese elites described Turkestanis as unindustrious and incapable of fully exploiting Xinjiang's resources on their own. One gazetteer characterized the region's people as "idle farmers prone to self-contentment" who used "poor, inferior tools which they have not changed for generations." In a region where "the heavens are moist even without rain and the earth is rich even without fertilizer," such people were "greedy to take the achievements of nature as the product of their own effort."[29] Other evaluations of the native inhabitants of Xinjiang were harsher and blunter.[30] In 1906, Guangdong native Pei Jingfu, who had been impeached from office and exiled to the borderland, cast aspersions on Turkestanis, calling them "stupid," "lazy," "greedy," and "uncivilized," and claimed they worked hard in agriculture only when heavy taxes were imposed upon them.[31] Certainly, Pei was not the first to describe Turkestanis in a pejorative manner; negative descriptions of them had appeared in texts since the eighteenth century.[32] Yet it seems that, for a variety of reasons, Chinese discourses about Turkic Muslims reached a new degree of derogation by the first decade of the twentieth century.[33] Such denigrating language was not unrelated to the larger project of colonial development, as it was mobilized to justify greater intervention in their lives.[34] Writing about how such people should be ruled, Pei Jingfu urged officials to implement a "form of governance to compel them to cherish work," to mold them into industrious laborers through a combination of coercion and education in institutions devoted to training in agriculture, commerce, and industry.[35]

When new institutions started to appear in Xinjiang in the following years, they became focal points for renewed attempts to disseminate technology to accelerate development. In 1907, the provincial governor initiated a new plan for sericulture, sending a native of Zhejiang to the Tarim Basin to establish training institutes and revive silk education among Turkestanis. Like the sericulture improvement project launched by Zuo Zongtang three decades earlier, this scheme was aimed at raising the quality and productivity of the region's silk industry so that rural households and merchants could take advantage of the demand for raw silk among buyers from Russian and British territory.[36] The new plan also reflected a more contemporary zeitgeist of institution-building in which activist officials sought to harness the government's capacity to expand education and propagate technical knowledge among the people, especially new knowledge drawn from European, American, and Japanese sources.[37] As in other regions of the empire, the provincial government in Xinjiang established research and teaching institutions, including experiment stations and schools for agriculture and forestry, with the goal of fostering more productive natural resource industries.[38] In Turkestani communities, though, such institutions took on an additional layer of meaning. Their creation was inseparable from the larger Chinese colonial project of controlling the territory, a project in which Turkestanis were seen as being incapable of exploiting local resources on their own without the help of Chinese bureaucrats, technicians, farmers, and workers from the east.

While these institutions were being erected, the frontiers of resource exploitation continued to expand in new directions, especially underground. Since the 1850s, when the Taiping war threw the Qing state into deep financial distress, Beijing had called upon officials in Xinjiang and Manchuria to encourage the mining of gold, silver, and other minerals and tax the output to make up for major shortfalls in government revenue.[39] In the ensuing decades, foreign scientists and their ideas about geology began to influence the policy-making of officials, who developed a much fuller appreciation for the magnitude and value of China's untapped underground resources.[40] Realizing the need to foster industrialization, they authorized the exploitation of stocks of coal, iron, and other minerals, often turning to foreign experts for technical assistance.[41] By the turn of the twentieth century, elites were championing mineral extraction as a cornerstone of national renewal. In Xinjiang, mining operations slowly expanded from gold into petroleum and industrial minerals. Although such operations faced many technical and financial difficulties in their early years, they served to increase the state's capacity to control the region in the long run. In the process, they created patterns of investment and infrastructure-building that ended up exacerbating inequalities between Han Chinese and Turkestanis because the latter were often excluded from enjoying the rewards of development.[42]

The foregoing evidence suggests that, by the early decades of the twentieth century, Chinese leaders were adopting new tactics to secure their domination of Xinjiang and its native inhabitants. To the extent that these tactics involved the use of foreign sciences and technologies to enhance agriculture, mining, forestry, and other resource industries, it may be said that patterns of colonial development in China and other empires had reached a new level of convergence. Without a doubt, over the course of the twentieth century, certain technologies such as railways eventually accelerated the pace of frontier colonization by Han people from the provinces. Future research may reveal additional ways in which certain scientific disciplines and technologies facilitated the Chinese colonial enterprise, not just in Xinjiang but also in Tibet, Inner Mongolia, and other borderlands. Nonetheless, questions about the country's convergence or divergence with global patterns of scientific, technological, or economic change, which so often frame discussions of Chinese history in this period, should not overshadow equally important questions about the enduring legacies of Qing politics in the twentieth century.[43] Throughout the century, Nationalist and Communist leaders echoed their nineteenth-century predecessors in expressing concerns about major imbalances between population and resources within the bounds of the country's territory. As Mao Zedong famously wrote in 1956: "We say China is a country vast in territory, rich in resources and large in population. As a matter of fact, it is the Han nationality whose population is large and the minority nationalities whose territory is vast and whose resources are rich, or at least in all probability their resources under the soil are rich."[44] Like their predecessors, these leaders employed such concerns to justify colonial projects, viewing Xinjiang and other frontier regions not just as territory worth defending, but as valuable spaces that could help resolve China's internal social and political problems through land settlement and capital investment. In this sense, while the state's capacity for carrying out campaigns in agriculture, industry, and infrastructure-building increased dramatically over the course of the twentieth century, leaving it quite different from the late Qing government in many regards, the underlying logic of colonial development persisted.

Acknowledgments

During the long course of writing this book, I have delighted in traveling to new places, meeting new people, and learning from so many generous mentors, colleagues, and friends along the way. I owe each of them a debt of gratitude, and I can only begin to offer a few words of thanks here. I am grateful to Andrew Hsieh for having introduced me to Chinese history and for providing his excellent guidance on sources and other matters over the years. I am thankful to Sherman Cochran for his outstanding teaching, sage advice, and steadfast encouragement. No one has done more than Sherm to help me think through questions about research, provide direction to the project, and foster my development as a scholar. I have also benefited greatly from the thoughtful counsel and kind support of Aaron Sachs, Bruce Rusk, Victor Koschmann, Ding Xiang Warner, and TJ Hinrichs, wonderful teachers all. Each made his or her own important contributions to my thinking and shaped the project when it was not yet a book.

Over the years, I have gained a great deal from scheduled or spontaneous meetings with scholars from other institutions, who have been generous with their questions, critiques, and suggestions regarding my research. I presented several chapters of the book manuscript at the annual meetings of the Agricultural History Society, the Association for Asian Studies, and the History of Science Society, as well as the "Knowing Nature" workshop cosponsored by the Rachel Carson Center and Renmin University in the spring of 2017. I thank the many participants at each of those gatherings for their feedback on my scholarship. In addition, a number of colleagues have been especially considerate in raising thought-provoking points of inquiry or offering assistance along the way. They include Mitchitake Aso, David Bello, Timothy Brook, Yan Gao, Shen Hou, Andrew Isenberg, Elisabeth Kaske, Aleksandra Kobiljski, Brian Lander, Joseph Lawson, Seung-joon Lee, James Lin, Micah Muscolino, Dagmar Schäfer, Sigrid Schmalzer, Grace Shen, Shellen Wu, and Li Zhang. Special thanks goes to Robert Marks for reading the entire manuscript and providing incisive comments on each of the chapters.

I could not have completed this book without the liberal support of institutions and communities of scholars around the world. Cornell University, Temple University, the Blakemore Foundation, the Fulbright Program, the U.S. Department of Education, the Association for Asian Studies, and the American Historical Association each provided funding for research or language training. In Taipei, the scholars at Academia Sinica graciously hosted me for a postdoctoral fellowship. Chang Li kindly sponsored my stay at the Institute of Modern History. Ts'ui-jung Liu and Michael Shiyung Liu welcomed me to Taiwan and into the environmental history working group. Lin Man-houng, Wu Jen-shu, Wu Zhe, and Marlon Zhu gave helpful advice at various points during my visit. Fellow postdocs Lin Ching-chih and Zhang Xueqian offered camaraderie and critical assistance on more than one occasion. In Beijing, Zhang Shiming and Xia Mingfang at Renmin University cheerfully provided guidance and assistance with letters of introduction, which opened doors to a number of archives and facilitated my research. In Urumchi, several Uyghur scholars generously invited me into their homes for meals and conversations about Xinjiang and its history. I am truly grateful for their hospitality. It is dreadful to think that they and their families may now be caught up in the government's systematic repression of Uyghur people and their culture. I sincerely hope they have escaped the worst of the tyranny.

Much of the work for this book project was completed after I moved to Philadelphia. I am happy to say that I could not have asked for a better group of colleagues than those at Temple University. It is a pleasure to recognize the members of my department and college for their support. Jay Lockenour kindly helped me navigate academic life at the university and apply for research funding. Travis Glasson, Jessica Roney, and Eileen Ryan read and commented upon a chapter in an earlier draft of the manuscript.

Petra Goedde and Priya Joshi made a year at the Center for the Humanities at Temple a productive and rewarding experience. I am grateful to these folks and many others for their help along the way.

Many librarians and archivists accommodated my requests for books, documents, and other materials that were necessary to complete this project. In this regard, my first thanks goes to the librarians at Temple University and Cornell University, who deserve much credit for helping me to obtain copies of numerous items on loan from other institutions. I would also like to recognize the help furnished by archivists at the First Historical Archives in Beijing, the National Palace Museum in Taipei, and the Xinjiang Uyghur Autonomous Region Archives in Urumchi, who gave me access to important unpublished sources. In the final stages of writing the book, I relied upon the assistance of people at the Alinari Archives, Toyo Bunko, the National Library of Brazil, the Getty Research Institute, Princeton University Libraries, Harvard University Libraries, Columbia University Libraries, and Cornell University Libraries to acquire copies of images that appear in the following pages.

This book would not have come to fruition without the diligent labor of people in the world of publishing. I am grateful to Caelyn Cobb for taking an interest in the manuscript and for helping it find a home at Columbia University Press. I would also like to thank other members of the staff at the press, including Monique Briones, Zack Friedman, and Susan Pensak, who spent time and effort bringing the book to completion. Others outside of the press made important contributions as well. Emily Shelton copyedited the manuscript, Erin Greb produced the maps, and Do Mi Stauber created the index. Two anonymous reviewers offered insightful suggestions for improving and streamlining the text. Thank you all for your work on this project.

Many friends have contributed to this book in large and small ways. From the time I moved to Ithaca, I benefitted from the intellectual camaraderie of numerous people, including Christopher Ahn, Tracy Barrett, Mari Crabtree, Matthew Erie, Franz Hofer, Noriaki Hoshino, Xiaojia Hou, Akiko Ishii, Christopher Jones, Taran Kang, Amy Kardos, Amy Kohout, Seok-Won Lee, Samson Lim, Oiyan Liu, Tze May Loo, Jorge Rivera Marín, Hajimu Masuda, Daegan Miller, Soon Keong Ong, Rebecca Tally, Lesley Turnbull, Yuanchong Wang, and Taomo Zhou. I am especially grateful to Claudine Ang, Wendy Leutert, Lisa Onaga, John Phan, and Ivan Small, each of whom helped to advance the project in his or her own way. I also extend my thanks to Michael Martina, for his munificent hospitality during multiple research visits to Beijing, and to Zhou Yuan, who shared several digital sources in the early years of the project. Friends in other parts of the world have offered moral support from afar.

My greatest debt of gratitude goes to the members of my family, who have been unfailingly supportive of my work on this book regardless of where or how long it has taken me. I thank Patrick, Bridget, and Tu-Uyen and each of their families for all of the lighthearted diversions from work over the years. I am grateful to my father-in-law and my late mother-in-law for always having welcomed me into their home and for generously supplying me with beer and bánh mì. My wife, Nu-Anh, deserves an immeasurable amount of credit for doing so much to support me while she tackles her own work. I cannot thank her enough. Above all, I wish to recognize my parents, Patty and Bill, who have always been generous with their love and encouragement. This book is dedicated to them.

Chinese Terms

A-bu-du-re-yi-mu 阿不都熱以木
A-bu-se-min 阿不色敏
A-sheng-mu 阿生木
Ai-ling-ba-hai 哎令八亥
Bao-ning 保寧 (?–1808)
Bi-chang 壁昌 (?–1854)
Bu-yan-tai 布彥泰 (1791–1880)
Cansang jiyao 蠶桑輯要
cansang ju 蠶桑局
Chen Baoshan 陳寶善
Chen Chi 陳熾 (1855–1900)
Chen Hongmou 陳宏謀 (1696–1771)
Chengnan Academy 城南書院
cun 寸
dan 石
Daoguang 道光 (r. 1821–1850)
dili 地利
Dushi fangyu jiyao 讀史方輿紀要
e'hui 惡卉
Feng Guifen 馮桂芬 (1809–1874)
fuqiang 富強
Ga-si-er 尕四爾
gengdu 耕讀

Gong Zizhen 龔自珍 (1792–1841)

Gong-tang 恭鏜 (1837–1889)

Guang qutian tushuo 廣區田圖說

Guangxu 光緒 (r. 1875–1908)

Gu Yanwu 顧炎武 (1613–1682)

Gu Zuyu 顧祖禹 (1631–1692)

Haiguo tuzhi 海國圖志

He Changling 賀長齡 (1785–1848)

He Xiling 賀熙齡 (1788–1846)

Hengchan suoyan 恆產瑣言

He-si-man 何四滿

Hong Liangji 洪亮吉 (1746–1809)

Hong Liangpin 洪良品 (1826–1896)

Hu Guangyong 胡光墉

Huang Xianyi 黃憲儀

huang 荒

Huangchao jingshi wenbian 皇朝經世文編

huangtian 荒田

huangwu 荒蕪

Husang 湖桑

Huijiang 回疆

Jia Sixie 賈思勰 (fl. 530)

jiahe 嘉禾

jianli 繭利

Jiaqing 嘉慶 (r. 1796–1820)

jiasang 家桑

jin 斤

jingshi 經世

jinshi 進士

ju 局

juren 舉人

kaiyuan jieliu 開源節流

kan'er 坎爾, 坎耳

kanjing 坎井

Kangxi 康熙 (r. 1662–1722)

kaozheng xue 考證學

kongxu 空虛

li 里

Li Hanzhang 李瀚章 (1821–1899)

Li Hongzhang 李鴻章 (1823–1901)

Li Jinxing 李晉興

Li Yunlin 李雲麟

Li Zongbin 李宗賓

liang 兩

Liang Qichao 梁啟超 (1873–1929)

lijin 釐金

Lin Zexu 林則徐 (1785–1850)

Liu Jintang 劉錦棠 (1844–1894)

Liu Mingchuan 劉銘傳 (1836–1896)

Lu Shiyi 陸世儀 (1611–1672)

Luo Dian 羅典 (1719–1808)

Ma Taihe 馬泰和

Ma Xinyi 馬新貽 (1821–1870)

Mao-sha-er 毛沙爾

Mao Xianglin 毛祥麟

Mian shu 棉書

mu 畝

Mumian pu 木棉譜

neidi 內地

Nongshu 農書

Nongzheng quanshu 農政全書

Pan Zengyi 潘曾沂 (1792–1852)

Pei Jingfu 裴景福 (1854–1926)

pengmin 棚民

Pucun 樸存

Pucun ge nongshu 樸存閣農書

qi 氣

Qianlong 乾隆 (r. 1736–1795)

Qimin yaoshu 齊民要術

Qinding huangyu xiyu tuzhi 欽定皇輿西域圖志

Qinding Xinjiang shilüe 欽定新疆識略

qingfu ju 清賦局

Qi-shi-yi 七十一

Quan-qing 全慶 (?–1882)

qutian fa 區田法

Qutian zhong fa 區田種法

sangmian ju 桑棉局

shanhou ju 善後局

Shen Bingcheng 沈秉成 (1823–1895)

Shen Yao 沈垚 (1798–1840)

sheng 升

Shengnü chuan 聖女川

shengsang 生桑
Shengshi weiyan 盛世危言
Shengyu 聖諭
Shengyu chuan 聖諭川
shixue 實學
Song-yun 松筠 (1754–1835)
Sunzi bingfa 孫子兵法
Tan Jixun 譚繼洵 (1823–1901)
Tang Jian 唐鑑 (1777–1861)
Tan Zhonglin 譚鍾麟 (1822–1905)
Tao Shu 陶澍 (1778–1839)
Te-yi-shun-bao 特依順保 (1768–1840)
tiandi ziran zhi li 天地自然之利
Tianxia junguo libing shu 天下郡國利病書
Tie-mu-er 鐵木爾
tongshan ju 同善局
Tongzhi 同治 (r. 1862–1874)
tunken zongju 屯墾總局
tuntian 屯田
Wang Shiduo 汪士鐸 (1802–1889)
Wang Zhen 王禎 (fl. 1290–1333)
Wei Guangtao 魏光燾 (1837–?)
Wei Yuan 魏源 (1794–1856)
weilü 尾閭
Wu Qijun 吳其濬 (1789–1847)
Wu-long-a 武隆阿 (?–1831)
Xianfeng 咸豐 (r. 1851–1861)
xiangdao 鄉導
Xiangyin xianzhi 湘陰縣志
Xia xiao zheng 夏小正
xinzheng 新政
Xiyu shuidao ji 西域水道記
Xiyu tuzhi 西域圖志
Xu Guangqi 徐光啟 (1562–1633)
Xu Song 徐松 (1781–1848)
Xunzi 荀子
yang can 養蠶
Yang Changjun 楊昌濬 (?–1897)
yang min 養民
yang sheng 養生
yesang 野桑

yili 遺利

yimin shibian 移民實邊

yixin 異心

Yongzheng 雍正 (r. 1723–1735)

Yu can shuo 育蠶說

Yu Zhi 余治 (1809–1874)

Yuelu Academy 岳麓書院

yujiang 腴疆

Yu-su-pu 玉蘇普

yuzhuma 裕珠瑪

Zhang Peilun 張佩綸 (1848–1903)

Zhang Yao 張曜 (1832–1891)

Zhang Ying 張英 (1637–1708)

Zheng Guanying 鄭觀應 (1842–1922)

Zhong mian shi yao 種棉十要

Zhongguo weilü 中國尾閭

Zhou Tingfen 周廷芬

Zhou Yiduan 周詒端 (1812–1870)

Zhu Yingtao 祝應橐

Zhuangzi 莊子

ziran zhi li 自然之利

Zi-ya-bu-dong 子牙不動

zulei 族類

Zuo Zongtang 左宗棠 (1812–1885)

Abbreviations

For sources

CBYWSM	*Chouban yiwu shimo*
FHA–GCA	Grand Council copies of memorials (*Junjichu lufu zouzhe*), First Historical Archives, Beijing
FHA–QPA	Rescripted palace memorials (*Gongzhong zhupi zouzhe*), First Historical Archives, Beijing
HJWB	He Changling, ed., *Huangchao jingshi wenbian*
LXGZ	Liu Jintang, *Liu Xiangqin gong zougao*
NPM–GCA	Memorials in the Grand Council archives (*Junjichu dang zhejian*), National Palace Museum, Taipei
QXDX	*Qingdai Xinjiang dang'an xuanji*
XUARA	Xinjiang Uyghur Autonomous Region Archives, Urumchi
ZWGN	Luo Zhengjun, ed., *Zuo Wenxiang gong nianpu*
ZZQJ	Zuo Zongtang, *Zuo Zongtang quanji*

For reign periods

KX	Kangxi (1662–1722)
YZ	Yongzheng (1723–35)

QL	Qianlong (1736–95)
JQ	Jiaqing (1796–1820)
DG	Daoguang (1821–50)
XF	Xianfeng (1851–61)
TZ	Tongzhi (1862–74)
GX	Guangxu (1875–1908)

Notes

Introduction

1. Wang Shiduo, *Wang Huiweng yibing riji*, 3 *juan* (n.p., 1936), 3.28a.
2. Wang, *Wang Huiweng yibing riji*, 3.26b; Frank Dikötter, "The Limits of Benevolence: Wang Shiduo (1802–1889) and Population Control," *Bulletin of the School of Oriental and African Studies* 55, no. 1 (February 1992): 112. On Wang, also see Chuck Wooldridge, *City of Virtues: Nanjing in an Age of Utopian Visions* (Seattle: University of Washington Press, 2015), 88–116; Wang Fansen, *Zhongguo jindai sixiang yu xueshu de xipu* (Taipei: Lianjing, 2003), 80–87; Arthur W. Hummel, ed., *Eminent Chinese of the Ch'ing Period (1644–1912)*, 2 vols. (Washington, DC: Government Printing Office, 1943), 834–35.
3. Hummel, ed., *Eminent Chinese of the Ch'ing Period*, 242.
4. Feng Guifen, *Jiaobinlu kangyi*, 2 *juan* (n.p., 1884), xia.45b. This translation is from Ssu-yü Teng and John K. Fairbank, eds., *China's Response to the West: A Documentary Survey, 1839–1923* (New York: Atheneum, 1971), 55.
5. Feng, *Jiaobinlu kangyi*, xia.2b.
6. Weitang zuoshuzhang, "Zhong xi pinfu qiangruo bian," *Shenbao*, October 16, 1876. Similar statements may be found in the works of prominent late Qing scholars. For example, see Zheng Guanying, *Shengshi weiyan houbian*, 15 *juan* (n.p., 1921), 6.7a.
7. James Z. Lee and Wang Feng, *One Quarter of Humanity: Malthusian Mythology and Chinese Realities, 1700–2000* (Cambridge, MA: Harvard University Press,

1999), 27; Ping-ti Ho, *Studies on the Population of China, 1368–1953* (Cambridge, MA: Harvard University Press, 1959), 64.

8. For examples of eyewitness accounts, see Anne Osborne, "Highlands and Lowlands: Economic and Ecological Interactions in the Lower Yangzi Region under the Qing," in *Sediments of Time: Environment and Society in Chinese History*, ed. Mark Elvin and Liu Ts'ui-jung (Cambridge: Cambridge University Press, 1998), 216–19; Christian Daniels, "Environmental Degradation, Forest Protection and Ethno-History in Yunnan: (I) The Uprising by Swidden Agriculturalists in 1821," *Chinese Environmental History Newsletter* 1, no. 2 (November 1994): 9.

9. Jiayan Zhang, *Coping with Calamity: Environmental Change and Peasant Response in Central China, 1736–1949* (Vancouver: University of British Columbia Press, 2014); Peter C. Perdue, *Exhausting the Earth: State and Peasant in Hunan, 1500–1850* (Cambridge, MA: Council on East Asian Studies, Harvard University, 1987); Osborne, "Highlands and Lowlands," 216–22.

10. R. Keith Schoppa, *Song Full of Tears: Nine Centuries of Chinese Life at Xiang Lake* (Boulder: Westview, 2002); Micah S. Muscolino, *Fishing Wars and Environmental Change in Late Imperial and Modern China* (Cambridge, MA: Harvard University Asia Center, 2009).

11. Jonathan Schlesinger, *A World Trimmed with Fur: Wild Things, Pristine Places, and the Natural Fringes of Qing Rule* (Stanford, CA: Stanford University Press, 2017); David A. Bello, *Across Forest, Steppe, and Mountain: Environment, Identity, and Empire in Qing China's Borderlands* (Cambridge: Cambridge University Press, 2016).

12. Robert B. Marks, *Tigers, Rice, Silk, and Silt: Environment and Economy in Late Imperial South China* (Cambridge: Cambridge University Press, 1998), 320; Kenneth Pomeranz, *The Making of a Hinterland: State, Society, and Economy in Inland North China, 1853–1937* (Berkeley: University of California Press, 1993), 123–37; S. A. M. Adshead, "An Energy Crisis in Early Modern China," *Ch'ing-shih wen-t'i* 3, no. 2 (December 1974): 20–28.

13. Lillian Li has written of "environmental decline" and an "ecological crisis of the nineteenth century." See Lillian M. Li, *Fighting Famine in North China: State, Market, and Environmental Decline, 1690s–1990s* (Stanford, CA: Stanford University Press, 2007), 3–4, 73. Robert Marks has argued that "environmental crisis" should be added to the list of "social, political, and intellectual crises that wracked China in the second half of the nineteenth century and helped to define what modern China was to become." See Marks, *Tigers, Rice, Silk, and Silt*, 333.

14. Feng, *Jiaobinlu kangyi, shang*.28a.

15. Zuo Zongtang to Zongli Yamen, GX 3, *ZZQJ*, 12:205.

16. William T. Rowe, *China's Last Empire: The Great Qing* (Cambridge, MA: Belknap Press of Harvard University Press, 2009), 150.

17. Pomeranz, *The Making of a Hinterland*, 3. See also Stephen R. Halsey, *Quest for Power: European Imperialism and the Making of Chinese Statecraft* (Cambridge, MA: Harvard University Press, 2015), 5–6.

18. Qing officials established these institutions during what has become known as the Self-Strengthening Movement. On this movement, see Ting-yee Kuo and Kwang-Ching Liu, "Self-Strengthening: The Pursuit of Western Technology," in *The Cambridge History of China*, vol. 10, *Late Ch'ing, 1800–1911*, pt. 1, ed. John K. Fairbank (Cambridge: Cambridge University Press, 1978), 491–542; and R. Bin Wong, "Self-Strengthening and Other Political Responses to the Expansion of European Economic and Political Power," in *The Cambridge World History*, vol. 7, *Production, Destruction, and Connection, 1750-Present*, pt. 1, *Structures, Spaces, and Boundary Making*, ed. J. R. McNeill and Kenneth Pomeranz (Cambridge: Cambridge University Press, 2015), 366–94.

19. For examples of scholarship on the administrative and ethnic pluralism of the Qing empire, see the essays in Pamela Kyle Crossley, Helen F. Siu, and Donald S. Sutton, eds., *Empire at the Margins: Culture, Ethnicity, and Frontier in Early Modern China* (Berkeley: University of California Press, 2006).

20. Edward B. Vermeer, "Population and Ecology along the Frontier in Qing China," in Elvin and Liu, *Sediments of Time*, 239–40. See also Schlesinger, *A World Trimmed with Fur*; Bello, *Across Forest, Steppe, and Mountain*; and Seonmin Kim, *Ginseng and Borderland: Territorial Boundaries and Political Relations between Qing China and Chosŏn Korea, 1636–1912* (Oakland: University of California Press, 2017).

21. For works on this field of scholarship, see Laura Hostetler, *Qing Colonial Enterprise: Ethnography and Cartography in Early Modern China* (Chicago: University of Chicago Press, 2001); Emma Jinhua Teng, *Taiwan's Imagined Geography: Chinese Colonial Travel Writing and Pictures, 1683–1895* (Cambridge, MA: Harvard University Asia Center, 2004); Hou Deren, *Qingdai xibei bianjiang shidi xue* (Beijing: Qunyan chubanshe, 2006); Guo Liping, *Jueyu yu juexue: Qingdai zhongye xibei shidi xue yanjiu* (Beijing: Sanlian shudian, 2007); and Jia Jianfei, *Qingdai xibei shidi xue yanjiu* (Urumchi: Xinjiang renmin chubanshe, 2010).

22. On the intertwining of ideas about resource scarcity and abundance in European thought, see Fredrik Albritton Jonsson, "The Origins of Cornucopianism: A Preliminary Genealogy," *Critical Historical Studies* 1, no. 1 (Spring 2014): 159–60.

23. John L. Rawlinson, *China's Struggle for Naval Development, 1839–1895* (Cambridge, MA: Harvard University Press, 1967), 38–39; Steven A. Leibo, *Transferring Technology to China: Prosper Giquel and the Self-Strengthening Movement*

(Berkeley: Institute of East Asian Studies, University of California, 1985), 75; David Pong, *Shen Pao-chen and China's Modernization in the Nineteenth Century* (Cambridge: Cambridge University Press, 1994), 109–12.

24. Douglas Reynolds has defined the nineteenth-century bureau (*ju*) as a "temporary or ad hoc agency outside of the formal bureaucracy and statutory budget." See Douglas R. Reynolds, *East Meets East: Chinese Discover the Modern World in Japan, 1854–1898* (Ann Arbor, MI: Association for Asian Studies, 2014), 668–69. On this type of institution, see also William T. Rowe, *Hankow: Commerce and Society in a Chinese City, 1796–1889* (Stanford, CA: Stanford University Press, 1984), 35–36; Kathryn Bernhardt, *Rents, Taxes, and Peasant Resistance: The Lower Yangzi Region, 1840–1950* (Stanford, CA: Stanford University Press, 1992), 122–23; and Susan Mann, *Local Merchants and the Chinese Bureaucracy, 1750-1950* (Stanford, CA: Stanford University Press, 1987), 110.

25. Hubu, "Kaiyuan jieliu shiyi ershisi tiao," in *Huangchao jingshi wen xu bian*, 120 *juan*, ed. Ge Shijun (Baoshan shuju, 1896), 26.4a-b.

26. James C. Scott, *Seeing Like a State: How Certain Schemes to Improve the Human Condition Have Failed* (New Haven, CT: Yale University Press, 1998), 219; Paul R. Josephson, *Resources under Regimes: Technology, Environment, and the State* (Cambridge, MA: Harvard University Press, 2005), 30–31; Arun Agrawal, *Environmentality: Technologies of Government and the Making of Subjects* (Durham, NC: Duke University Press, 2005), 12.

27. For an example, see Agrawal, *Environmentality*, 48–49.

28. On this period of reform and state building, see Douglas R. Reynolds, *China, 1898–1912: The Xinzheng Revolution and Japan* (Cambridge, MA: Council on East Asian Studies, Harvard University, 1993).

29. Francesca Bray, "Science, Technique, Technology: Passages between Matter and Knowledge in Imperial Chinese Agriculture," *British Journal for the History of Science* 41, no. 3 (September 2008): 343. On the dissemination of agricultural technology in late imperial China, see also Timothy Brook, "Growing Rice in North Zhili," in *The Chinese State in Ming Society* (London: Routledge-Curzon, 2005), 94–96; William T. Rowe, "Political, Social, and Economic Factors Affecting the Transmission of Technical Knowledge in Early Modern China," in *Cultures of Knowledge: Technology in Chinese History*, ed. Dagmar Schäfer (Leiden: Brill, 2012), 26–30; and Francesca Bray, "Chinese Literati and the Transmission of Technological Knowledge: The Case of Agriculture," in Schäfer, *Cultures of Knowledge*, 299–325.

30. On the distribution of vegetable seeds in this period, see Peter Lavelle, "The Aesthetics and Politics of Chinese Horticulture in Late Qing Borderlands," in *Environmental History in East Asia: Interdisciplinary Perspectives*, ed. Ts'ui-jung Liu (London: Routledge, 2014), 227–28.

31. In the past, this story was given greater validity by a historical paradigm that took China's inability to develop modern science and technology on its own as the crux of its modern predicament. For examples, see Ho, *Studies on the Population of China*, 204–6; Joseph Needham, *The Grand Titration: Science and Society in East and West* (London: George Allen & Unwin, 1969), 16; and Mark Elvin, *The Pattern of the Chinese Past* (Stanford, CA: Stanford University Press, 1973), 203–4. Much has been written on the problematic nature of these paradigms. For example, see Nathan Sivin's widely circulated "Why the Scientific Revolution Did Not Take Place in China—Or Didn't It?," *Chinese Science* 5 (June 1982): 45–66.

32. On the history of science in this period, see Benjamin A. Elman, *On Their Own Terms: Science in China, 1550–1900* (Cambridge, MA: Harvard University Press, 2005).

33. Gideon Chen, *Tso Tsung T'ang: Pioneer Promoter of the Modern Dockyard and the Woollen Mill in China* (Beijing: Department of Economics, Yenching University, 1938), 49–76.

34. Daniel R. Headrick, *The Tentacles of Progress: Technology Transfer in the Age of Imperialism, 1850–1940* (New York: Oxford University Press, 1988), 261–62; James Beattie, "Eco-Cultural Networks in Southern China and Colonial New Zealand: Cantonese Market Gardening and Environmental Exchange, 1860s–1910s," in *Eco-Cultural Networks and the British Empire: New Views on Environmental History*, ed. James Beattie, Edward Melillo, and Emily O'Gorman (London: Bloomsbury Academic, 2015), 159–60.

35. Such machines no doubt played a critical role in transforming relationships on a global scale. See Daniel R. Headrick, *The Tools of Empire: Technology and European Imperialism in the Nineteenth Century* (Oxford: Oxford University Press, 1981); and Michael Adas, *Machines as the Measure of Men: Science, Technology, and Ideologies of Western Dominance* (Ithaca, NY: Cornell University Press, 1989). Francesca Bray has explored the problematic nature of histories of technology that focus on such revolutionary moments. See Francesca Bray, "Towards a Critical History of Non-Western Technology," in *China and Historical Capitalism: Genealogies of Sinological Knowledge*, ed. Timothy Brook and Gregory Blue (Cambridge: Cambridge University Press, 1999), 160–61.

36. On Qing rule in Xinjiang in earlier periods, see James A. Millward, *Beyond the Pass: Economy, Ethnicity, and Empire in Qing Central Asia, 1759–1864* (Stanford, CA: Stanford University Press, 1998); Peter C. Perdue, *China Marches West: The Qing Conquest of Central Eurasia* (Cambridge, MA: Belknap Press of Harvard University Press, 2005); and Kwangmin Kim, *Borderland Capitalism: Turkestan Produce, Qing Silver, and the Birth of an Eastern Market* (Stanford, CA: Stanford University Press, 2016).

37. For examples of studies that explore the influence of foreign colonialism on Chinese society, see James L. Hevia, *English Lessons: The Pedagogy of Imperialism in Nineteenth-Century China* (Durham, NC: Duke University Press, 2003); and Ruth Rogaski, *Hygienic Modernity: Meanings of Health and Disease in Treaty-Port China* (Berkeley: University of California Press, 2004).

38. Zheng, *Shengshi weiyan houbian*, 6.8a; *Xinjiang tuzhi*, 116 *juan*, ed. Yuan Dahua (Tianjin: Dongfang xuehui, 1923; reprint, Shanghai: Shanghai guji chubanshe, 1996), 29.16a.

39. Edward B. Barbier, *Scarcity and Frontiers: How Economies Have Developed through Natural Resource Exploitation* (Cambridge: Cambridge University Press, 2011), 369. On environmental history in this period, see Corey Ross, *Ecology and Power in the Age of Empire: Europe and the Transformation of the Tropical World* (Oxford: Oxford University Press, 2017).

40. James Belich, *Replenishing the Earth: The Settler Revolution and the Rise of the Anglo-World, 1783–1939* (Oxford: Oxford University Press, 2009), 394; John C. Weaver, *The Great Land Rush and the Making of the Modern World, 1650–1900* (Montreal: McGill-Queen's University Press, 2003), 311–13.

41. For several studies of the British case, see Michael Havinden and David Meredith, *Colonialism and Development: Britain and Its Tropical Colonies, 1850–1960* (London: Routledge, 1993); and Joseph Morgan Hodge, *Triumph of the Expert: Agrarian Doctrines of Development and the Legacies of British Colonialism* (Athens: Ohio University Press, 2007).

42. On the global "developmentalist project," see Kenneth Pomeranz, "Introduction: World History and Environmental History," in *The Environment and World History*, ed. Edmund Burke III and Kenneth Pomeranz (Berkeley: University of California Press, 2009), 3–32. Similar comparisons have been extended to the case of the late Ottoman empire. See Jacob Norris, *Land of Progress: Palestine in the Age of Colonial Development, 1905–1948* (Oxford: Oxford University Press, 2013), 15–17.

43. For records of such disasters, see Li Wenhai et al., *Jindai Zhongguo zaihuang jinian* (Changsha: Hunan jiaoyu chubanshe, 1990); Li Wenhai et al., *Zhongguo jindai shi da zaihuang* (Shanghai: Shanghai renmin chubanshe, 1994); and Tan Xuming, ed., *Qingdai ganhan dang'an shiliao*, 2 vols. (Beijing: Zhongguo shuji chubanshe, 2013).

44. Andrew C. Isenberg, *The Destruction of the Bison: An Environmental History, 1750–1920* (Cambridge: Cambridge University Press, 2000), 11–12, 195–96. For an analysis of the origins of ideas about disorder in nature, see Donald Worster, "The Ecology of Order and Chaos," in *The Wealth of Nature: Environmental History and the Ecological Imagination* (Oxford: Oxford University Press, 1993), 156–70.

1. Agriculture in an Era of Crisis

1. Hummel, ed., *Eminent Chinese of the Ch'ing Period*, 762.
2. *ZWGN*, 1.7a.
3. *Xiangyin xianzhi*, 39 *juan*, ed. Weng Yuanqi (n.p., 1823), *shou*.3b.
4. *Xiangyin xianzhi* (1823), *fanli*.2a. For the image, see *Xiangyin xianzhi* (1823), 2.25b–26a. Note that a different version of this image appeared in an earlier edition of the gazetteer. See *Xiangyin xianzhi*, 32 *juan*, ed. Chen Zhongli and Yang Maolun (n.p., 1757; reprint, Haikou: Hainan chubanshe, 2001), 1.14b–15a.
5. Zuo to sons, TZ 11/11/22, *ZZQJ*, 13:176; Zuo Zongzhi, *Shen'an wen chao*, 2 *juan* (n.p., 1875), *shang*.22a.
6. Perdue, *Exhausting the Earth*, 197–233; Kang Chao, *Man and Land in Chinese History: An Economic Analysis* (Stanford, CA: Stanford University Press, 1986), 204–5.
7. Fu Shaohui and Liu Chunyang, eds., *Hunan nongye shi* (Changsha: Hunan renmin chubanshe, 2012), 414.
8. *Xiangyin xianzhi* (1823), 17.2b.
9. *Xiangyin xian tuzhi*, 34 *juan*, ed. Guo Songtao (Xiangyin xianzhiju, 1880), 29.5a, 29.8b; Yang Pengcheng, *Hunan zaihuang shi* (Changsha: Yuelu shushe, 2008), 147, 152, 163, 169, 183; Tan, ed., *Qingdai ganhan dang'an shiliao*, 524–29.
10. Shuji Cao, Yushang Li, and Bin Yang, "Mt. Tambora, Climatic Changes, and China's Decline in the Nineteenth Century," *Journal of World History* 23, no. 3 (September 2012): 596–603; Marks, *Tigers, Rice, Silk, and Silt*, 197–99.
11. Jürgen Osterhammel, *The Transformation of the World: A Global History of the Nineteenth Century* (Princeton, NJ: Princeton University Press, 2014), 205–6.
12. Li Bozhong, "The 'Daoguang Depression' and the 'Guiwei Great Flood': Economic Decline and Climatic Cataclysm in Early Nineteenth-Century Songjiang in a New Perspective," *Études chinoises* 34, no. 2 (2015): 89–119; Li Bozhong, "19 shiji Jiangnan de jingji xiaotiao yu qihou bianhua," in *Zhongguo lishi shang de huanjing yu shehui*, ed. Wang Lihua (Beijing: Sanlian shudian, 2007), 117–25.
13. Richard von Glahn, *The Economic History of China: From Antiquity to the Nineteenth Century* (Cambridge: Cambridge University Press, 2016), 364–65.
14. Man-houng Lin, *China Upside Down: Currency, Society, and Ideologies, 1808–1856* (Cambridge, MA: Harvard University Asia Center, 2006), 2–4; Richard von Glahn, "Cycles of Silver in Chinese Monetary History," in *The Economy of Lower Yangzi Delta in Late Imperial China: Connecting Money, Markets, and Institutions*, ed. Billy K. L. So (London: Routledge, 2013), 55.

15. Lin, *China Upside Down*, 124–33; Perdue, *Exhausting the Earth*, 238–39; Wang Jiping, *Wan Qing Hunan shi* (Changsha: Hunan renmin chubanshe, 2004), 25; R. Bin Wong, *China Transformed: Historical Change and the Limits of the European Experience* (Ithaca, NY: Cornell University Press, 1997), 238–44; Ho-fung Hung, *Protest with Chinese Characteristics: Demonstrations, Riots, and Petitions in the Mid-Qing Dynasty* (New York: Columbia University Press, 2011), 135. On the connection to environmental crisis, see Zhang Yanli, *Jia Dao shiqi de zai- huang yu shehui* (Beijing: Renmin chubanshe, 2008), 76–78.

16. Benjamin A. Elman, *A Cultural History of Civil Examinations in Late Imperial China* (Berkeley: University of California Press, 2000), 191.

17. *ZWGN*, 1.14a, 1.18b.

18. On practical learning, see Chen Guying, Xin Guanjie, and Ge Rongjin, eds., *Ming Qing shixue sichao shi*, 3 vols. (Jinan: Qi Lu shushe, 1989); Chen Guying, Xin Guanjie, and Ge Rongjin, eds., *Ming Qing shixue jianshi* (Beijing: Shehui kexue wenxian chubanshe, 1994); Lü Yuancong and Ge Rongjin, *Qingdai shehui yu shixue* (Hong Kong: Xianggang daxue chubanshe, 2000).

19. Geoffrey Parker, *Global Crisis: War, Climate Change and Catastrophe in the Sev- enteenth Century* (New Haven, CT: Yale University Press, 2013).

20. Timothy Brook, *The Troubled Empire: China in the Yuan and Ming Dynasties* (Cambridge, MA: Belknap Press of Harvard University Press, 2010), 242–55; Parker, *Global Crisis*, 115–51.

21. The emergence of practical learning in China may have reflected a more general trend among intellectual elites worldwide, who pursued new forms of scholarship as they dealt with the aftermath of the social and political crises of the Little Ice Age. For this argument, see Parker, *Global Crisis*, 647–53.

22. For a survey of evidential learning, see Benjamin A. Elman, *From Philosophy to Philology: Intellectual and Social Aspects of Change in Late Imperial China* (Cam- bridge, MA: Council on East Asian Studies, Harvard University, 1984).

23. Liang Qichao, *Qingdai xueshu gailun* (Shanghai, 1921; reprint, Taipei: Shangwu yinshuguan, 2008), 14. This translation is from Liang Ch'i-ch'ao, *Intellectual Trends in the Ch'ing Period*, trans. Immanuel C. Y. Hsü (Cambridge, MA: Har- vard University Press, 1959), 31.

24. Peng Minghui, *Wan Qing de jingshi shixue* (Taipei: Maitian, 2002), 5.

25. Elman, *On Their Own Terms*.

26. Susan Mann and Philip A. Kuhn, "Dynastic Decline and the Roots of Rebellion," in Fairbank, *Late Ch'ing*, 146–54; Benjamin Elman, "Ch'ing Dynasty 'Schools' of Scholarship," *Ch'ing-shih wen-t'i* 4, no. 6 (December 1981): 33–34.

27. Daniel McMahon, "The Yuelu Academy and Hunan's Nineteenth-Century Turn toward Statecraft," *Late Imperial China* 26, no. 1 (June 2005): 79;

William T. Rowe, *Saving the World: Chen Hongmou and Elite Consciousness in Eighteenth-Century China* (Stanford, CA: Stanford University Press, 2001), 148–51.

28. McMahon, "The Yuelu Academy," 84.

29. For an overview, see Frederic Wakeman, "The Huang-ch'ao ching-shih wen-pien," *Ch'ing-shih wen-t'i* 1, no. 10 (February 1969): 8–22.

30. Benjamin A. Elman,"The Relevance of Sung Learning in the Late Ch'ing: Wei Yuan and the Huang-ch'ao ching-shih wen-pien," *Late Imperial China* 9, no. 2 (December 1988): 58.

31. *ZWGN*, 1.7b–8a.

32. Zuo, DG 18, *ZZQJ*, 13:446.

33. Zuo, GX 13, *ZZQJ*, 13:408; Zuo, GX 15, *ZZQJ*, 13:420.

34. Francesca Bray, *Technology and Gender: Fabrics of Power in Late Imperial China* (Berkeley: University of California Press, 1997), 32n54.

35. Susan Mann, *Precious Records: Women in China's Long Eighteenth Century* (Stanford, CA: Stanford University Press, 1997), 148.

36. Peng Yuxin, ed., *Qingdai tudi kaiken shi ziliao huibian* (Wuhan: Wuhan daxue chubanshe, 1992), 1–8.

37. Bray, "Chinese Literati and the Transmission of Technological Knowledge," 299–325; Bray, "Science, Technique, Technology," 319–44; Rowe, "Political, Social and Economic Factors Affecting the Transmission of Technical Knowledge in Early Modern China," 27–30.

38. For overviews of premodern agricultural scholarship in China, see Francesca Bray, *Agriculture*, vol. 6, pt. 2, *Science and Civilisation in China*, ed. Joseph Needham (Cambridge: Cambridge University Press, 1984), 47–85; Zeng Xiongsheng, *Zhongguo nongxue shi*, revised ed. (Fuzhou: Fujian renmin chubanshe, 2012); and Wang Yuhu, *Zhongguo nongxue shulu* (Beijing: Zhonghua shuju, 2006).

39. On the multiplication, specialization, and regionalization of agricultural texts in this period, see Zhang Yan, *17–19 shiji Zhongguo de renkou yu shengcun huanjing* (Hefei: Huangshan shushe, 2008), 193–95; You Xiuling, *Nongshi yanjiu wenji* (Beijing: Zhongguo nongye chubanshe, 1999), 228–31; and Zeng, *Zhongguo nongxue shi*, 455–57.

40. Zuo, DG 18, *ZZQJ*, 13:446.

41. On Xu's ideas about agriculture as the source of wealth, see Richard von Glahn, *Fountain of Fortune: Money and Monetary Policy in China, 1000–1700* (Berkeley: University of California Press, 1996), 199–200. On the relationship between natural disasters and Xu's agricultural research, see Zeng Xiongsheng, "'Gao xiang li wen': yi ze xin faxian de Xu Guangqi yiwen ji qi jiedu," *Ziran kexue shi yanjiu* 29, no. 1 (2010): 1–12.

42. Xu Guangqi, *Nongzheng quanshu*, 60 *juan*, annot. Shi Shenghan (Shanghai: Shanghai guji chubanshe, 2011). For an overview of Xu's work, see Zeng, *Zhongguo nongxue shi*, 554–57.

43. Francesca Bray and Georges Métailié, "Who Was the Author of the *Nongzheng quanshu*?," in *Statecraft and Intellectual Renewal in Late Ming China: The Cross-Cultural Synthesis of Xu Guangqi (1562–1633)*, ed. Catherine Jami, Peter Engelfriet, and Gregory Blue (Leiden: Brill, 2001), 351–56.

44. Xiao Kezhi, *Nongye guji banben congtan* (Beijing: Zhongguo nongye chubanshe, 2007), 73; Ren Shusen, preface to *Nongzheng quanshu*, by Xu Guangqi, annot. Shi Shenghan (Shanghai: Shanghai guji chubanshe, 2011), 1470.

45. Zuo, DG 18, *ZZQJ*, 13:446.

46. Zuo, Memorial, GX 3/3/29, *ZZQJ*, 6:637; *ZWGN*, 1.16a.

47. Bray, *Agriculture*, 61; William Y. Chen, *An Annotated Bibliography of Chinese Agriculture* (San Francisco: Chinese Materials Center Publications, 1993), 14–15; Zeng, *Zhongguo nongxue shi*, 358.

48. Zeng, *Zhongguo nongxue shi*, 493–94.

49. Zuo, DG 18, *ZZQJ*, 13:446.

50. T'ung-tsu Ch'ü, *Local Government in China under the Ch'ing* (Stanford, CA: Stanford University Press, 1962), 21–22, 320n28.

51. Zuo, DG 18, *ZZQJ*, 13:446.

52. Zuo, DG 18, *ZZQJ*, 13:447.

53. Yang Bojun, ed., *Lunyu yizhu*, 3rd ed. (Beijing: Zhonghua shuju, 2009), 133 (13.4). Other early Chinese thinkers discussed the utility of consulting locals for insights about land use owing to their deep understanding of places and environments. For example, Sunzi advised readers of his *Art of War* (*Sunzi bingfa*) to consult with "native guides" (*xiangdao*) if they wanted to maximize their ability to use terrain in strategic ways. See Li Ling, ed., *Sunzi yizhu*, 2nd ed. (Beijing: Zhonghua shuju, 2009), 115 (11.11).

54. On experiential knowledge, see Carla Nappi, *The Monkey and the Inkpot: Natural History and Its Transformations in Early Modern China* (Cambridge, MA: Harvard University Press, 2009), 34, 174n7; Willard Peterson, "Confucian Learning in Late Ming Thought," in *The Cambridge History of China*, vol. 8, *The Ming Dynasty, 1368–1644*, pt. 2, ed. Dennis Twitchett and Frederick Mote (Cambridge: Cambridge University Press, 1998), 781–84; and Dagmar Schäfer, *The Crafting of the 10,000 Things: Knowledge and Technology in Seventeenth-Century China* (Chicago: University of Chicago Press, 2011), 133–34.

55. The seventeenth-century literatus Gu Zuyu followed Sunzi's lead in asserting that native guides were an indispensable source of information for outsiders who sought to know about geography, topography, and landforms in particular places but who possessed no more than a textual—and thus only partial—understanding of how to use land to their advantage. Gu made

such assertions in his *Essentials of Geography for Reading History* (*Dushi fangyu jiyao*), a work that Zuo purchased in 1829. See Gu Zuyu, *Dushi fangyu jiyao*, 130 *juan* (n.p., 1811; reprint, Shanghai: Zhonghua shuju, 1955), 11, 14; *ZWGN*, 1.7a.

56. Zuo, DG 18, *ZZQJ*, 13:446.

57. Zuo to Zhou Yiduan, DG 18, *ZZQJ*, 15:247–48.

58. Zuo to Zhou Ruchong, DG 25/1/19, *ZZQJ*, 15:53; Zuo to Hu Linyi, DG 25/1/19, in Zuo Zongtang, *Zuo Zongtang weikan shudu*, comp. Ren Guangliang and Zhu Zhongyue (Changsha: Yuelu shushe, 1989), 2.

59. Zuo, GX 7/1, *ZZQJ*, 13:266; *ZWGN*, 1.1b.

60. Zhang Ying, *Hengchan suoyan* (Jinhe guangrentang, 1882), 5a, 7b–8a; Hilary J. Beattie, *Land and Lineage in China: A Study of T'ung-ch'eng County, Anhwei, in the Ming and Ch'ing Dynasties* (Cambridge: Cambridge University Press, 1979), 144, 146–47.

61. Zhang Ying, "Hengchan suoyan," in *HJWB*, 36.42a–47b.

62. *ZWGN*, 1.10a.

63. Zuo to He Xiling, DG 21, *ZZQJ*, 10:30.

64. Zuo to Zuo Zongzhi, DG 22, *ZZQJ*, 15:252. See also Zuo to He Xiling, DG 22, *ZZQJ*, 10:34; and Zuo to He Xiling, DG 24, *ZZQJ*, 10:46.

65. Zuo to He Xiling, DG 22, *ZZQJ*, 10:35.

66. Zuo to Zuo Zongzhi, DG 22, *ZZQJ*, 15:252; Zuo to Zhang Shengjie, DG 24, *ZZQJ*, 15:41; *ZWGN*, 1.21b–22a.

67. Beattie, *Land and Lineage in China*, 12, 36.

68. Yin Hongqun, *Hunan chuantong shanglu* (Changsha: Hunan shifan daxue chubanshe, 2010), 75–76.

69. *Xiangyin xianzhi* (1823), 17.3a; Yin, *Hunan chuantong shanglu*, 102.

70. Zuo to He Xiling, DG 22, *ZZQJ*, 10:34.

71. Zuo to He Xiling, DG 21, *ZZQJ*, 10:27.

72. Perdue, *Exhausting the Earth*, 100; Chen Xi, *Wan Qing Hunan zibenzhuyi yanjiu* (Changsha: Hunan renmin chubanshe, 2006), 51; Yin, *Hunan chuantong shanglu*, 216–27; Fu and Liu, eds., *Hunan nongye shi*, 435.

73. Zuo to He Xiling, DG 22, *ZZQJ*, 10:35.

74. Zuo to Zhang Shengjie, DG 26, *ZZQJ*, 15:54; Zuo to Zhou Ruchong, DG 26/2/29, *ZZQJ*, 15:48; *ZWGN*, 1.22b–23a.

75. Zuo to Zhou Yiduan, DG 18, *ZZQJ*, 15:248; *ZWGN*, 1.16a.

76. He Xiling, *Hanxiangguan shi chao*, 4 *juan* (n.p., 1848), 4.3b; *ZWGN*, 1.17a, 1.18b.

77. Zuo to Zhou Yiduan, DG 18, *ZZQJ*, 15:248.

78. Luo Ruhuai, *Lüyi caotang shiji*, 20 *juan* (Changsha, 1883), 12.10a; *ZWGN*, 1.17b; Zuo, "Er shi jiu sui zi ti xiao xiang ba shou," DG 20, *ZZQJ*, 13:458.

79. Zuo to Li Guangshu, DG 20, *ZZQJ*, 10:22.

80. Zuo to Zhou Ruchong, DG 20/4/27, *ZZQJ*, 15:33. See also Zuo to Zhou Yiduan, DG 18, *ZZQJ*, 15:248; and Zuo to He Xiling, DG 21, *ZZQJ*, 10:28.

81. Xu, *Nongzheng quanshu*, 98; Wang Xinjing, "Qutian putian shuo," in *HJWB*, 36.35b. On crop yields in Jiangnan, see Bozhong Li, *Agricultural Development in Jiangnan, 1620–1850* (New York: St. Martin's, 1998), 122–32.

82. Cho-yun Hsu, *Han Agriculture: The Formation of Early Chinese Agrarian Economy (206 B.C.-A.D. 220)*, ed. Jack L. Dull (Seattle: University of Washington Press, 1980), 117; Zeng, *Zhongguo nongxue shi*, 191.

83. Sun Zhaikui, "Qutian shuo," Wang Xinjing, "Qutian putian shuo," and Lu Shiyi, "Lun qutian," in *HJWB*, 36.33a–41b.

84. Tang Jian, the Guizhou provincial judge at the time, wrote a preface to He's work, which was entitled *Cultivation Methods of Plot Farming (Qutian zhong fa)*. See Tang Jian, *Tang Queshen gong ji*, 10 *juan* (n.p., 1875), 2.32a–33a.

85. Lu, "Lun qutian," in *HJWB*, 36.37a–41b.

86. Lu Shiyi, *Sibianlu jiyao*, 35 *juan*, ed. Zhang Boxing (Jiangsu shuju, 1877), 11.1a.

87. Lu, *Sibianlu jiyao*, 11.8a; Perdue, *Exhausting the Earth*, 13–14; Li, *Agricultural Development in Jiangnan*, 77.

88. Lu, *Sibianlu jiyao*, 11.1b–2a.

89. Lu, 11.11b.

90. Pan Zengyi, *Fengyu zhuang benshu*, in *Qu zhong wu zhong*, 5 *juan*, ed. Zhao Mengling (Lianhuachi, 1878), 5.1a; Li, *Agricultural Development in Jiangnan*, 76.

91. Pan, *Fengyu zhuang benshu*, 5.3a, 6a.

92. Pan, 5.1b, 4b–14a.

93. Pan, 5.17a–18a.

94. Zuo to He Xiling, DG 20, *ZZQJ*, 10:19.

95. Zuo to He Xiling, DG 21, *ZZQJ*, 10:29.

96. Zuo to Zhang Shengjie, DG 24, *ZZQJ*, 15:41.

97. Zuo to He Xiling, DG 26, *ZZQJ*, 10:58.

98. *ZWGN*, 1.16a. The title of this tract was *Illustrated Explanations for Expanding Plot Farming (Guang qutian tushuo)*.

99. Only the preface to this work remains extant. For the preface, see Zuo, "'Guang qutian zhi tushuo' xu," *ZZQJ*, 13:244–47.

100. *ZWGN*, 1.22b; Zuo to Zhang Shengjie, DG 26, *ZZQJ*, 15:55; Zuo to Luo Ruhuai, DG 25, *ZZQJ*, 10:49–50. The title of the text borrowed one of Zuo's style names, Pucun.

101. Zuo to Luo Ruhuai, DG 25, *ZZQJ*, 10:50.

102. *Hunan tongzhi*, 288 *juan*, ed. Zeng Guoquan (Changsha: Fuxuegong, 1885), 244.43b; *ZWGN*, 1.23b.

103. *Hunan tongzhi*, 244.43b; Yang, *Hunan zaihuang shi*, 266, 280.

104. *Xiangyin xian tuzhi*, 29.5a.

105. *ZWGN*, 1.23b.

106. Yang, *Hunan zaihuang shi*, 281–83; *Hunan tongzhi*, 244.44a.

107. Yang, *Hunan zaihuang shi*, 281–82.

108. Yang, 380.

109. *ZWGN*, 1.24b–25a.

110. Zuo to Zhang Shengjie, DG 26, *ZZQJ*, 15:55; Zuo to Luo Ruhuai, DG 25, *ZZQJ*, 10:49.

111. Perdue, *Exhausting the Earth*, 12. See also Helen Dunstan, "Official Thinking on Environmental Issues and the State's Environmental Roles in Eighteenth-Century China," in Elvin and Liu, *Sediments of Time*, 587; and Rowe, *Saving the World*, 217, 221.

112. Shu-he-de, "Baqi kaiken biandi shu," in *HJWB*, 35.9a; Shellen Xiao Wu, *Empires of Coal: Fueling China's Entry into the Modern World Order, 1860–1920* (Stanford, CA: Stanford University Press, 2015), 24.

113. Zuo to Zhang Shengjie, DG 26, *ZZQJ*, 15:54.

2. Geography in a Growing Empire

1. Philip A. Kuhn, *Rebellion and Its Enemies in Late Imperial China: Militarization and Social Structure, 1796–1864* (Cambridge, MA: Harvard University Press, 1970), 183–85.

2. Hsin-pao Chang, *Commissioner Lin and the Opium War* (Cambridge, MA: Harvard University Press, 1964).

3. *ZWGN*, 1.25a–26a; Wei Yingqi, *Lin Wenzhong gong Zexu nianpu* (Shanghai, 1935; reprint, Taipei: Shangwu yinshuguan, 1981), 192.

4. *Qingshi gao*, 534 *juan*, ed. Zhao Erxun (n.p., 1928; reprint, Shanghai: Shanghai guji chubanshe, 1995), 375.3b, 388.2ab, 396.4ab; DG 25/1/14, *Xuanzong Cheng huangdi shilu*, 476 *juan* (Tokyo, 1937; reprint, Taipei: Hualian chubanshe, 1964), 413.9b–10a; Wang Xilong, *Qingdai xibei tuntian yanjiu* (Urumchi: Xinjiang renmin chubanshe, 2012), 170–71.

5. Lin Zexu, *Lin Zexu quanji*, 10 vols., ed. Lin Zexu quanji bianji weiyuanhui (Fuzhou: Haixia wenyi chubanshe, 2002), 9:533–80.

6. Zuo to Liu Jintang, GX 2, *ZZQJ*, 12:140.

7. On Lin's ideas for expanding riziculture in other regions of the empire, see Brook, "Growing Rice in North Zhili," 98.

8. Zuo to Zhang Yao, GX 2, *ZZQJ*, 12:134. Regarding an earlier plan to develop riziculture in southern Xinjiang, see David A. Bello, "Transformation through Inundation: Riziculturing Muslim Identity in Qing Dynasty Khotan," in *Landscape Change and Resource Utilization in East Asia: Perspectives from*

Environmental History, ed. Ts'ui-jung Liu, Andrea Janku, and David Pietz (New York: Routledge, 2018), 79–93.

9. Such concerns and criticisms prompted the Qianlong emperor to fabricate a justification for the expenditures. See Millward, *Beyond the Pass*, 41–43.

10. Millward, *Beyond the Pass*, 58–61; Lin Yingru, "Xiexiang yu Qing ting de Xinjiang zhili (1759–1884)" (master's thesis, National Taiwan Normal University, 2010), 58–59.

11. Joanna Waley-Cohen, *Exile in Mid-Qing China: Banishment to Xinjiang, 1758–1820* (New Haven, CT: Yale University Press, 1991), 7.

12. Zuo to Xu Faji, DG 13, *ZZQJ*, 10:1–2; *ZWGN*, 1.11a. On these issues, see Jane Kate Leonard, *Controlling from Afar: The Daoguang Emperor's Management of the Grand Canal Crisis, 1824–1826* (Ann Arbor: Center for Chinese Studies, University of Michigan, 1996); and Randall A. Dodgen, *Controlling the Dragon: Confucian Engineers and the Yellow River in Late Imperial China* (Honolulu: University of Hawaii Press, 2001).

13. Zuo bought Gu Zuyu's *Essentials of Geography for Reading History (Dushi fangyu jiyao)* and Gu Yanwu's *Strengths and Weaknesses of the Various Regions of the Realm (Tianxia junguo libing shu)*. See *ZWGN*, 1.7a.

14. *ZWGN*, 1.7a.

15. *ZWGN*, 1.13b; Zuo, "Wang qi Zhou furen muzhiming," TZ 9, *ZZQJ*, 13:356.

16. On the production of scholarship related to Xinjiang, see Nailene Josephine Chou, "Frontier Studies and Changing Frontier Administration in Late Ch'ing China: The Case of Sinkiang, 1759–1911" (PhD diss., University of Washington, 1976), 26–51, 81–145; Zhao Lisheng, *Zhao Lisheng shixue lunzhu zixuanji* (Jinan: Shandong daxue chubanshe, 1996), 461–91; L. J. Newby, "The Chinese Literary Conquest of Xinjiang," *Modern China* 25, no. 4 (October 1999): 451–74; James A. Millward, "'Coming onto the Map': 'Western Regions' Geography and Cartographic Nomenclature in the Making of Chinese Empire in Xinjiang," *Late Imperial China* 20, no. 2 (December 1999): 61–98; Hou, *Qingdai xibei bianjiang shidi xue*; Guo, *Jueyu yu juexue*; and Jia, *Qingdai xibei shidi xue yanjiu*.

17. *ZWGN*, 1.16a. The formal title of this work is the *Imperially Commissioned Illustrated Gazetteer of the Western Regions of the Imperial Realm (Qinding huangyu xiyu tuzhi)*.

18. Jia, *Qingdai xibei shidi xue yanjiu*, 11–12; Hou, *Qingdai xibei bianjiang shidi xue*, 92–96.

19. On the history of gazetteers, see Joseph Dennis, *Writing, Publishing, and Reading Local Gazetteers in Imperial China, 1100–1700* (Cambridge, MA: Harvard University Asia Center, 2015).

20. On the usefulness of gazetteers for revealing information about local products and food, see Mark Swislocki, *Culinary Nostalgia: Regional Food Culture*

and the Urban Experience in Shanghai (Stanford, CA: Stanford University Press, 2009), 12–14.

21. Stanley W. Toops, "The Ecology of Xinjiang: A Focus on Water," in *Xinjiang: China's Muslim Borderland*, ed. S. Frederick Starr (Armonk, NY: M. E. Sharpe, 2004), 265–66.

22. For accounts of Xinjiang's resources and local products in this period, see *Qinding huangyu xiyu tuzhi*, 48 *juan*, ed. Fu-heng et al. (n.p., 1782), 43.1a–30b; and Qi-shi-yi, *Xiyu ji*, 8 *juan* (n.p., 1885), 7.8a–12a. For analyses of Qi-shi-yi and his writings, see Matthew W. Mosca, "Cišii's Description of Xinjiang: Its Context and Circulation," in *Xinjiang in the Context of Central Eurasian Transformations*, ed. Onuma Takahiro, David Brophy, and Shinmen Yasushi (Tokyo: Toyo Bunko, 2018), 169–200; and Dorothy V. Borei, "Images of the Northwest Frontier: A Study of the *Hsi-yü wen chien lu* (1777)," *American Asian Review* 5, no. 2 (Summer 1987): 26–45.

23. Qi-shi-yi, *Xiyu ji*, 2.15a–b; Millward, *Beyond the Pass*, 180–84.

24. Song-yun, ed., *Qinding Xinjiang shilüe*, 12 *juan* (n.p., 1821), *shou*.38a.

25. Perdue, *China Marches West*, 304–7.

26. For examples of such claims, see Qi-shi-yi, *Xiyu ji*, 1.5b, 1.7a–b, 1.12a, 5.6a; Wang, *Qingdai xibei tuntian yanjiu*, 157–58. On the problems with official accounts of the conquest, see Benjamin Levey, "Jungar Refugees and the Making of Empire on Qing China's Kazakh Frontier, 1759–1773" (PhD diss., Harvard University, 2014).

27. *Qinding huangyu xiyu tuzhi*, 43.3b.

28. Song-yun, ed., *Qinding Xinjiang shilüe*, 6.23b; Fang Yingkai, *Xinjiang tunken shi* (Urumchi: Xinjiang qingshaonian chubanshe, 1989), 659.

29. Qi-shi-yi, *Xiyu ji*, 1.8a; Song-yun, ed., *Qinding Xinjiang shilüe*, 9.1a, 3b–4a, 6a; Song-yun, ed., *Xichui zongtong shilüe*, 12 *juan* (n.p., 1809), 8.7b–15b.

30. Qi-shi-yi, *Xiyu ji*, 1.9a; Hong Liangji, *Tianshan kehua* (E'yuan, 1877), 3b.

31. Qi-shi-yi, *Xiyu ji*, 1.6b, 7.12a.

32. Wang, *Qingdai xibei tuntian yanjiu*, 160.

33. Ji Yun, *Wulumuqi zashi* (n.p., 1771; reprint, Yangzhou: Guangling shushe, 2003), 9a.

34. Wang, *Qingdai xibei tuntian yanjiu*, 163.

35. *Qinding huangyu xiyu tuzhi*, 32.16b.

36. For example, see Yong Xue, "'Treasure Nightsoil as If It Were Gold': Economic and Ecological Links between Urban and Rural Areas in Late Imperial Jiangnan," *Late Imperial China* 26, no. 1 (June 2005): 41–71.

37. QL 24/11/18, *Gaozong Chun huangdi shilu*, 1500 *juan* (Tokyo, 1937; reprint, Taipei: Hualian chubanshe, 1964), 601.8a; QL 24/11/30, *Gaozong Chun huangdi shilu*, 601.32b; Saguchi Tōru, *18–19 seiki higashi Torukisutan shakaishi kenkyū* (Tokyo: Yoshikawa kōbunkan, 1963), 217.

38. Ji, *Wulumuqi zashi*, 14a; Song-yun, ed., *Qinding Xinjiang shilüe*, 6.15a, 6.38a.

39. Song-yun, ed., *Qinding Xinjiang shilüe*, 6.12b; *Qinding huangyu xiyu tuzhi*, 32.1a.

40. Song-yun, ed., *Qinding Xinjiang shilüe*, 6.36a–37b.

41. Millward, *Beyond the Pass*, 52.

42. Song-yun, ed., *Qinding Xinjiang shilüe*, 9.1b; Qi-shi-yi, *Xiyu ji*, 1.10a, 2.6b, 2.7b–8a, 2.13a–b, 2.16b.

43. Qi-shi-yi, *Xiyu ji*, 1.10a.

44. Song-yun, ed., *Qinding Xinjiang shilüe*, 9.1b; Qi-shi-yi, *Xiyu ji*, 1.10a; Perdue, *China Marches West*, 355. On the Qing-Kazakh trade, see also Jin Noda, *The Kazakh Khanates between the Russian and Qing Empires: Central Eurasian International Relations during the Eighteenth and Nineteenth Centuries* (Leiden: Brill, 2016), 215–59.

45. Millward, *Beyond the Pass*, 79.

46. Hummel, ed., *Eminent Chinese of the Ch'ing Period*, 432.

47. Waley-Cohen, *Exile in Mid-Qing China*, 82–83, 146; Hou, *Qingdai xibei bianjiang shidi xue*, 154–55. Xu eventually compiled three of his own works about the territory, including a major treatise on its waterways entitled *Record of Waterways in the Western Regions* (*Xiyu shuidao ji*). He also conducted surveys and gathered information to assist in the compilation of a major new geographical guide to the territory, the *Imperially Commissioned Survey of Xinjiang* (*Qinding Xinjiang shilüe*). Gong was particularly impressed with Xu's knowledge of geography and his expertise on the territory's Kazakh and Kyrgyz populations. See Wu Changshou, *Ding'an xiansheng nianpu* (Shanghai: Zhongguo tushu gongsi, 1909), 11a.

48. Gong Zizhen, *Ding'an quanji*, 10 *juan* (Shanghai: Saoye shanfang, 1920), 3.11b. For an English translation of Gong's essay, see David C. Wright, "Gong Zizhen and His Essay on the 'Western Regions,'" in *Opuscula Altaica: Essays Presented in Honor of Henry Schwarz*, ed. Edward H. Kaplan and Donald W. Whisenhunt (Bellingham: Center for East Asian Studies, Western Washington University, 1994), 655–85.

49. Gong, *Ding'an quanji*, 3.11b.

50. On this period of tension, see Wensheng Wang, *White Lotus Rebels and South China Pirates: Crisis and Reform in the Qing Empire* (Cambridge, MA: Harvard University Press, 2014), 17–34.

51. Gong, *Ding'an quanji*, 3.11b–12a.

52. James Legge, trans., *Confucius: Confucian Analects, the Great Learning, and the Doctrine of the Mean* (Oxford: Clarendon, 1893; reprint, New York: Dover, 1971), 379.

53. Although Gong did not closely address the relationship between prosperity and landlessness in his 1820 essay, he later wrote about the problem of

inequality between rich and poor, identifying it as a major cause of social decay. See Gong, *Ding'an quanji*, 2.18a–19b; Dorothy V. Borei, "Eccentricity and Dissent: The Case of Kung Tzu-chen," *Ch'ing-shih wen-t'i* 3, no. 4 (December 1975): 55; and Helen Dunstan, *Conflicting Counsels to Confuse the Age: A Documentary Study of Political Economy in Qing China, 1644–1840* (Ann Arbor: Center for Chinese Studies, University of Michigan, 1996), 117–23.

54. KX 48/11/14, *Shengzu Ren huangdi shilu*, 300 *juan* (Tokyo, 1937; reprint, Taipei: Hualian chubanshe, 1964), 240.6b; Zhang, *17–19 shiji Zhongguo de renkou yu shengcun huanjing*, 107.

55. Kung-chuan Hsiao, *Rural China: Imperial Control in the Nineteenth Century* (Seattle: University of Washington Press, 1960), 380. For other estimates, see Thomas M. Buoye, *Manslaughter, Markets, and Moral Economy: Violent Disputes over Property Rights in Eighteenth-Century China* (Cambridge: Cambridge University Press, 2000), 61.

56. On changes in agricultural technology and land use, see Li, *Agricultural Development in Jiangnan*.

57. Marks, *Tigers, Rice, Silk, and Silt*, 292; Rowe, *Saving the World*, 56.

58. QL 5/7/26, *Gaozong Chun huangdi shilu*, 123.22b; Marks, *Tigers, Rice, Silk, and Silt*, 306.

59. Chen Hongmou, "Yu Yuexi dangshi shu," in *HJWB*, 16.35a; Rowe, *Saving the World*, 156.

60. Rowe, *Saving the World*, 216–31.

61. QL 13/6/10, *Gaozong Chun huangdi shilu*, 316.15a.

62. QL 25/5/9, *Gaozong Chun huangdi shilu*, 612.21a–b; Hua Li, *Qingdai Xinjiang nongye kaifa shi* (Harbin: Heilongjiang jiaoyu chubanshe, 1995), 41–42; Ge Jianxiong, *Zhongguo yimin shi* (Taipei: Wunan tushu chubanshe, 2005), 375.

63. QL 41/7/2, *Gaozong Chun huangdi shilu*, 1012.1b–2b; Fang, *Xinjiang tunken shi*, 586–87.

64. Hua, *Qingdai Xinjiang nongye kaifa shi*, 61.

65. Hong Liangji, *Juanshige ji*, 40 *juan* (E'yuan, 1877), *wenyaji*.1.9a.

66. Hong Liangji, *Yili riji* (E'yuan, 1877), 14a; Jia, *Qingdai xibei shidi xue yanjiu*, 83.

67. Gong, *Ding'an quanji*, 3.11b, 12a–b, 14b, 15a.

68. Gong, 6.11b.

69. On Wei's life and later scholarship, see Jane Kate Leonard, *Wei Yuan and China's Rediscovery of the Maritime World* (Cambridge, MA: Council on East Asian Studies, Harvard University, 1984); and Matthew W. Mosca, *From Frontier Policy to Foreign Policy: The Question of India and the Transformation of Geopolitics in Qing China* (Stanford, CA: Stanford University Press, 2013), 271–304.

70. Wei Yuan, "Da ren wen xibei bianyu shu," in *HJWB*, 80.3b.

71. In a later restatement of these claims, Wei added the common refrain of eighteenth-century leaders that, in regard to China, "land has not increased

but the population is ever growing." See Wei Yuan, *Sheng wu ji*, 14 *juan* (n.p., 1842), 4.14b.

72. Wei, "Da ren wen xibei bianyu shu," in *HJWB*, 80.3b.

73. In a chapter on autumnal flooding, the text states: "Among all the waters of the world, none is larger than the ocean. Ten thousand rivers flow into it without end, yet it does not overflow. It incessantly drains off at the outlet, yet it is never empty." This translation is based upon Burton Watson, trans., *The Complete Works of Chuang Tzu* (New York: Columbia University Press, 1968), 176; and Herbert A. Giles, trans., *Chuang Tzŭ: Mystic, Moralist, and Social Reformer*, 2nd ed. (New York: AMS, 1974), 201.

74. Wei, "Da ren wen xibei bianyu shu," in *HJWB*, 80.1a–4b; Gong Zizhen, "Xiyu zhi xingsheng yi," in *HJWB*, 81.17a–23a.

75. Zuo to Tao Guang, GX 6, *ZZQJ*, 12:595–96. Zuo also later composed a preface for a reprint edition of Wei Yuan's widely read *Illustrated Gazetteer of Maritime Countries (Haiguo tuzhi)*, a source offering an integrated perspective on geography and politics beyond China's shores. See Zuo, "Haiguo tuzhi xu," *ZZQJ*, 13:255–57.

76. Zuo, "Guisi Yantai zagan ba shou," DG 13, *ZZQJ*, 13:456.

77. Joseph Fletcher, "The Heyday of the Ch'ing Order in Mongolia, Sinkiang and Tibet," in Fairbank, *Late Ch'ing*, 363–71; L. J. Newby, *The Empire and the Khanate: A Political History of Qing Relations with Khoqand, c. 1760–1860* (Leiden: Brill, 2005), 95–101; Scott C. Levi, *The Rise and Fall of Khoqand, 1709–1876: Central Asia in the Global Age* (Pittsburgh: University of Pittsburgh Press, 2017), 137–47.

78. Millward, *Beyond the Pass*, 117, 138.

79. DG 11/9/29, *Xuanzong Cheng huangdi shilu*, 197.18a–19a; Saguchi, *18–19 seiki higashi Torukisutan*, 241.

80. Wu-long-a, DG 7/12/2, in *Qinding pingding Huijiang jiaoqin niyi fanglüe*, 80 *juan*, ed. Cao Zhenyong et al. (n.p., 1830), 55.10a; Saguchi, *18–19 seiki higashi Torukisutan*, 240.

81. Shen Yao, *Luofanlou wenji*, 24 *juan* (n.p., 1918), 1.3b–12b.

82. DG 11/9/29, *Xuanzong Cheng huangdi shilu*, 197.18a–19a; Saguchi, *18–19 seiki higashi Torukisutan*, 241.

83. Wu-long-a, DG 7/12/2, in Cao, *Qinding pingding Huijiang jiaoqin niyi fanglüe*, 55.10b–11a.

84. Na-yan-cheng and Wu-long-a, DG 8/9/15, in Na-yan-cheng, *Na Wenyi gong zouyi*, 80 *juan* (n.p., 1834), 76.31b–32a; DG 8/10/17, *Xuanzong Cheng huangdi shilu*, 145.7a–b.

85. DG 14/11/15, *Xuanzong Cheng huangdi shilu*, 260.14a–15a; DG 15/8/27, *Xuanzong Cheng huangdi shilu*, 270.33b–34a; Saguchi, *18–19 seiki higashi Torukisutan*, 244–45; Kim, *Borderland Capitalism*, 140–43.

86. For this argument, see Kim, *Borderland Capitalism*.

87. Song-yun, ed., *Qinding Xinjiang shilüe*, 3.29a–30a; Zuo, Memorial, GX 4/12/6, *ZZQJ*, 7:227. There is evidence that the population was indeed growing robustly. In Yarkand, for example, the population is estimated to have increased by nearly 80 percent in the decades after the conquest, reaching almost 120,000 people by the 1820s. See Saguchi, *18–19 seiki higashi Torukisutan*, 235.

88. DG 13/7/16, *Xuanzong Cheng huangdi shilu*, 241.1b; Saguchi, *18–19 seiki higashi Torukisutan*, 249.

89. Fletcher, "The Heyday of the Ch'ing Order in Mongolia, Sinkiang and Tibet," 374.

90. Shen Yao to Xu Song, in Shen, *Luofanlou wenji*, 2.25b; Guo, *Jueyu yu juexue*, 9.

91. DG 7/9/6, *Xuanzong Cheng huangdi shilu* 125.7b–8b; DG 7/11/17, *Xuanzong Cheng huangdi shilu*, 130.1b–2b; Saguchi, *18–19 seiki higashi Torukisutan*, 239–40.

92. DG 14/5/23, *Xuanzong Cheng huangdi shilu*, 252.25a-b; DG 14/7/7, *Xuanzong Cheng huangdi shilu*, 254.9b–10a; Saguchi, *18–19 seiki higashi Torukisutan*, 244; DG 14/11/15, *Xuanzong Cheng huangdi shilu*, 260.14a–15a; DG 15/6/21, *Xuanzong Cheng huangdi shilu*, 267.20a–21b; DG 15/8/27, *Xuanzong Cheng huangdi shilu*, 270.33b–34a.

93. Xu Song, *Xiyu shuidao ji*, 5 *juan* (n.p., 1823), 1.15a-b.

94. John Biddulph, "Visit to Maralbashi," in Thomas D. Forsyth, *Report of a Mission to Yarkund in 1873, under Command of Sir T. D. Forsyth, with Historical and Geographical Information regarding the Possessions of the Ameer of Yarkund* (Calcutta: Foreign Department Press, 1875), 218.

95. DG 14/5/23, *Xuanzong Cheng huangdi shilu*, 252.25a-b; DG 14/8/29, *Xuanzong Cheng huangdi shilu*, 255.38a–39a; DG 14/11/15, *Xuanzong Cheng huangdi shilu*, 260.14a–15a; Saguchi, *18–19 seiki higashi Torukisutan*, 244; Xing-de, DG 14/7/13, NPM-GCA 068834; Chang-qing, DG 14/8/8, NPM-GCA 068824.

96. Bi-chang, *Ye'erqiang shoucheng jilüe* (Fuzhou, 1848; reprint, 1859), 10b; DG 11/12/11, *Xuanzong Cheng huangdi shilu*, 202.21a-b; DG 14/2/1, *Xuanzong Cheng huangdi shilu*, 249.4a. A government checkpoint had existed in Barchuk in the late eighteenth century, but it was abandoned by the start of the nineteenth century. See Xu, *Xiyu shuidao ji*, 1.15a.

97. DG 11/11/25, *Xuanzong Cheng huangdi shilu*, 201.21a; DG 13/1/24, *Xuanzong Cheng huangdi shilu*, 230.25a; DG 13/4/23, *Xuanzong Cheng huangdi shilu*, 236.23b.

98. DG 12/10/25, *Xuanzong Cheng huangdi shilu*, 224.23a-b; DG 15/11/15, *Xuanzong Cheng huangdi shilu*, 274.17a–18a; DG 16/7/20, *Xuanzong Cheng huangdi shilu*, 286.8b–11a.

99. Te-yi-shun-bao, DG 16/7/4, NPM-GCA 071679; Te-yi-shun-bao et al., DG 16/6/3, NPM-GCA 071663; Chang-qing and Xing-de, DG 14/4/15, NPM-GCA 067971; Chang-qing, DG 13/12/26, NPM-GCA 066857.

100. DG 14/2/1, *Xuanzong Cheng huangdi shilu*, 249.1a–2b.

101. On these problems, see DG 18/10/17, *Xuanzong Cheng huangdi shilu*, 315.12a–13a; and DG 18/10/30, *Xuanzong Cheng huangdi shilu*, 315.32b–34a. On the repairs, see DG 19/5/18, *Xuanzong Cheng huangdi shilu*, 322.30a-b.

102. Lin, *Lin Zexu quanji*, 9:552. Each *mu* was taxed annually at a rate of three *sheng* of grain, less than half the standard tax rate for farmland in the Urumchi region. The tax rate was set purposefully low to encourage Chinese farmers, especially those with families, to move to Barchuk. See DG 14/5/17, *Xuanzong Cheng huangdi shilu*, 252.12a–13b.

103. For a list of such projects, see Kim, *Borderland Capitalism*, 139–40.

104. *Qingshi gao*, 395.4b.

105. Estimates suggest that Xinjiang's total farmland before this surge of development was between three and six million *mu*. See Millward, *Beyond the Pass*, 51; Kim, *Borderland Capitalism*, 202.

106. DG 24/5/25, *Xuanzong Cheng huangdi shilu*, 405.19b; DG 24/9/23, *Xuanzong Cheng huangdi shilu*, 409.21a–22a; Saguchi, *18–19 seiki higashi Torukisutan*, 250.

107. On such conditions, see Yi-shan and Tu-qie-bu, XF 4/10/12, FHA-QPA 04-01-22-0060-015.

108. Song-yun, ed., *Qinding Xinjiang shilüe*, 6.14b, 16a; Qi-shi-yi, *Xiyu ji*, 7.2a; JQ 15/10/25, *Qingdai zouzhe huibian: nongye, huanjing*, comp. Zhongguo diyi lishi dang'anguan (Beijing: Shangwu yinshuguan, 2005), 366–67; James A. Millward, "Towards a Xinjiang Environmental History: Evidence from Space, the Ground, and in Between," in *Studies on Xinjiang Historical Sources in 17-20th Centuries*, ed. James A. Millward, Shinmen Yasushi, and Sugawara Jun (Tokyo: Toyo Bunko, 2010), 288.

109. Te-yi-shun-bao, DG 16/7/4, NPM-GCA 071679.

110. DG 25/7/18, *Xuanzong Cheng huangdi shilu*, 419.18b–19a; Saguchi, *18–19 seiki higashi Torukisutan*, 251.

111. DG 16/7/20, *Xuanzong Cheng huangdi shilu*, 286.8b–11a; DG 25/11/5, *Xuanzong Cheng huangdi shilu*, 423.8a-b.

3. Reclaiming the Land

1. Kuhn, *Rebellion and Its Enemies in Late Imperial China*, 136–37; Perdue, *Exhausting the Earth*, 238.

2. Franz Michael, *The Taiping Rebellion: History* (Seattle: University of Washington Press, 1966), 69; Philip A. Kuhn, "The Taiping Rebellion," in Fairbank, *Late Ch'ing*, 275.

3. *ZWGN*, 1.29a; Stephen R. Platt, *Provincial Patriots: The Hunanese and Modern China* (Cambridge, MA: Harvard University Press, 2007), 20.

4. *ZWGN*, 1.29a–b; Hu Linyi, *Hu Wenzhong gong yiji*, 86 *juan* (Shanghai: Zhuyitang, 1888), 54.1a; Platt, *Provincial Patriots*, 23.

5. On the rise of these armies, see Kuhn, *Rebellion and Its Enemies in Late Imperial China*, 105–64.

6. Wen-djang Chu, *The Moslem Rebellion in Northwest China, 1862–1878: A Study of Government Minority Policy* (The Hague: Mouton, 1966); Jonathan N. Lipman, *Familiar Strangers: A History of Muslims in Northwest China* (Seattle: University of Washington Press, 1997), 115–29.

7. Hodong Kim, *Holy War in China: The Muslim Rebellion and State in Chinese Central Asia, 1864–1877* (Stanford, CA: Stanford University Press, 2004).

8. Elizabeth J. Perry, *Rebels and Revolutionaries in North China, 1845–1945* (Stanford, CA: Stanford University Press, 1980); Robert D. Jenks, *Insurgency and Social Disorder in Guizhou: The "Miao" Rebellion, 1854–1873* (Honolulu: University of Hawaii Press, 1994); David G. Atwill, *The Chinese Sultanate: Islam, Ethnicity, and the Panthay Rebellion in Southwest China, 1856–1873* (Stanford, CA: Stanford University Press, 2005).

9. Lin, *China Upside Down*, 133–35.

10. Yeh-chien Wang, *Land Taxation in Imperial China, 1750–1911* (Cambridge, MA: Harvard University Press, 1973), 89.

11. Millward, *Beyond the Pass*, 235; Lin, "Xiexiang yu Qing ting de Xinjiang zhili," 67.

12. On these policies, see Edwin George Beal Jr., *The Origin of Likin, 1853–1864* (Cambridge, MA: Chinese Economic and Political Studies, Harvard University, 1958); Kuhn, "The Taiping Rebellion," 288–89; Wenkai He, *Paths toward the Modern Fiscal State: England, Japan, and China* (Cambridge, MA: Harvard University Press, 2013), 131–56; Halsey, *Quest for Power*, 81–112; and Elizabeth Kaske, "Fund-Raising Wars: Office Selling and Interprovincial Finance in Nineteenth-Century China," *Harvard Journal of Asiatic Studies* 71, no. 1 (June 2011): 69–141. On the financial situation in Xinjiang, see Millward, *Beyond the Pass*, 236–37; and Kim, *Borderland Capitalism*, 158–59.

13. Beal, *The Origin of Likin*, 25.

14. On Xinjiang, see Yi Tang, XF 4/7/29, FHA-QPA 04-01-22-0060-011; Yi Tang, "Chouyi Xinjiang shiyi shu," in *Hunan wenzheng*, 190 *juan*, ed. Luo Ruhuai (n.p., 1869), *guochao*.6.23a–28a; XF 4/R7/20, *Wenzong Xian huangdi shilu*, 356 *juan* (Tokyo, 1937; reprint, Taipei: Hualian chubanshe, 1964), 139.27b–28b; Bao-heng, XF 6/11/15, FHA-GCA 03-4469-075; Bao-heng, XF 7/4/20, FHA-GCA 03-4469-085; and *Qingchao xu wenxian tongkao*, 400 *juan*, comp. Liu Jinzao (Shanghai: Shangwu yinshuguan, 1936), 7516. On

Manchuria, see Mary Clabaugh Wright, *The Last Stand of Chinese Conservatism: The T'ung-Chih Restoration, 1862–1874* (Stanford, CA: Stanford University Press, 1957), 160; *Qingchao xu wenxian tongkao*, 7516, 7518, 7520; Wu Taishou, TZ 2/2/26, FHA-GCA 03-9559-019; and Wu Taishou, TZ 2/2/26, FHA-GCA 03-9559-020.

15. Ho, *Studies on the Population of China*, 160; Christopher Mills Isett, *State, Peasant, and Merchant in Qing Manchuria, 1644–1862* (Stanford, CA: Stanford University Press, 2007), 32; Robert H. G. Lee, *The Manchurian Frontier in Ch'ing History* (Cambridge, MA: Harvard University Press, 1970), 103; James Reardon-Anderson, *Reluctant Pioneers: China's Expansion Northward, 1644–1937* (Stanford, CA: Stanford University Press, 2005), 72–75; Kim, *Ginseng and Borderland*, 133–34; Victor Zatsepine, *Beyond the Amur: Frontier Encounters between China and Russia, 1850–1930* (Vancouver: University of British Columbia Press, 2017), 72–74.

16. Ho, *Studies on the Population of China*, 246–47; Cao Shuji, *Zhongguo renkou shi, di wu juan, Qing shiqi* (Shanghai: Fudan daxue chubanshe, 2000), 832.

17. Officials used numerous terms to describe wasteland (e.g., *huang, huangtian, huangwu*). Chinese conceptions of wasteland seem to have overlapped to a large degree with the connotations of wasteland in the Atlantic world. For a comparative reference, see Vittoria Di Palma, *Wasteland: A History* (New Haven, CT: Yale University Press, 2014), 3–4.

18. Wang Wenshao, *Tuipu laoren Xuannan zouyi*, 2 *juan* (n.p., 1896; reprint, Taipei: Taiwan xuesheng shuju, 1986), 210.

19. Liu Qing, TZ 1, FHA-GCA 03-4955-080; *Qingchao xu wenxian tongkao*, 7519; Wright, *The Last Stand of Chinese Conservatism*, 159.

20. A growing literature on the environmental history of warfare reveals strong connections between wartime violence, human population losses, and environmental change. For some recent examples, see Richard P. Tucker and Edmund Russell, eds., *Natural Enemy, Natural Ally: Toward an Environmental History of Warfare* (Corvallis: Oregon State University Press, 2004); Chris Pearson, *Scarred Landscapes: War and Nature in Vichy France* (New York: Palgrave Macmillan, 2008); Lisa M. Brady, *War upon the Land: Military Strategy and the Transformation of Southern Landscapes during the American Civil War* (Athens: University of Georgia Press, 2012); and Micah S. Muscolino, *The Ecology of War in China: Henan Province, the Yellow River, and Beyond, 1938–1950* (Cambridge: Cambridge University Press, 2015).

21. Augustus F. Lindley, *Ti-ping Tien-kwoh: The History of the Ti-ping Revolution, Including a Narrative of the Author's Personal Adventure*, 2 vols. (London: Day & Son, 1866), 2:684–85.

22. Laurence Oliphant, *Narrative of the Earl of Elgin's Mission to China and Japan in the Years 1857, '58, '59*, 2 vols., 2nd ed. (Edinburgh: William Blackwood and

Sons, 1860), 2:299; Thomas W. Blakiston, *Five Months on the Yang-tsze; with a Narrative of the Exploration of Its Upper Waters, and Notices of the Present Rebellions in China* (London: John Murray, 1862), 7.

23. Blakiston, *Five Months on the Yang-tsze*, 7–8, 59; Lindley, *Ti-ping Tien-kwoh*, 2:684–85; Inspector General of Customs, *Reports on Trade at the Treaty Ports in China, for the Year 1869* (Shanghai: Imperial Maritime Customs Press, 1870), 58. For a discussion of the relationship between warfare and forests, see J. R. McNeill, "Woods and Warfare in World History," *Environmental History* 9, no. 3 (July 2004): 388–410.

24. Blakiston, *Five Months on the Yang-tsze*, 8.

25. Blakiston, *Five Months on the Yang-tsze*, 7–9, 13–14; "Royal Asiatic Society," *North-China Herald*, August 6, 1864; Wright, *The Last Stand of Chinese Conservatism*, 122; Thomas W. Kingsmill, "Retrospect of Events in China and Japan during the Year 1865," *Journal of the North China Branch of the Royal Asiatic Society*, n.s., no. 2 (December 1865): 143.

26. Jiyun shanren, *Jiangnan tielei tu* (n.p., n.d.; reprint, Taipei: Xuesheng shuju, 1969), 5b–6a. On Yu Zhi's philanthropic mission after the war, see Tobie Meyer-Fong, *What Remains: Coming to Terms with Civil War in 19th Century China* (Stanford, CA: Stanford University Press, 2013), 23.

27. Jiyun shanren, *Jiangnan tielei tu*, 31b–32a; Prosper Giquel, *A Journal of the Chinese Civil War, 1864*, trans. Steven A. Leibo and Debbie Weston, ed. Steven A. Leibo (Honolulu: University of Hawaii Press, 1985), 63; "Retrospect of Events which Occurred in the North of China during 1865," *North-China Herald*, January 6, 1866; Kingsmill, "Retrospect of Events in China and Japan during the Year 1865," 143; Robert J. Forrest, "Tigers at Ningpo," *North-China Herald and Supreme Court & Consular Gazette*, January 14, 1875; "Ningpo," *North-China Herald and Supreme Court & Consular Gazette*, January 14, 1875; "Ningpo," *North-China Herald and Supreme Court & Consular Gazette*, June 15, 1878; "Notes from Native Papers," *North-China Herald and Supreme Court & Consular Gazette*, February 10, 1888.

28. For perspectives on tiger attacks and their relationship to agricultural expansion and habitat loss, see Marks, *Tigers, Rice, Silk, and Silt*, 323–27; and Zhang, *17–19 shiji Zhongguo de renkou yu shengcun huanjing*, 266–68.

29. Joseph Edkins, "Narrative of a Visit to Nanking," in Jane R. Edkins, *Chinese Scenes and People: with Notices of Christian Missions and Missionary Life in a Series of Letters from Various Parts of China* (London: James Nisbet, 1863), 252.

30. Mao Xianglin, *Duishan shuwu mo yu lu*, 16 *juan* (Huzhou: Zuiliutang, 1870), 2.3b–4a. For similar statements, see William Muirhead (May 22, 1866), Archives of the London Missionary Society, quoted in Prescott Clarke and J. S. Gregory, eds., *Western Reports on the Taiping: A Selection of Documents* (Honolulu: University of Hawaii Press, 1982), 426; Kingsmill, "Retrospect

of Events in China and Japan during the Year 1865," 143; Edkins, "Narrative of a Visit to Nanking," 259; and Jiyun shanren, *Jiangnan tielei tu*, 13b.

31. Ferdinand von Richthofen, *Baron Richthofen's Letters, 1870–1872* (Shanghai: North-China Herald Office, 1903), 50.

32. Zuo, Memorial, TZ 1/4/24, *ZZQJ*, 1:54.

33. Zuo, Memorial, TZ 1/6/16, *ZZQJ*, 1:74–75.

34. Zuo, Memorial, TZ 2/2/4, *ZZQJ*, 1:178.

35. Cao, *Zhongguo renkou shi*, 489, 492; Mary Backus Rankin, *Elite Activism and Political Transformation in China: Zhejiang Province, 1865–1911* (Stanford, CA: Stanford University Press, 1986), 55. For estimates in neighboring Jiangsu province, see Hou Zhuqing, *Taiping Tianguo zhanzheng shiqi Jiangsu renkou sunshi yanjiu, 1853–1864* (Beijing: Zhongguo shehui kexue chubanshe, 2016).

36. In February 1864, Zuo Zongtang reported the proportion of survivors was perilously small, just "one or two in a hundred." See Zuo to Xia Xianyun, TZ 2/12/25, *ZZQJ*, 10:551. Nearly a decade later, Ferdinand von Richthofen heard that in some places only 3 percent of the population had survived the chaos, many perishing not from violence but from starvation as they fled into the mountains. See Richthofen, *Baron Richthofen's Letters*, 50.

37. Zuo, Memorial, TZ 3/4/13, *ZZQJ*, 1:421.

38. Cao, *Zhongguo renkou shi*, 492.

39. In some areas of Yanzhou, as little as 20 percent of all people survived the war. Dai Pan, *Yanling jilüe* (n.p., 1866; reprint, Taipei: Wenhai chubanshe, 1980), 23a. In the northern Zhejiang district of Anji, the population reportedly fell from over 130,000 to fewer than 7000 between 1860 and 1864. See *Anji xianzhi*, 18 *juan*, ed. Zhang Xingfu and Wang Rong (n.p., 1874), 4-*hukou*.4a-b.

40. On famine-relief manuals, see Xia Mingfang, *Jinshi jitu: shengtai bianqian zhong de Zhongguo xiandaihua jincheng* (Beijing: Zhongguo renmin daxue chubanshe, 2012), 317–66.

41. Zuo, Memorial, TZ 3/4/13, *ZZQJ*, 1:421.

42. Zuo, Memorial, TZ 1/6/16, *ZZQJ*, 1:75.

43. Zuo, Memorial, TZ 2/2/4, *ZZQJ*, 1:178.

44. For an overview of such industries, see Xu Dixin and Wu Chengming, eds., *Chinese Capitalism, 1522–1840* (New York: St. Martin's, 2000).

45. Zuo, Memorial, TZ 2/2/4, *ZZQJ*, 1:178; Qin Xiangye, *Ping Zhe jilüe*, 16 *juan* (Zhejiang shuju, 1873), 13.3a; Li Yingjue, *Zhe zhong fafei jilüe* (n.p., n.d.; reprint, Nanjing: Jiangsu renmin chubanshe, 1983), 228.

46. There were prewar precedents for such welfare bureaus, but their numbers greatly increased in the post-Taiping era as gentry took on larger roles in matters of local governance. See Rankin, *Elite Activism and Political Transformation in China*, 94.

47. Qin, *Ping Zhe jilüe*, 13.3a–5b.

48. Qin, *Ping Zhe jilüe*, 13.7a-b; Li, *Zhe zhong fafei jilüe*, 228; Zuo, Memorial, TZ 3/4/13, *ZZQJ*, 1:421.

49. Qin, *Ping Zhe jilüe*, 13.3b.

50. Zuo to Liu Changyou, TZ 2, *ZZQJ*, 10:493. See also Bernhardt, *Rents, Taxes, and Peasant Resistance*, 119.

51. Qin, *Ping Zhe jilüe*, 13.5b.

52. Zuo, Memorial, TZ 3/4/13, *ZZQJ*, 1:421.

53. Peng, ed., *Qingdai tudi kaiken shi ziliao huibian*, 194.

54. Huang Tong, *Yiwu bingshi jilüe* (n.p., n.d.; reprint, Taipei: Wenhai chubanshe, 1980), 25b.

55. On sets of regulations for land reclamation in other provinces, which came from the Board of Revenue and governors in Shandong, Anhui, and Shaanxi, see Peng, ed., *Qingdai tudi kaiken shi ziliao huibian*, 172–73, 192–98.

56. Ma Xinyi, *Ma Duanmin gong zouyi*, 8 *juan* (Min Zhe du shu, 1894; reprint, Taipei: Chengwen chubanshe, 1969), 3.49a–57b; Ma Xinyi, TZ 5/9/20, FHA-GCA 03-9552-017.

57. Ma, *Ma Duanmin gong zouyi*, 3.57a; Ma Xinyi, TZ 5/9/20, FHA-GCA 03-9552-017.

58. Zuo, Memorial, TZ 2/2/4, *ZZQJ*, 1:178.

59. Ma, *Ma Duanmin gong zouyi*, 1.6a, 3.53b; Ma Xinyi, TZ 5/9/20, FHA-GCA 03-9552-017.

60. Dai, *Yanling jilüe*, 1b.

61. On the shack people, see Ho, *Studies on the Population of China*, 146–48; Stephen C. Averill, "The Shed People and the Opening of the Yangzi Highlands," *Modern China* 9, no. 1 (January 1983): 84–126; Anne Osborne, "The Local Politics of Land Reclamation in the Lower Yangzi Highlands," *Late Imperial China* 15, no. 1 (June 1994): 1–46; and Sow-Theng Leong, *Migration and Ethnicity in Chinese History: Hakkas, Pengmin, and Their Neighbors*, ed. Tim Wright (Stanford, CA: Stanford University Press, 1997), 147–62. For examples of officials blaming shack people, see Chang Dachun, XF 1/4/11, FHA-GCA 03-4489-023; and *Qinding gongbu zeli*, 116 *juan* (n.p., 1884), 63.1a.

62. Zuo, Memorial, TZ 2/2/25, *ZZQJ*, 1:199–200; Zuo, Memorial, TZ 2/2/4, *ZZQJ*, 1:178; Zuo, Memorial, TZ 2/6/10, *ZZQJ*, 1:243–44.

63. Zuo, Memorial, TZ 3/6/27, *ZZQJ*, 1:466–67; Zuo, TZ 3, *ZZQJ*, 14:37.

64. *Qingdai zouzhe huibian: nongye, huanjing*, 507.

65. Jiang Yili, TZ 3/11/29, FHA-GCA 03-4955-125; Jiang Yili, TZ 3/11/29, FHA-GCA 03-4955-126; *Jiande xianzhi*, 21 *juan*, ed. Yu Guanxu (n.p., 1892), 20.9b.

66. Zuo, Memorial, TZ 3/10/1, *ZZQJ*, 1:524.

67. Zuo to Zuo Xiaowei, TZ 8/12/16, *ZZQJ*, 13:145.

68. Zuo to Jiang Zhizhang, TZ 9, *ZZQJ*, 11:188. See also Zuo, Memorial, TZ 8/4/1, *ZZQJ*, 4:74.

69. Pavel Piassetsky, *Russian Travellers in Mongolia and China*, 2 vols., trans. J. Gordon-Cumming (London: Chapman & Hall, 1884), 2:90.

70. Piassetsky, *Russian Travellers in Mongolia and China*, 2:104.

71. Piassetsky, 2:226. See also *Anxi caifang diben* (n.p., n.d.; reprint, Nanjing: Fenghuang chubanshe, 2008), 401.

72. One Chinese report from early 1874 suggested that 80 to 90 percent of all farmers had perished or departed during war in these areas. See Zuo, Memorial, TZ 13/2/16, *ZZQJ*, 6:19. A German traveler who passed through these towns in 1879 reported similar damage. See Gustav Kreitner, *Im fernen Osten: Reisen des Grafen Bela Széchenyí in Indien, Japan, China, Tibet und Birma in den Jahren 1877–1880* (Vienna: Alfred Hölder, 1881), 676–77.

73. Zuo, Memorial, TZ 8/8/11, *ZZQJ*, 4:135.

74. *Chongxin xianzhi*, 4 *juan*, ed. Zhang Mingdao and Ren Yinghan (Jingchuan: Fusheng yinshuguan, 1928), 4.37b.

75. Piassetsky, *Russian Travellers in Mongolia and China*, 2:91, 97–98, 100–101; Fuke, "Xi xing suo lu," in *Xiaofanghuzhai yudi congchao*, 12 *zhi*, ed. Wang Xiqi (Shanghai: Zhuyitang, 1877–1897), 6.301a, 302a; Kreitner, *Im fernen Osten*, 536, 562, 611–12, 628, 648.

76. E. Delmar Morgan, "Introductory Remarks to 'Journey of Carey and Dalgleish in Chinese Turkistan and Northern Tibet; and General Prejevalsky on the Orography of Northern Tibet,'" *Royal Geographical Society Supplementary Papers*, vol. 3 (London: John Murray, 1893), 4–5.

77. For a similar case, see Kathryn Edgerton-Tarpley, *Tears from Iron: Cultural Responses to Famine in Nineteenth-Century China* (Berkeley: University of California Press, 2008), 51.

78. Zuo to Zuo Xiaowei, TZ 8/12/16, *ZZQJ*, 13:145.

79. Zuo, Memorial, TZ 13/11/3, *ZZQJ*, 6:123.

80. *Chongxin xianzhi*, 4.46a–b.

81. *Suzhou xinzhi*, ed. Wu Renshou and He Yanqing (n.p., 1897; reprint, Nanjing: Fenghuang chubanshe, 2008), 511.

82. *Pingyuan xianzhi*, 10 *juan*, ed. Chen Rixin (n.p., 1879), 10.47a.

83. The price offered in Jingzhou was four thousand copper cash per dead wolf. See *Jingzhou xiangtu zhi*, ed. Zhang Yuanchan (n.p., 1907; reprint, Nanjing: Fenghuang chubanshe, 2008), 5a–b; *Jingzhou caifang xinzhi*, ed. Yang Bingrong (n.p., 1909; reprint, Nanjing: Fenghuang chubanshe, 2008), 594. On policies for dealing with wolves, see also *Suzhou xinzhi*, 511; *Jingchuan xianzhi*, ed. Jingchuan xian xianzhi bianzuan weiyuanhui (Lanzhou: Gansu renmin chubanshe, 1996), 25.

84. Fang Rong and Zhang Ruilan, *Gansu renkou shi* (Lanzhou: Gansu renmin chubanshe, 2003), 377; Cao, *Zhongguo renkou shi*, 635; Ho, *Studies on the Population of China*, 248. Zuo's estimates of population losses in Gansu ranged from 50 to 90 percent. See Zuo to Zuo Zongzhi, TZ 5/12/11, *ZZQJ*, 13:117; Zuo, Memorial, GX 2/1/5, *ZZQJ*, 6:379–80; and Zuo, Memorial, GX 2/1/6, *ZZQJ*, 6:381.

85. Cao, *Zhongguo renkou shi*, 616. See also Zuo, Memorial, TZ 10/3/3, *ZZQJ*, 5:43.

86. Zuo, Memorial, TZ 8/5/19, *ZZQJ*, 4:109; *Lingtai zhuanji*, 4 *juan*, ed. Zhang Dongye (Nanjing: Jinghua yinshuguan, 1935), 3.49a.

87. On the history of Hui people in Gansu, see Lipman, *Familiar Strangers*.

88. Zuo, TZ 6, *ZZQJ*, 14:581–82; Zuo, TZ 7, *ZZQJ*, 14:133; Zuo, TZ 8, *ZZQJ*, 14:586.

89. Zuo, Memorial, TZ 13/12/17, *ZZQJ*, 6:141.

90. Zuo, TZ 10, *ZZQJ*, 14:259; Zuo, TZ 13, *ZZQJ*, 14:346.

91. Zuo, TZ 10, *ZZQJ*, 14:256.

92. Zuo, Memorial, TZ 11/6/25, *ZZQJ*, 5:281–82.

93. Zuo, "Fu hou jinling," TZ 10, *ZZQJ*, 14:592; Zuo, "Ancha Huimin gaoshi," TZ 12, *ZZQJ*, 14:593–96. For cases regarding the travel policy, see Zuo, TZ 13, *ZZQJ*, 14:347; Zuo, GX 2, *ZZQJ*, 14:386–87; and Zuo, GX 2, *ZZQJ*, 14:388–89.

94. Fang and Zhang, *Gansu renkou shi*, 378–79; Zuo, Memorial, TZ 12/12/10, *ZZQJ*, 5:545.

95. Zuo, Memorial, TZ 10/1/25, *ZZQJ*, 5:17. On Huapingchuan's later population history, see Cao, *Zhongguo renkou shi*, 609–10.

96. Zuo, Memorial, TZ 9/12/11, *ZZQJ*, 4:499–500; Zuo, Memorial, TZ 10/1/25, *ZZQJ*, 5:17–18; *Huaping zhili fumin ting zunzhang caifang bianji quanzhi* (n.p., n.d.; reprint, Taipei: Taiwan xuesheng shuju, 1987), 217, 225; *Jingyuan xianzhi*, ed. Jingyuan xianzhi bianzuan weiyuanhui (Yinchuan: Ningxia renmin chubanshe, 1995), 74–74, 94.

97. *Huaping zhili fumin ting zunzhang caifang bianji quanzhi*, 211–14. Perhaps inspired by Huapingchuan's eponymous river, whose name refers to pacification, Zuo tried to make the surrounding landscape more fully evocative of the principle of righteous obedience to imperial authority by renaming two other nearby rivers, including the Sacred Woman River (*Shengnü chuan*), which became the Sacred Edict River (*Shengyu chuan*) after the Kangxi emperor's famous dictum. See Zuo, Memorial, TZ 10/1/25, *ZZQJ*, 5:17–18.

98. *Tongzhi nianjian Shaanxi Huimin qiyi lishi diaocha jilu*, comp. Xibei daxue lishixi minzu yanjiushi (Xi'an: Shaanxi renmin chubanshe, 1993), 432.

99. *Huaping zhili fumin ting zunzhang caifang bianji quanzhi*, 221, 302.

100. *Tongzhi nianjian Shaanxi Huimin qiyi lishi diaocha jilu,* 432, 434, 444; GX 7/12/6, QXDX, 52:224.

101. Zuo, TZ 9, *ZZQJ,* 14:232–33.

102. Zuo, TZ 12, *ZZQJ,* 14:328; Zuo, TZ 12, *ZZQJ,* 14:329–30.

103. *Xinxiu Guyuan zhouzhi,* 12 *juan,* ed. Wang Xueyi (n.p., 1909), 10.22a.

104. Zuo, Memorial, TZ 12/12/10, *ZZQJ,* 5:538; Zuo to Tan Zhonglin, TZ 13, *ZZQJ,* 11:466.

105. Zuo, Memorial, TZ 12/12/10, *ZZQJ,* 5:538. See also Zuo, Memorial, TZ 13/2/16, *ZZQJ,* 6:6.

106. Zuo, TZ 10, *ZZQJ,* 14:259; Zuo, TZ 10, *ZZQJ,* 14:275; Zuo, Memorial, TZ 11/2, *ZZQJ,* 5:223–25; Zuo, Memorial, TZ 12/10/7, *ZZQJ,* 5:504; Zuo, TZ 12, *ZZQJ,* 14:342. In certain cases, reconstruction bureaus lasted more than a decade: the bureau in Lanzhou was not disbanded until 1883. See Liu Jintang, GX 12/9/18, *LXGZ,* 11.44a. Also note that Yang Changjun, a native of Hunan who had worked on reconstruction projects with Zuo Zongtang in Zhejiang in the early 1860s, arrived in Lanzhou at the end of 1878 to head up reconstruction efforts. See Zuo, Memorial, GX 4/12/21, *ZZQJ,* 7:247.

107. Between 1867 and 1873, government funding for resettlement and land reclamation projects, including money for seeds, tools, animals, and other equipment, totaled over 385,000 taels, or roughly 1 percent of all expenses incurred by armies under Zuo's supervision in this period. See Zuo, Memorial, TZ 13/6/29, *ZZQJ,* 6:77.

108. Zuo, TZ 10, *ZZQJ,* 14:271.

109. Zuo, TZ 13/7, *ZZQJ,* 14:355–56; Zuo, TZ 12, *ZZQJ,* 14:321.

110. Zuo, Memorial, TZ 12/12/10, *ZZQJ,* 5:539.

111. Zuo, "Zhun fu tiaogui," TZ 10, *ZZQJ,* 14:591–92.

112. Zuo, Memorial, TZ 11/3/25, *ZZQJ,* 5:233–34; Zuo to Zuo Xiaowei, TZ 11/5/17, *ZZQJ,* 13:170; Zuo, Memorial, TZ 11/6/25, *ZZQJ,* 5:281; Zuo to Yushi, TZ 12, *ZZQJ,* 11:311.

113. Zuo, TZ 8, *ZZQJ,* 14:200.

114. Zuo, TZ 8, *ZZQJ,* 14:176; Zuo, Memorial, TZ 9/6/8, *ZZQJ,* 4:382; Zuo, TZ 10, *ZZQJ,* 14:289; *Chongxiu Gaolan xianzhi,* 30 *juan,* ed. Zhang Guochang (Longyou leshan shuju, 1917), 14.11b.

115. Zuo, Memorial, GX 2/1/5, *ZZQJ,* 6:379–80; Zuo, Memorial, GX 3/3/29, *ZZQJ,* 6:637; Zuo, Memorial, GX 5/12/17, *ZZQJ,* 7:463.

116. Zuo, TZ 8, *ZZQJ,* 14:168; Zuo, TZ 10, *ZZQJ,* 14:284.

117. Zuo, Memorial, TZ 13/11/3, *ZZQJ,* 6:122–23.

118. Zuo, TZ 9, *ZZQJ,* 14:217; Zuo, Memorial, TZ 6/1/10, *ZZQJ,* 3:372; Zuo, Memorial, TZ 9/3/7, *ZZQJ,* 4:336; Zuo, TZ 13, *ZZQJ,* 14:351; Zuo, Memorial, GX 2/1/5, *ZZQJ,* 6:379–80.

119. *Haicheng xianzhi*, 10 *juan*, ed. Yang Jingeng (n.p., 1908), 3.16a; Zuo, TZ 13, ZZQJ, 14:355–56; *Lingtai zhuanji*, 4.52a–53a; Zuo, Memorial, GX 2/2/21, ZZQJ, 6:433.

120. Jingji xuehui, *Gansu quansheng caizheng shuoming shu* (n.p., n.d.; reprint, Guangzhou: Guangdong renmin chubanshe, 2009), 207; Zhao Weixi, *Xiangjun jituan yu xibei Huimin da qiyi zhi shanhou yanjiu: yi Gan Ning Qing diqu wei zhongxin* (Shanghai: Shanghai guji chubanshe, 2014), 249–50; Jixiang yufu, *Jiuhuang baice* (Qinzhou, 1884), 45a–b.

121. Zuo, Memorial, GX 3/4/15, ZZQJ, 6:653–54; Zuo Zongtang, GX 3/4/15, XUARA 15-11-0026.

122. Zuo to Zuo Xiaowei, TZ 1/5/17, ZZQJ, 13:53; Zuo to Zuo Xiaowei, TZ 2/1/17, ZZQJ, 13:70.

123. In 1885, Zhejiang officials reported 4.5 million *mu* of wasteland in the province, down from 7.1 million *mu* in 1877. For reports on wasteland in Zhejiang in these years, see Mei Qizhao, GX 3/11/26, FHA-GCA 03-7068-041; Tan Zhonglin, GX 6/12/21, FHA-GCA 03-6712-006; Chen Shijie, GX 8/11/23, FHA-GCA 03-9554-004; and Liu Bingzhang, GX 11/12/9, FHA-GCA 03-6716-064. Regarding incoming migrants, see Ho, *Studies on the Population of China*, 156; and Bernhardt, *Rents, Taxes, and Peasant Resistance*, 130.

124. Shi Zhihong, *Agricultural Development in Qing China: A Quantitative Study, 1661–1911* (Leiden: Brill, 2018), 215–16; Liang Fangzhong, *Zhongguo lidai hukou, tiandi, tianfu tongji* (Shanghai: Shanghai renmin chubanshe, 1980), 380.

125. Cao, *Zhongguo renkou shi*, 432; Ho, *Studies on the Population of China*, 248.

126. Wright, *The Last Stand of Chinese Conservatism*, 160; Chao, *Man and Land in Chinese History*, 32. For data on farmland acreage in the Qing period and problems with the data, see Ho, *Studies on the Population of China*, 101–23; Zhang, *17–19 shiji Zhongguo de renkou yu shengcun huanjing*, 155–81; and Shi, *Agricultural Development in Qing China*, 12–58, 214–17. For estimates of China's population, see Cao, *Zhongguo renkou shi*, 832.

127. Ho, *Studies on the Population of China*, 157.

4. Promoting Profitable Crops

1. Zuo to Tan Zhonglin, TZ 13, ZZQJ, 11:444.

2. Sven Beckert, *Empire of Cotton: A Global History* (New York: Alfred A. Knopf, 2014); Carl A. Trocki, *Opium, Empire and the Global Political Economy: A Study of the Asian Opium Trade, 1750–1950* (New York: Routledge, 1999).

3. On the relationship between transport costs and patterns of development, see G. William Skinner, "Regional Urbanization in Nineteenth-Century

China," in *The City in Late Imperial China*, ed. G. William Skinner (Stanford, CA: Stanford University Press, 1977), 216–17.

4. On Gansu's tobacco, see Carol Benedict, *Golden-Silk Smoke: A History of Tobacco in China, 1550–2010* (Berkeley: University of California Press, 2011), 28–31. On rhubarb from Xining, see Clifford M. Foust, *Rhubarb: The Wondrous Drug* (Princeton, NJ: Princeton University Press, 1992), 164; and Nikolay Prejevalsky, *Mongolia, the Tangut Country, and the Solitudes of Northern Tibet: Being a Narrative of Three Years' Travel in Eastern High Asia*, 2 vols., trans. E. Delmar Morgan (London: Sampson Low, Marston, Searle & Rivington, 1876), 2:81–83. For a description of foraged and cultivated commodities in late nineteenth-century Gansu, see Gustav Kreitner, "Geographie," in Béla Széchenyi, *Die wissenschaftlichen Ergebnisse der Reise des Grafen Béla Széchenyi in Ostasien, 1877–1880*, 3 vols. (Vienna: E. Hölzel, 1893), 1:153–56.

5. Hubu, *Qinding Hubu xuzuan zeli*, 15 *juan* (n.p., 1838), 2.8a–8b; Hubu, *Qinding Hubu zeli*, 100 *juan* (n.p., 1874), 8.27a–b.

6. Jonathan Spence, "Opium Smoking in Ch'ing China," in *Conflict and Control in Late Imperial China*, ed. Frederic Wakeman Jr. and Carolyn Grant (Berkeley: University of California Press, 1975), 151.

7. Zheng Yangwen, *The Social Life of Opium in China* (Cambridge: Cambridge University Press, 2005), 11–24.

8. Man-houng Lin, "China's 'Dual Economy' in International Trade Relations, 1842–1949," in *Japan, China, and the Growth of the Asian International Economy, 1850–1949*, ed. Kaoru Sugihara (Oxford: Oxford University Press, 2005), 182; Man-houng Lin, "Late Qing Perceptions of Native Opium," *Harvard Journal of Asiatic Studies* 64, no. 1 (June 2004): 120.

9. David A. Bello, *Opium and the Limits of Empire: Drug Prohibition in the Chinese Interior, 1729–1850* (Cambridge, MA: Harvard University Asia Center, 2005), 125–27.

10. *Qinzhou zhili zhou xinzhi*, 24 *juan*, ed. Yu Zechun (Longnan shuyuan, 1889), 3.13a; Jonathan N. Lipman, "The Border World of Gansu, 1895–1935" (PhD diss., Stanford University, 1980), 227; Bello, *Opium and the Limits of Empire*, 194; Zheng, *The Social Life of Opium in China*, 102. Opium poppies were listed in gazetteers from Gansu as early as the seventeenth century. See David Bello, "Opium in Xinjiang and Beyond," in *Opium Regimes: China, Britain, and Japan, 1839–1952*, ed. Timothy Brook and Bob Tadashi Wakabayashi (Berkeley: University of California Press, 2000), 145n8.

11. *Chongxiu Zhenyuan xianzhi*, 19 *juan*, ed. Qian Shitong and Jiao Guoli (Lanzhou: Junhua yinshuguan, 1935; reprint, Nanjing: Fenghuang chubanshe, 2008), 9.29a.

12. *Qinzhou zhili zhou xinzhi*, 3.13a.

13. Zuo to sons, TZ 8/12/16, *ZZQJ*, 13:145.

14. Zuo, TZ 11, *ZZQJ*, 14:539; Zuo, Memorial, GX 4/7/4, *ZZQJ*, 7:142.

15. Hubu, *Qinding Hubu zeli*, 8.28b; Trocki, *Opium, Empire and the Global Political Economy*, 123–24.

16. Zuo, TZ 8, *ZZQJ*, 14:587.

17. Zuo, Memorial, GX 4/7/4, *ZZQJ*, 7:142; Zuo to Wang Siyi, GX 5, *ZZQJ*, 12:531; Zuo to officials, GX 5, *ZZQJ*, 14:561; *Qinzhou zhili zhou xinzhi*, 3.13b; GX 5/4/5, *QXDX*, 51:91–92.

18. Hubu, *Qinding Hubu zeli*, 8.27b–28b.

19. Zuo, Memorial, GX 4/7/4, *ZZQJ*, 7:143. See also GX 4/10/15, *QXDX*, 37:149.

20. *Qinzhou zhili zhou xinzhi*, 3.13a-b; Tan Jixun, *Tan Jixun ji*, 2 vols., ed. Jia Wei and Tan Zhihong (Changsha: Yuelu shushe, 2015), 624. See also *Chongxiu Zhenyuan xianzhi*, 9.29a–30a.

21. Zuo, Memorial, GX 4/7/4, *ZZQJ*, 7:143.

22. Zuo, TZ 10, *ZZQJ*, 14:529; Zuo, TZ 11, *ZZQJ*, 14:539; Zuo, GX 4, *ZZQJ*, 14:556.

23. Tan Zhonglin, *Tan Wenqin gong zougao*, 20 *juan* (n.p., 1911; reprint, Taipei: Wenhai chubanshe, 1969), 6.3b.

24. Zuo, TZ 8, *ZZQJ*, 14:173.

25. Zuo, Memorial, GX 4/7/4, *ZZQJ*, 7:146. See also Zuo, GX 4, *ZZQJ*, 14:453.

26. On the history of environmental change in China's Loess Plateau, see Ruth Mostern, "Sediment and State in Imperial China: The Yellow River Watershed as an Earth System and a World System," *Nature and Culture* 11, no. 2 (Summer 2016): 121–47.

27. Zuo, Memorial, GX 4/7/4, *ZZQJ*, 7:143; Zuo, GX 4, *ZZQJ*, 14:453.

28. Zuo, Memorial, TZ 13/5/6, *ZZQJ*, 6:45.

29. Tan, *Tan Wenqin gong zougao*, 6.3a.

30. Zuo, Memorial, GX 4/7/4, *ZZQJ*, 7:143. William Rockhill, who traveled through Gansu over a decade later, also noted that Muslims observed a rule against the use of opium. See William Woodville Rockhill, *The Land of the Lamas: Notes of a Journey through China, Mongolia and Tibet* (New York: Century, 1891), 39.

31. Zuo, Memorial, GX 4/7/4, *ZZQJ*, 7:143.

32. Trocki cites lectures by Man-houng Lin on this point. See Trocki, *Opium, Empire and the Global Political Economy*, 123.

33. Zuo to Liu Dian, GX 3, *ZZQJ*, 12:214. See also Zuo to He Xiling, DG 26, *ZZQJ*, 10:58; Zuo to Zhang Yao, GX 4, *ZZQJ*, 12:417; Zuo to Yang Changjun, GX 5, *ZZQJ*, 12:458; and Zuo to Zongli Yamen, GX 9, *ZZQJ*, 12:796.

34. Zuo, Memorial, GX 4/7/4, *ZZQJ*, 7:142.

35. For a comparative case, see William T. Rowe, *Speaking of Profit: Bao Shichen and Reform in Nineteenth-Century China* (Cambridge, MA: Harvard University Asia Center, 2018).

36. Zuo, Memorial, GX 4/7/4, *ZZQJ*, 7:143.

37. Zuo to Tan Zhonglin, TZ 13, *ZZQJ*, 11:445.

38. Beckert, *Empire of Cotton*, 242–73.

39. Isaac Watts, *The Cotton Supply Association: Its Origin and Progress* (Manchester: Tubbs & Brook, 1871), 7, 9.

40. *Report of the Delegates of the Shanghai General Chamber of Commerce on the Trade of the Upper Yangtsze and Report of the Naval Surveyors on the River above Hankow* (Shanghai: Shanghai Recorder Office, 1869), 17. See also Yen-p'ing Hao, *The Commercial Revolution in Nineteenth-Century China: The Rise of Sino-Western Mercantile Capitalism* (Berkeley: University of California Press, 1986), 291.

41. Prosper Giquel, "Ningpo et son Commerce pendant l'année 1864," in Inspector General of Customs, *Reports on Trade at the Ports of Shanghai, Canton, Swatow, Amoy, Ningpo, Hankow, Kiukiang, Chefoo, and Newchwang, for the Year 1864* (Shanghai: Imperial Maritime Customs Press, 1865), 3; S. Wells Williams, *The Chinese Commercial Guide, Containing Treaties, Tariffs, Regulations, Tables, Etc., Useful in the Trade to China & Eastern Asia; with an Appendix of Sailing Directions for Those Seas and Coasts*, 5th ed. (Hong Kong: A. Shortrede, 1863), 88; Inspector General of Customs, *Reports on Trade at the Ports in China Open by Treaty to Foreign Trade, for the Year 1866* (Shanghai: Imperial Maritime Customs Press, 1867), 25; Inspector General of Customs, *Reports on Trade at the Treaty Ports in China, for the Year 1868* (Shanghai: Imperial Maritime Customs Press, 1869), 50; Inspector General of Customs, *Reports on Trade at the Treaty Ports in China, for the Year 1869* (Shanghai: Imperial Maritime Customs Press, 1870), 63.

42. Inspector General of Customs, *Reports on Trade at the Treaty Ports in China, for the Year 1869*, 63.

43. Christopher T. Gardner, "Notes to the 'Journey from Ningpo to Shanghai,'" *Proceedings of the Royal Geographical Society* 13, no. 3 (March 22, 1869): 249.

44. Inspector General of Customs, *Reports on Trade at the Ports in China Open by Treaty to Foreign Trade, for the Year 1866*, 94.

45. Zuo, Memorial, TZ 5/3/10, *ZZQJ*, 3:16. Fujian historically had grown cotton, but the expansion of sugarcane and tea farming after the seventeenth century led to the demise of local cotton farming. See Zhao Gang and Chen Zhongyi, *Zhongguo mianye shi* (Taipei: Lianjing, 1977), 49.

46. Zuo, Memorial, TZ 5/9/8, *ZZQJ*, 3:125; Zuo to Yang Changjun, TZ 5, *ZZQJ*, 10:717.

47. Zuo, Memorial, TZ 5/10/12, *ZZQJ*, 3:184; Inspector General of Customs, *Silk* (Shanghai: Statistical Department of the Inspectorate General, 1881), 134; *Min xian xiangtu zhi*, ed. Zheng Zugeng (n.p., 1903), 28b, 340b–341a.

48. Inspector General of Customs, *Reports on Trade at the Treaty Ports in China, for the Year 1867* (Shanghai: Imperial Maritime Customs Press, 1868), 63; "Silk in Fohkien," *North-China Herald*, December 22, 1866.

49. Zuo, TZ 10, *ZZQJ*, 14:528; Zuo, Memorial, TZ 13/3/22, *ZZQJ*, 6:27; Zuo Zongtang, TZ 13/3/22, NPM-GCA 114834.

50. Zuo, TZ 10, *ZZQJ*, 14:528; Zuo to Tan Zhonglin, TZ 12, *ZZQJ*, 11:379; Zuo to Shen Yingkui, TZ 10/2/4, in Zuo, *Zuo Zongtang weikan shudu*, 99–100.

51. Zuo, TZ 10, *ZZQJ*, 14:528.

52. Zuo, TZ 10, *ZZQJ*, 14:529.

53. Zuo to Jiang Zhizhang, TZ 10, *ZZQJ*, 11:231.

54. Zuo, TZ 10, *ZZQJ*, 14:528–29.

55. Zuo, Memorial, TZ 13/3/22, *ZZQJ*, 6:27; Zuo Zongtang, TZ 13/3/22, NPM-GCA 114834. See also Zuo to Tan Zhonglin, TZ 13, *ZZQJ*, 11:444; and Zuo to Zongli Yamen, GX 5, *ZZQJ*, 12:464.

56. Zuo, TZ 10, *ZZQJ*, 14:529.

57. Zuo to Shen Yingkui, TZ 10/2/4, in Zuo, *Zuo Zongtang weikan shudu*, 99–100.

58. Ho, *Studies on the Population of China*, 186; Bray and Métailié, "Who Was the Author of the *Nongzheng Quanshu*?," 342.

59. He Changling, *Nai'an zouyi*, 12 *juan* (n.p., 1882; reprint, Taipei: Chengwen chubanshe, 1968), 6.1b; Bello, *Opium and the Limits of Empire*, 279.

60. He, *Nai'an zouyi*, 6.25a.

61. Zuo, TZ 10, *ZZQJ*, 14:528.

62. Zuo, TZ 10, *ZZQJ*, 14:528. For comparisons, see Li, *Agricultural Development in Jiangnan*, 122–27; and Shi, *Agricultural Development in Qing China*, 74.

63. Zuo, TZ 10, *ZZQJ*, 14:528. On the development of rice agriculture in Gansu, see also *Chongxin xianzhi*, 1.26a.

64. Zuo, TZ 10, *ZZQJ*, 14:529; GX 5/6/15, *QXDX*, 7:416–17.

65. Zuo, Memorial, TZ 13/3/22, *ZZQJ*, 6:27; Zuo Zongtang, TZ 13/3/22, NPM-GCA 114834.

66. Zuo to Tan Zhonglin, TZ 13, *ZZQJ*, 11:444.

67. Zuo, Memorial, TZ 13/3/22, *ZZQJ*, 6:28; Zuo Zongtang, TZ 13/3/22, NPM-GCA 114834; Zuo to Zongli Yamen, GX 5, *ZZQJ*, 12:464; *ZWGN*, 7.1a; Qin Hancai, *Zuo Wenxiang gong zai xibei* (Changsha: Yuelu shushe, 1984), 243–44.

68. Because this text no longer exists, it is impossible to determine its content or potential use.

69. *Mian shu* (Fujian fanshu, 1866; reprint, Shanghai: Shanghai guji chubanshe, 1996). See also Xiao, *Nongye guji banben congtan*, 130–35.

70. Xiao, *Nongye guji banben congtan*, 129. One of the sources of its information, the eighteenth-century *Treatise on Cotton* (*Mumian pu*), was republished by Zuo's mentor He Changling in Guizhou in 1837. See He, *Nai'an zouyi*, 6.1a.

71. Bray, "Science, Technique, Technology," 334.

72. *Mian shu*, 1a, 12a.

73. *Dali xian xuzhi*, 12 *juan*, ed. Zhou Mingqi (n.p., 1879), 4.20a.

74. GX 4/8/29, QXDX, 7:231; GX 5/6/15, QXDX, 7:416–17.

75. *Suzhou xinzhi*, 506, 665.

76. GX 4/3/25, XUARA 15-21-0113.

77. Analyses of the famine and its relation to Qing politics can be found in Paul Richard Bohr, *Famine in China and the Missionary: Timothy Richard as Relief Administrator and Advocate of National Reform, 1876–1884* (Cambridge, MA: East Asian Research Center, Harvard University, 1972); He Hanwei, *Guangxu chunian (1876–79) Huabei de da hanzai* (Hong Kong: Zhongwen daxue chubanshe, 1980); Mike Davis, *Late Victorian Holocausts: El Niño Famines and the Making of the Third World* (New York: Verso, 2001); Andrea Janku, "'Heaven-Sent Disasters' in Late Imperial China: The Scope of the State and Beyond," in *Natural Disasters, Cultural Responses: Case Studies toward a Global Environmental History*, ed. Christof Mauch and Christian Pfister (Lanham, MD: Lexington, 2009), 233–64; Edgerton-Tarpley, *Tears from Iron*; and Li, *Fighting Famine in North China*, 272–77. For documentation of the extent of the drought underlying the famine, see Tan, ed., *Qingdai ganhan dang'an shiliao*, 664–806.

78. Zuo, Memorial, GX 4/7/4, ZZQJ, 7:143; Zuo, GX 4, ZZQJ, 14:450.

79. Zuo, Memorial, GX 4/7/4, ZZQJ, 7:147.

80. Zuo, GX 4, ZZQJ, 14:450.

81. Spence, "Opium Smoking in Ch'ing China," 153.

82. Richthofen, *Baron Richthofen's Letters*, 22; Piassetsky, *Russian Travellers in Mongolia and China*, 2:225.

83. Zuo reported that the richest farmlands in Ningxia, located on the more fertile eastern bank of the Yellow River, could yield as much as seventy to eighty ounces (*liang*) of unprocessed opium per *mu*, while land on the western bank produced about half as much opium per *mu*. See Zuo, GX 4, ZZQJ, 14:450. In the early 1870s, Richthofen reported that Gansu opium cost about nine hundred to one thousand coins of copper cash per ounce (*liang*) in Henan and Shanxi, 0.4 taels of silver per ounce in Xi'an, and 0.38 taels of silver per ounce in Gansu. See Richthofen, *Baron Richthofen's Letters*, 22, 109.

84. Edgerton-Tarpley, *Tears from Iron*, 107–112; Davis, *Late Victorian Holocausts*, 346.

85. Inspector General of Customs, *Reports on Trade at the Treaty Ports in China, for the Year 1876* (Shanghai: Statistical Department of the Inspectorate General of Customs, 1877), 24. On the damage done to opium crops in India, see Foreign Office, *Commercial Reports by Her Majesty's Consuls in China, 1877–78* (London: Harrison & Sons, 1879), 4–5; and Davis, *Late Victorian Holocausts*, 322.

86. Zuo reported that the price of opium reached sixty to seventy taels of silver for one hundred ounces of the drug. Zuo to Wang Siyi, GX 5, ZZQJ, 12:531.

87. Zuo, TZ 10, ZZQJ, 14:270.

88. Zuo, Memorial, TZ 13/5/6, ZZQJ, 6:45; Zuo Zongtang, TZ 13/3/22, NPM-GCA 114837.

89. Zuo, GX 4, ZZQJ, 14:450; Zuo, GX 4, ZZQJ, 14:556.

90. Zuo, Memorial, GX 4/7/4, ZZQJ, 7:144–45; Zuo, Memorial, GX 4/10/23, ZZQJ, 7:201; Zuo to Liu Dian, GX 4, ZZQJ, 12:369.

91. Zuo to Zhu Zhi, GX 4, ZZQJ, 12:367. See also Zuo, Memorial, GX 4/7/4, ZZQJ, 7:143; and Zuo, Memorial, GX 4/7/4, ZZQJ, 7:147.

92. Zuo, Memorial, GX 4/7/4, ZZQJ, 7:143.

93. David A. Bello, "Qing Opium Dependency and Republican Opium Autonomy," in Early Modern East Asia: War, Commerce, and Cultural Exchange, ed. Kenneth M. Swope and Tonio Andrade (New York: Routledge, 2018), 20.

94. Lin, "Late Qing Perceptions of Native Opium," 121; Edgerton-Tarpley, Tears from Iron, 105–6.

95. Zuo to Wang Siyi, GX 5, ZZQJ, 12:531. See also Kreitner, "Geographie," 154.

96. Zuo, Memorial, GX 7/5/5, ZZQJ, 8:31.

97. Zuo, Memorial, GX 7/5/5, ZZQJ, 8:30–33. See also Zuo, Memorial, GX 7/8/27, ZZQJ, 8:45–48.

98. Joyce A. Madancy, The Troublesome Legacy of Commissioner Lin: The Opium Trade and Opium Suppression in Fujian Province, 1820s to 1920s (Cambridge, MA: Harvard University Asia Center, 2003), 59.

99. Zuo to Liu Jintang, GX 7, ZZQJ, 12:722.

100. Qinzhou zhili zhou xinzhi, 3.13b.

101. Kreitner, "Geographie," 154.

102. Trocki, Opium, Empire and the Global Political Economy, 126.

103. This decline may have been part of a longer slump in agricultural commodity prices that characterized the late decades of the nineteenth century. For reference to the longer slump, see Eric Hobsbawm, The Age of Capital, 1848–1875 (New York: Vintage, 1996), 5, 68. On the global convergence of prices over the course of the nineteenth century, see Ronald Findlay and Kevin H. O'Rourke, Power and Plenty: Trade, War, and the World Economy in the Second Millennium (Princeton, NJ: Princeton University Press, 2007), 402–7.

104. Beckert, Empire of Cotton, 335–37. On the integration of the Chinese and international markets for agricultural commodities in the late nineteenth century, see Loren Brandt, Commercialization and Agricultural Development: Central and Eastern China, 1870–1937 (Cambridge: Cambridge University Press, 1989).

105. Zuo to Tan Zhonglin, TZ 13, ZZQJ, 11:444; Zuo to Zongli Yamen, GX 5, ZZQJ, 12:464.

106. Jingji xuehui, *Gansu quansheng caizheng shuoming shu*, 128. On the creation of cotton weaving bureaus in Gansu in the 1880s, see Rao Yingqi, *Xinjiang xunfu Rao Yingqi gaoben wenxian jicheng*, 37 vols., ed. Li Delong (Beijing: Xueyuan chubanshe, 2008), 37:421–22, 429–31, 435–36, 439–40.

5. Water in a Fertile Frontier

1. Imperial edict, GX 1/2/3, *ZZQJ*, 6:154–55; Imperial edict, GX 1/2/3, in *Guangxu chao shangyu dang*, 34 vols., comp. Zhongguo diyi lishi dang'anguan (Guilin: Guangxi shifan daxue chubanshe, 2008), 1:42–44.

2. On this episode, see Robert Eskildsen, *Transforming Empire in Japan and East Asia: The Taiwan Expedition and the Birth of Japanese Imperialism* (Singapore: Palgrave Macmillan, 2019); Leonard H. D. Gordon, *Confrontation over Taiwan: Nineteenth-Century China and the Powers* (Lanham, MD: Lexington, 2007), 77–131; and Norihito Mizuno, "Qing China's Reaction to the 1874 Japanese Expedition to the Taiwanese Aboriginal Territories," *Sino-Japanese Studies* 16 (2009): 100–125.

3. Wang Wenshao, TZ 13/11/11, *CBYWSM*, 99.61a; Ding Baozhen, TZ 13/11/25, *CBYWSM*, 100.41a-b.

4. S. C. M. Paine, *Imperial Rivals: China, Russia, and Their Disputed Frontier* (Armonk, NY: M. E. Sharpe, 1996), 90–91. See also Chen Weixin, *Shiluo de jiangyu: Qingji xibei bianjie bianqian tiaoyue yutu tezhan* (Taipei: Guoli gugong bowuyuan, 2010).

5. Immanuel C. Y. Hsü, *The Ili Crisis: A Study of Sino-Russian Diplomacy, 1871–1881* (Oxford: Clarendon, 1965), 30–32; Paine, *Imperial Rivals*, 120–22.

6. On the debate, see Immanuel C. Y. Hsü, "The Great Policy Debate in China, 1874: Maritime Defense vs. Frontier Defense," *Harvard Journal of Asiatic Studies* 25 (1964–65): 212–28; and Kwang-Ching Liu and Richard J. Smith, "The Military Challenge: The North-West and the Coast," in *The Cambridge History of China*, vol. 11, *Late Ch'ing, 1800–1911*, pt. 2, ed. John K. Fairbank and Kwang-Ching Liu (Cambridge: Cambridge University Press, 1980), 202–73.

7. Li Hongzhang, TZ 13/11/4, *CBYWSM*, 99.24a-b.

8. Li Hongzhang, TZ 13/11/4, *CBYWSM*, 99.23b.

9. Zuo, Memorial, GX 1/3/7, *ZZQJ*, 6:192.

10. Zuo, Memorial, GX 1/3/7, *ZZQJ*, 6:191. On earlier claims about the so-called "forward defense dividend," see Millward, *Beyond the Pass*, 41–42.

11. Jack A. Dabbs, *History of the Discovery and Exploration of Chinese Turkestan* (The Hague: Mouton, 1963).

12. Henry W. Bellew and Edward Chapman, "General Description of Kashghar," in Forsyth, *Report of a Mission to Yarkund*, 26.

13. Biddulph, "Visit to Maralbashi," 221. For similar sentiments, see W. H. Johnson, "Report on His Journey to Ilchí, the Capital of Khotan, in Chinese Tartary," *Journal of the Royal Geographical Society* 37 (1867): 6.

14. A. N. Kuropatkin, *Kashgaria: Eastern or Chinese Turkistan: Historical and Geographical Sketch of the Country; Its Military Strength, Industries and Trade*, trans. Walter E. Gowan (Calcutta: Thacker, Spink, 1882), 23, 24.

15. The court appointed Zuo "Imperial Commissioner for Xinjiang Military Affairs," a title he held concurrently with the office he retained, governor-general of Shaanxi and Gansu. See Imperial edict, GX 1/3/28, *ZZQJ*, 6:205; GX 1/3/28, *Dezong Jing huangdi shilu*, 597 *juan* (Tokyo, 1937; reprint, Taipei: Hualian chubanshe, 1964), 6.9b–10a.

16. Hubu, "Tongzhou Xinjiang quanju yi gui jiuyuan shu," in *Huangchao Dao Xian Tong Guang zouyi*, 64 *juan*, ed. Wang Yanxi and Wang Shumin (Shanghai: Jiujingzhai, 1902), 26.*xia*.11a. From 1874 to 1880, total expenses reached a staggering 52.3 million taels. For expense reports, see Zuo, Memorial, TZ 13/6/29, *ZZQJ*, 6:65–78; Zuo, Memorial, GX 5/4/11, *ZZQJ*, 7:326–34; Zuo, Memorial, GX 5/11/8, *ZZQJ*, 7:439–51; and Zuo, Memorial, GX 8/6/4, *ZZQJ*, 8:104–14. On international bank loans which supported the reconquest, see C. John Stanley, *Late Ch'ing Finance: Hu Kuang-yung as an Innovator* (Cambridge, MA: East Asian Research Center, Harvard University, 1961), 51.

17. Edgerton-Tarpley, *Tears from Iron*, 38.

18. Zuo, Memorial, GX 3/3/29, *ZZQJ*, 6:639; Zuo, Memorial, GX 3/6/16, *ZZQJ*, 6:703; Zuo, Memorial, GX 4/10/22, *ZZQJ*, 7:193. The Board of Revenue later reported that Ili's best land could produce yields with a harvest-to-seed ratio of over thirty to one. See Hubu, GX 10/9/29, FHA-GCA 03-8105-013.

19. Zuo, Memorial, GX 4/10/22, *ZZQJ*, 7:195–96. On market prices in Xinjiang, see Zuo, Memorial, GX 4/1/7, *ZZQJ*, 7:5. Claims about low market prices were corroborated by others. See "Lun Xinjiang qingxing," *Shenbao*, March 30, 1878. See also Zuo, Memorial, GX 3/6/16, *ZZQJ*, 6:703; and Zuo, Memorial, GX 4/10/22, *ZZQJ*, 7:193.

20. Zuo, Memorial, GX 4/10/22, *ZZQJ*, 7:196.

21. This phrase originated in Warring States-era discourses on statecraft and wealth. In a chapter about "enriching the state," Xunzi advised rulers to promote the production of goods among the people and reduce the extent of state exactions in order to generate prosperity. See Eric L. Hutton, trans., *Xunzi: The Complete Text* (Princeton, NJ: Princeton University Press, 2014), 95.

22. Li Hanzhang, TZ 13/11/14, *CBYWSM*, 100.16b.

23. For these discussions, see Ding Richang, "Haifang tiaoyi," in *Bianshi xuchao*, 8 *juan*, ed. Zhu Kejing (Changsha, 1880), 3.15b–16a; Li Hanzhang, TZ 13/11/14, *CBYWSM*, 100.16b; Liu Kunyi, TZ 13/11/17, *CBYWSM*, 100.25a-b; Li Hongzhang, TZ 13/11/4, *CBYWSM*, 99.26a; and Li Zongxi, TZ 13/11/12, *CBYWSM*, 100.9a.

24. Zuo spoke about such projects using the language of "opening up springs and restricting the outflow." For example, see Zuo, Memorial, GX 4/1/7, *ZZQJ*, 7:6.

25. On hydraulic development in Xinjiang, see Hori Sunao, "Shindai kaikyō no suiri kangai: 19–20 seiki no Yārukando o chūshin to shite," *Ōtemae joshi daigaku ronshū* 14 (1980): 72–99.

26. Zuo to Liu Jintang, GX 4, *ZZQJ*, 12:387.

27. For recent examples of state-environment entanglements, see David Biggs, *Quagmire: Nation-Building and Nature in the Mekong Delta* (Seattle: University of Washington Press, 2010); and Ling Zhang, *The River, the Plain, and the State: An Environmental Drama in Northern Song China, 1048–1128* (Cambridge: Cambridge University Press, 2016).

28. Mark Fiege, *Irrigated Eden: The Making of an Agricultural Landscape in the American West* (Seattle: University of Washington Press, 1999), 6, 8–9; Emmanuel Kreike, *Environmental Infrastructure in African History: Examining the Myth of Natural Resource Management in Namibia* (Cambridge: Cambridge University Press, 2013), 21–22; David Gilmartin, *Blood and Water: The Indus River Basin in Modern History* (Berkeley: University of California Press, 2015), 150; Timothy Mitchell, *Rule of Experts: Egypt, Techno-Politics, Modernity* (Berkeley: University of California Press, 2002), 52.

29. Zuo, Memorial, TZ 12/12/10, *ZZQJ*, 5:542–43; Zuo, Memorial, TZ 13/10/4, *ZZQJ*, 6:109.

30. Zuo, Memorial, TZ 13/11/3, *ZZQJ*, 6:123; Cao, *Zhongguo renkou shi*, 701.

31. Zuo to Zhang Yao, TZ 13, *ZZQJ*, 11:439.

32. Zuo, Memorial, GX 1/8/25, *ZZQJ*, 6:319; Zuo, Memorial, GX 1/8/25, *ZZQJ*, 6:324; Wei Guangtao, *Kanding Xinjiang ji*, 8 *juan* (n.p., 1899; reprint, Taipei: Wenhai chubanshe, 1968), 8.11b. See also Zuo, Memorial, GX 2/1/3, *ZZQJ*, 6:374–75.

33. Zuo, Memorial, GX 1/8/25, *ZZQJ*, 6:324.

34. Zuo, Memorial, GX 2/7/18, *ZZQJ*, 6:497.

35. GX 3/12/4, *QXDX*, 6:398.

36. Cao, *Zhongguo renkou shi*, 701; Gong-tang, GX 5/R3/21, FHA-GCA 03-9553-047.

37. Zuo, Memorial, GX 4/2/1, *ZZQJ*, 7:29.

38. Zuo, GX 4, *ZZQJ*, 14:454; Zuo, GX 4, *ZZQJ*, 14:558.

39. Zuo, Memorial, GX 4/10/22, *ZZQJ*, 7:192; Zuo, Memorial, GX 6/4/17, *ZZQJ*, 7:518; Gong-tang, GX 5/2/30, FHA-GCA 03-9553-044.

40. Zuo, Memorial, GX 4/1/7, *ZZQJ*, 7:5; Zuo, Memorial, GX 4/4/2, *ZZQJ*, 7:95–96.

41. Zuo, Memorial, GX 3/10/14, *ZZQJ*, 6:759.

42. There were head bureaus in Kashgar and Aksu; regular bureaus in Turpan, Urumchi, Karashahr, Kucha, Uchturpan, Yangihissar, Yarkand, and Khotan; and branch bureaus in Shayar, Bay, and Maralbashi. See Liu, GX 10/2/28, *LXGZ*, 6.48b.

43. Liu, GX 9/7/1, *LXGZ*, 5.62b–63a.

44. Liu, GX 11/3/6, *LXGZ*, 8.53b.

45. Kim, *Borderland Capitalism*, 55.

46. For an example of one such register produced in this era, see GX 4/11/18, *QXDX*, 7:37–56.

47. For land tax regulations in Xinjiang prior to the reconquest, see Hubu, *Qinding hubu zeli*, 6.16a–20a. On the history of the grading system, see Ho, *Studies on the Population of China*, 102–4.

48. Zuo, Memorial, GX 6/4/17, *ZZQJ*, 7:518.

49. Zuo, Memorial, GX 6/4/17, *ZZQJ*, 7:518; GX 8/4/7, *QXDX*, 8:440–41; Wei, *Kanding Xinjiang ji*, 8.12b.

50. GX 7/2/9, *QXDX*, 77:220; GX 8/2/28, *QXDX*, 77:396.

51. GX 5/11/30, *QXDX*, 8:19–21.

52. Zuo, Memorial, GX 4/12/6, *ZZQJ*, 7:232; Zuo, Memorial, GX 6/4/18, *ZZQJ*, 7:529; Zuo, Memorial, GX 6/12/2, *ZZQJ*, 7:630; GX 6/9/3, *QXDX*, 77:124.

53. Zuo to Jin-shun, GX 3, *ZZQJ*, 12:271; Zuo to Liu Jintang, GX 3, *ZZQJ*, 12:274.

54. Zuo, Memorial, GX 3/10/14, *ZZQJ*, 6:755–56.

55. Zuo, Memorial, GX 4/12/6, *ZZQJ*, 7:229–30; Wei, *Kanding Xinjiang ji*, 8.12b; GX 7/2/19, *QXDX*, 38:237; GX 7/2/24, *QXDX*, 38:239.

56. Liu, GX 7/7/2, *LXGZ*, 2.52a–53a; Wei, *Kanding Xinjiang ji*, 8.12b.

57. Liu, GX 7/7/2, *LXGZ*, 2.53b–54b; *Xinjiang tuzhi*, 78.16b–17a, 18a, 19a, 20b–21b.

58. Zuo, Memorial, GX 6/4/17, *ZZQJ*, 7:517; Zuo, Memorial, GX 6/4/17, *ZZQJ*, 7:524–25; Zuo, GX 5, *ZZQJ*, 14:479; Wei, *Kanding Xinjiang ji*, 8.11b–12b; GX 10/8/10, *QXDX*, 9:401.

59. *Bachu zhou xiangtu zhi*, ed. Zhang Zaoguang (n.p., 1908; reprint, Lanzhou: Lanzhou guji shudian, 1990), 267.

60. *Xinjiang tuzhi*, j. 73–78; Hua, *Qingdai Xinjiang nongye kaifa shi*, 222–25; Zhao Zhen, *Qingdai xibei shengtai bianqian yanjiu* (Beijing: Renmin chubanshe, 2005), 280.

61. Wei Guangtao, GX 17/11/28, in *Gongzhongdang Guangxu chao zouzhe*, 26 vols., comp. Guoli gugong bowuyuan (Taipei: Guoli gugong bowuyuan, 1973–75), 6:778–79; GX 18/4/29, *QXDX*, 13:85–86.

62. Nikolay Prejevalsky, "Letters from Colonel Prejevalsky," *Proceedings of the Royal Geographical Society* 7, no. 12 (December 1885): 814.

63. For one description of water allocation practices in Turkestani communities in Xinjiang, see Ildikó Bellér-Hann, *Community Matters in Xinjiang, 1880–1949: Towards a Historical Anthropology of the Uyghur* (Leiden: Brill, 2008), 107–8.

64. On begs, see L. J. Newby, "The Begs of Xinjiang: Between Two Worlds," *Bulletin of the School of Oriental and African Studies* 61, no. 2 (June 1998): 278–97; and James A. Millward and Laura J. Newby, "The Qing and Islam on the Western Frontier," in Crossley, Siu, and Sutton, *Empire at the Margins*, 117–23. On the benefits they received for their collaboration, see Kim, *Borderland Capitalism*, 7, 58.

65. Newby, "The Begs of Xinjiang," 283; Kim, *Holy War in China*, 12.

66. GX 3/12, *QXDX*, 6:396–97; GX 13, *QXDX*, 11:118–19.

67. Zuo, Memorial, GX 4/9/24, *ZZQJ*, 7:176.

68. Some begs were rewarded for their willingness to provide assistance to Qing forces during the reconquest. Others found employment in the reconstruction bureaus. See Zuo, Memorial, GX 4/9/24, *ZZQJ*, 7:175; and Zuo, Memorial, GX 6/4/18, *ZZQJ*, 7:534–35.

69. Liu, GX 7/7/2, *LXGZ*, 2.56a; Zuo, Memorial, GX 6/4/17, *ZZQJ*, 7:517; GX 13/2/23, *QXDX*, 79:382–83. Daily wages for workers were generally lower in more populous southern Xinjiang. See Liu, GX 13/7/26, *LXGZ*, 13.31a.

70. GX 6/10/20, *QXDX*, 8:202–3. The Qing state also seems to have gotten involved in certain cases of misbehavior by local officials who governed community water resources. For an example, see GX 12/4/21, *QXDX*, 79:234. For insights into the legal system in late Qing Xinjiang, see Eric T. Schluessel, "Muslims at the Yamen Gate: Translating Justice in Late-Qing Xinjiang," in *Kashgar Revisited: Uyghur Studies in Memory of Ambassador Gunnar Jarring*, ed. Ildikó Bellér-Hann, Birgit N. Schlyter, and Jun Sugawara (Leiden: Brill, 2016), 116–38.

71. The term *karez*, from Persian, was often transliterated in Chinese-language documents as *kan'er* or *kanjing*. For examples, see Zuo to Liu Dian, GX 3, *ZZQJ*, 12:307; Zuo, Memorial, GX 6/4/17, *ZZQJ*, 7:517; and GX 4/4/17, XUARA 15-4-96. For a study of the history of karez in Turpan, see Zhong Xingqi and Chu Huaizhen, eds., *Tulufan kan'erjing* (Urumchi: Xinjiang daxue chubanshe, 1993).

72. Iwao Kobori, "Notes from the Turpan Basin: Pioneering Research on the Karez," in *Water and Sustainability in Arid Regions: Bridging the Gap between*

Physical and Social Sciences, ed. Graciela Schneier-Madanes and Marie-Françoise Courel (Dordrecht: Springer, 2010), 142–44.

73. Éric Trombert, "The Karez Concept in Ancient Chinese Sources: Myth or Reality?" *T'oung Pao* 94 (2008): 119–23, 142–47; Shimazaki Akira, "Higashi Tōrukisutān ni okeru kārēzu kangai no kigen ni tsuite," *Shikagu zasshi* 63, no. 12 (December 1954): 1074–114; Ellsworth Huntington, "The Depression of Turfan, in Central Asia," *The Geographical Journal* 30, no. 3 (September 1907): 270–71; M. Aurel Stein, *Ruins of Desert Cathay: Personal Narrative of Explorations in Central Asia and Westernmost China,* 2 vols. (London: Macmillan, 1912), 2:354–57.

74. For a case of death from karez construction work, see GX 5/4/15, QXDX, 51:98–99.

75. Lin, *Lin Zexu quanji,* 9:537.

76. Le-bin, XF 2/10/8, NPM-GCA 087290.

77. Liu, GX 10/4/28, LXGZ, 7.15a-b.

78. Hua, *Qingdai Xinjiang nongye kaifa shi,* 185–86.

79. GX 8/3, QXDX, 8:431–32.

80. Kim, *Borderland Capitalism,* 73.

81. GX 3/12/24, QXDX, 6:392. An 1883 report tallied approximately 49,700 residents in Turpan, most of them men. See GX 11/11/30, QXDX, 10:297–98.

82. Kim, *Holy War in China,* 58.

83. Numerous Han survivors of the uprising or their children returned to Turpan after 1877 to report their losses to Qing authorities and seek compensation or the reinstatement of prior rental agreements. For examples, see GX 7/5/20, QXDX, 8:114–15; GX 8/3, QXDX, 8:431–32; GX 8/3, QXDX, 8:434; GX 11/7/8, QXDX, 10:204–206; and GX 15/6/1, QXDX, 11:423–25. Some Han seem to have filed fraudulent claims against Turkestani property-owners, seeking to use the arm of the law to cheat locals out of their land. For example, see GX 7/5/4, QXDX, 8:302.

84. Kim, *Borderland Capitalism,* 180.

85. Zuo to Liu Dian, GX 3, ZZQJ, 12:307; GX 4/4/17, XUARA 15-4-96; GX 4/4/17, QXDX, 7:133–34.

86. Zuo, Memorial, GX 6/4/17, ZZQJ, 7:524; Zuo, Memorial, GX 6/4/17, ZZQJ, 7:517.

87. GX 10/5/13, QXDX, 78:289; GX 10/5, QXDX, 78:301–2; GX 10/6, QXDX, 78:323–24.

88. GX 11/9/19, QXDX, 79:130–31; GX 12/10/4, QXDX, 79:311; GX 12, QXDX, 79:368–69.

89. GX 3/6/27, QXDX, 6:268.

90. For example, see GX 9/8/9, QXDX, 9:196.

91. GX 6/6/3, *QXDX*, 8:48. The original request was for fifty *dan* of sorghum and twenty *dan* of wheat.

92. GX 8/2/8, *QXDX*, 8:399. For similar requests, see GX 8/2/13, *QXDX*, 8:402; and GX 8/2/17, *QXDX*, 8:403.

93. GX 10/8/19, *QXDX*, 78:350–51.

94. GX 8/2/21, *QXDX*, 8:405; GX 8/2/28, *QXDX*, 8:407–8.

95. GX 12/7/22, *QXDX*, 10:412–13.

96. GX 7/2/14, *QXDX*, 77:221. See also GX 7/2/15, *QXDX*, 77:225; GX 7/2/20, *QXDX*, 77:226; GX 7/2/22, *QXDX*, 77:226; and GX 7/2/23, *QXDX*, 77:227.

97. Liu, GX 10/4/28, *LXGZ*, 7.15b.

98. Bellew and Chapman, "General Description of Kashghar," 39, 50. See also Henry W. Bellew, *Kashmir and Kashghar: A Narrative of the Journey of the Embassy to Kashghar in 1873–74* (London: Trübner, 1875), 9–10.

99. Nikolay Prejevalsky, *From Kulja, across the Tian Shan to Lob-Nor*, trans. E. Delmar Morgan (London: Sampson Low, Marston, Searle & Rivington, 1879), 54, 87.

100. Gong-tang, GX 5/1/27, FHA-GCA 03-8105-011; Gong-tang, GX 5/2/30, FHA-GCA 03-9553-044.

101. Liu, GX 7/7/2, *LXGZ*, 2.56a.

102. Wentai Zhang et al., "Characteristics of Water Erosion and Conservation Practice in Arid Regions of Central Asia: Xinjiang, China as an Example," *International Soil and Water Conservation Research* 3, no. 2 (June 2015): 102.

103. Henry Trotter, "Geographical Report," in Forsyth, *Report of a Mission to Yarkund*, 264, 254.

104. Trotter, "Geographical Report," 260, 265.

105. Liu, GX 10/4/28, *LXGZ*, 7.15b.

106. GX 7/2/14, *QXDX*, 77:221.

107. Liu, GX 10/4/28, *LXGZ*, 7.15b.

108. Wei, *Kanding Xinjiang ji*, 8.11b; *Hami zhili ting xiangtu zhi*, ed. Liu Rundao (n.p., 1909; reprint, Lanzhou: Lanzhou guji shudian, 1990), 168.

109. Zuo to Zhang Yao, GX 1, *ZZQJ*, 11:515–16.

110. GX 5/11/30, *QXDX*, 8:19–21; *Xinjiang tuzhi*, 74.18a.

111. *Xinjiang tuzhi*, 73.4b–5a. See also Hua, *Qingdai Xinjiang nongye kaifa shi*, 228.

112. Z. W. Kundzewicz et al., "Analysis of Changes in Climate and River Discharge with Focus on Seasonal Runoff Predictability in the Aksu River Basin," *Environmental Earth Sciences* 73, no. 2 (January 2015): 505; Jianhua Xu, Yaning Chen, and Weihong Li, "The Nonlinear Hydro-Climatic Process: A Case Study of the Tarim Headwaters, NW China," in *Water Resources Research in Northwest China*, ed. Yaning Chen (Dordrecht: Springer, 2014), 291–92.

113. *Xinjiang tuzhi*, 78.20b–21b.

114. *Xinjiang tuzhi*, 78.21a.

115. *Xinjiang tuzhi*, 78.20b–21b.

116. GX 6/6/26, *QXDX*, 8:136; Liu, GX 9/11/4, *LXGZ*, 6.26a.

117. Gong-tang, GX 5/9/29, FHA-GCA 03-9553-057. On rainmaking ceremonies as political performance, see Jeffrey Snyder-Reinke, *Dry Spells: State Rainmaking and Local Governance in Late Imperial China* (Cambridge, MA: Harvard University Asia Center, 2009).

118. Gong-tang, GX 5/12/10, FHA-GCA 03-9553-065.

119. For the court's request and Zuo's initial response, see GX 3/5/10, *Dezong Jing huangdi shilu*, 51.5b–6a; and Zuo, Memorial, GX 3/6/16, *ZZQJ*, 6:701–4. For the subsequent proposals, see Zuo, Memorial, GX 4/1/7, *ZZQJ*, 7:3–6; Zuo, Memorial, GX 4/10/22, *ZZQJ*, 7:190–98; Zuo, Memorial, GX 6/4/18, *ZZQJ*, 7:527–30; and Zuo, Memorial, GX 8/9/7, *ZZQJ*, 8:147–51. For his perspective on Gong's earlier proposal, see Zuo to Tao Guang, GX 6, *ZZQJ*, 12:596.

120. Imperial edict, GX 4/9/30, *ZZQJ*, 7:173; GX 4/9/30, *Dezong Jing huangdi shilu*, 78.17a–18a.

121. Liu Hai'ao, GX 8/8/3, in *Qinding pingding Shaan Gan Xinjiang Huifei fanglüe*, 320 *juan*, ed. Yi-xin et al. (n.p., 1896), 315.23b–26a; Zhu Fengjia, "Xinjiang she xingsheng yi," in Wang, *Xiaofanghuzhai yudi congchao*, 2.119b.

122. Li Yunlin, *Xichui shilüe* (n.p., 1878; reprint, Beijing: Xianzhuang shuju, 2003), 68.

123. Li, *Xichui shilüe*, 52–53. Another opponent of provincialization, Liu Hai'ao, also supported colonization. See Liu Hai'ao, GX 8/8/3, in Yi-xin, *Qinding pingding Shaan Gan Xinjiang Huifei fanglüe*, 315.25a-b.

124. Tan, *Tan Wenqin gong zougao*, 9.5b. See also Tan Zhonglin, GX 8/2/27, in Yi-xin, *Qinding pingding Shaan Gan Xinjiang Huifei fanglüe*, 315.11b. Liu Jintang, another supporter of the plan, was similarly concerned about the specific arrangements of administrative divisions and civil offices. See Liu, GX 8/7/3, *LXGZ*, 3.51a; Liu, GX 8/7/3, *LXGZ*, 3.44a–47b; Liu Jintang and Tan Zhonglin, GX 8, in *Dao Xian Tong Guang sichao zouyi*, 12 vols., comp. Wang Yunwu (Taipei: Taiwan shangwu yinshuguan, 1970), 10:4521; and Liu Jintang and Tan Zhonglin, GX 8/7/22, in Yi-xin, *Qinding pingding Shaan Gan Xinjiang Huifei fanglüe*, 315.12b–15b.

125. GX 10/9/30, *Dezong Jing huangdi shilu*, 194.27a–28a.

126. For various interpretations of this transition, see Ping-ti Ho, "In Defense of Sinicization: A Rebuttal of Evelyn Rawski's 'Reenvisioning the Qing,'" *Journal of Asian Studies* 57, no. 1 (February 1998): 148; Kataoka Kazutada, *Shinchō Shinkyō tōchi kenkyū* (Tokyo: Yūzankaku 1991), 202–13; and Millward, *Beyond the Pass*, 250. After this decision, the official recognition given to local elites by the empire gradually ended. By September 1888, Liu Jintang was reporting to Beijing that all Turkic officials except for three Muslims "kings" in the oases of Hami, Turpan, and Kucha had been removed from their posts. See Liu Jintang, GX 14/7/26, FHA-GCA 03-8099-025.

127. Liu, GX 12/1/21, *LXGZ*, 10.37b.

128. Liu, GX 13/2/12, *LXGZ*, 12.16a.

129. XUARA 15-34-3258. This document is undated and only partially preserved, but a comparison of its contents with a memorial written by Liu Jintang suggests a production date prior to early 1887. See Liu, GX 13/2/12, *LXGZ*, 12:16a–18a; and *Qingdai zouzhe huibian: nongye, huanjing*, 553. On tax remission and land reclamation policies in these years, see GX 10/11, *QXDX*, 39:424–25; and GX 11/9/15, *QXDX*, 79:125–26.

130. Liu, GX 13/2/12, *LXGZ*, 12.17a. On the problems of land reclamation in the north, see GX 13/2/21, *QXDX*, 2:127–29.

131. GX 13, *QXDX*, 11:118–19; Hua, *Qingdai Xinjiang nongye kaifa shi*, 219; Cao, *Zhongguo renkou shi*, 701.

132. Data on cultivated land in Qing Xinjiang was only irregularly reported to Beijing. Estimates of the total arable land in the territory during the last three decades of imperial rule range from 9.3 million *mu* (1887) to 11.2 million *mu* (1894) to 10.5 million *mu* (1911). For these figures, see Hori Sunao, "Shindai kaikyō no kōchi menseki: nagareru mizu kara, ugokanu daichi e," *Kōnan daigaku kiyō, bungakuhen* 90 (1993): 32n21; Hua, *Qingdai Xinjiang nongye kaifa shi*, 229–30; and *Xinjiang tuzhi*, 30.5a. In 1887, Liu Jintang reported a total of 11.4 million *mu* of "waste and cultivated land" in Xinjiang. See *Xinjiang tuzhi*, 30.4b; and GX 13, *QXDX*, 11:118–19. For an overview of estimates during the entire Qing period, see Kim, *Borderland Capitalism*, 202.

133. E. Delmar Morgan, "Expedition of the Brothers Grijimailo to the Tian Shan Oases and Lob-nor," *Proceedings of the Royal Geographical Society* 13, no. 4 (April 1891): 220.

134. Diana K. Davis, "Deserts," in *The Oxford Handbook of Environmental History*, ed. Andrew C. Isenberg (Oxford: Oxford University Press, 2014), 114–19. See also Richard H. Grove, *Green Imperialism: Colonial Expansion, Tropical Island Edens and the Origins of Environmentalism, 1600–1860* (Cambridge: Cambridge University Press, 1995).

135. On official recognition of the problems of water scarcity caused by agrarian development in late Qing Xinjiang, see Xie Li, *Qingdai zhi minguo shiqi nongye kaifa dui Talimu pendi nanyuan shengtai huanjing de yingxiang* (Shanghai: Shanghai renmin chubanshe, 2008), 48.

6. Sericulture in a Colonial Borderland

1. Hsü, *The Ili Crisis*, 57, 185; Paine, *Imperial Rivals*, 134, 152.

2. Zuo, Memorial, GX 6/4/17, *ZZQJ*, 7:521.

3. Hsiao Liang-lin, *China's Foreign Trade Statistics, 1864–1949* (Cambridge, MA: East Asian Research Center, Harvard University, 1974), 109; Jerome Ch'en, *State Economic Policies of the Ch'ing Government, 1840–1895* (New York: Garland, 1980), 69.

4. Philip C. C. Huang, *The Peasant Economy and Social Change in North China* (Stanford, CA: Stanford University Press, 1985), 122; Dwight H. Perkins, *Agricultural Development in China, 1368–1968* (Chicago: Aldine, 1969), 132.

5. Debin Ma, "The Modern Silk Road: The Global Raw-Silk Market, 1850–1930," *Journal of Economic History* 56, no. 2 (June 1996): 332–33; Giovanni Federico, *An Economic History of the Silk Industry, 1830–1930* (Cambridge: Cambridge University Press, 1997), 36–41, 76–77.

6. Feng, *Jiaobinlu kangyi*, *xia*.2b; Zheng Guanying, *Yi yan*, 2 *juan* (Hong Kong: Zhonghua yinwu zongju, 1880), *shang*.10b.

7. GX 5/3/23, QXDX, 7:357; Zuo, Memorial, GX 5/12/17, ZZQJ, 7:468; Zuo, Memorial, GX 6/4/17, ZZQJ, 7:521.

8. Zuo to Yang Changjun, GX 6, ZZQJ, 12:618.

9. GX 5/3/23, QXDX, 7:357; Zuo, Memorial, GX 5/12/17, ZZQJ, 7:468. For other comments on the purported inferiority of Turkestani knowledge as it related to sericulture, see QXDX, 25:95–96.

10. On the late nineteenth-century promotion of sericulture, see Gao Guojin, *Wan Qing cansangju ji cansangye fazhan yanjiu* (Beijing: Zhongguo nongye kexue jishu chubanshe, 2017).

11. Zuo, Memorial, GX 6/4/18, ZZQJ, 7:527.

12. Liu, GX 9/7/1, LXGZ, 5.64b–65b; Zuo, Memorial, GX 6/4/17, ZZQJ, 7:519; James A. Millward, *Eurasian Crossroads: A History of Xinjiang* (New York: Columbia University Press, 2007), 142–43.

13. For examples of this literature, see Alfred W. Crosby, *Ecological Imperialism: The Biological Expansion of Europe, 900–1900* (Cambridge: Cambridge University Press, 1986); and J. R. McNeill, *Mosquito Empires: Ecology and War in the Greater Caribbean, 1620–1914* (Cambridge: Cambridge University Press, 2010).

14. Edmund Russell, *Evolutionary History: Uniting History and Biology to Understand Life on Earth* (Cambridge: Cambridge University Press, 2011).

15. Timothy J. LeCain, *The Matter of History: How Things Create the Past* (Cambridge: Cambridge University Press, 2017), 213–15.

16. Edmund Russell, "The Garden in the Machine: Toward an Evolutionary History of Technology," in *Industrializing Organisms: Introducing Evolutionary History*, ed. Susan R. Schrepfer and Philip Scranton (New York: Routledge, 2004), 1. For useful analyses of sericulture through this lens, see Edmund Russell, "Spinning Their Way into History: Silkworms, Mulberries and Manufacturing Landscapes in China," *Global Environment* 10, no. 1 (April 2017): 21–53; and Jacqueline Field, "Silk Production: Moths, Mulberry and

Metamorphosis," in *Making and Growing: Anthropological Studies of Organisms and Artefacts*, ed. Elizabeth Hallam and Tim Ingold (London: Routledge, 2014), 25–43.

17. Millward, *Beyond the Pass*, 45–48.

18. Qi-shi-yi, *Xiyu ji*, 2.16a; Ch. Ch. Valikhanov et al., *The Russians in Central Asia: Their Occupation of the Kirghiz Steppe and the Line of the Syr-Daria; Their Political Relations with Khiva, Bokhara, and Kokan; Also Descriptions of Chinese Turkestan and Dzungaria*, trans. John Mitchell and Robert Mitchell (London: Edward Stanford, 1865), 145, 159.

19. Bellew and Chapman, "General Description of Kashghar," 33; J. E. T. Aitchison, *Hand-Book of the Trade Products of Leh, with the Statistics of the Trade, from 1867 to 1872 Inclusive* (Calcutta: Wyman, 1874), 324; Kim, *Borderland Capitalism*, 52, 175–80.

20. Bellew and Chapman, "General Description of Kashghar," 79–80.

21. Kuropatkin, *Kashgaria*, 86–87; Bellew and Chapman, "General Description of Kashghar," 79; Edward Chapman, "Yarkand to Khotan," in Forsyth, *Report of a Mission to Yarkund*, 448; Edward Chapman, "Commerce," in Forsyth, *Report of a Mission to Yarkund*, 477, 485; Aitchison, *Hand-book of the Trade Products of Leh*, 217–18, 302–303.

22. Kuropatkin, *Kashgaria*, 86–87; Li Sheng, *Xinjiang dui Su (E) maoyi shi, 1600–1990* (Urumchi: Xinjiang renmin chubanshe, 1993), 90–91.

23. Edward Chapman, "Sericulture," in Forsyth, *Report of a Mission to Yarkund*, 510; "Sketches in Eastern Turkestan," *Illustrated London News*, November 21, 1874.

24. Chapman, "Yarkand to Khotan," 448; Chapman, "Commerce," 477. For an early twentieth-century description of silk production in the Tarim Basin, see Gunnar Jarring, *Materials to the Knowledge of Eastern Turki: Tales, Poetry, Proverbs, Riddles, Ethnological and Historical Texts from the Southern Parts of Eastern Turkestan*, 4 vols. (Lund: C. W. K. Gleerup, 1951), 4:54–56.

25. Other regional sericulture industries received similar scrutiny. For an appraisal of sericulture in Russian Turkestan in the 1870s, see Eugene Schuyler, *Turkistan: Notes of a Journey in Russian Turkistan, Khokand, Bukhara, and Kuldja*, 2 vols. (London: Sampson Low, Marston, Searle & Rivington, 1876), 1:190–201.

26. Kuropatkin, *Kashgaria*, 86.

27. "Sketches in Eastern Turkestan," November 21, 1874. On his praise for local silkworm breeding, see Chapman, "Sericulture," 511.

28. Chapman, "Sericulture," 510; Chapman, "Commerce," 477. See also Thomas E. Gordon, *The Roof of the World: Being the Narrative of a Journey over the High Plateau of Tibet to the Russian Frontier and the Oxus Sources on Pamir* (Edinburgh: Edmonston & Douglas, 1876), 51–52; and Bellew, *Kashmir and Kashghar*, 12.

29. Robert B. Shaw, "Trade Report, Ladakh, 1871," in Aitchison, *Hand-Book of the Trade Products of Leh,* 354–55.

30. Zuo, Memorial, GX 5/12/17, *ZZQJ,* 7:468. Zuo was hardly the first to make such a claim based upon transimperial comparisons. Nearly thirty-five years earlier, while conducting surveys of farmland in the Tarim Basin oases, Lin Zexu had found Khotanese silk to be "coarse and far inferior to silks from the innerland." See Lin, *Lin Zexu quanji,* 9:557.

31. Zuo, Memorial, GX 6/12/2, *ZZQJ,* 7:631; GX 8/4/27, *QXDX,* 8:449–50. See also *QXDX,* 25:95–96.

32. Zuo, Memorial, GX 5/12/17, *ZZQJ,* 7:468.

33. Ye Shizhuo, *Zengke sangcan xuzhi* (n.p., 1872), 45b; Shen Bingcheng, *Cansang jiyao* (Chang Zhen tonghaidao shu, 1871; reprint, Shanghai: Shanghai guji chubanshe, 1995), *zashuo*.2a-b, 16a–20b.

34. *QXDX,* 25:95–96.

35. "Sketches in Eastern Turkestan," November 21, 1874.

36. Chapman, "Sericulture," 510.

37. Vivienne Lo, "The Influence of Nurturing Life Culture on the Development of Western Han Acumoxa Therapy," in *Innovation in Chinese Medicine,* ed. Elizabeth Hsu (Cambridge: Cambridge University Press, 2001), 19–50; Rogaski, *Hygenic Modernity,* 25; Constance A. Cook, "The Pre-Han Period," in *Chinese Medicine and Healing: An Illustrated History,* ed. TJ Hinrichs and Linda L. Barnes (Cambridge, MA: Belknap Press of Harvard University Press, 2013), 14.

38. On the system for keeping people nourished in Qing China, see Pierre-Étienne Will and R. Bin Wong, *Nourish the People: The State Civilian Granary System in China, 1650–1850* (Ann Arbor: Center for Chinese Studies, University of Michigan, 1991).

39. *Xiyu tuzhi,* 43.10b.

40. *Xinjiang Huibu zhi,* 4 *juan,* ed. Yong-gui and Su-er-de (Nanpingli, 1794; reprint, Beijing: Beijing chubanshe, 2000), 2.16b.

41. Qi-shi-yi, *Xiyu zhi,* 7.4a.

42. Lin, *Lin Zexu quanji,* 3:511; Wei, *Kanding Xinjiang ji,* 8.15b; Xiao Xiong, *Xijiang zashu shi,* 4 *juan* (n.p., 1892; reprint, Yangzhou: Guangling shushe, 2003), 3.28a, 3.39a.

43. Xiao, *Xijiang zashu shi,* 3.34b; C. G. Mannerheim, *Across Asia from West to East in 1906–1908,* 2 vols. (Oosterhout: Anthropological Publications, 1969), 1:81–82.

44. Zuo, Memorial, GX 6/4/17, *ZZQJ,* 7:521.

45. Liu Jintang, GX 8/4/21, *QXDX,* 1:218–20.

46. Zuo, Memorial, GX 6/4/17, *ZZQJ,* 7:521.

47. Ye, *Zengke sangcan xuzhi,* 30a.

48. GX 5/3/23, *QXDX,* 7:357.

49. Chapman, "Sericulture," 510.

50. George Henderson and Allan O. Hume, *Lahore to Yārkand: Incidents of the Route and Natural History of the Countries Traversed by the Expedition of 1870, under T. D. Forsyth* (London: L. Reeve, 1873), 111.

51. Zuo, Memorial, GX 6/4/17, ZZQJ, 7:521.

52. GX 5/3/23, QXDX, 7:357.

53. Zuo, Memorial, GX 6/4/17, ZZQJ, 7:520.

54. This description is based upon Lillian M. Li, *China's Silk Trade: Traditional Industry in the Modern World, 1842–1937* (Cambridge, MA: Council on East Asian Studies, Harvard University, 1981), 138–62.

55. Wei Jie, *Cansang cuibian*, 15 *juan* (Zhejiang shuju, 1900), 2.15b–16a.

56. *Huzhou shizhi*, ed. Wang Kewen (Beijing: Kunlun chubanshe, 1999), 617; Dieter Kuhn, *Textile Technology: Spinning and Reeling*, vol. 5, pt. 9, *Science and Civilisation in China*, ed. Joseph Needham (Cambridge: Cambridge University Press, 1988), 289. On grafting, see Georges Métailié, "Grafting as an Agricultural and Cultural Practice in Ancient China," in *Botanical Progress, Horticultural Innovations and Cultural Changes*, ed. Michel Conan and W. John Kress (Washington: Dumbarton Oaks Research Library and Collection, 2007), 147–57.

57. Cheng Dai'an, *Xi Wu canlüe*, 2 *juan* (n.p., n.d.; reprint, Shanghai: Shanghai guji chubanshe, 1995), *shang*.4a-b; Wang Yuezhen, *Hu can shu*, 4 *juan* (n.p., 1880; reprint, Shanghai: Shanghai guji chubanshe, 1995), 1.12b. See also Ye, *Zengke sangcan xuzhi*, 17a.

58. Liang Jiamian, ed., *Zhongguo nongye kexue jishu shigao* (Beijing: Nongye chubanshe, 1989), 544.

59. *Huzhou shizhi*, 618.

60. Shen, *Cansang jiyao*, zashuo.12a.

61. Wu Qijun, *Zhiwu mingshi tukao*, 38 *juan* (Taiyuan, 1848), 33.34b.

62. *Huzhou shizhi*, 624–25; Liang, ed., *Zhongguo nongye kexue jishu shigao*, 546–47.

63. For an example of regulations promoting sericulture in this period, see Yu Zhi, *Deyi lu*, 16 *juan* (Suzhou: Dejianzhai, 1869; reprint, Hefei: Huangshan shushe, 1997), 6.1a–3a.

64. Shen, *Cansang jiyao*, xu.1b.

65. Li, *China's Silk Trade*, 105; Ch'en, *State Economic Policies of the Ch'ing Government*, 32.

66. Shen, *Cansang jiyao*, xu.1a.

67. Shen, *Cansang jiyao*, xu.1b, guitiao.1b; *Dantu xianzhi*, 60 *juan*, ed. He Shaozhang (n.p., 1879; reprint, Taipei: Chengwen chubanshe, 1970), 17.19a; Li Wenzhi, ed., *Zhongguo jindai nongye shi ziliao*, 3 vols. (Beijing: Sanlian shudian, 1957), 1:883.

68. Xiao, *Nongye guji banben congtan*, 180–87; Zeng, *Zhongguo nongxue shi*, 524–26. For an overview of sericulture scholarship in this period, see Hua Degong, ed., *Zhongguo cansang shulu* (Beijing: Nongye chubanshe, 1990); and Gao, *Wan Qing cansangju ji cansangye fazhan yanjiu*, 127–39.

69. Wang, *Zhongguo nongxue shulu*, 275; Zeng, *Zhongguo nongxue shi*, 526.

70. Zuo, Memorial, GX 6/4/17, *ZZQJ*, 7:521.

71. Zuo to Tan Zhonglin, TZ 12, *ZZQJ*, 11:379; Zuo, Memorial, GX 5/12/17, *ZZQJ*, 7:468; GX 6/1/26, *Dezong Jing huangdi shilu*, 108.18a.

72. Zuo, Memorial, GX 6/4/17, *ZZQJ*, 7:521; *Cansang zhiwu jiyao* (Henan cansang zhiwu ju, 1881), 63a–b.

73. GX, QXDX, 8:96.

74. Aside from the head bureau in Aksu, sericulture bureaus were located in Aykol, Yarkand, Khotan, Kashgar, Yangihissar, Kucha, Korla, Turpan, Hami, and Dunhuang. See Liu, GX 9/7/1, *LXGZ*, 5.63a. By the fall of 1883, the bureau in Dunhuang had been scrapped and a new one established in Bugur. See Liu, GX 10/2/28, *LXGZ*, 6.49b–50a. On staffing in the bureaus, see Hubu, *Hubu Shaanxi si zougao*, 8 juan (n.p., n.d.; reprint, Urumchi: Xinjiang renmin chubanshe, 1997), 3.18b–19a; and Liu, GX 9/7/1, *LXGZ*, 5.63a.

75. Liu, GX 9/7/1, *LXGZ*, 5.64a–b.

76. GX 6/3/17, QXDX, 8:94–95; GX 6/3/18, QXDX, 8:95.

77. GX 6/3/18, QXDX, 8:95.

78. Subbranch bureaus were located in Lukchun, Buluyuk (Putaogou), Toksun, Yargul, Karakhoja (Erbao), and Pichan. See GX 6/6/24, QXDX, 8:135; GX 6/7/13, QXDX, 8:159; GX 6/8/1, QXDX, 8:179–80; GX 6/8/9, QXDX, 8:180–81; GX 8/6, XUARA 15-29-0383; and GX 8/6, QXDX, 77:440–42.

79. GX 6/7/13, QXDX, 8:159.

80. *Cansang zhiwu jiyao*, 47b, 59a; Fang Dashi, *Sangcan tiyao*, 2 juan (Nanjing: Hua'elou, 1900), 2.9a.

81. Zuo to Yang Changjun, GX 6, *ZZQJ*, 12:659–60.

82. GX 8/2/18, QXDX, 8:404; GX 8/4/27, QXDX, 8:449–50.

83. GX 8/4/27, QXDX, 8:449–50.

84. GX 7/3/26, QXDX, 8:272–73; GX 8/5/22, QXDX, 1:227–28.

85. GX 7/R7/2, QXDX, 8:321–22. See also GX 8/5/1, QXDX, 9:3–4; and GX, QXDX, 24:294.

86. GX 7/3/26, QXDX, 8:271–72; GX 7, QXDX, 8:280. The Chaghatay title of this manual is recorded in Martin Hartmann, "Das Buchwesen in Turkestan und die Türkischen Drucke der Sammlung Hartmann," *Mitteilungen des Seminars für Orientalische Sprachen zu Berlin, Westasiatische Studien* 7 (1904): 101. Thanks to Rian Thum for bringing Hartmann's work to my attention.

87. GX 8/5/1, QXDX, 9:3–4.

88. GX 10/4/6, *QXDX*, 9:326; GX 10/8/14, *QXDX*, 9:404; GX 10/4/15, *QXDX*, 1:328–29; GX 10/9/19, *QXDX*, 9:437; GX 10/10/11, *QXDX*, 39:411–12.

89. GX 10/4/6, *QXDX*, 9:326–27; GX 11/9/6, *QXDX*, 10:239–40.

90. GX 10/2, *QXDX*, 39:252.

91. On the distribution of eggs, see GX 10/4/15, *QXDX*, 9:329–32; and GX, *QXDX*, 10:40–43. On the monitoring process, see GX 10/4/6, *QXDX*, 9:326–27.

92. GX 10/4/15, XUARA 15-30-624.

93. On prices of mulberry saplings, see *Cansang zhiwu jiyao*, 60a. For transport costs, see *Cansang jiyao hebian* (Henan cansang ju, 1880), *buyi*.48b; and *Cansang zhiwu jiyao*, 11b, 47b, 59a.

94. *Cansang zhiwu jiyao*, 61a-b.

95. *Xinjiang tuzhi*, 28.5b. On the transport of the trees, see *Cansang zhiwu jiyao*, 28a.

96. Zuo to Yang Changjun, GX 6, *ZZQJ*, 12:595; Liu Jintang, GX, XUARA 15-34-3297.

97. Zuo to Yang Changjun, GX 7, *ZZQJ*, 12:693.

98. Zuo, Memorial, GX 6/12/2, *ZZQJ*, 7:631.

99. Liu Jintang, GX 7/3/26, *QXDX*, 8:272–73; Liu Jintang, GX, XUARA 15-34-3297.

100. Liu Jintang, GX 7/1/13, *QXDX*, 8:257–58; Liu Jintang, GX, XUARA 15-34-3297.

101. Liu also advised bureau officials to consult information in Shen Bingcheng's *Collected Essentials of Sericulture* to learn more about leaf picking. See Liu Jintang, GX, XUARA 15-34-3297.

102. Liu Jintang, GX, XUARA 15-34-3297.

103. GX 6/6/24, *QXDX*, 8:135; GX 6/7/13, *QXDX*, 8:159.

104. Liu Jintang, GX 7/1/13, *QXDX*, 8:257–58.

105. Liu Jintang, GX 7/1/13, *QXDX*, 8:257–58. See also Liu Jintang, GX 8/1/29, *QXDX*, 8:393; and GX 8/2/8, *QXDX*, 8:399.

106. GX 7/7/2, *QXDX*, 8:323. For other reports from 1881, see GX 7/6/21, *QXDX*, 8:314; GX 7/6, *QXDX*, 8:318–19; GX 7/7/13, *QXDX*, 8:327–28; GX 7/7/13, *QXDX*, 8:328; GX 7/7, *QXDX*, 8:336; GX 7/7, *QXDX*, 8:337; GX 7/7, *QXDX*, 8:379–80; and GX 7, *QXDX*, 8:380.

107. For example, reports from 1883 and 1884 noted that over 21,000 mulberry trees were planted in the Turpan oasis. See GX 11/3, *QXDX*, 10:159–61. For seed distribution, see GX 11/3/14, *QXDX*, 10:155–56.

108. GX 8/4/5, *QXDX*, 8:438.

109. GX 13/2, *QXDX*, 11:69.

110. For these figures, see GX 8/5, XUARA 15-29-0422; GX 10/4/6, *QXDX*, 9:326–27; GX 10/10/8, *QXDX*, 9:441–42; GX 10/11/9, *QXDX*, 10:38–39; GX

11/3/14, *QXDX*, 10:155–56; GX 11/3, *QXDX*, 10:161–64; GX 14/1/24, *QXDX*, 11:217–18; GX, *QXDX*, 25:84–85; and Zhao Yi, "Qingmo Tulufan cansang ye," *Xibei minzu luncong* 14, no. 2 (2016): 202.

111. For these figures, see GX 7/6/15, *QXDX*, 8:313–14; GX 8/6, XUARA 15-29-0383; GX 8/6/27, *QXDX*, 9:18; GX 9/7/22, *QXDX*, 9:186; GX 10/11/9, *QXDX*, 10:38–39; and GX 11/9/6, *QXDX*, 10:239–40.

112. Zuo, GX 6/12/2, *ZZQJ*, 7:631. See also GX 5/6/3, *QXDX*, 76:318.

113. Zuo to Yang Changjun, GX 7, *ZZQJ*, 12:693; Fu-ke, "Xi xing suo lu," 6.303b.

114. GX 8/9/29, XUARA 15-29-0448. See also GX 8/6/27, *QXDX*, 9:18; GX 8/9, *QXDX*, 78:23–24; GX 8/11/29, *QXDX*, 78:37; and GX 8/11, *QXDX*, 78:50.

115. GX, XUARA 15-34-3525. On the returning workers, see GX 9/1/21, *QXDX*, 9:108–109; GX 9/1/21, XUARA 15-4-0471; GX 9/3/10, XUARA 15-29-0510; GX 9/3/10, *QXDX*, 78:113; GX 10/4/13, XUARA 15-30-0614; and GX 10/4, *QXDX*, 78:279. On the workers who stayed, see *Xinjiang tuzhi*, 28.6b.

116. GX 11/2/26, *QXDX*, 79:367–68; GX 11/2, *QXDX*, 79:17; GX 11/2/26, *QXDX*, 79:17–18; GX 11/2/26, *QXDX*, 79:219–20; GX 11/7/20, *QXDX*, 79:90–99; GX 11/7/29, *QXDX*, 10:216–18.

117. GX 10/4/15, XUARA 15-30-624; GX 10/7/11, *QXDX*, 78:328–29; GX 11/3/14, *QXDX*, 10:155–56; GX 11/2, *QXDX*, 79:17; GX 10/10/8, *QXDX*, 9:441–42.

118. GX 10/5/9, *QXDX*, 9:348–50; GX 10/8/14, *QXDX*, 9:403–404; Liu Jintang, GX 10/9/14, *QXDX*, 9:427–28; GX 10/9/19, *QXDX*, 9:436–37; GX 11/9/21, *QXDX*, 79:131–32; GX 11/11/17, *QXDX*, 79:165; GX 12/1/29, *QXDX*, 79:198–99; GX 12/2/5, *QXDX*, 79:200–201.

119. GX 12/2/10, *QXDX*, 79:202–203.

120. GX 14/1/24, *QXDX*, 11:217–18.

121. For examples, see Wang, *Tuipu laoren Xuannan zouyi*, 197–98; and GX, *QXDX*, 8:62–63.

122. Hubu, "Zouchen kaiyuan jieliu zhangcheng shu," in Ge, *Huangchao jingshi wen xu bian*, 26.1a.

123. Liu, GX 11/9/5, *LXGZ*, 9.58b–59a.

124. Liu, GX 11/8/12, *LXGZ*, 9.49a-b; Liu, GX 11/12/19, *LXGZ*, 10.27a–35b; Hubu, "Kaiyuan jieliu shiyi ershisi tiao," 26.1b–5b.

125. Wei Guangtao, GX 16/3/4, in *Gongzhongdang Guangxu chao zouzhe*, 5:166–67.

126. GX 15/5/1, XUARA 15-30-1009.

127. Martin Reuss and Stephen H. Cutcliffe, eds., *The Illusory Boundary: Environment and Technology in History* (Charlottesville: University of Virginia Press, 2010).

Conclusion

1. Li et al., *Jindai Zhongguo zaihuang jinian*, 413, 417, 428–29, 432–33, 453, 454–55, 466–68; Zuo to Li Wenmin and Qing-yu, GX 8, *ZZQJ*, 12:755; Zuo, Memorial, GX 9/8/26, *ZZQJ*, 8:338–41; Zuo, Memorial, GX 10/2/12, *ZZQJ*, 8:452–53; Zuo, Memorial, GX 10/2/23, *ZZQJ*, 8:453–54; Ho, *Studies on the Population of China*, 255.

2. In regard to refugees, see Zuo, Memorial, GX 9/12/14, *ZZQJ*, 8:412–14; and Zuo, Memorial, GX 10/3/4, *ZZQJ*, 8:459–61. For an estimate of the number of refugees, see Li et al., *Jindai Zhongguo zaihuang jinian*, 447. For discussions of hydraulic solutions to regional flooding, see Zuo, Memorial, GX 9/10/17, *ZZQJ*, 8:361–62; Zuo, Memorial, GX 9/10/28, *ZZQJ*, 8:368–69; Zuo, Memorial, GX 10/2/10, *ZZQJ*, 8:446; and Zuo, Memorial, GX 10/2/10, *ZZQJ*, 8:447–50.

3. Zuo, Memorial, GX 9/8/26, *ZZQJ*, 8:340.

4. On this problem, see Pomeranz, *The Making of a Hinterland*, 154–68. On the river's avulsion, see David A. Pietz, *The Yellow River: The Problem of Water in Modern China* (Cambridge, MA: Harvard University Press, 2015), 64–69; Dodgen, *Controlling the Dragon*, 144; and David A. Pietz, *Engineering the State: The Huai River and Reconstruction in Nationalist China, 1927–1937* (New York: Routledge, 2002), 17–18, 26–28.

5. Lloyd E. Eastman, *Throne and Mandarins: China's Search for a Policy during the Sino-French Controversy, 1880–1885* (Cambridge, MA: Harvard University Press, 1967), 162–73.

6. Zuo, Memorial, GX 11/6/18, *ZZQJ*, 8:597.

7. Zuo, Memorial, GX 10/12/23, *ZZQJ*, 8:538–40. On sugar in Taiwan in this period, see Sucheta Mazumdar, *Sugar and Society in China: Peasants, Technology, and the World Market* (Cambridge, MA: Harvard University Asia Center, 1998), 370–74.

8. Robert Gardella, "From Treaty Ports to Provincial Status, 1860–1894," in *Taiwan: A New History*, expanded ed., ed. Murray A. Rubinstein (Armonk, NY: M. E. Sharpe, 2007), 187–94; William M. Speidel, "The Administrative and Fiscal Reforms of Liu Ming-ch'uan in Taiwan, 1884–1891: Foundation for Self-Strengthening," *Journal of Asian Studies* 35, no. 3 (May 1976): 441–59; Samuel C. Chu, "Liu Ming-ch'uan and Modernization of Taiwan," *Journal of Asian Studies* 23, no. 1 (November 1963): 37–53; Gordon, *Confrontation over Taiwan*, 164–70.

9. Liu Mingchuan, *Liu Zhuangsu gong zouyi*, 10 juan (n.p., 1906), 2.21a.

10. The use of the provincial system of territorial rule increased after the fall of the Qing. At least six other provinces were created in the first three decades of the twentieth century. See Justin Tighe, *Constructing Suiyuan: The Politics*

of Northwestern Territory and Development in Early Twentieth-Century China (Leiden: Brill, 2005), 5, 72. On provincialization in the late Qing period, see Adili Aini, *Qingmo bianjiang jiansheng yanjiu* (Harbin: Heilongjiang jiaoyu chubanshe, 2012).

11. Zuo to Tao Guang, GX 6, *ZZQJ*, 12:596.

12. Gardella, "From Treaty Ports to Provincial Status, 1860–1894," 193; William M. Speidel, "Liu Ming-ch'uan in Taiwan, 1884–1891" (PhD diss., Yale University, 1967), 109–10.

13. On the declining condition of Manchu livelihoods in the capital going back to the eighteenth century, see Mark C. Elliott, *The Manchu Way: The Eight Banners and Ethnic Identity in Late Imperial China* (Stanford, CA: Stanford University Press, 2001), 313–22.

14. Zhang Peilun, *Jianyu ji* (Fengrun: Jianyu caotang, 1918), *zouyi*.1.5b; Zhang Peilun, GX 2/11/7, FHA-GCA 03-9553-019. Zuo Zongtang rejected Zhang's proposal largely because he believed urban Manchus lacked the agrarian skills necessary to survive on the frontier. See Zuo, Memorial, GX 3/3/29, *ZZQJ*, 6:635–40.

15. Hong Liangpin, GX 9, in *Dao Xian Tong Guang sichao zouyi*, 11:4636–37.

16. Zheng Guanying, *Shengshi weiyan*, 5 *juan* (Shanghai: Shanghai shuju, 1896), 3.47a–49b.

17. Chen Chi, *Yong shu*, 4 *juan* (n.p., 1896), *nei.xia*.21a–22b.

18. Examples of this logic of colonialism can be found across the nineteenth-century world. For Britain, see Henry William Spiegel, *The Growth of Economic Thought*, 3rd ed. (Durham, NC: Duke University Press, 1991), 357–58. For France, see Mahfoud Bennoune, *The Making of Contemporary Algeria, 1830–1987: Colonial Upheavals and Post-Independence Development* (Cambridge: Cambridge University Press, 1988), 35. For the United States, see Robert V. Hine and John Mack Faragher, *The American West: A New Interpretive History* (New Haven, CT: Yale University Press, 2000), 330–33. For Russia, see Jeff Sahadeo, *Russian Colonial Society in Tashkent, 1865–1923* (Bloomington: Indiana University Press, 2007), 148.

19. Kenneth Pomeranz, *The Great Divergence: China, Europe, and the Making of the Modern World Economy* (Princeton, NJ: Princeton University Press, 2000). While historians generally agree on the existence of a divergence, they disagree on when the divergence appeared. For example, see Andre Gunder Frank, *ReOrienting the 19th Century: Global Economy in the Continuing Asian Age*, ed. Robert A. Denemark (Boulder, CO: Paradigm, 2015).

20. Jürgen Osterhammel, "Semi-Colonialism and Informal Empire in Twentieth-Century China: Towards a Framework of Analysis," in *Imperialism and After: Continuities and Discontinuities*, ed. Wolfgang J. Mommsen and Jürgen Osterhammel (London: Allen & Unwin, 1986), 290–314.

21. Angus Maddison, *Contours of the World Economy, 1–2030 AD: Essays in Macro-Economic History* (Oxford: Oxford University Press, 2007), 164.

22. On the decline of interprovincial assistance for Xinjiang, see Halsey, *Quest for Power*, 100–103; and Judd C. Kinzley, *Natural Resources and the New Frontier: Constructing Modern China's Borderlands* (Chicago: University of Chicago Press, 2018), 32–34.

23. On the response to the scramble for mining and railroad concessions in China, see En-Han Lee, "China's Response to Foreign Investment in Her Mining Industry (1902–1911)," *Journal of Asian Studies* 28, no. 1 (November 1968): 55–76; and Joseph W. Esherick, *Reform and Revolution in China: The 1911 Revolution in Hunan and Hubei* (Berkeley: University of California Press, 1976), 70–91.

24. Liang Qichao, *Yinbingshi quanji*, 48 *ce* (Shanghai: Zhonghua shuju, 1916), 1.3b. It is highly unlikely that Liang's choice of the term "outlet" (*weilü*) to describe the colonies of the new imperial powers was mere coincidence. It was the same term that Wei Yuan had chosen to characterize Xinjiang in its relation to the Chinese provinces eighty years earlier. For another translation of this passage, see Colin Mackerras, *China in Transformation, 1900–1949*, 2nd ed. (London: Routledge, 2013), 122–23. For an analysis of this passage in the context of Liang's thought, see Xiaobing Tang, *Global Space and the Nationalist Discourse of Modernity: The Historical Thinking of Liang Qichao* (Stanford, CA: Stanford University Press, 1996), 25–26. For Liang's views on colonialism, see Wang Jianwei, "The Chinese Interpretation of the Concept of Imperialism in the Anti-Imperialist Context of the 1920s," *Journal of Modern Chinese History* 6, no. 2 (December 2012): 165–67. Liang was not alone in seeking to illuminate the connections between imperialism and nationalism. In 1902, the very same year that Liang wrote the tract in which he discussed "national imperialism," the English economist John Hobson published his famed analysis of imperialism in which he stated that colonialism amounted to a "natural overflow of nationality." See J. A. Hobson, *Imperialism: A Study* (New York: James Pott, 1902), 6.

25. "Lun Zhongguo zhi qiantu ji guomin yingjin zhi zeren," in *Xinhai geming qian shi nian jian shilun xuanji*, 2 vols., ed. Zhang Nan and Wang Renzhi (Beijing: Sanlian shudian, 1960), 1-*shang*:460. My translation is based on the translation in Wang, "The Chinese Interpretation of the Concept of Imperialism," 166.

26. Justin M. Jacobs, *Xinjiang and the Modern Chinese State* (Seattle: University of Washington Press, 2016), 3–4; Xu Xiangbian, "Shu Guoyang Yuan zhongcheng gong Fu Xin jicheng hou," in Yuan Dahua, *Fu Xin jicheng* (n.p., 1911; reprint, Taipei: Wenhai chubanshe, 1967), 1b–2a.

27. Jingji xuehui, *Xinjiang quansheng caizheng shuoming shu* (n.p., n.d.; reprint, Guangzhou: Guangdong renmin chubanshe, 2009), 529.

28. Joseph Lawson, "The Chinese State and Agriculture in an Age of Global Empires, 1880–1949," in Beattie, Melillo, and O'Gorman, *Eco-Cultural Networks and the British Empire*, 50; Scott Relyea, "Conceiving the 'West': Early Twentieth-Century Visions of Kham," *Twentieth-Century China* 40, no. 3 (October 2015): 196.

29. *Xinjiang tuzhi*, 28.4b–5a. This claim bore a certain resemblance to tropes of native indolence and the fecundity of nature within European colonial discourses about the tropical world. On this subject, see David Arnold, *The Problem of Nature: Environment, Culture and European Expansion* (Oxford: Blackwell, 1996), 142–49; David Arnold, *The Tropics and the Traveling Gaze: India, Landscape, and Science, 1800–1856* (Seattle: University of Washington Press, 2006); and Syed Hussein Alatas, *The Myth of the Lazy Native: A Study of the Image of the Malays, Filipinos and Javanese from the 16th to the 20th Century and Its Function in the Ideology of Colonial Capitalism* (London: Frank Cass, 1977).

30. *Xinjiang tuzhi*, 28.3b, 52.11a; Xie Bin, *Xinjiang youji* (n.p., 1923; reprint, Taipei: Wenhai chubanshe, 1969), 164–65. See also Shen Songqiao, "Jiangshan ruci duo jiao: 1930 niandai de xibei lüxing shuxie yu guozu xiangxiang," *Taida lishi xuebao* 37 (June 2006): 192–93.

31. Pei Jingfu, *Hehai kunlun lu*, 4 *juan* (Anhui, 1914), 2.52a–b.

32. Millward, *Beyond the Pass*, 194–96. On literary depictions of life in Qing Xinjiang, see also Newby, "The Chinese Literary Conquest of Xinjiang"; and Laura Newby, "Lines of Vision: Qing Representations of the Turkic Muslim Peoples of Xinjiang," in *Looking at the Coloniser: Cross-Cultural Perceptions in Central Asia and the Caucasus, Bengal, and Related Areas*, ed. Beate Eschment and Hans Harder (Würzburg: Ergon, 2004), 339–55.

33. Chou, "Frontier Studies," 77; Millward, *Beyond the Pass*, 197.

34. On the power of development discourses to shape politics in the twentieth-century world, see Arturo Escobar, *Encountering Development: The Making and Unmaking of the Third World* (Princeton, NJ: Princeton University Press, 1995).

35. Pei, *Hehai kunlun lu*, 2.52b.

36. On this project and its impact, see *Xinjiang tuzhi*, 8.5a–7b, 52.11a; *Xinjiang tongzhi* (n.p., n.d.; reprint, Beijing: Guojia tushuguan chubanshe, 2014), 27:78.

37. Peter Lavelle, "Agricultural Improvement at China's First Agricultural Experiment Stations," in *New Perspectives on the History of Life Sciences and Agriculture*, ed. Denise Phillips and Sharon Kingsland (Cham, Switzerland: Springer, 2015), 323–44. For such institutions elsewhere in the empire, see Lawson, "The Chinese State and Agriculture in an Age of Global Empires," 52–53; Xiuyu Wang, *China's Last Imperial Frontier: Late Qing Expansion in Sichuan's Tibetan Borderlands* (Lanham, MD: Lexington, 2011), 235n27; and Patrick Fuliang Shan, *Taming China's Wilderness: Immigration, Settlement and the Shaping of the*

Heilongjiang Frontier, 1900–1931 (Burlington, VT: Ashgate, 2014), 72. For a general assessment of institutional changes in borderland areas during the "New Policies" period, see Zhao Yuntian, *Qingmo xinzheng yanjiu* (Harbin: Heilongjiang jiaoyu chubanshe, 2014).

38. On such institutions in Xinjiang, see *Qingchao xu wenxian tongkao*, 382.11287; Hua, *Qingdai Xinjiang nongye kaifa shi*, 251–52; and Zhao, *Qingmo xinzheng yanjiu*, 186–96.

39. Lee, *The Manchurian Frontier in Ch'ing History*, 91; Judd Kinzley, "Turning Prospectors into Settlers: Gold, Immigrant Miners and the Settlement of the Frontier in Late Qing Xinjiang," in *China on the Margins*, ed. Sherman Cochran and Paul G. Pickowicz (Ithaca, NY: East Asia Program, Cornell University, 2010), 25.

40. On the arrival of foreign geological knowledge in China in the late nineteenth and early twentieth centuries, see Grace Yen Shen, *Unearthing the Nation: Modern Geology and Nationalism in Republican China* (Chicago: University of Chicago Press, 2014); and Wu, *Empires of Coal*.

41. On the most famous of these enterprises, see Ellsworth C. Carlson, *The Kaiping Mines, 1877–1912*, 2nd ed. (Cambridge, MA: East Asian Research Center, Harvard University, 1971). On Zuo Zongtang's involvement with mining in the final years of his life, see Zuo, Memorial, GX 8/11/14, *ZZQJ*, 8:171–72; Zuo, Memorial, GX 9/3/5, *ZZQJ*, 8:244–45; and Zuo, Memorial, GX 9/12/7, *ZZQJ*, 8:407–408.

42. Kinzley, *Natural Resources and the New Frontier*, 181–85.

43. In recent years, historians have explored the legacies of the imperial past in the twentieth century, especially in the realm of ethnopolitics. On China as a whole, see James Leibold, *Reconfiguring Chinese Nationalism: How the Qing Frontier and Its Indigenes Became Chinese* (New York: Palgrave Macmillan, 2007). On the case of Xinjiang, see Jacobs, *Xinjiang and the Modern Chinese State*; and David Brophy, *Uyghur Nation: Reform and Revolution on the Russia-China Frontier* (Cambridge, MA: Harvard University Press, 2016).

44. Mao Tse-tung, *Selected Works of Mao Tse-tung*, 5 vols. (Beijing: Foreign Languages Press, 1977), 5:295. Other political elites purveyed similar logic about colonial development. In 1921, Nationalist leader Sun Yat-sen had proposed to move ten million people from the "congested provinces" to Xinjiang and Mongolia in order to spur national economic growth. In 1999, Jiang Zemin announced the "Open Up the West" campaign to send waves of domestic investment to Gansu, Xinjiang, and other western provinces and autonomous regions. These examples suggest that China's leaders have been captivated by their own claims about the promise of colonial development to rectify uneven patterns of growth within the country that stemmed from concentrations of labor or capital in the east. For Sun's proposal, see Sun Yat-sen,

The International Development of China (New York: G. P. Putnam's Sons, 1922), 23–24. On the "Open Up the West" campaign and its repercussions in Xinjiang, see Nicolas Becquelin, "Staged Development in Xinjiang," *China Quarterly* 178 (June 2004): 358–78; and Henryk Szadziewski, "The Open Up the West Campaign among Uyghurs in Xinjiang: Exploring a Rights-Based Approach," in *On the Fringes of the Harmonious Society: Tibetans and Uyghurs in Socialist China*, ed. Trine Brox and Ildikó Bellér-Hann (Copenhagen: Nordic Institute of Asian Studies, 2014), 69–97. Certainly, these are not the only cases in which China's leaders looked upon the northwest borderlands as a geographical solution for crises of political economy in the eastern provinces. For other examples, see Justin Tighe, "From Borderland to Heartland: The Discourse of the North-West in Early Republican China," *Twentieth-Century China* 35, no. 1 (November 2009): 69–70; and Jeremy Tai, "The Northwest Question: Capitalism in the Sands of Nationalist China," *Twentieth-Century China* 40, no. 3 (October 2015): 214–15.

Bibliography

Archives

First Historical Archives, Beijing
National Palace Museum, Taipei
Xinjiang Uyghur Autonomous Region Archives, Urumchi

Published Sources

Adas, Michael. *Machines as the Measure of Men: Science, Technology, and Ideologies of Western Dominance*. Ithaca, NY: Cornell University Press, 1989.

Adshead, S. A. M. "An Energy Crisis in Early Modern China." *Ch'ing-shih wen-t'i* 3, no. 2 (December 1974): 20–28.

Agrawal, Arun. *Environmentality: Technologies of Government and the Making of Subjects*. Durham, NC: Duke University Press, 2005.

Aini, Adili. *Qingmo bianjiang jiansheng yanjiu*. Harbin: Heilongjiang jiaoyu chubanshe, 2012.

Aitchison, J. E. T. *Hand-Book of the Trade Products of Leh, with the Statistics of the Trade, from 1867 to 1872 Inclusive*. Calcutta: Wyman, 1874.

Alatas, Syed Hussein. *The Myth of the Lazy Native: A Study of the Image of the Malays, Filipinos and Javanese from the 16th to the 20th Century and Its Function in the Ideology of Colonial Capitalism*. London: Frank Cass, 1977.

Anji xianzhi. 18 *juan*. Edited by Zhang Xingfu and Wang Rong. N.p., 1874.

Anxi caifang diben. N.p., n.d. Reprint in *Zhongguo difang zhi jicheng, Gansu fu xian zhi ji*, vol. 47.

Arnold, David. *The Problem of Nature: Environment, Culture and European Expansion.* Oxford: Blackwell, 1996.

——. *Tropics and the Traveling Gaze: India, Landscape, and Science, 1800–1856.* Seattle: University of Washington Press, 2014.

Atwill, David G. *The Chinese Sultanate: Islam, Ethnicity, and the Panthay Rebellion in Southwest China, 1856–1873.* Stanford, CA: Stanford University Press, 2005.

Averill, Stephen C. "The Shed People and the Opening of the Yangzi Highlands." *Modern China* 9, no. 1 (January 1983): 84–126.

Bachu zhou xiangtu zhi. Edited by Zhang Zaoguang. N.p., 1908. Reprint in *Xinjiang xiangtu zhigao ershijiu zhong*, 267–75.

Barbier, Edward B. *Scarcity and Frontiers: How Economies Have Developed through Natural Resource Exploitation.* Cambridge: Cambridge University Press, 2011.

Beal, Edwin George, Jr. *The Origin of Likin, 1853–1864.* Cambridge, MA: Chinese Economic and Political Studies, Harvard University, 1958.

Beattie, Hilary J. *Land and Lineage in China: A Study of T'ung-ch'eng County, Anhwei, in the Ming and Ch'ing Dynasties.* Cambridge: Cambridge University Press, 1979.

Beattie, James. "Eco-Cultural Networks in Southern China and Colonial New Zealand: Cantonese Market Gardening and Environmental Exchange, 1860s–1910s." In *Eco-Cultural Networks and the British Empire: New Views on Environmental History*, edited by James Beattie, Edward Melillo, and Emily O'Gorman, 151–79. London: Bloomsbury Academic, 2015.

——, Edward Melillo, and Emily O'Gorman, eds. *Eco-Cultural Networks and the British Empire: New Views on Environmental History.* London: Bloomsbury Academic, 2015.

Beckert, Sven. *Empire of Cotton: A Global History.* New York: Alfred A. Knopf, 2014.

Becquelin, Nicolas. "Staged Development in Xinjiang." *China Quarterly* 178 (June 2004): 358–78.

Belich, James. *Replenishing the Earth: The Settler Revolution and the Rise of the Anglo-World, 1783–1939.* Oxford: Oxford University Press, 2009.

Bellér-Hann, Ildikó. *Community Matters in Xinjiang, 1880–1949: Towards a Historical Anthropology of the Uyghur.* Leiden: Brill, 2008.

Bellew, Henry W. *Kashmir and Kashghar: A Narrative of the Journey of the Embassy to Kashghar in 1873–74.* London: Trübner, 1875.

——, and Edward Chapman. "General Description of Kashghar." In Thomas D. Forsyth, *Report of a Mission to Yarkund in 1873, under Command of Sir T. D. Forsyth, with Historical and Geographical Information regarding the Possessions of the Ameer of Yarkund*, 23–105. Calcutta: Foreign Department, 1875.

Bello, David A. *Across Forest, Steppe, and Mountain: Environment, Identity, and Empire in Qing China's Borderlands.* Cambridge: Cambridge University Press, 2016.

———. *Opium and the Limits of Empire: Drug Prohibition in the Chinese Interior, 1729–1850*. Cambridge, MA: Harvard University Asia Center, 2005.

———. "Opium in Xinjiang and Beyond." In *Opium Regimes: China, Britain, and Japan, 1839–1952*, edited by Timothy Brook and Bob Tadashi Wakabayashi, 127–51. Berkeley: University of California Press, 2000.

———. "Qing Opium Dependency and Republican Opium Autonomy." In *Early Modern East Asia: War, Commerce, and Cultural Exchange*, edited by Kenneth M. Swope and Tonio Andrade, 11–33. New York: Routledge, 2018.

———. "Transformation through Inundation: Riziculturing Muslim Identity in Qing Dynasty Khotan." In *Landscape Change and Resource Utilization in East Asia: Perspectives from Environmental History*, edited by Ts'ui-jung Liu, Andrea Janku, and David Pietz, 79–93. New York: Routledge, 2018.

Benedict, Carol. *Golden-Silk Smoke: A History of Tobacco in China, 1550–2010*. Berkeley: University of California Press, 2011.

Bennoune, Mahfoud. *The Making of Contemporary Algeria, 1830–1987: Colonial Upheavals and Post-Independence Development*. Cambridge: Cambridge University Press, 1988.

Bernhardt, Kathryn. *Rents, Taxes, and Peasant Resistance: The Lower Yangzi Region, 1840–1950*. Stanford, CA: Stanford University Press, 1992.

Bi-chang. *Ye'erqiang shoucheng jilüe*. Fuzhou, 1848. Reprinted in Bi-chang, *Bi Qinxiang gong yishu*. N.p., 1859.

Biddulph, John. "Visit to Maralbashi." In Forsyth, *Report of a Mission to Yarkund*, 217–21.

Biggs, David. *Quagmire: Nation-Building and Nature in the Mekong Delta*. Seattle: University of Washington Press, 2010.

Blakiston, Thomas W. *Five Months on the Yang-tsze; with a Narrative of the Exploration of Its Upper Waters, and Notices of the Present Rebellions in China*. London: John Murray, 1862.

Bohr, Paul Richard. *Famine in China and the Missionary: Timothy Richard as Relief Administrator and Advocate of National Reform, 1876–1884*. Cambridge, MA: East Asian Research Center, Harvard University, 1972.

Borei, Dorothy V. "Eccentricity and Dissent: The Case of Kung Tzu-chen." *Ch'ing-shih wen-t'i* 3, no. 4 (December 1975): 50–62.

———. "Images of the Northwest Frontier: A Study of the *Hsi-yü wen chien lu* (1777)." *American Asian Review* 5, no. 2 (Summer 1987): 26–45.

Brady, Lisa M. *War upon the Land: Military Strategy and the Transformation of Southern Landscapes during the American Civil War*. Athens: University of Georgia Press, 2012.

Brandt, Loren. *Commercialization and Agricultural Development: Central and Eastern China, 1870–1937*. Cambridge: Cambridge University Press, 1989.

Bray, Francesca. *Agriculture*. Vol. 6, pt. 2 of *Science and Civilisation in China*, edited by Joseph Needham. Cambridge: Cambridge University Press, 1984.

——. "Chinese Literati and the Transmission of Technological Knowledge: The Case of Agriculture." In *Cultures of Knowledge: Technology in Chinese History*, edited by Dagmar Schäfer, 299–325. Leiden: Brill, 2012.

——. "Science, Technique, Technology: Passages between Matter and Knowledge in Imperial Chinese Agriculture." *British Journal for the History of Science* 41, no. 3 (September 2008): 319–44.

——. *Technology and Gender: Fabrics of Power in Late Imperial China*. Berkeley: University of California Press, 1997.

——. "Towards a Critical History of Non-Western Technology." In *China and Historical Capitalism: Genealogies of Sinological Knowledge*, edited by Timothy Brook and Gregory Blue, 158–209. Cambridge: Cambridge University Press, 1999.

——, and Georges Métailié. "Who Was the Author of the *Nongzheng quanshu?*" In *Statecraft and Intellectual Renewal in Late Ming China: The Cross-Cultural Synthesis of Xu Guangqi (1562–1633)*, edited by Catherine Jami, Peter Engelfriet, and Gregory Blue, 322–59. Leiden: Brill, 2001.

Brook, Timothy. "Growing Rice in North Zhili." In *The Chinese State in Ming Society*, 81–98. London: RoutledgeCurzon, 2005.

——. *The Troubled Empire: China in the Yuan and Ming Dynasties*. Cambridge, MA: Belknap Press of Harvard University Press, 2010.

Brophy, David. *Uyghur Nation: Reform and Revolution on the Russia-China Frontier*. Cambridge, MA: Harvard University Press, 2016.

Buoye, Thomas M. *Manslaughter, Markets, and Moral Economy: Violent Disputes over Property Rights in Eighteenth-Century China*. Cambridge: Cambridge University Press, 2000.

Cansang jiyao hebian. Henan cansang ju, 1880.

Cansang zhiwu jiyao. Henan cansang zhiwu ju, 1881.

Cao Shuji. *Zhongguo renkou shi, di wu juan, Qing shiqi*. Shanghai: Fudan daxue chubanshe, 2000.

——, Yushang Li, and Bin Yang. "Mt. Tambora, Climatic Changes, and China's Decline in the Nineteenth Century." *Journal of World History* 23, no. 3 (September 2012): 587–607.

Cao Zhenyong, et al., eds. *Qinding pingding Huijiang jiaoqin niyi fanglüe*. 80 *juan*. N.p., 1830.

Carlson, Ellsworth C. *The Kaiping Mines, 1877–1912*. 2nd ed. Cambridge, MA: East Asian Research Center, Harvard University, 1971.

CBYWSM. See *Chouban yiwu shimo*.

Chang, Hsin-pao. *Commissioner Lin and the Opium War*. Cambridge, MA: Harvard University Press, 1964.

Chao, Kang. *Man and Land in Chinese History: An Economic Analysis*. Stanford, CA: Stanford University Press, 1986.

Chapman, Edward. "Commerce." In Forsyth, *Report of a Mission to Yarkund*, 474–90.

——. "Sericulture." In Forsyth, *Report of a Mission to Yarkund*, 510–11.

——. "Yarkand to Khotan." In Forsyth, *Report of a Mission to Yarkund*, 445–51.

Chen Chi. *Yong shu*. 4 *juan*. N.p., 1896.

Chen, Gideon. *Tso Tsung T'ang: Pioneer Promoter of the Modern Dockyard and the Woollen Mill in China*. Beijing: Department of Economics, Yenching University, 1938.

Chen Guying, Xin Guanjie, and Ge Rongjin, eds. *Ming Qing shixue jianshi*. Beijing: Shehui kexue wenxian chubanshe, 1994.

——. *Ming Qing shixue sichao shi*. 3 vols. Jinan: Qi Lu shushe, 1989.

Chen Hongmou. "Yu Yuexi dangshi shu." In *HJWB*, 16.35a–b.

Ch'en, Jerome. *State Economic Policies of the Ch'ing Government, 1840–1895*. New York: Garland, 1980.

Chen Weixin. *Shiluo de jiangyu: Qingji xibei bianjie bianqian tiaoyue yutu tezhan*. Taipei: Guoli gugong bowuyuan, 2010.

Chen, William Y. *An Annotated Bibliography of Chinese Agriculture*. San Francisco: Chinese Materials Center, 1993.

Chen Xi. *Wan Qing Hunan zibenzhuyi yanjiu*. Changsha: Hunan renmin chubanshe, 2006.

Cheng Dai'an. *Xi Wu canlüe*. 2 *juan*. N.p., n.d. Reprint in *Xuxiu siku quanshu*, vol. 978.

Chongxin xianzhi. 4 *juan*. Edited by Zhang Mingdao and Ren Yinghan. Jingchuan: Fusheng yinshuguan, 1928.

Chongxiu Gaolan xianzhi. 30 *juan*. Edited by Zhang Guochang. Longyou leshan shuju, 1917.

Chongxiu Zhenyuan xianzhi. 19 *juan*. Edited by Qian Shitong and Jiao Guoli. Lanzhou: Junhua yinshuguan, 1935. Reprint in *Zhongguo difang zhi jicheng, Gansu fu xian zhi ji*, vols. 25–28.

Chou, Nailene Josephine. "Frontier Studies and Changing Frontier Administration in Late Ch'ing China: The Case of Sinkiang, 1759–1911." PhD diss., University of Washington, 1976.

Chouban yiwu shimo. 260 *juan*. Beijing, 1929–1931. Reprint, Taipei: Guofeng chubanshe, 1963.

Chu, Samuel C. "Liu Ming-ch'uan and Modernization of Taiwan." *Journal of Asian Studies* 23, no. 1 (November 1963): 37–53.

Chu, Wen-djang. *The Moslem Rebellion in Northwest China, 1862–1878: A Study of Government Minority Policy*. The Hague: Mouton, 1966.

Ch'ü, T'ung-tsu. *Local Government in China under the Ch'ing*. Stanford, CA: Stanford University Press, 1962.

Clarke, Prescott, and J. S. Gregory, eds. *Western Reports on the Taiping: A Selection of Documents*. Honolulu: University of Hawaii Press, 1982.

Cook, Constance A. "The Pre-Han Period." In *Chinese Medicine and Healing: An Illustrated History*, edited by TJ Hinrichs and Linda L. Barnes, 5–29. Cambridge, MA: Belknap Press of Harvard University Press, 2013.

Crosby, Alfred W. *Ecological Imperialism: The Biological Expansion of Europe, 900–1900.* Cambridge: Cambridge University Press, 1986.

Crossley, Pamela Kyle, Helen F. Siu, and Donald S. Sutton, eds. *Empire at the Margins: Culture, Ethnicity, and Frontier in Early Modern China.* Berkeley: University of California Press, 2006.

Da Qing lichao shilu. 94 vols. Tokyo, 1937. Reprint, Taipei: Hualian chubanshe, 1964.

Dabbs, Jack A. *History of the Discovery and Exploration of Chinese Turkestan.* The Hague: Mouton, 1963.

Dai Pan. *Yanling jilüe.* N.p., 1866. In *Liang Zhe huanyou jilüe*, 1–68. Reprint in *Jindai Zhongguo shiliao congkan xubian*, vol. 76. Taipei: Wenhai chubanshe, 1980.

Dali xian xuzhi. 12 *juan*. Edited by Zhou Mingqi. N.p., 1879.

Daniels, Christian. "Environmental Degradation, Forest Protection and Ethno-History in Yunnan: (I) The Uprising by Swidden Agriculturalists in 1821." *Chinese Environmental History Newsletter* 1, no. 2 (November 1994): 8–10.

Dantu xianzhi. 60 *juan*. Edited by He Shaozhang et al. N.p., 1879. Reprint in *Zhongguo fangzhi congshu, Huazhong difang*, vol. 11. Taipei: Chengwen chubanshe, 1970.

Dao Xian Tong Guang sichao zouyi. 12 vols. Compiled by Wang Yunwu. Taipei: Taiwan shangwu yinshuguan, 1970.

Davis, Diana K. "Deserts." In *The Oxford Handbook of Environmental History*, edited by Andrew C. Isenberg, 108–32. Oxford: Oxford University Press, 2014.

Davis, Mike. *Late Victorian Holocausts: El Niño Famines and the Making of the Third World.* London: Verso, 2001.

Dennis, Joseph. *Writing, Publishing, and Reading Local Gazetteers in Imperial China, 1100–1700.* Cambridge, MA: Harvard University Asia Center, 2015.

Dezong Jing huangdi shilu. 597 *juan*. In *Da Qing lichao shilu*, vols. 85–92.

Di Palma, Vittoria. *Wasteland: A History.* New Haven, CT: Yale University Press, 2014.

Dikötter, Frank. "The Limits of Benevolence: Wang Shiduo (1802–1889) and Population Control." *Bulletin of the School of Oriental and African Studies* 55, no. 1 (February 1992): 110–15.

Ding Richang. "Haifang tiaoyi." In *Bianshi xuchao*, 8 *juan*, edited by Zhu Kejing, 3.1a–32a. Changsha, 1880.

Dodgen, Randall A. *Controlling the Dragon: Confucian Engineers and the Yellow River in Late Imperial China.* Honolulu: University of Hawaii Press, 2001.

Dong Gao, et al. *Qinding shouyi guangxun.* 2 *juan*. N.p., 1808.

Dunstan, Helen. *Conflicting Counsels to Confuse the Age: A Documentary Study of Political Economy in Qing China, 1644–1840.* Ann Arbor: Center for Chinese Studies, University of Michigan, 1996.

———. "Official Thinking on Environmental Issues and the State's Environmental Roles in Eighteenth-Century China." In Elvin and Liu, *Sediments of Time*, 585–614.

Eastman, Lloyd E. *Throne and Mandarins: China's Search for a Policy during the Sino-French Controversy, 1880–1885.* Cambridge, MA: Harvard University Press, 1967.

Edgerton-Tarpley, Kathryn. *Tears from Iron: Cultural Responses to Famine in Nineteenth-Century China.* Berkeley: University of California Press, 2008.

Edkins, Joseph. "Narrative of a Visit to Nanking." In Jane R. Edkins, *Chinese Scenes and People: With Notices of Christian Missions and Missionary Life in a Series of Letters from Various Parts of China*, 239–307. London: James Nisbet, 1863.

Elliott, Mark C. *The Manchu Way: The Eight Banners and Ethnic Identity in Late Imperial China.* Stanford, CA: Stanford University Press, 2001.

Elman, Benjamin A. "Ch'ing Dynasty 'Schools' of Scholarship." *Ch'ing-shih wen-t'i* 4, no. 6 (December 1981): 1–44.

———. *A Cultural History of Civil Examinations in Late Imperial China.* Berkeley: University of California Press, 2000.

———. *From Philosophy to Philology: Intellectual and Social Aspects of Change in Late Imperial China.* Cambridge, MA: Council on East Asian Studies, Harvard University, 1984.

———. *On Their Own Terms: Science in China, 1550–1900.* Cambridge, MA: Harvard University Press, 2005.

———. "The Relevance of Sung Learning in the Late Ch'ing: Wei Yuan and the Huang-ch'ao ching-shih wen-pien." *Late Imperial China* 9, no. 2 (December 1988): 56–85.

Elvin, Mark. *The Pattern of the Chinese Past.* Stanford, CA: Stanford University Press, 1973.

———, and Liu Ts'ui-jung, eds. *Sediments of Time: Environment and Society in Chinese History.* Cambridge: Cambridge University Press, 1998.

Escobar, Arturo. *Encountering Development: The Making and Unmaking of the Third World.* Princeton, NJ: Princeton University Press, 1995.

Esherick, Joseph W. *Reform and Revolution in China: The 1911 Revolution in Hunan and Hubei.* Berkeley: University of California Press, 1976.

Eskildsen, Robert. *Transforming Empire in Japan and East Asia: The Taiwan Expedition and the Birth of Japanese Imperialism.* Singapore: Palgrave Macmillan, 2019.

Fairbank, John K., ed. *Late Ch'ing, 1800–1911.* Vol. 10, pt. 1 of *The Cambridge History of China.* Cambridge: Cambridge University Press, 1978.

Fang Dashi. *Sangcan tiyao. 2 juan.* Nanjing: Hua'elou, 1900.

Fang Rong and Zhang Ruilan. *Gansu renkou shi.* Lanzhou: Gansu renmin chubanshe, 2003.

Fang Yingkai. *Xinjiang tunken shi.* Urumchi: Xinjiang qingshaonian chubanshe, 1989.

Federico, Giovanni. *An Economic History of the Silk Industry, 1830–1930.* Cambridge: Cambridge University Press, 1997.

Feng Guifen. *Jiaobinlu kangyi.* 2 *juan.* N.p., 1884.

Fiege, Mark. *Irrigated Eden: The Making of an Agricultural Landscape in the American West.* Seattle: University of Washington Press, 1999.

Field, Jacqueline. "Silk Production: Moths, Mulberry and Metamorphosis." In *Making and Growing: Anthropological Studies of Organisms and Artefacts,* edited by Elizabeth Hallam and Tim Ingold, 25–43. London: Routledge, 2014.

Findlay, Ronald, and Kevin H. O'Rourke. *Power and Plenty: Trade, War, and the World Economy in the Second Millennium.* Princeton, NJ: Princeton University Press, 2007.

Fletcher, Joseph. "The Heyday of the Ch'ing Order in Mongolia, Sinkiang and Tibet." In Fairbank, *Late Ch'ing,* 351–408.

Foreign Office. *Commercial Reports by Her Majesty's Consuls in China, 1877–78.* London: Harrison & Sons, 1879.

Forrest, Robert J. "Tigers at Ningpo." *North-China Herald and Supreme Court & Consular Gazette,* January 14, 1875.

Forsyth, Thomas D. *Report of a Mission to Yarkund in 1873, under Command of Sir T. D. Forsyth, with Historical and Geographical Information regarding the Possessions of the Ameer of Yarkund.* Calcutta: Foreign Department Press, 1875.

Foust, Clifford M. *Rhubarb: The Wondrous Drug.* Princeton, NJ: Princeton University Press, 1992.

Frank, Andre Gunder. *ReOrienting the 19th Century: Global Economy in the Continuing Asian Age.* Edited by Robert A. Denemark. Boulder, CO: Paradigm, 2015.

Fu Shaohui and Liu Chunyang, eds. *Hunan nongye shi.* Changsha: Hunan renmin chubanshe, 2012.

Fu-ke (Otto Fock). "Xi xing suo lu." N.p., 1881. In Wang, *Xiaofanghuzhai yudi congchao,* 6.300a–304b.

Fuqiang xian xuzhi. 6 *juan.* Edited by Fang Chengxuan. N.p., 1872.

Gao Guojin. *Wan Qing cansangju ji cansangye fazhan yanjiu.* Beijing: Zhongguo nongye kexue jishu chubanshe, 2017.

Gaozong Chun huangdi shilu. 1500 *juan.* In *Da Qing lichao shilu,* vols. 17–46.

Gardella, Robert. "From Treaty Ports to Provincial Status, 1860–1894." In *Taiwan: A New History,* expanded ed., edited by Murray A. Rubinstein, 163–200. Armonk, NY: M. E. Sharpe, 2007.

Gardner, Christopher T. "Notes to the 'Journey from Ningpo to Shanghai.'" *Proceedings of the Royal Geographical Society* 13, no. 3 (March 22, 1869): 249–51.

Ge Jianxiong. *Zhongguo yimin shi.* Taipei: Wunan tushu chubanshe, 2005.

Ge Shijun, ed. *Huangchao jingshi wen xu bian.* 120 *juan.* Baoshan shuju, 1896.

Giles, Herbert A., trans. *Chuang Tzŭ: Mystic, Moralist, and Social Reformer.* 2nd ed. New York: AMS, 1974.

Gilmartin, David. *Blood and Water: The Indus River Basin in Modern History.* Berkeley: University of California Press, 2015.

Giquel, Prosper. *A Journal of the Chinese Civil War, 1864.* Translated by Steven A. Leibo and Debbie Weston. Edited by Steven A. Leibo. Honolulu: University of Hawaii Press, 1985.

———. "Ningpo et son Commerce pendant l'année 1864." In Inspector General of Customs, *Reports on Trade at the Ports of Shanghai, Canton, Swatow, Amoy, Ningpo, Hankow, Kiukiang, Chefoo, and Newchwang, for the Year 1864.* Shanghai: Imperial Maritime Customs Press, 1865.

Gong Zizhen. *Ding'an quanji.* 10 *juan.* Shanghai: Saoye shanfang, 1920.

———. "Xiyu zhi xingsheng yi." In *HJWB*, 81.17a–23a.

Gongzhongdang Guangxu chao zouzhe. 26 vols. Compiled by Guoli gugong bowuyuan. Taipei: Guoli gugong bowuyuan, 1973–75.

Gordon, Leonard H. D. *Confrontation over Taiwan: Nineteenth-Century China and the Powers.* Lanham, MD: Lexington, 2007.

Gordon, Thomas E. *The Roof of the World: Being the Narrative of a Journey over the High Plateau of Tibet to the Russian Frontier and the Oxus Sources on Pamir.* Edinburgh: Edmonston & Douglas, 1876.

Grove, Richard H. *Green Imperialism: Colonial Expansion, Tropical Island Edens and the Origins of Environmentalism, 1600–1860.* Cambridge: Cambridge University Press, 1995.

Gu Yanwu. *Tianxia junguo libing shu.* 120 *juan.* N.p., n.d. Reprint in *Xuxiu siku quanshu*, vols. 595–97.

Gu Zuyu. *Dushi fangyu jiyao.* 130 *juan.* N.p., 1811. Reprint, Shanghai: Zhonghua shuju, 1955.

Guangxu chao shangyu dang. 34 vols. Compiled by Zhongguo diyi lishi dang'anguan. Guilin: Guangxi shifan daxue chubanshe, 2008.

Guo Liping. *Jueyu yu juexue: Qingdai zhongye xibei shidi xue yanjiu.* Beijing: Sanlian shudian, 2007.

Haicheng xianzhi. 10 *juan.* Edited by Yang Jingeng. N.p., 1908.

Halsey, Stephen R. *Quest for Power: European Imperialism and the Making of Chinese Statecraft.* Cambridge, MA: Harvard University Press, 2015.

Hami zhili ting xiangtu zhi. Edited by Liu Rundao. N.p., 1909. Reprint in *Xinjiang xiangtu zhigao ershijiu zhong*, 161–72.

Hao, Yen-p'ing. *The Commercial Revolution in Nineteenth-Century China: The Rise of Sino-Western Capitalism.* Berkeley: University of California Press, 1986.

Hartmann, Martin. "Das Buchwesen in Turkestan und die Türkischen Drucke der Sammlung Hartmann." *Mitteilungen des Seminars für Orientalische Sprachen zu Berlin, Westasiatische Studien* 7 (1904): 69–103.

Havinden, Michael, and David Meredith. *Colonialism and Development: Britain and Its Tropical Colonies, 1850–1960.* London: Routledge, 1993.

He Changling, ed. *Huangchao jingshi wenbian.* 120 *juan.* N.p., 1827.

———. *Nai'an zouyi.* 12 *juan.* N.p., 1882. Reprint in *Qingmo minchu shiliao congkan,* vol. 27. Taipei: Chengwen chubanshe, 1968.

He Hanwei. *Guangxu chunian (1876–79) Huabei de da hanzai.* Hong Kong: Zhongwen daxue chubanshe, 1980.

He, Wenkai. *Paths toward the Modern Fiscal State: England, Japan, and China.* Cambridge, MA: Harvard University Press, 2013.

He Xiling. *Hanxiangguan shi chao.* 4 *juan.* N.p., 1848.

Headrick, Daniel R. *The Tentacles of Progress: Technology Transfer in the Age of Imperialism, 1850–1940.* New York: Oxford University Press, 1988.

———. *The Tools of Empire: Technology and European Imperialism in the Nineteenth Century.* Oxford: Oxford University Press, 1981.

Henderson, George, and Allan O. Hume. *Lahore to Yārkand: Incidents of the Route and Natural History of the Countries Traversed by the Expedition of 1870, under T. D. Forsyth.* London: L. Reeve, 1873.

Hevia, James L. *English Lessons: The Pedagogy of Imperialism in Nineteenth-Century China.* Durham, NC: Duke University Press, 2003.

Hine, Robert V., and John Mack Faragher. *The American West: A New Interpretive History.* New Haven, CT: Yale University Press, 2000.

HJWB. See He Changling, ed., *Huangchao jingshi wenbian.*

Ho, Ping-ti. "In Defense of Sinicization: A Rebuttal of Evelyn Rawski's 'Reenvisioning the Qing.'" *Journal of Asian Studies* 57, no. 1 (February 1998): 123–55.

———. *Studies on the Population of China, 1368–1953.* Cambridge, MA: Harvard University Press, 1959.

Hobsbawm, Eric. *The Age of Capital, 1848–1875.* New York: Vintage, 1996.

Hobson, J. A. *Imperialism: A Study.* New York: James Pott, 1902.

Hodge, Joseph Morgan. *Triumph of the Expert: Agrarian Doctrines of Development and the Legacies of British Colonialism.* Athens: Ohio University Press, 2007.

Hong Liangji. *Juanshige ji.* 40 *juan.* E'yuan, 1877.

———. *Tianshan kehua.* E'yuan, 1877.

———. *Yili riji.* E'yuan, 1877.

Hori Sunao. "Shindai kaikyō no kōchi menseki: nagareru mizu kara, ugokanu daichi e." *Kōnan daigaku kiyō, bungaku-hen* 90 (1993): 16–35.

———. "Shindai kaikyō no suiri kangai: 19–20 seiki no Yārukando o chūshin to shite." *Ōtemae joshi daigaku ronshū* 14 (1980): 72–99.

Hostetler, Laura. *Qing Colonial Enterprise: Ethnography and Cartography in Early Modern China.* Chicago: University of Chicago Press, 2001.

Hou Deren. *Qingdai xibei bianjiang shidi xue.* Beijing: Qunyan chubanshe, 2006.

Hou Zhuqing. *Taiping Tianguo zhanzheng shiqi Jiangsu renkou sunshi yanjiu, 1853–1864.* Beijing: Zhongguo shehui kexue chubanshe, 2016.

Hsiao, Kung-chuan. *Rural China: Imperial Control in the Nineteenth Century.* Seattle: University of Washington Press, 1960.

Hsiao Liang-lin. *China's Foreign Trade Statistics, 1864–1949.* Cambridge, MA: East Asian Research Center, Harvard University, 1974.

Hsu, Cho-yun. *Han Agriculture: The Formation of Early Chinese Agrarian Economy (206 B.C.–A.D. 220).* Edited by Jack L. Dull. Seattle: University of Washington Press, 1980.

Hsü, Immanuel C. Y. "The Great Policy Debate in China, 1874: Maritime Defense vs. Frontier Defense." *Harvard Journal of Asiatic Studies* 25 (1964–65): 212–28.

——. *The Ili Crisis: A Study of Sino-Russian Diplomacy, 1871–1881.* Oxford: Clarendon, 1965.

Hu Linyi. *Hu Wenzhong gong yiji.* 86 *juan.* Shanghai: Zhuyitang, 1888.

Hua Degong, ed. *Zhongguo cansang shulu.* Beijing: Nongye chubanshe, 1990.

Hua Li. *Qingdai Xinjiang nongye kaifa shi.* Harbin: Heilongjiang jiaoyu chubanshe, 1995.

Huang, Philip C. C. *The Peasant Economy and Social Change in North China.* Stanford, CA: Stanford University Press, 1985.

Huang Tong. *Yiwu bingshi jilüe.* N.p., n.d. Reprint in *Jindai Zhongguo shiliao congkan xu bian,* vol. 76. Taipei: Wenhai chubanshe, 1980.

Huaping zhili fumin ting zunzhang caifang bianji quanzhi. N.p., n.d. Reprint in *Zhongguo shixue congshu sanbian,* vol. 32. Taipei: Taiwan xuesheng shuju, 1987.

Hubu. *Hubu Shaanxi si zougao.* 8 *juan.* N.p., n.d. Reprint in Ma, *Qingdai Xinjiang xijian zoudu huibian,* vol. 2.

——. "Kaiyuan jieliu shiyi ershisi tiao." In Ge, *Huangchao jingshi wen xu bian,* 26.1b–5b.

——. *Qinding Hubu xuzuan zeli.* 15 *juan.* N.p., 1838.

——. *Qinding Hubu zeli.* 100 *juan.* N.p., 1874.

——. "Tongchou Xinjiang quanju yi gui jiuyuan shu." In Wang and Wang, *Huangchao Dao Xian Tong Guang zouyi,* 26.xia.11a–13a.

——. "Zouchen kaiyuan jieliu zhangcheng shu." In Ge, *Huangchao jingshi wen xu bian,* 26.1a–b.

Hummel, Arthur W., ed. *Eminent Chinese of the Ch'ing Period (1644–1912).* 2 vols. Washington, DC: Government Printing Office, 1943.

Hunan tongzhi. 288 *juan.* Edited by Zeng Guoquan. Changsha: Fuxuegong, 1885.

Hung, Ho-fung. *Protest with Chinese Characteristics: Demonstrations, Riots, and Petitions in the Mid-Qing Dynasty.* New York: Columbia University Press, 2011.

Huntington, Ellsworth. "The Depression of Turfan, in Central Asia." *Geographical Journal* 30, no. 3 (September 1907): 254–73.

Hutton, Eric L., trans. *Xunzi: The Complete Text.* Princeton, NJ: Princeton University Press, 2014.

Huzhou shizhi. Edited by Wang Kewen. Beijing: Kunlun chubanshe, 1999.

Inspector General of Customs. *Reports on Trade at the Ports of Shanghai, Canton, Swatow, Amoy, Ningpo, Hankow, Kiukiang, Chefoo, and Newchwang, for the Year 1864*. Shanghai: Imperial Maritime Customs Press, 1865.

——. *Reports on Trade at the Ports in China Open by Treaty to Foreign Trade, for the Year 1866*. Shanghai: Imperial Maritime Customs Press, 1867.

——. *Reports on Trade at the Treaty Ports in China, for the Year 1867*. Shanghai: Imperial Maritime Customs Press, 1868.

——. *Reports on Trade at the Treaty Ports in China, for the Year 1868*. Shanghai: Imperial Maritime Customs Press, 1869.

——. *Reports on Trade at the Treaty Ports in China, for the Year 1869*. Shanghai: Imperial Maritime Customs Press, 1870.

——. *Reports on Trade at the Treaty Ports in China, for the Year 1876*. Shanghai: Statistical Department of the Inspectorate General of Customs, 1877.

——. *Silk*. China Imperial Maritime Customs, Special Series No. 3. Shanghai: Statistical Department of the Inspectorate General, 1881.

Isenberg, Andrew C. *The Destruction of the Bison: An Environmental History, 1750–1920*. Cambridge: Cambridge University Press, 2000.

Isett, Christopher Mills. *State, Peasant, and Merchant in Qing Manchuria, 1644–1862*. Stanford, CA: Stanford University Press, 2007.

Jacobs, Justin M. *Xinjiang and the Modern Chinese State*. Seattle: University of Washington Press, 2016.

Janku, Andrea. "'Heaven-Sent Disasters' in Late Imperial China: The Scope of the State and Beyond." In *Natural Disasters, Cultural Responses: Case Studies toward a Global Environmental History*, edited by Christof Mauch and Christian Pfister, 233–64. Lanham, MD: Lexington, 2009.

Jarring, Gunnar. *Materials to the Knowledge of Eastern Turki: Tales, Poetry, Proverbs, Riddles, Ethnological and Historical Texts from the Southern Parts of Eastern Turkestan*. 4 vols. Lund: C. W. K. Gleerup, 1951.

Jenks, Robert D. *Insurgency and Social Disorder in Guizhou: The "Miao" Rebellion, 1854–1873*. Honolulu: University of Hawaii Press, 1994.

Ji Yun. *Wulumuqi zashi*. N.p., 1771. Reprint in *Zhongguo fengtu zhi congkan*, vol. 25. Yangzhou: Guangling shushe, 2003.

Jia Jianfei. *Qingdai xibei shidi xue yanjiu*. Urumchi: Xinjiang renmin chubanshe, 2010.

Jiande xianzhi. 21 juan. Edited by Yu Guanxu. N.p., 1892.

Jingchuan xianzhi. Edited by Jingchuan xian xianzhi bianzuan weiyuanhui. Lanzhou: Gansu renmin chubanshe, 1996.

Jingji xuehui. *Gansu quansheng caizheng shuoming shu*. N.p., n.d. Reprint in *Qingdai gao chao ben xu bian*, vol. 96. Guangzhou: Guangdong renmin chubanshe, 2009.

———. *Xinjiang quansheng caizheng shuoming shu*. N.p., n.d. Reprint in *Qingdai gao chao ben xu bian*, vol. 100. Guangzhou: Guangdong renmin chubanshe, 2009.

Jingyuan xianzhi. Edited by Jingyuan xianzhi bianzuan weiyuanhui. Yinchuan: Ningxia renmin chubanshe, 1995.

Jingzhou caifang xinzhi. Edited by Yang Bingrong. N.p., 1909. Reprint in *Zhongguo difang zhi jicheng, Gansu fu xian zhi ji*, vol. 20.

Jingzhou xiangtu zhi. Edited by Zhang Yuanchan. N.p., 1907. Reprint in *Zhongguo difang zhi jicheng, Gansu fu xian zhi ji*, vol. 20.

Jixiang yufu. *Jiuhuang baice*. Qinzhou, 1884.

Jiyun shanren (Yu Zhi). *Jiangnan tielei tu*. N.p., n.d. Reprint, Taipei: Xuesheng shuju, 1969.

Johnson, W. H. "Report on His Journey to Ilchí, the Capital of Khotan, in Chinese Tartary." *Journal of the Royal Geographical Society* 37 (1867): 1–47.

Jonsson, Fredrik Albritton. "The Origins of Cornucopianism: A Preliminary Genealogy." *Critical Historical Studies* 1, no. 1 (Spring 2014): 151–68.

Josephson, Paul R. *Resources under Regimes: Technology, Environment, and the State*. Cambridge, MA: Harvard University Press, 2005.

Kaske, Elizabeth. "Fund-Raising Wars: Office Selling and Interprovincial Finance in Nineteenth-Century China." *Harvard Journal of Asiatic Studies* 71, no. 1 (June 2011): 69–141.

Kataoka Kazutada. *Shinchō Shinkyō tōchi kenkyū*. Tokyo: Yūzankaku, 1991.

Kim, Hodong. *Holy War in China: The Muslim Rebellion and State in Chinese Central Asia, 1864–1877*. Stanford, CA: Stanford University Press, 2004.

Kim, Kwangmin. *Borderland Capitalism: Turkestan Produce, Qing Silver, and the Birth of an Eastern Market*. Stanford, CA: Stanford University Press, 2016.

Kim, Seonmin. *Ginseng and Borderland: Territorial Boundaries and Political Relations between Qing China and Chosŏn Korea, 1636–1912*. Oakland: University of California Press, 2017.

Kingsmill, Thomas W. "Retrospect of Events in China and Japan during the Year 1865." *Journal of the North China Branch of the Royal Asiatic Society*, n.s., no. 2 (December 1865): 134–70.

Kinzley, Judd C. *Natural Resources and the New Frontier: Constructing Modern China's Borderlands*. Chicago: University of Chicago Press, 2018.

———. "Turning Prospectors into Settlers: Gold, Immigrant Miners and the Settlement of the Frontier in Late Qing Xinjiang." In *China on the Margins*, edited by Sherman Cochran and Paul G. Pickowicz, 17–41. Ithaca, NY: East Asia Program, Cornell University, 2010.

Kobori, Iwao. "Notes from the Turpan Basin: Pioneering Research on the Karez." In *Water and Sustainability in Arid Regions: Bridging the Gap between Physical and Social Sciences*, edited by Graciela Schneier-Madanes and Marie-Françoise Courel, 139–49. Dordrecht: Springer, 2010.

Kreike, Emmanuel. *Environmental Infrastructure in African History: Examining the Myth of Natural Resource Management in Namibia.* Cambridge: Cambridge University Press, 2013.

Kreitner, Gustav. "Geographie." In Széchenyi, *Die wissenschaftlichen Ergebnisse der Reise des Grafen Béla Széchenyi in Ostasien,* 1:1–304.

——. *Im fernen Osten: Reisen des Grafen Bela Széchenyi in Indien, Japan, China, Tibet und Birma in den Jahren 1877–1880.* Vienna: Alfred Hölder, 1881.

Kuhn, Dieter. *Textile Technology: Spinning and Reeling.* Vol. 5, pt. 9 of *Science and Civilisation in China,* edited by Joseph Needham. Cambridge: Cambridge University Press, 1988.

Kuhn, Philip A. *Rebellion and Its Enemies in Late Imperial China: Militarization and Social Structure, 1796–1864.* Cambridge, MA: Harvard University Press, 1970.

——. "The Taiping Rebellion." In Fairbank, *Late Ch'ing,* 264–317.

Kundzewicz, Z. W., B. Merz, S. Vorogushyn, H. Hartmann, D. Duethmann, M. Wortmann, Sh. Huang, B. Su, T. Jiang, and V. Krysanova. "Analysis of Changes in Climate and River Discharge with Focus on Seasonal Runoff Predictability in the Aksu River Basin." *Environmental Earth Sciences* 73, no. 2 (January 2015): 501–16.

Kuo, Ting-yee, and Kwang-Ching Liu. "Self-Strengthening: The Pursuit of Western Technology." In Fairbank, *Late Ch'ing,* 491–542.

Kuropatkin, A. N. *Kashgaria: Eastern or Chinese Turkistan: Historical and Geographical Sketch of the Country; Its Military Strength, Industries and Trade.* Translated by Walter E. Gowan. Calcutta: Thacker, Spink, 1882.

Lavelle, Peter. "The Aesthetics and Politics of Chinese Horticulture in Late Qing Borderlands." In *Environmental History in East Asia: Interdisciplinary Perspectives,* edited by Ts'ui-jung Liu, 213–42. London: Routledge, 2014.

——. "Agricultural Improvement at China's First Agricultural Experiment Stations." In *New Perspectives on the History of Life Sciences and Agriculture,* edited by Denise Phillips and Sharon Kingsland, 323–44. Cham, Switzerland: Springer, 2015.

Lawson, Joseph. "The Chinese State and Agriculture in an Age of Global Empires, 1880–1949." In Beattie, Melillo, and O'Gorman, *Eco-Cultural Networks and the British Empire,* 44–67.

LeCain, Timothy J. *The Matter of History: How Things Create the Past.* Cambridge: Cambridge University Press, 2017.

Lee, En-Han. "China's Response to Foreign Investment in Her Mining Industry (1902–1911)." *Journal of Asian Studies* 28, no. 1 (November 1968): 55–76.

Lee, James Z., and Wang Feng. *One Quarter of Humanity: Malthusian Mythology and Chinese Realities, 1700–2000.* Cambridge, MA: Harvard University Press, 1999.

Lee, Robert H. G. *The Manchurian Frontier in Ch'ing History.* Cambridge, MA: Harvard University Press, 1970.

Legge, James, trans. *Confucius: Confucian Analects, the Great Learning, and the Doctrine of the Mean*. Oxford: Clarendon, 1893. Reprint, New York: Dover, 1971.

Leibo, Steven A. *Transferring Technology to China: Prosper Giquel and the Self-Strengthening Movement*. Berkeley: Institute of East Asian Studies, University of California, 1985.

Leibold, James. *Reconfiguring Chinese Nationalism: How the Qing Frontier and Its Indigenes Became Chinese*. New York: Palgrave Macmillan, 2007.

Leonard, Jane Kate. *Controlling from Afar: The Daoguang Emperor's Management of the Grand Canal Crisis, 1824–1826*. Ann Arbor: Center for Chinese Studies, University of Michigan, 1996.

——. *Wei Yuan and China's Rediscovery of the Maritime World*. Cambridge, MA: Council on East Asian Studies, Harvard University, 1984.

Leong, Sow-Theng. *Migration and Ethnicity in Chinese History: Hakkas, Pengmin, and Their Neighbors*. Edited by Tim Wright. Stanford, CA: Stanford University Press, 1997.

Levey, Benjamin. "Jungar Refugees and the Making of Empire on Qing China's Kazakh Frontier, 1759–1773." PhD diss., Harvard University, 2014. Proquest (AAT 3611551).

Levi, Scott C. *The Rise and Fall of Khoqand, 1709–1876: Central Asia in the Global Age*. Pittsburgh: Univeristy of Pittsburgh Press, 2017.

Li, Bozhong. *Agricultural Development in Jiangnan, 1620–1850*. New York: St. Martin's, 1998.

——. "The 'Daoguang Depression' and the 'Guiwei Great Flood': Economic Decline and Climatic Cataclysm in Early Nineteenth-Century Songjiang in a New Perspective." *Études chinoises* 34, no. 2 (2015): 89–119.

——. "19 shiji Jiangnan de jingji xiaotiao yu qihou bianhua." In *Zhongguo lishi shang de huanjing yu shehui*, edited by Wang Lihua, 117–25. Beijing: Sanlian shudian, 2007.

Li, Lillian M. *China's Silk Trade: Traditional Industry in the Modern World, 1842–1937*. Cambridge, MA: Council on East Asian Studies, Harvard University, 1981.

——. *Fighting Famine in North China: State, Market, and Environmental Decline, 1690s–1990s*. Stanford, CA: Stanford University Press, 2007.

Li Ling, ed. *Sunzi yizhu*. 2nd ed. Beijing: Zhonghua shuju, 2009.

Li Sheng. *Xinjiang dui Su (E) maoyi shi, 1600–1990*. Urumchi: Xinjiang renmin chubanshe, 1993.

Li Wenhai, Lin Dunkui, Zhou Yuan, and Gong Ming. *Jindai Zhongguo zaihuang jinian*. Changsha: Hunan jiaoyu chubanshe, 1990.

——, Cheng Xiao, Liu Yangdong, and Xia Mingfang. *Zhongguo jindai shi da zaihuang*. Shanghai: Shanghai renmin chubanshe, 1994.

Li Wenzhi, ed. *Zhongguo jindai nongye shi ziliao*. 3 vols. Beijing: Sanlian shudian, 1957.

Li Yingjue. *Zhe zhong fafei jilüe.* N.p., n.d. Reprint in *Jiang Zhe Yu Wan Taiping Tianguo shiliao xuanbian*, edited by Nanjing daxue lishixi Taiping Tianguo shi yanjiushi, 201–30. Nanjing: Jiangsu renmin chubanshe, 1983.

Li Yunlin. *Xichui shilüe.* N.p., 1878. Reprint in *Qingdai bianjiang shiliao chao gaoben huibian*, vol. 22. Beijing: Xianzhuang shuju, 2003.

Liang Ch'i-ch'ao. See Liang Qichao.

Liang Fangzhong. *Zhongguo lidai hukou, tiandi, tianfu tongji.* Shanghai: Shanghai renmin chubanshe, 1980.

Liang Jiamian, ed. *Zhongguo nongye kexue jishu shigao.* Beijing: Nongye chubanshe, 1989.

Liang Qichao (Liang Ch'i-ch'ao). *Intellectual Trends in the Ch'ing Period.* Translated by Immanuel C. Y. Hsü. Cambridge, MA: Harvard University Press, 1959.

——. *Qingdai xueshu gailun.* Shanghai, 1921. Reprint, Taipei: Shangwu yinshuguan, 2008.

——. *Yinbingshi quanji.* 48 *ce.* Shanghai: Zhonghua shuju, 1916.

Lin, Man-houng. "China's 'Dual Economy' in International Trade Relations, 1842–1949." In *Japan, China, and the Growth of the Asian International Economy, 1850–1949*, edited by Kaoru Sugihara, 179–97. Oxford: Oxford University Press, 2005.

——. *China Upside Down: Currency, Society, and Ideologies, 1808–1856.* Cambridge, MA: Harvard University Asia Center, 2006.

——. "Late Qing Perceptions of Native Opium." *Harvard Journal of Asiatic Studies* 64, no. 1 (June 2004): 117–44.

Lin Yingru. "Xiexiang yu Qing ting de Xinjiang zhili (1759–1884)." Master's thesis, National Taiwan Normal University, 2010.

Lin Zexu. *Lin Zexu quanji.* 10 vols. Edited by Lin Zexu quanji bianji wenyuanhui. Fuzhou: Haixia wenyi chubanshe, 2002.

Lindley, Augustus F. *Ti-ping Tien-kwoh: The History of the Ti-ping Revolution, Including a Narrative of the Author's Personal Adventures.* 2 vols. London: Day & Son, 1866.

Lingtai zhuanji. 4 *juan.* Edited by Zhang Dongye. Nanjing: Jinghua yinshuguan, 1935.

Lipman, Jonathan N. "The Border World of Gansu, 1895–1935." PhD diss., Stanford University, 1980.

——. *Familiar Strangers: A History of Muslims in Northwest China.* Seattle: University of Washington Press, 1997.

Liu Jintang. *Liu Xiangqin gong zougao.* 16 *juan.* Changsha, 1898. Reprint in Ma, *Qingdai Xinjiang xijian zoudu huibian*, vol. 1.

Liu, Kwang-Ching, and Richard J. Smith. "The Military Challenge: The Northwest and the Coast." In *The Cambridge History of China*, vol. 11, *Late Ch'ing, 1800–1911*, pt. 2, edited by John K. Fairbank and Kwang-Ching Liu, 202–73. Cambridge: Cambridge University Press, 1980.

Liu Mingchuan. *Liu Zhuangsu gong zouyi.* 10 *juan.* N.p., 1906.

Lo, Vivienne. "The Influence of Nurturing Life Culture on the Development of Western Han Acumoxa Therapy." In *Innovation in Chinese Medicine*, edited by Elizabeth Hsu, 19–50. Cambridge: Cambridge University Press, 2001.

Lóczy, Ludwig. "Geologie." In Széchenyi, *Die wissenschaftlichen Ergebnisse der Reise des Grafen Béla Széchenyi in Ostasien*, 1:305–837.

Lu Shiyi. "Lun qutian." In *HJWB*, 36.37a–41b.

——. *Sibianlu jiyao*. 35 *juan*. Edited by Zhang Boxing. Jiangsu shuju, 1877.

Lü Yuancong, and Ge Rongjin. *Qingdai shehui yu shixue*. Hong Kong: Xianggang daxue chubanshe, 2000.

"Lun Xinjiang qingxing." *Shenbao*, March 30, 1878.

"Lun Zhongguo zhi qiantu ji guomin yingjin zhi zeren." *Hubei xuesheng jie* 3 (1903). Reprint in *Xinhai geming qian shi nian jian shilun xuanji*, 2 vols., edited by Zhang Nan and Wang Renzhi. Beijing: Sanlian shudian, 1960.

Luo Ruhuai, ed. *Hunan wenzheng*. 190 *juan*. N.p., 1869.

——. *Lüyi caotang shiji*. 20 *juan*. Changsha, 1883.

Luo Zhengjun, ed. *Zuo Wenxiang gong nianpu*. 10 *juan*. N.p., 1897. Reprint in *Jindai Zhongguo shiliao congkan*, vol. 145. Taipei: Wenhai chubanshe, 1967.

LXGZ. See Liu Jintang, *Liu Xiangqin gong zougao*.

Ma Dazheng, ed. *Qingdai Xinjiang xijian zoudu huibian: Tongzhi, Guangxu, Xuantong chao juan*. 3 vols. Urumchi: Xinjiang renmin chubanshe, 1997.

Ma, Debin. "The Modern Silk Road: The Global Raw-Silk Market, 1850–1930." *Journal of Economic History* 56, no. 2 (June 1996): 330–55.

Ma Xinyi. *Ma Duanmin gong zouyi*. 8 *juan*. Min Zhe du shu, 1894. Reprint in *Jindai Zhongguo shiliao congkan xubian*, vol. 171. Taipei: Chengwen chubanshe, 1969.

Mackerras, Colin. *China in Transformation, 1900–1949*. 2nd ed. London: Routledge, 2013.

Madancy, Joyce A. *The Troublesome Legacy of Commissioner Lin: The Opium Trade and Opium Suppression in Fujian Province, 1820s to 1920s*. Cambridge, MA: Harvard University Asia Center, 2003.

Maddison, Angus. *Contours of the World Economy, 1–2030 AD: Essays in Macro-Economic History*. Oxford: Oxford University Press, 2007.

Mann, Susan. *Local Merchants and the Chinese Bureaucracy, 1750–1950*. Stanford, CA: Stanford University Press, 1987.

——. *Precious Records: Women in China's Long Eighteenth Century*. Stanford, CA: Stanford University Press, 1997.

——, and Philip A. Kuhn. "Dynastic Decline and the Roots of Rebellion." In Fairbank, *Late Ch'ing*, 107–62.

Mannerheim, C. G. *Across Asia from West to East in 1906–1908*. 2 vols. Oosterhout: Anthropological Publications, 1969.

Mao Tse-tung. *Selected Works of Mao Tse-tung*. 5 vols. Beijing: Foreign Languages Press, 1977.

Mao Xianglin. *Duishan shuwu mo yu lu. 16 juan.* Huzhou: Zuiliutang, 1870.

Marks, Robert B. *Tigers, Rice, Silk, and Silt: Environment and Economy in Late Imperial South China.* Cambridge: Cambridge University Press, 1998.

Mazumdar, Sucheta. *Sugar and Society in China: Peasants, Technology, and the World Market.* Cambridge, MA: Harvard University Asia Center, 1998.

McMahon, Daniel. "The Yuelu Academy and Hunan's Nineteenth-Century Turn toward Statecraft." *Late Imperial China* 26, no. 1 (June 2005): 72–109.

McNeill, J. R. *Mosquito Empires: Ecology and War in the Greater Caribbean, 1620–1914.* Cambridge: Cambridge University Press, 2010.

——. "Woods and Warfare in World History." *Environmental History* 9, no. 3 (July 2004): 388–410.

Métailié, Georges. "Grafting as an Agricultural and Cultural Practice in Ancient China." In *Botanical Progress, Horticultural Innovations and Cultural Changes*, edited by Michel Conan and W. John Kress, 147–57. Washington, DC: Dumbarton Oaks Research Library and Collection, 2007.

Meyer-Fong, Tobie. *What Remains: Coming to Terms with Civil War in 19th Century China.* Stanford, CA: Stanford University Press, 2013.

Mian shu. Fujian fanshu, 1866. Reprint in *Xuxiu siku quanshu*, vol. 977.

Michael, Franz. *The Taiping Rebellion: History.* Seattle: University of Washington Press, 1966.

Millward, James A. *Beyond the Pass: Economy, Ethnicity, and Empire in Qing Central Asia, 1759–1864.* Stanford, CA: Stanford University Press, 1998.

——. "'Coming onto the Map': 'Western Regions' Geography and Cartographic Nomenclature in the Making of Chinese Empire in Xinjiang." *Late Imperial China* 20, no. 2 (December 1999): 61–98.

——. *Eurasian Crossroads: A History of Xinjiang.* New York: Columbia University Press, 2007.

——. "Towards a Xinjiang Environmental History: Evidence from Space, the Ground, and in Between." In *Studies on Xinjiang Historical Sources in 17–20th Centuries*, edited by James A. Millward, Shinmen Yasushi, and Sugawara Jun, 279–303. Tokyo: Toyo Bunko, 2010.

——, and Laura J. Newby. "The Qing and Islam on the Western Frontier." In Crossley, Siu, and Sutton, *Empire at the Margins*, 113–34.

Min xian xiangtu zhi. Edited by Zheng Zugeng. N.p., 1903.

Mitchell, Timothy. *Rule of Experts: Egypt, Techno-Politics, Modernity.* Berkeley: University of California Press, 2002.

Mizuno, Norihito. "Qing China's Reaction to the 1874 Japanese Expedition to the Taiwanese Aboriginal Territories." *Sino-Japanese Studies* 16 (2009): 100–125.

Morgan, E. Delmar. "Expedition of the Brothers Grijimailo to the Tian Shan Oases and Lob-nor." *Proceedings of the Royal Geographical Society* 13, no. 4 (April 1891): 208–26.

———. "Introductory Remarks to 'Journey of Carey and Dalgleish in Chinese Turkistan and Northern Tibet; and General Prejevalsky on the Orography of Northern Tibet.'" *Royal Geographical Society Supplementary Papers*, vol. 3, 1–88. London: John Murray, 1893.

Mosca, Matthew W. "Cišii's Description of Xinjiang: Its Context and Circulation." In *Xinjiang in the Context of Central Eurasian Transformations*, edited by Onuma Takahiro, David Brophy, and Shinmen Yasushi, 169–200. Tokyo: Toyo Bunko, 2018.

———. *From Frontier Policy to Foreign Policy: The Question of India and the Transformation of Geopolitics in Qing China.* Stanford, CA: Stanford University Press, 2013.

Mostern, Ruth. "Sediment and State in Imperial China: The Yellow River Watershed as an Earth System and a World System." *Nature and Culture* 11, no. 2 (Summer 2016): 121–47.

Muscolino, Micah S. *The Ecology of War in China: Henan Province, the Yellow River, and Beyond, 1938–1950.* Cambridge: Cambridge University Press, 2015.

———. *Fishing Wars and Environmental Change in Late Imperial and Modern China.* Cambridge, MA: Harvard University Asia Center, 2009.

Nappi, Carla. *The Monkey and the Inkpot: Natural History and Its Transformations in Early Modern China.* Cambridge, MA: Harvard University Press, 2009.

Na-yan-cheng. *Na Wenyi gong zouyi.* 80 *juan.* N.p., 1834.

Needham, Joseph. *The Grand Titration: Science and Society in East and West.* London: George Allen & Unwin, 1969.

Newby, Laura J. "The Begs of Xinjiang: Between Two Worlds." *Bulletin of the School of Oriental and African Studies* 61, no. 2 (June 1998): 278–97.

———. "The Chinese Literary Conquest of Xinjiang." *Modern China* 25, no. 4 (October 1999): 451–74.

———. *The Empire and the Khanate: A Political History of Qing Relations with Khoqand, c. 1760–1860.* Leiden: Brill, 2005.

———. "Lines of Vision: Qing Representations of the Turkic Muslim Peoples of Xinjiang." In *Looking at the Coloniser: Cross-Cultural Perceptions in Central Asia and the Caucasus, Bengal, and Related Areas,* edited by Beate Eschment and Hans Harder, 339–55. Würzburg: Ergon, 2004.

"Ningpo." *North-China Herald and Supreme Court & Consular Gazette,* January 14, 1875.

"Ningpo." *North-China Herald and Supreme Court & Consular Gazette,* June 15, 1878.

Noda, Jin. *The Kazakh Khanates between the Russian and Qing Empires: Central Eurasian International Relations during the Eighteenth and Nineteenth Centuries.* Leiden: Brill, 2016.

Norris, Jacob. *Land of Progress: Palestine in the Age of Colonial Development, 1905–1948.* Oxford: Oxford University Press, 2013.

"Notes from Native Papers." *North-China Herald and Supreme Court & Consular Gazette*, February 10, 1888.

Oliphant, Laurence. *Narrative of the Earl of Elgin's Mission to China and Japan in the Years 1857, '58, '59.* 2 vols. 2nd ed. Edinburgh: William Blackwood & Sons, 1860.

Osborne, Anne. "Highlands and Lowlands: Economic and Ecological Interactions in the Lower Yangzi Region under the Qing." In Elvin and Liu, *Sediments of Time*, 203–34.

———. "The Local Politics of Land Reclamation in the Lower Yangzi Highlands." *Late Imperial China* 15, no. 1 (June 1994): 1–46.

Osterhammel, Jürgen. "Semi-Colonialism and Informal Empire in Twentieth-Century China: Towards a Framework of Analysis." In *Imperialism and After: Continuities and Discontinuities*, edited by Wolfgang J. Mommsen and Jürgen Osterhammel, 290–314. London: Allen & Unwin, 1986.

———. *The Transformation of the World: A Global History of the Nineteenth Century.* Princeton, NJ: Princeton University Press, 2014.

Paine, S. C. M. *Imperial Rivals: China, Russia, and Their Disputed Frontier.* Armonk, NY: M. E. Sharpe, 1996.

Pan Zengyi. *Fengyu zhuang benshu.* N.p., 1829. In *Qu zhong wu zhong, 5 juan*, edited by Zhao Mengling, 5.1a–16b. Lianhuachi, 1878.

———. *Kenong quzhong fa tu.* N.p., 1834. In Zhao, *Qu zhong wu zhong*, 5.17a–18a.

Parker, Geoffrey. *Global Crisis: War, Climate Change and Catastrophe in the Seventeenth Century.* New Haven, CT: Yale University Press, 2013.

Pearson, Chris. *Scarred Landscapes: War and Nature in Vichy France.* New York: Palgrave Macmillan, 2008.

Pei Jingfu. *Hehai kunlun lu.* 4 juan. Anhui, 1914.

Peng Minghui. *Wan Qing de jingshi shixue.* Taipei: Maitian, 2002.

Peng Yuxin, ed. *Qingdai tudi kaiken shi ziliao huibian.* Wuhan: Wuhan daxue chubanshe, 1992.

Perdue, Peter C. *China Marches West: The Qing Conquest of Central Eurasia.* Cambridge, MA: Belknap Press of Harvard University Press, 2005.

———. *Exhausting the Earth: State and Peasant in Hunan, 1500–1850.* Cambridge, MA: Council on East Asian Studies, Harvard University, 1987.

Perkins, Dwight H. *Agricultural Development in China, 1368–1968.* Chicago: Aldine, 1969.

Perry, Elizabeth J. *Rebels and Revolutionaries in North China, 1845–1945.* Stanford, CA: Stanford University Press, 1980.

Peterson, Willard. "Confucian Learning in Late Ming Thought." In *The Cambridge History of China*, vol. 8, *The Ming Dynasty, 1368–1644*, pt. 2, edited by Dennis Twitchett and Frederick Mote, 708–88. Cambridge: Cambridge University Press, 1998.

Piassetsky, Pavel. *Russian Travellers in Mongolia and China*. 2 vols. Translated by J. Gordon-Cumming. London: Chapman & Hall, 1884.

Pietz, David A. *Engineering the State: The Huai River and Reconstruction in Nationalist China, 1927–1937*. New York: Routledge, 2002.

——. *The Yellow River: The Problem of Water in Modern China*. Cambridge, MA: Harvard University Press, 2015.

Pingyuan xianzhi. 10 *juan*. Edited by Chen Rixin. N.p., 1879.

Platt, Stephen R. *Provincial Patriots: The Hunanese and Modern China*. Cambridge, MA: Harvard University Press, 2007.

Pomeranz, Kenneth. *The Great Divergence: China, Europe, and the Making of the Modern World Economy*. Princeton, NJ: Princeton University Press, 2000.

——. "Introduction: World History and Environmental History." In *The Environment and World History*, edited by Edmund Burke III and Kenneth Pomeranz, 3–32. Berkeley: University of California Press, 2009.

——. *The Making of a Hinterland: State, Society, and Economy in Inland North China, 1853–1937*. Berkeley: University of California Press, 1993.

Pong, David. *Shen Pao-chen and China's Modernization in the Nineteenth Century*. Cambridge: Cambridge University Press, 1994.

Prejevalsky, Nikolay. *From Kulja, across the Tian Shan to Lob-Nor*. Translated by E. Delmar Morgan. London: Sampson Low, Marston, Searle & Rivington, 1879.

——. "Letters from Colonel Prejevalsky." *Proceedings of the Royal Geographical Society* 7, no. 12 (December 1885): 807–15.

——. *Mongolia, the Tangut Country, and the Solitudes of Northern Tibet: Being a Narrative of Three Years' Travel in Eastern High Asia*. 2 vols. Translated by E. Delmar Morgan. London: Sampson Low, Marston, Searle & Rivington, 1876.

Qin Hancai. *Zuo Wenxiang gong zai xibei*. Changsha: Yuelu shushe, 1984.

Qin Xiangye. *Ping Zhe jilüe*. 16 *juan*. Zhejiang shuju, 1873.

Qinding gongbu zeli. 116 *juan*. N.p., 1884.

Qinding huangyu xiyu tuzhi. 48 *juan*. Edited by Fu-heng et al. N.p., 1782.

Qingchao xu wenxian tongkao. 400 *juan*. Compiled by Liu Jinzao. Shanghai: Shangwu yinshuguan, 1936.

Qingdai Xinjiang dang'an xuanji. 91 vols. Compiled by Xinjiang Weiwu'er zizhiqu dang'anju and Zhongguo bianjiang shidi yanjiu zhongxin. Guilin: Guangxi shifan daxue chubanshe, 2012.

Qingdai zouzhe huibian: nongye, huanjing. Compiled by Zhongguo diyi lishi dang'anguan. Beijing: Shangwu yinshuguan, 2005.

Qingshi gao. 534 *juan*. Edited by Zhao Erxun. N.p., 1928. Reprint in *Xuxiu siku quanshu*, vols. 295–300.

Qinzhou zhili zhou xinzhi. 24 *juan*. Edited by Yu Zechun. Longnan shuyuan, 1889.

Qi-shi-yi. *Xiyu ji*. 8 *juan*. N.p., 1885.

QXDX. See *Qingdai Xinjiang dang'an xuanji*.

Rankin, Mary Backus. *Elite Activism and Political Transformation in China: Zhejiang Province, 1865–1911*. Stanford, CA: Stanford University Press, 1986.

Rao Yingqi. *Xinjiang xunfu Rao Yingqi gaoben wenxian jicheng*. 37 vols. Edited by Li Delong. Beijing: Xueyuan chubanshe, 2008.

Rawlinson, John L. *China's Struggle for Naval Development, 1839–1895*. Cambridge, MA: Harvard University Press, 1967.

Reardon-Anderson, James. *Reluctant Pioneers: China's Expansion Northward, 1644–1937*. Stanford, CA: Stanford University Press, 2005.

Relyea, Scott. "Conceiving the 'West': Early Twentieth-Century Visions of Kham." *Twentieth-Century China* 40, no. 3 (October 2015): 181–200.

Ren Shusen. Preface to *Nongzheng quanshu*, by Xu Guangqi, 1470–71. Annotated by Shi Shenghan. Shanghai: Shanghai guji chubanshe, 2011.

Report of the Delegates of the Shanghai General Chamber of Commerce on the Trade of the Upper Yangtsze and Report of the Naval Surveyors on the River above Hankow. Shanghai: Shanghai Recorder Office, 1869.

"Retrospect of Events which Occurred in the North of China during 1865." *North-China Herald*, January 6, 1866.

Reuss, Martin, and Stephen H. Cutcliffe, eds. *The Illusory Boundary: Environment and Technology in History*. Charlottesville: University of Virginia Press, 2010.

Reynolds, Douglas R. *China, 1898–1912: The Xinzheng Revolution and Japan*. Cambridge, MA: Council on East Asian Studies, Harvard University, 1993.

——. *East Meets East: Chinese Discover the Modern World in Japan, 1854–1898*. Ann Arbor: Association for Asian Studies, 2014.

Richthofen, Ferdinand von. *Baron Richthofen's Letters, 1870–1872*. Shanghai: North-China Herald Office, 1903.

Rockhill, William Woodville. *The Land of the Lamas: Notes of a Journey through China, Mongolia and Tibet*. New York: Century, 1891.

Rogaski, Ruth. *Hygienic Modernity: Meanings of Health and Disease in Treaty-Port China*. Berkeley: University of California Press, 2004.

Ross, Corey. *Ecology and Power in the Age of Empire: Europe and the Transformation of the Tropical World*. Oxford: Oxford University Press, 2017.

Rowe, William T. *China's Last Empire: The Great Qing*. Cambridge, MA: Belknap Press of Harvard University Press, 2009.

——. *Hankow: Commerce and Society in a Chinese City, 1796–1889*. Stanford, CA: Stanford University Press, 1984.

——. "Political, Social and Economic Factors Affecting the Transmission of Technical Knowledge in Early Modern China." In Schäfer, *Cultures of Knowledge*, 25–44.

——. *Saving the World: Chen Hongmou and Elite Consciousness in Eighteenth-Century China*. Stanford, CA: Stanford University Press, 2001.

———. *Speaking of Profit: Bao Shichen and Reform in Nineteenth-Century China*. Cambridge, MA: Harvard University Asia Center, 2018.

"Royal Asiatic Society." *North-China Herald*, August 6, 1864.

Russell, Edmund. *Evolutionary History: Uniting History and Biology to Understand Life on Earth*. Cambridge: Cambridge University Press, 2011.

———. "The Garden in the Machine: Toward an Evolutionary History of Technology." In *Industrializing Organisms: Introducing Evolutionary History*, edited by Susan R. Schrepfer and Philip Scranton, 1–16. New York: Routledge, 2004.

———. "Spinning Their Way into History: Silkworms, Mulberries and Manufacturing Landscapes in China." *Global Environment* 10, no. 1 (April 2017): 21–53.

Saguchi Tōru. *18–19 seiki higashi Torukisutan shakaishi kenkyū*. Tokyo: Yoshikawa kōbunkan, 1963.

Sahadeo, Jeff. *Russian Colonial Society in Tashkent, 1865–1923*. Bloomington: Indiana University Press, 2007.

Schäfer, Dagmar. *The Crafting of the 10,000 Things: Knowledge and Technology in Seventeenth-Century China*. Chicago: University of Chicago Press, 2011.

———, ed. *Cultures of Knowledge: Technology in Chinese History*. Leiden: Brill, 2012.

Schlesinger, Jonathan. *A World Trimmed with Fur: Wild Things, Pristine Places, and the Natural Fringes of Qing Rule*. Stanford, CA: Stanford University Press, 2017.

Schluessel, Eric T. "Muslims at the Yamen Gate: Translating Justice in Late-Qing Xinjiang." In *Kashgar Revisited: Uyghur Studies in Memory of Ambassador Gunnar Jarring*, edited by Ildikó Bellér-Hann, Birgit N. Schlyter, and Jun Sugawara, 116–38. Leiden: Brill, 2016.

Schoppa, R. Keith. *Song Full of Tears: Nine Centuries of Chinese Life at Xiang Lake*. Boulder, CO: Westview, 2002.

Schuyler, Eugene. *Turkistan: Notes of a Journey in Russian Turkistan, Khokand, Bukhara, and Kuldja*. 2 vols. London: Sampson Low, Marston, Searle & Rivington, 1876.

Scott, James C. *Seeing Like a State: How Certain Schemes to Improve the Human Condition Have Failed*. New Haven, CT: Yale University Press, 1998.

Shan, Patrick Fuliang. *Taming China's Wilderness: Immigration, Settlement and the Shaping of the Heilongjiang Frontier, 1900–1931*. Burlington, VT: Ashgate, 2014.

Shaw, Robert B. "Trade Report, Ladakh, 1871." In Aitchison, *Hand-Book of the Trade Products of Leh*, 336–55.

———. *Visits to High Tartary, Yarkand, and Kashghar (Formerly Chinese Tartary), and Return Journey over the Karakoram Pass*. London: John Murray, 1871.

Shen Bingcheng. *Cansang jiyao*. Chang Zhen tonghaidao shu, 1871. Reprint in *Xuxiu siku quanshu*, vol. 789.

Shen, Grace Yen. *Unearthing the Nation: Modern Geology and Nationalism in Republican China*. Chicago: University of Chicago Press, 2014.

Shen Songqiao. "Jiangshan ruci duo jiao: 1930 niandai de xibei lüxing shuxie yu guozu xiangxiang." *Taida lishi xuebao* 37 (June 2006): 145–216.

Shen Yao. *Luofanlou wenji*. 24 *juan*. N.p., 1918.

Shengzu Ren huangdi shilu. 300 *juan*. In *Da Qing lichao shilu*, vols. 8–13.

Shi Zhihong. *Agricultural Development in Qing China: A Quantitative Study, 1661–1911*. Leiden: Brill, 2018.

Shimazaki Akira. "Higashi Tōrukisutān ni okeru kārēzu kangai no kigen ni tsuite." *Shikagu zasshi* 63, no. 12 (December 1954): 1074–114.

Shu-he-de. "Baqi kaiken biandi shu." In *HJWB*, 35.9a–11a.

"Silk in Fohkien." *North-China Herald*, December 22, 1866.

Sivin, Nathan. "Why the Scientific Revolution Did Not Take Place in China—Or Didn't It?" *Chinese Science* 5 (June 1982): 45–66.

"Sketches in Eastern Turkestan." *Illustrated London News*, November 21, 1874.

Skinner, G. William. "Regional Urbanization in Nineteenth-Century China." In *The City in Late Imperial China*, edited by G. William Skinner, 211–49. Stanford, CA: Stanford University Press, 1977.

Snyder-Reinke, Jeffrey. *Dry Spells: State Rainmaking and Local Governance in Late Imperial China*. Cambridge, MA: Harvard University Asia Center, 2009.

Song-yun, ed. *Qinding Xinjiang shilüe*. 12 *juan*. N.p., 1821.

——, ed. *Xichui zongtong shilüe*. 12 *juan*. N.p., 1809.

Speidel, William M. "The Administrative and Fiscal Reforms of Liu Ming-ch'uan in Taiwan, 1884–1891: Foundation for Self-Strengthening." *Journal of Asian Studies* 35, no. 3 (May 1976): 441–59.

——. "Liu Ming-ch'uan in Taiwan, 1884–1891." PhD diss., Yale University, 1967.

Spence, Jonathan. "Opium Smoking in Ch'ing China." In *Conflict and Control in Late Imperial China*, edited by Frederic Wakeman Jr. and Carolyn Grant, 143–73. Berkeley: University of California Press, 1975.

Spiegel, Henry William. *The Growth of Economic Thought*. 3rd ed. Durham, NC: Duke University Press, 1991.

Stanley, C. John. *Late Ch'ing Finance: Hu Kuang-yung as an Innovator*. Cambridge, MA: East Asian Research Center, Harvard University, 1961.

Stein, M. Aurel. *Ruins of Desert Cathay: Personal Narrative of Explorations in Central Asia and Westernmost China*. 2 vols. London: Macmillan, 1912.

Suzhou xinzhi. Edited by Wu Renshou and He Yanqing. N.p., 1897. Reprint in *Zhongguo difang zhi jicheng, Gansu fu xian zhi ji*, vol. 48.

Sun Yat-sen. *The International Development of China*. New York: G. P. Putnam's Sons, 1922.

Sun Zhaikui. "Qutian shuo." In *HJWB*, 36.33a–34b.

Swislocki, Mark. *Culinary Nostalgia: Regional Food Culture and the Urban Experience in Shanghai*. Stanford, CA: Stanford University Press, 2009.

Szadziewski, Henryk. "The Open Up the West Campaign among Uyghurs in Xinjiang: Exploring a Rights-Based Approach." In *On the Fringes of the Harmonious Society: Tibetans and Uyghurs in Socialist China*, edited by Trine Brox and Ildikó Bellér-Hann, 69–97. Copenhagen: Nordic Institute of Asian Studies, 2014.

Széchenyi, Béla. *Die wissenschaftlichen Ergebnisse der Reise des Grafen Béla Széchenyi in Ostasien, 1877–1880.* 3 vols. Vienna: E. Hölzel, 1893–99.

Tai, Jeremy. "The Northwest Question: Capitalism in the Sands of Nationalist China." *Twentieth-Century China* 40, no. 3 (October 2015): 201–19.

Tan Jixun. *Tan Jixun ji.* 2 vols. Edited by Jia Wei and Tan Zhihong. Changsha: Yuelu shushe, 2015.

Tan Xuming, ed. *Qingdai ganhan dang'an shiliao.* 2 vols. Beijing: Zhongguo shuji chubanshe, 2013.

Tan Zhonglin. *Tan Wenqin gong zougao.* 20 *juan*. N.p., 1911. Reprint in *Jindai Zhongguo shiliao congkan*, vol. 33. Taipei: Wenhai chubanshe, 1969.

Tang Jian. *Tang Queshen gong ji.* 10 *juan*. N.p., 1875.

Tang, Xiaobing. *Global Space and the Nationalist Discourse of Modernity: The Historical Thinking of Liang Qichao.* Stanford, CA: Stanford University Press, 1996.

Teng, Emma Jinhua. *Taiwan's Imagined Geography: Chinese Colonial Travel Writing and Pictures, 1683–1895.* Cambridge, MA: Harvard University Asia Center, 2004.

Teng, Ssu-yü, and John K. Fairbank, eds. *China's Response to the West: A Documentary Survey, 1839–1923.* New York: Atheneum, 1971.

Tighe, Justin. *Constructing Suiyuan: The Politics of Northwestern Territory and Development in Early Twentieth-Century China.* Leiden: Brill, 2005.

———. "From Borderland to Heartland: The Discourse of the North-West in Early Republican China." *Twentieth-Century China* 35, no. 1 (November 2009): 54–74.

Tongzhi nianjian Shaanxi Huimin qiyi lishi diaocha jilu. Compiled by Xibei daxue lishixi minzu yanjiushi. Xi'an: Shaanxi renmin chubanshe, 1993.

Toops, Stanley W. "The Ecology of Xinjiang: A Focus on Water." In *Xinjiang: China's Muslim Borderland*, edited by S. Frederick Starr, 264–75. Armonk, NY: M. E. Sharpe, 2004.

Trocki, Carl A. *Opium, Empire and the Global Political Economy: A Study of the Asian Opium Trade, 1750–1950.* London: Routledge, 1999.

Trombert, Éric. "The Karez Concept in Ancient Chinese Sources: Myth or Reality?" *T'oung Pao* 94 (2008): 115–50.

Trotter, Henry. "Geographical Report." In Forsyth, *Report of a Mission to Yarkund*, 233–93.

Tucker, Richard P., and Edmund Russell, eds. *Natural Enemy, Natural Ally: Toward an Environmental History of Warfare.* Corvallis: Oregon State University Press, 2004.

Valikhanov, Ch. Ch. et al. *The Russians in Central Asia: Their Occupation of the Kirghiz Steppe and the Line of the Syr-Daria; Their Political Relations with Khiva, Bokhara, and Kokan; Also Descriptions of Chinese Turkestan and Dzungaria*. Translated by John Mitchell and Robert Mitchell. London: Edward Stanford, 1865.

Vermeer, Eduard B. "Population and Ecology along the Frontier in Qing China." In Elvin and Liu, *Sediments of Time*, 235–79.

von Glahn, Richard. "Cycles of Silver in Chinese Monetary History." In *The Economy of Lower Yangzi Delta in Late Imperial China: Connecting Money, Markets, and Institutions*, edited by Billy K. L. So, 17–71. London: Routledge, 2013.

——. *The Economic History of China: From Antiquity to the Nineteenth Century*. Cambridge: Cambridge University Press, 2016.

——. *Fountain of Fortune: Money and Monetary Policy in China, 1000–1700*. Berkeley: University of California Press, 1996.

Wakeman, Frederic. "The Huang-ch'ao ching-shih wen-pien." *Ch'ing-shih wen-t'i* 1, no. 10 (February 1969): 8–22.

Waley-Cohen, Joanna. *Exile in Mid-Qing China: Banishment to Xinjiang, 1758–1820*. New Haven, CT: Yale University Press, 1991.

Wang Fansen. *Zhongguo jindai sixiang yu xueshu de xipu*. Taipei: Lianjing, 2003.

Wang Jianwei. "The Chinese Interpretation of the Concept of Imperialism in the Anti-Imperialist Context of the 1920s." *Journal of Modern Chinese History* 6, no. 2 (December 2012): 164–81.

Wang Jiping. *Wan Qing Hunan shi*. Changsha: Hunan renmin chubanshe, 2004.

Wang Shiduo. *Wang Huiweng yibing riji*. 3 *juan*. N.p., 1936.

Wang Wenshao. *Tuipu laoren Xuannan zouyi*. 2 *juan*. N.p., 1896. Reprint in *Zhongguo shixue congshu sanbian*, vol. 1. Taipei: Taiwan xuesheng shuju, 1986.

Wang, Wensheng. *White Lotus Rebels and South China Pirates: Crisis and Reform in the Qing Empire*. Cambridge, MA: Harvard University Press, 2014.

Wang Xilong. *Qingdai xibei tuntian yanjiu*. Urumchi: Xinjiang renmin chubanshe, 2012.

Wang Xinjing. "Qutian putian shuo." In *HJWB*, 36.35a–36a.

Wang Xiqi, ed. *Xiaofanghuzhai yudi congchao*. 12 *zhi*. Shanghai: Zhuyitang, 1877–1897.

Wang, Xiuyu. *China's Last Imperial Frontier: Late Qing Expansion in Sichuan's Tibetan Borderlands*. Lanham, MD: Lexington, 2011.

Wang Yanxi and Wang Shumin, eds. *Huangchao Dao Xian Tong Guang zouyi*. 64 *juan*. Shanghai: Jiujingzhai, 1902.

Wang, Yeh-chien. *Land Taxation in Imperial China, 1750–1911*. Cambridge, MA: Harvard University Press, 1973.

Wang Yuezhen. *Hu can shu*. 4 *juan*. N.p., 1880. Reprint in *Xuxiu Siku quanshu*, vol. 978.

Wang Yuhu. *Zhongguo nongxue shulu*. Beijing: Zhonghua shuju, 2006.

Watson, Burton, trans. *The Complete Works of Chuang Tzu*. New York: Columbia University Press, 1968.

Watts, Isaac. *The Cotton Supply Association: Its Origin and Progress*. Manchester: Tubbs & Brook, 1871.

Weaver, John C. *The Great Land Rush and the Making of the Modern World, 1650–1900*. Montreal: McGill-Queen's University Press, 2003.

Wei Guangtao. *Kanding Xinjiang ji*. 8 juan. N.p., 1899. Reprint in *Jindai Zhongguo shiliao congkan*, vol. 17. Taipei: Wenhai chubanshe, 1968.

Wei Jie. *Cansang cuibian*. 15 juan. Zhejiang shuju, 1900.

——. *Cansang tushuo*. 3 ce. N.p., 1895.

Wei Yingqi. *Lin Wenzhong gong Zexu nianpu*. Shanghai, 1935. Reprint in *Xinbian Zhongguo mingren nianpu jicheng*, vol. 12. Taipei: Shangwu yinshuguan, 1981.

Wei Yuan. "Da ren wen xibei bianyu shu." In *HJWB*, 80.1a–4b.

——. *Sheng wu ji*. 14 juan. N.p., 1842.

Weitang zuoshuzhang. "Zhong xi pinfu qiangruo bian." *Shenbao*, October 16, 1876.

Wenzong Xian huangdi shilu. 356 juan. In *Da Qing lichao shilu*, vols. 67–74.

Wilkinson, Endymion. *Chinese History: A New Manual*. Cambridge, MA: Harvard University Asia Center, 2013.

Will, Pierre-Étienne, and R. Bin Wong. *Nourish the People: The State Civilian Granary System in China, 1650–1850*. Ann Arbor: Center for Chinese Studies, University of Michigan, 1991.

Williams, S. Wells. *The Chinese Commercial Guide, Containing Treaties, Tariffs, Regulations, Tables, Etc., Useful in the Trade to China & Eastern Asia; with an Appendix of Sailing Directions for Those Seas and Coasts*. 5th ed. Hong Kong: A. Shortrede, 1863.

Wong, R. Bin. *China Transformed: Historical Change and the Limits of the European Experience*. Ithaca, NY: Cornell University Press, 1997.

——. "Self-Strengthening and Other Political Responses to the Expansion of European Economic and Political Power." In *The Cambridge World History*, vol. 7, *Production, Destruction, and Connection, 1750-Present*, pt. 1, *Structures, Spaces, and Boundary Making*, edited by J. R. McNeill and Kenneth Pomeranz, 366–94. Cambridge: Cambridge University Press, 2015.

Wooldridge, Chuck. *City of Virtues: Nanjing in an Age of Utopian Visions*. Seattle: University of Washington Press, 2015.

Worster, Donald. "The Ecology of Order and Chaos." In *The Wealth of Nature: Environmental History and the Ecological Imagination*, 156–70. Oxford: Oxford University Press, 1993.

Wright, David C. "Gong Zizhen and His Essay on the 'Western Regions.'" In *Opuscula Altaica: Essays Presented in Honor of Henry Schwarz*, edited by Edward H. Kaplan and Donald W. Whisenhunt, 655–85. Bellingham: Center for East Asian Studies, Western Washington University, 1994.

Wright, Mary Clabaugh. *The Last Stand of Chinese Conservatism: The T'ung-Chih Restoration, 1862–1874*. Stanford, CA: Stanford University Press, 1957.

Wu Changshou. *Ding'an xiansheng nianpu*. Shanghai: Zhongguo tushu gongsi, 1909.

Wu Qijun. *Zhiwu mingshi tukao*. 38 *juan*. Taiyuan, 1848.

Wu, Shellen Xiao. *Empires of Coal: Fueling China's Entry into the Modern World Order, 1860–1920*. Stanford, CA: Stanford University Press, 2015.

Xia Mingfang. *Jinshi jitu: shengtai bianqian zhong de Zhongguo xiandaihua jincheng*. Beijing: Zhongguo renmin daxue chubanshe, 2012.

Xiangyin xian tuzhi. 34 *juan*. Edited by Guo Songtao. Xiangyin xianzhiju, 1880.

Xiangyin xianzhi. 39 *juan*. Edited by Weng Yuanqi. N.p., 1823.

Xiangyin xianzhi. 32 *juan*. Edited by Chen Zhongli and Yang Maolun. N.p., 1757. Reprint in *Gugong zhenben congkan*, vol. 146. Haikou: Hainan chubanshe, 2001.

Xiao Kezhi. *Nongye guji banben congtan*. Beijing: Zhongguo nongye chubanshe, 2007.

Xiao Xiong. *Xijiang zashu shi*. 4 *juan*. N.p., 1892. Reprint in *Zhongguo fengtu zhi congkan*, vol. 25. Yangzhou: Guangling shushe, 2003.

Xie Bin. *Xinjiang youji*. N.p., 1923. Reprint in *Jindai Zhongguo shiliao congkan*, vol. 31. Taipei: Wenhai chubanshe, 1969.

Xie Li. *Qingdai zhi minguo shiqi nongye kaifa dui Talimu pendi nanyuan shengtai huanjing de yingxiang*. Shanghai: Shanghai renmin chubanshe, 2008.

Xinjiang Huibu zhi. 4 *juan*. Edited by Yong-gui and Su-er-de. Nanpingli, 1794. Reprint in *Siku weishou shu jikan*, ser. 9, vol. 7. Beijing: Beijing chubanshe, 2000.

Xinjiang tongzhi. N.p., n.d. Reprint in *Zhongguo kexueyuan wenxian qingbao zhongxin cang xijian fangzhi congkan*, vols. 26–27. Beijing: Guojia tushuguan chubanshe, 2014.

Xinjiang tuzhi. 116 *juan*. Edited by Yuan Dahua. Tianjin: Dongfang xuehui, 1923. Reprint in *Xuxiu siku quanshu*, vols. 649–650.

Xinjiang xiangtu zhigao ershijiu zhong. N.p., n.d. Reprint in *Xibei xijian fangzhi wenxian*, vol. 61. Lanzhou: Lanzhou guji shudian, 1990.

Xinxiu Guyuan zhouzhi. 12 *juan*. Edited by Wang Xueyi. N.p., 1909.

Xu Dixin and Wu Chengming, eds. *Chinese Capitalism, 1522–1840*. New York: St. Martin's, 2000.

Xu Guangqi. *Nongzheng quanshu*. 60 *juan*. Annotated by Shi Shenghan. Shanghai: Shanghai guji chubanshe, 2011.

Xu, Jianhua, Yaning Chen, and Weihong Li. "The Nonlinear Hydro-Climatic Process: A Case Study of the Tarim Headwaters, NW China." In *Water Resources Research in Northwest China*, edited by Yaning Chen, 289–310. Dordrecht: Springer, 2014.

Xu Song. *Xiyu shuidao ji*. 5 *juan*. N.p., 1823.

Xu Xiangbian. "Shu Guoyang Yuan zhongcheng gong Fu Xin jicheng hou." In Yuan Dahua, *Fu Xin jicheng*. N.p., 1911. Reprint in *Jindai Zhongguo shiliao congkan*, vol. 95. Taipei: Wenhai chubanshe, 1967.

Xuanzong Cheng huangdi shilu. 476 juan. In *Da Qing lichao shilu*, vols. 55–66.

Xuxiu siku quanshu. 1800 vols. Shanghai: Shanghai guji chubanshe, 1995–99.

Xue, Yong. "'Treasure Nightsoil as If It Were Gold': Economic and Ecological Links between Urban and Rural Areas in Late Imperial Jiangnan." *Late Imperial China* 26, no. 1 (June 2005): 41–71.

Yang Bojun, ed. *Lunyu yizhu*. 3rd ed. Beijing: Zhonghua shuju, 2009.

Yang Pengcheng. *Hunan zaihuang shi*. Changsha: Yuelu shushe, 2008.

Ye Shizhuo. *Zengke sangcan xuzhi*. N.p., 1872.

Yi Tang. "Chouyi Xinjiang shiyi shu." In Luo, *Hunan wenzheng, guochao*.6.23a–28a.

Yi-xin et al., eds. *Qinding pingding Shaan Gan Xinjiang Huifei fangliie*. 320 juan. N.p., 1896.

Yin Hongqun. *Hunan chuantong shanglu*. Changsha: Hunan shifan daxue chubanshe, 2010.

You Xiuling. *Nongshi yanjiu wenji*. Beijing: Zhongguo nongye chubanshe, 1999.

Yu Zui. *Deyi lu*. 16 juan. Suzhou: Dejianzhai, 1869. Reprint in *Guan zhen shu jicheng*, vol. 8. Hefei: Huangshan shushe, 1997.

———. See also Jiyun shanren.

Yuan Dahua. *Fu Xin jicheng*. N.p., 1911.

Zatsepine, Victor. *Beyond the Amur: Frontier Encounters between China and Russia, 1850–1930*. Vancouver: University of British Columbia Press, 2017.

Zeng Xiongsheng. "'Gao xiang li wen': yi ze xin faxian de Xu Guangqi yiwen ji qi jiedu." *Ziran kexue shi yanjiu* 29, no. 1 (2010): 1–12.

———. *Zhongguo nongxue shi*. Revised ed. Fuzhou: Fujian renmin chubanshe, 2012.

Zhang, Jiayan. *Coping with Calamity: Environmental Change and Peasant Response in Central China, 1736–1949*. Vancouver: University of British Columbia Press, 2014.

Zhang, Ling. *The River, the Plain, and the State: An Environmental Drama in Northern Song China, 1048–1128*. Cambridge: Cambridge University Press, 2016.

Zhang Peilun. *Jianyu ji*. Fengrun: Jianyu caotang, 1918.

Zhang, Wentai, Jianqin Zhou, Guanglong Feng, David C. Weindorf, Guiqing Hu, and Jiandong Sheng. "Characteristics of Water Erosion and Conservation Practice in Arid Regions of Central Asia: Xinjiang, China as an Example." *International Soil and Water Conservation Research* 3, no. 2 (June 2015): 97–111.

Zhang Yan. *17–19 shiji Zhongguo de renkou yu shengcun huanjing*. Hefei: Huangshan shushe, 2008.

Zhang Yanli. *Jia Dao shiqi de zaihuang yu shehui*. Beijing: Renmin chubanshe, 2008.

Zhang Ying. "Hengchan suoyan." In *HJWB*, 36.42a–47b.

——. *Hengchan suoyan.* Jinhe guangrentang, 1882.

Zhao Gang and Chen Zhongyi. *Zhongguo mianye shi.* Taipei: Lianjing, 1977.

Zhao Lisheng. *Zhao Lisheng shixue lunzhu zixuanji.* Jinan: Shandong daxue chubanshe, 1996.

Zhao Mengling, ed. *Qu zhong wu zhong.* 5 *juan.* Lianhuachi, 1878.

Zhao Weixi. *Xiangjun jituan yu xibei Huimin da qiyi zhi shanhou yanjiu: yi Gan Ning Qing diqu wei zhongxin.* Shanghai: Shanghai guji chubanshe, 2014.

Zhao Yi. "Qingmo Tulufan cansang ye." *Xibei minzu luncong* 14, no. 2 (2016): 196–206.

Zhao Yuntian. *Qingmo xinzheng yanjiu.* Harbin: Heilongjiang jiaoyu chubanshe, 2014.

Zhao Zhen. *Qingdai xibei shengtai bianqian yanjiu.* Beijing: Renmin chubanshe, 2005.

Zheng Guanying. *Shengshi weiyan.* 5 *juan.* Shanghai: Shanghai shuju, 1896.

——. *Shengshi weiyan houbian.* 15 *juan.* N.p., 1921.

——. *Yi yan.* 2 *juan.* Hong Kong: Zhonghua yinwu zongju, 1880.

Zheng Yangwen. *The Social Life of Opium in China.* Cambridge: Cambridge University Press, 2005.

Zhong Xingqi and Chu Huaizhen, eds. *Tulufan kan'erjing.* Urumchi: Xinjiang daxue chubanshe, 1993.

Zhongguo difang zhi jicheng, Gansu fu xian zhi ji. 49 vols. Compiled by Wang Jian and Xue Fei. Nanjing: Fenghuang chubanshe, 2008.

Zhu Fengjia. "Xinjiang she xingsheng yi." In Wang, *Xiaofanghuzhai yudi congchao,* 2.119a–b.

Zuo Zongtang. *Zuo Zongtang quanji.* 15 vols. Edited by Li Runying. Changsha: Yuelu shushe, 1986–96.

——. *Zuo Zongtang weikan shudu.* Compiled by Ren Guangliang and Zhu Zhongyue. Changsha: Yuelu shushe, 1989.

Zuo Zongzhi. *Shen'an wen chao.* 2 *juan.* N.p., 1875.

ZWGN. See Luo Zhengjun, ed., *Zuo Wenxiang gong nianpu.*

ZZQJ. See Zuo Zongtang, *Zuo Zongtang quanji.*

Index

agrarian ideology: agricultural development projects and, 23–24; on natural resource exploitation, 7, 20, 23, 37–38, 45, 169; opium poppy cultivation ban and, 92

agrarian technologies, 10, 11, 24

agricultural development projects: agrarian ideology and, 23–24; agricultural treatise dissemination, 10, 24; cost of, 86, 218n107; Gansu province, 11, 67, 81, 82, 83–85, 85; Hui Muslim forced resettlement and, 81, 82; labor supply and, 61–62, 75–76, 86–87; and laws of avoidance, 27; local knowledge sources for, 27–28, 200–1nn53, 55; post–Taiping Rebellion reconstruction and, 73, 74, 75; profit motive and, 96–97; prominence of, 9, 23–24; Qing soldiers as labor for, 84–85, 123, 128, 131–32; reconstruction bureaus and, 10, 83–84; regional conditions and, 28; seed dissemination, 10–11, 102.

See also land reclamation policies; Xinjiang agricultural development

Agricultural Treatise (Nongshu), 26

Agricultural Treatise from the Pavilion of Pucun (Pucun ge nongshu), 36, 202n100

agricultural treatises: on cotton cultivation, 103–4, 106; limitations of, 26–27; on plot farming, 33–35; Qing state dissemination, 10, 24; on sericulture, 153–54, 157, 240n101; by Zuo Zongtang, 36, 202n100; Zuo Zongtang's studies, 24–26, 30–32

agriculture: civil war impact on, 69, 71, 90; experimentation in, 100, 101; exports, 30–31; plot farming, 32–33, 33, 34–35; population loss and, 66; regional styles, 26, 28. *See also* agricultural development projects; land reclamation policies; Zuo Zongtang's agricultural studies

Anhua, 31

Anhui province, 1, 73, 167

Maralbashi, 59, 122–23

Marks, Robert, 192n13

Ming dynasty: agricultural treatises, 25–26; decline of, 20–21; sericulture, 151

mining, 176

moral philosophy, 21

mulberry cultivation, 98–99

Muslim Rebellions (1862–78), 5–6; animal confiscation and, 84; depopulation and, 78, 80, 118, 127, 216n72, 217n84, 231nn81, 83; end of, 88; impacts of, 64, 77–80; opium smoking and, 92; silk trade and, 142. *See also* postwar reconstruction

nationalism, 174, 244n24

natural disasters: accumulation of, 13–14, 167–68; agricultural impacts of, 19, 90; flooding in Anhui and Jiangsu provinces, 167; global context of, 17, 20, 198n21; Hunan province, 36–37, 63; North China Famine, 13, 106, 107, 116; opium poppy cultivation and, 106, 107; post–Taiping Rebellion reconstruction and, 76; Taiping Rebellion and, 63; Zuo Zongtang's agricultural studies and, 19–20

natural resource exploitation: colonialism/imperialism and, 174; crises and, 3; difficulty of, 170–71; Feng Guifen on, 2, 191n6; mining, 176; postwar reconstruction and, 116, 146–49, 227nn19, 21; Qing colonialism/imperialism and, 3, 170–71, 177; Qing statecraft and, 7, 20, 23, 37–38, 45, 168–69; Xinjiang reconquest and, 116; Xinjiang sericulture and, 139–40, 146–49; Zuo

Zongtang on, 67, 116, 139–40, 148–49, 169, 227nn19, 21; Zuo Zongtang's agricultural studies and, 7, 36

Ningxia region, 106–8, 224n83

North China Famine (1876–79), 13, 106, 107, 116

Northern Song dynasty, 149, 151

On Raising Silkworms (Yu can shuo; Pila baqadurghan bajani), 157

opium poppy cultivation, 90–96; banning of, 88, 89–90, 91, 92–95, 107–8; as cash crop, 88, 91–92; Gansu province expansion, 106–8, 110, 111, 224n83; grain shortages and, 92, 93, 106; history of, 90–92, 220n10; Hui Muslims and, 95–96, 221n30; labor recruitment and, 95–96; opium smoking and, 91, 92, 107; profit motive and, 96; taxation and, 108, 109–10; wars based on, 30, 91

Opium War (1839–42), 30, 39, 91

overpopulation: Gong Zizhen on, 49, 50; Hong Liangji on, 52; land reclamation policies and, 50–51; Wang Shiduo on, 1–2; Wei Yuan on, 53–54, 207–8nn71, 73; Xinjiang colonial settlement as solution to, 41–42, 52–54, 207–8nn71, 73; Zhang Peilun on, 171

Pan Zengyi, 35, 36

Pei Jingfu, 175

Perdue, Peter, 37

Piasetskii, Pavel, 78

plot farming (*qutian fa*), 32–33, *33, 34*–35

plowing and reading strategy, 29

Pomeranz, Kenneth, 6

postwar reconstruction: agricultural development projects, 73, *74,* 75, 83–85, 116, 117–20, 228*n*24; environmental impacts of, 136–37; Hui Muslim forced resettlement, 80–83; labor recruitment, 75–76, 85–87, 136, 234*n*129; labor scarcity and, 135–36; land reclamation policies, 65–66, 67, 75, 81, 82, 86, 136, 218*n*107, 219*n*123, 234*n*132; land surveys, 85–86, 120–22; natural resource exploitation and, 116, 146–49, 227*nn*19, 21; Western technology imports, 11; Xinjiang provincial status and, 134–35, 233*nn*124, 126. *See also* reconstruction bureaus

practical learning (*shixue*), 19, 20–21, 23, 198*n*21

provincial system: Gong Zizhen on, 48; Hong Liangpin on, 171; Liu Jintang on, 233*n*124; Taiwan and, 169, 170; Turkestani reduced role in governance, 135, 233*n*126; twentieth-century expansion, 242*n*10; Zuo Zongtang on, 12, 54, 134–35, 169

Przhevalskii, Nikolai, 124, 130

Qianlong emperor, 42, 49, 51–52

Qing colonialism/imperialism: derogation of Turkestanis and, 140, 144, 145, 146, 175, 176; frontier geography scholarship and, 42–43; frontier settlement prohibitions, 6–7, 8; global context of, 12–13; late nineteenth-century intellectual analysis of, 174; Manchuria settlement, 51–52, 65; natural resource exploitation and, 3, 170–71, 177; provincial system and, 12, 48, 54, 134–35, 169, 170, 171, 233*n*126,

242*n*10; Taiwan, 169–70; twentieth-century support for, 177, 246–47*n*44. *See also* Chinese-Turkestani relationships; Xinjiang colonial settlement; Xinjiang, Qing governance of

Qing empire: conquest of Zunghars, 45; environmental crises, 2–3, 192*n*13; financial crises, 6, 17–19, 64–65, 86, 164–65, 173; map, *8*; overview of crises, 4–6, 167–68; political economy of, 49–50, 206–7*n*53; Sino-French War, 164; Sino-Japanese War, 173; Western technology narrative, 11, 195*nn*31, 35. *See also* agricultural development projects; land reclamation policies; Muslim Rebellions; natural disasters; Qing colonialism/imperialism; Qing empire, territorial threats to; Qing governance; Taiping Rebellion

Qing empire, territorial threats to: colonial settlement and, 56; great divergence and, 172–73, 243*n*9; Japan, 112, 173; natural disasters and, 168; Opium War and, 30, 39, 91; Russia, 6, 65, 112, 114, 138–39; treaty ports, 6, 12

Qing governance: and agrarian ideology, 7, 20, 23, 37–38, 45, 168–69; commercial tax (*lijin*), 65; late nineteenth-century reforms, 173; laws of avoidance, 27; opium economy and, 109–10; statecraft innovations, 6, 9; *xinzheng* (New Policy) reforms, 10. *See also* bureaus; postwar reconstruction; provincial system; Xinjiang postreconquest reconstruction; Xinjiang, Qing governance of

Qi-shi-yi, 44

on, 52–53; Hong Liangji on, 52; land reclamation policies and, 56–57, 59, 60, 210n105; late nineteenth-century support for, 171–72; Lin Zexu on, 40; provincial status and, 135, 171, 233n126; Qianlong emperor on, 51–52; as solution to overpopulation, 41–42, 52–54, 207–8nn71, 73; Tarim Basin, 55–56, 58, 60; Wei Yuan on, 53–54, 207–8nn71, 73, 244n24; Zunghar conquest and, 45–46; Zuo Zongtang on, 54–55

Xinjiang hydraulic infrastructure, 121–29; flooding, 122–23; hybrid nature of, 117–18; karez, 31, 125–29, 131, 162–63, 230n71; land surveys and, 121–22; local investment in, 124; Qing soldiers as labor for, 123, 128, 131–32; soil characteristics and, 129–32; Turkestani collaboration, 124–25, 128, 129, 133–34, 230n70

Xinjiang natural resources: Gong Zizhen on, 48–49; mining, 176; sericulture and, 139–40, 146–48; Western explorers on, 114–15; Zunghars and, 45; Zuo Zongtang on, 116, 227nn18–19, 21; Zuo Zongtang's study of, 8–9, 41, 43–44

Xinjiang postreconquest reconstruction: agricultural development projects and, 9, 116, 117–20, 228n24; bureaus for, 118–19, 121–22, 121, 128, 229n42; environmental impacts of, 136–37; labor recruitment, 136, 234n129; labor scarcity and, 135–36; land reclamation, 136, 234n132; land surveys, 120–22; natural resource exploitation and, 116, 146–49, 227nn19, 21; provincial status and, 134–35, 233nn124, 126. See also Xinjiang hydraulic infrastructure

Xinjiang, Qing governance of: cost of, 40–41, 47–48, 49, 113, 174, 204n9; Ili as base of, 46; provincial status, 12, 48, 54, 134–35, 171, 233n126; sericulture and, 140; Turkestani collaboration, 125, 230nn68, 70; Turkestani reduced role in, 12, 135, 233n126

Xinjiang reconquest: agricultural development projects and, 116, 117–20, 228n24; cost of Qing governance and, 113; costs of, 115–16, 227n16; debate on, 112–13, 116; governance and, 12; Turkestani headmen roles in, 230n68; Zuo Zongtang leadership role in, 4, 115, 227n15

Xinjiang sericulture, 138–49; bureaus for, 153, 154, 155, 156, 156, 157–58, 163, 165, 239n74; Chinese derogation of Turkestanis and, 140, 144, 145, 146, 176; as cottage industry, 142–43, 143; early twentieth-century, 175–76; extension agents and, 157–58; labor problems, 165; mulberry tree imports and, 158–59; natural resource exploitation and, 139–40, 146–49; organism variations and, 140–41, 144–45, 166; privatization, 163, 164; Russian territorial threats and, 138–39; silk quality and, 144–45, 157, 236nn25, 30; silk weaving and, 163–64; tensions over resources, 159–60, 162–63; tree planting campaigns, 160, 161, 162; Turkestani roles, 143–44, 145–46, 155, 157–58, 159, 162–64, 165; Turpan, 155–58, 156

xinzheng (New Policy) reforms, 10

Xu Guangqi, 25–26, 32, 101

Xu Song, 48, 58, 206n47

Xunzi, 227n21